A HISTORY OF WOMEN PHILOSOPHERS

A History of Women Philosophers

MARGARET LUCAS CAVENDISH, DUCHESS OF NEWCASTLE
School of van Dyck, Margaret Lucas c. 1635, oil on canvas, 119.0 × 99.2 cm,
Felton Bequest 1934.
(By permission of National Gallery of Victoria, Melbourne, Victoria, Australia)

A History of Women Philosophers

Volume III

Modern Women Philosophers, 1600–1900

Edited by

MARY ELLEN WAITHE

University of Minnesota, U.S.A.

Kluwer Academic Publishers

Dordrecht / Boston / London

Library of Congress Cataloging-in-Publication Data

```
Modern women philosophers, 1600-1900 / edited by Mary Ellen Waithe.
      p.   cm. -- (A History of women philosophers ; v. 3)
   Includes bibliographical references and index.
   ISBN 0-7923-0930-8 (alk. paper)
   1. Women philosophers. 2. Philosophy, Modern.   I. Waithe, Mary
Ellen.  II. Series.
   B105.W6M63  1991
   190'.82--dc20                                          90-45345
```

ISBN 0-7923-0930-8 (HB)
ISBN 0-7923-0931-6 (PB)

Published by Kluwer Academic Publishers,
P.O. Box 17, 3300 AA Dordrecht, The Netherlands.

Kluwer Academic Publishers incorporates
the publishing programmes of
D. Reidel, Martinus Nijhoff, Dr W. Junk and MTP Press.

Sold and distributed in the U.S.A. and Canada
by Kluwer Academic Publishers,
101 Philip Drive, Norwell, MA 02061, U.S.A.

In all other countries, sold and distributed
by Kluwer Academic Publishers,
P.O. Box 322, 3300 AH Dordrecht, The Netherlands.

Printed on acid-free paper

Printed in the Netherlands

In memory of
Paul Kirchner, 1933–1989

Contents

CHRONOLOGY OF MODERN WOMEN PHILOSOPHERS AND THEIR MALE CONTEMPORARIES

ANNA MARIA VAN SCHURMAN   ANNE FINCH, VISCOUNTESS CONWAY   CATHARINE TROTTER
1607-1678   1631-1679   COCKBURN
1679-1749

BATHSUA PELL MAKIN   HELENA CORNARO
fl. 1612   PISCOPIA
1646-1684   DAMARIS
CUDWORTH MASHAM
ELISABETH OF BOHEMIA   1659-1708
1618-1680

MARGARET CAVENDISH   SOR JUANA INÉS DE LA CRUZ   LAURA BASSI
1623-1673   1648-1695   1711-1778

KRISTINA WASA
QUEEN OF SWEDEN   MARY ASTELL
1626-1689   1666-1731

ÉMILIE   CATHARINE
DU CHÂTELET   MACAULAY GRAHAM
1706-1749   1731-1791

| Suarez | Grotius | Comenius | Cudworth | Locke | Leibniz | Vico | deMontesquieu | Voltaire |
| Hume | Rousseau | Bacon | Hobbes | Descartes | Pascal | Spinoza | Malebranche | Berkeley |

"SOPHIA"	MARY SOMERVILLE	CATHARINE WARD	CLEMENCE ROYER		
fl. 1739	1780-1872	BEECHER	1830-1902		
		1800-1878			

OLYMPE DE GOUGES
1748-1793

GEORGE ELIOT   JULIE VELTEN FAVRE   CHRISTINE LADD
1819-1880   1834-1896   FRANKLIN
1847-1930

MARY WOLLSTONECRAFT
1759-1797

HARRIET MARTINEAU
1802-1876

ANNA DOYLE
WHEELER
1785-1848

JULIETTE LAMBERT   HORTENSE ALLART
ADAM   DE MERITENS
1836-1936   fl. 1850

HARRIET TAYLOR MILL
1807-1858

JENNY POINSARD
D'HÉRICOURT
1809-1875

CLARISSE COIGNET
b. 1823

ANTOINETTE BROWN
BLACKWELL
1825-1921

Butler   Reid   Diderot   Mendelsohn   Kant   Schleiermacher   Helvetius   Bentham
Fichte   Comte   Emerson   Mill   Kierkegaard   Marx   Spencer   Sidgwick   Pierce   Nietzsche   Poincaré

Acknowledgements

A volume of this scope, spanning three centuries of the history of philosophy, cannot be developed without the capable assistance of many other people. Indeed, work on it could not even have been started without their unsolicited, generously-offered help. Some have shared source materials that came to their attention, others have shared the fruits of their own research, and still others have offered their own special skills and insights.

Among those who shared source materials was Professor Jeffner Allen who kindly supplied me with a copy of Angeline Goreau's modern English translation of Anna Maria van Schurman's *The Learned Maid, or, Whether a Maid may be a Scholar?* Kathryn M. Kendall, a former graduate student at the University of Texas, discovered Catharine Trotter Cockburn's philosophical works while researching sixteenth-century women playwrights. I wish to express my thanks to Dr. Kendall for providing me with copies of her work in progress on Trotter's dramatic writings, and a draft bibliography of works by and about Trotter Cockburn.

Among those who shared the fruits of their labors were Professors Elizabeth Stich and Al Nephew. Her preliminary research on Bathsua Makin, and his on Harriet Martineau was undertaken as part of my workshop, "Reclaiming our Heritage," April 1986, and became the basis for the sections on Makin and Martineau in the final chapter. Project member Nancy Weber provided me with her "Bibliography on Women in Philosophy: 20th Century." Completed more than a decade ago under a National Endowment for the Humanities Youthgrant, this valuably annotated bibliography contains a special section on Harriet Taylor Mill which greatly facilitated my research on that philosopher.

Still others requested work assignments suited to their special skills. Anne F. Robertson, a graduate student at New York University Department of Near Eastern Languages, spent countless hours in the New York Public Library and in New York University Bobst Library, compiling and annotating an extensive bibliography of the known editions of the works of Anna Maria van Schurmann. In addition to the work on the van Schurmann bibliography, and armed only with a list of names of women of the period who were alleged to be philosophers, Ms. Robertson compiled extensive bibliographies on a half-dozen women philosophers. Those bibliographies were then shared with other Project members who completed the research and prepared chapters for inclusion in this volume.

Comelli's article on the Italian philosopher Laura Bassi was the sole available resource on Bassi, and without Ms. Alba Scholz' oral translation of that work the section on Bassi in the final chapter would not have been possible. Ms. Judy Maier Voshell was particularly generous and volunteered considerable time as copyeditor of several chapters for this volume, including those authored by me. Her background in literature rather than in philosophy proved to be of great value when there was a need for tighter definition or explanation of philosophic terminology, and when technical jargon was used imprecisely.

There comes a time in a professional career when it is appropriate to thank one's teachers. Bernard S. Baumrin of the City University of New York Graduate School was my first undergraduate philosophy teacher. And although he provided me with early support for entering the profession, in recent years, he has provided me with an intriguing hypothesis regarding Ralph Cudworth, Damaris Masham, and John Locke's reasons for delaying publication of the *Essay*, and with general information concerning Christine Ladd-Franklin. In addition, he has introduced me to two historians of philosophy who have had different influences upon my work. He encouraged me to take a history of philosophy course from then-visiting Professor Richard Popkin. From Popkin I learned how the combined use of solid detective work and empathic identification with one's subject-philosopher could yield interesting new insights into the philosopher's motivation for saying what he did, and thereby make his meaning clearer. And although the question of women philosophers never arose, Professor Popkin's attitude and approach was extremely valuable not only for identifying why particular writings are important, but for identifying the connections between individual philosophers. More recently, Professor Baumrin has introduced me to Professor Jerome B. Schneewind, who was busy working on a book about Samuel Pufendorf. As things would have it, there are tenuous connections between Pufendorf and Catharine Trotter Cockburn, but more interestingly, we explored the reasons why philosophers who were important and well-known among contemporary philosophic circles managed to be excluded from the histories of philosophy. It is encouraging to know women were not alone in their exclusion from the histories of philosophy, and that factors other than sexism must play a role in their omission.

I remain indebted to Lloyd Waithe for his support in administering the Project on the History of Women in Philosophy and its several writing projects. Mr. Philip Jago of the National Gallery of Victoria in Melbourne kindly gave permission to reproduce *Margaret Lucas* by the School of Van Dyck as the frontispiece for this volume. My thanks to him, and to all who have made the completion of this volume possible.

MARY ELLEN WAITHE

Introduction to Volume III

MARY ELLEN WAITHE

The seventeenth through the nineteenth centuries were marked by several important kinds of changes that in part affected women's abilities to study and publish philosophy and in part were affected by the kinds of philosophy they pursued. The earlier transition from monasticism to scholasticism had changed the locus of education and therefore women's opportunities for learning. Similar transitions occurred in the 300-year period included in the scope of this volume. More than thirty women philosophers took part in and gave shape to the three-centuries-long transition from religious to secular rule, from colonization to self-government, from slavery and subjection to emancipation and suffrage, and from speculative to empirical science.

The scientific and social transformations of the seventeenth, eighteenth and nineteenth centuries were accompanied by marked changes in women's interests in, and opportunities for, philosophy. Academies, not convents, had become the centers of learning. Early in this period, only Italian universities ever made exceptions and admitted women. With the closing of convents and the wholesale transfer of convent libraries to male monasteries and to male universities, women's need to obtain an education required new approaches. Many were largely self-educated and were part of non-academic philosophical circles which included men as well as women. Descartes, Bayle, Pascal, Locke, Leibniz, Newton, van Helmont, More, Norris, Voltaire, Saint-Simon, Fourier, Mill, Pierce, and other male philosophers of this period had women colleagues with whom they discussed and often wrote philosophy.

The response of some eighteenth- and nineteenth-century women to patriarchal exclusion from formal education was to form their own intellectual institutions, the *salons*. The *salonistes* were almost always

Mary Ellen Waithe (ed.), A History of Women Philosophers/Volume 3, xix–xl.
© 1991 *Kluwer Academic Publishers. Printed in the Netherlands.*

women. Male intellectuals addressed a largely female *salon*, thereby keeping women appraised of intellectual currents in the closed universities and the exclusionary *sociétés littéraires*. Like the French *salons*, English intellectual circles included both men and women philosophers and non-philosophers. Scientists, literary writers, medical practitioners, and other learned persons created what we would now call an interdisciplinary environment. The lines between the disciplines were left largely undrawn. The convention of seeking one's colleagues within intellectual organizations provided opportunities for advanced philosophical and other learning for both men and women. By the last half of the nineteenth century women's colleges became more common. Occasionally, European and American men's colleges admitted women of extraordinary talent. But this period was far less notable for increasing opportunities for women to formally pursue philosophy than it was for other social, political, and scientific transformations.

This was an era of expansion and contraction of empires, of fractionalization and disintegration of ecclesiastical political power, and of subtle shifts from the philosophical to the technological emphasis in science. The sheer pace and complexity of philosophical, scientific, and technological developments that accompanied the industrial age is astonishing. This was the age of Descartes, Malebranche, Hobbes, Spinoza, Leibniz, Locke, and Newton. Philosophy proposed new ways of looking at the world, at our place in it, and at our social, political, and religious institutions. Like philosophy, science contributed to a similar reexamination. The seventeenth century witnessed the discovery of the circulatory system and the microscope. It was in this century that body temperature was first measured and cranial neurology was first diagrammed. The invention of the barometer, the magic lantern, and the reflecting telescope all occurred then. Discoveries were made of the finite velocity and polarization of light, of the nature of combustion, of the elasticity of gasses, and of the gravitational effect of the sun, moon, and earth on tides. These discoveries opened new universes of knowledge beyond this planet. At the same time, the mapping of weather systems and of the Americas permitted expansion of trade and empire.

Such great scientific discoveries occurred amidst even greater social and political strife. The civil state had replaced the church as the primary source of political authority, and state persecution of religious minorities resulted in massive emigrations to the new world. Bacon's *Instauratio magna: novum organum Scientiarum* appeared in 1620, the year the Mayflower set sail, and his *Historia naturalis et experimentalis* followed two years later. With the publication of Newton's *Optics* and *Principia*, other natural philosophers moved from purely theoretical to more empirically based science, testing, as it were, aspects of epistemology, metaphysics, and even ethical theory with newly gained and ingeniously analyzed data from medicine, physics, biology, and astronomy. At the same time, humanitarian reform in Prussia, Austria, and elsewhere resulted in more humane penal systems and in compulsory public education for all children. Theories about who can learn, how learning occurs, and what should be taught came from philosophers including John Locke, Anna Maria van Schurman, and Bathsua Makin.

Philosophy of Education was not the only area of philosophy in which women engaged. Metaphysics in the seventeenth century is in part represented by the vitalism of Anne Finch Conway, the materialism of Margaret Cavendish, and the Aristotelianism of Laura Bassi. Metaphysics and philosophy of science are the central subjects of Emilie du Châtelet's *Analytical Institutions* as well as her edited translation of Newton's *Principia*. Philosophy of religion is variously encountered in the skepticism of Kristina of Sweden and in the neoplatonic mysticism of Sor Juana Inés de la Cruz. Other women of this century made fewer contributions to written philosophy: Elisabeth of Bohemia critiqued Descartes' draft manuscripts, and Helena Cornaro Piscopia became known throughout Italy for her expertise in Aristotelian philosophy.

In the seventeenth century, women gradually stopped trying to prove that their souls were as capable of intellectual virtue as those of men. Instead, they focussed on undermining men's assumptions that women's bodies were incapable of withstanding the rigors of philosophizing without abdicating their preordained roles of wife and mother. Following Anna Maria van Schurman's intellectual reputation and her argument that women were capable of scholarship, Bathsua Makin called for liberal education of women. With the dissemination of van Schurman's *Whether a Maid may be a Scholar?* and Makin's *Essay to Revive the Antient Education of Gentlewomen*, women who earlier had been viewed as prodigies were represented as models to which many women could realistically aspire. Makin specifically argued that education of women contributed to their fulfilling their socially prescribed roles. In contrast, Kristina of Sweden considered most women unfit for anything else, while herself rejecting heterosexual stereotypes along with her throne in favor of a life of learning, non-conformity, and political intrigue.

By the eighteenth century, the debates over Locke's epistemology accompanied an increase in philosophy publications by women. Damaris Cudworth Masham, Catharine Trotter Cockburn, and Mary Astell were among the many late seventeenth-century and early eighteenth-century writers to defend or dispute Locke's views. They explored the consequences of Locke's epistemology for the certainty of religious knowledge and for the question of women's intellectual abilities. Other writers such as "Sophia," Catharine Macaulay, Olympe de Gouges, and Mary Wollstonecraft insisted that women's education and suffrage was an enterprise consistent with human, rather than male, nature. At the same time that Kant elaborated upon the central role of reason in morality, women's claims to having innately equal intellectual potential with men renewed women's demands for full social and political equality.

In the writings of women philosophers of the seventeenth and eighteenth centuries, foremothers were less frequently viewed as prodigious examples of Mother Nature's mistaken allocation of male intellects to female physiques. More often, they were viewed through a complex new understanding of human nature. Mary Wollstonecraft's *A Vindication of the Rights of Men* and *A Vindication of the Rights of Woman* reflected that new understanding. Monarchies were becoming republics, and empires were dissolving into democracies as the great French and American revolutions incorporated egalitarian and libertarian social philosophies into their founding constitutions. In this intellectual and political climate, Olympe de Gouges and Jenny Poinsard d'Héricourt joined Wollstonecraft and others providing arguments to justify universal suffrage. De Gouges was among those French women who waged the war of the pamphlets, papering Paris with well-argued demands that the new Republic treat women as full and equal citizens. The Paris riots of 1795 resulted in the General Assembly's crackdown on women's activism and the arrest and trial of activist feminist pamphleteers. Olympe de Gouges was among those women who were guillotined by the Terror because of their views.

The eighteenth century was the century of revolution, but it was also the century of industrial development. Recent scientific advances were combined with technological innovations to improve manufacturing, agriculture, navigation, and trade. The development of hosiery-ribbing machinery gave new economic importance to the silk industry and, therefore, to European control of silk-producing nations. The invention of the condenser gave rise to the steam engine, which would later permit far-flung shores to be connected by rail. The development of modern canning techniques expanded European markets for exotic foodstuffs from the Americas and the Orient, while enhancing the potential for survival in the wilderness. Frontiers were pushed back. As the land-intensive logging, rubber, mining, and agricultural industries grew, so did the demand for expanded frontiers beyond Europe. Programs to decimate and displace Native Americans decreased the risk of territorial expansion as the bondage of African and Oriental peoples increased its yield. In marked contrast to these facts stood philosophies which proclaimed that *all* persons had equal potential for rational action and were of equal moral worth. Equally incongruous with the facts were political philosophies that proclaimed the rights of all to self-determination.

In the nineteenth century, the emergence of a scientific anthropology of human nature accompanied the shrinking of empires as the moral justification for slavery and colonization crumbled. Persons of other races and cultures were now considered to be surprisingly similar to Europeans, and all were considered to be astonishingly similar to other higher primates. Mill was further developing Bentham's utilitarianism into a libertarian theory which would require the enfranchisement of women and the abolition of slavery. The popularization of Auguste Comte's positivist philosophy by Harriet Martineau gave a new, sociological perspective to the historical relationships between religion, philosophy, and science. The utopian theories of Fourier, Saint-Simon, and Owen revived discussions of the nature of ideal societies. Philosophers including Clarisse Coignet, Juliette Lambert Adam, and Harriet Taylor Mill took active roles in those discussions. Others, including Anna Doyle Wheeler and Catharine Ward Beecher, not only wrote social and political philosophy but became political activists.

The philosophy of human nature held by nineteenth-century women philosophers including Julie Favre, Clarisse Coignet, and Antoinette

Brown Blackwell held that women were different from men in a way which made women morally superior to men. They rejected a rationalism that denied the epistemological and moral role of the passions, senses, and emotions. They glorified motherhood as both a natural and morally virtuous state for women. Female perceptiveness, insight, intuition, and inductive reasoning were as essential in the ethical and political domain as deductive reasoning was in the scientific domain. Moral caring, nurturance, and concern were the first virtues of social institutions, and family was the first social institution. It was argued that men were deficient in these virtues and that women could and should teach them to children of both sexes. Antoinette Brown Blackwell argued that feminine perception, insight, and unselfishness evolved from women's biological role as mothers. Catharine Ward Beecher was among those who promoted the view of female moral superiority and the incumbent duties of women to fight social injustice.

Nineteenth-century feminist activists are at the end of a long tradition of (largely female) love mysticism and mariologies which depicted Mary as a model for women's salvation. These theologies emphasized the role of the moral emotions and the development of virtue. Against this background, nineteenth-century American romantic evangelism emphasized the role of intuition, subjectivity, love, and the senses: empiricism plus emotivism. Religious experience was valued above rationalist extrapolations from official doctrine. Sensorium, experience, and emotion were central to this antirationalist and antispeculative theology. It is a philosophical humanism which identified women, blacks, children, and other so-called "primitives" as valid sources of experiential knowledge. Their knowledge was immediate and natural. It was not stifled by a repressive rationalism that denied the role and significance of the moral emotions. These feminist humanistic reevaluations of rationalist moral philosophy contributed to the development of three women-led reform movements in the United States: abolition, temperance, and women's suffrage. In the nineteenth century, suffrage movements attempted to do for the legal status of women what emancipation movements were then doing for slaves and indentured persons. Jenny d'Héricourt, Harriet Taylor Mill, Antoinette Brown Blackwell, Julie Velten Favre, and Clarisse Coignet argued in favor of women's rights to education and career. The social and political writings of Harriet Taylor Mill expressly demanded full equality for women and other oppressed peoples.

As important as this wave of philosophical feminism was, nineteenth-century women philosophers, like their predecessors, were not all feminist philosophers. Some turned from speculation to experimentation as a source of knowledge of the physical sciences. Mary Somerville's *On the Connexion of the Physical Sciences* was on a subject which until then was called "natural philosophy." Indeed it is her account of the nature of scientific knowledge that prompted William Whewell to suggest the substitution of the term "scientist" for "natural philosopher." The philosopher Christine Ladd-Franklin made contributions to theories of perception and color, as well as logic. Both Somerville and Ladd-Franklin came from a long tradition of women philosopher-scientists which began with Hypatia of Alexandria nearly fifteen centuries earlier. Many others were part of that important philosophical tradition.

* * *

Margaret Cavendish (1623–1673) was one of the most prolific women philosophers of the seventeenth century, and although some of her works criticized those of male philosophers, she was one of the first to produce original natural philosophy. She critiqued Hobbes in her *Philosophical Letters*, and Descartes, van Helmont, and More in her *Elements of Philosophy*. She deliberately addressed her rigorous writings to women, as if to belie the popular view that her intended female audience needed complex arguments simplified. Her view that matter is atomistic, intelligent, and self-moving markedly contrasted with Descartes' dualism and with Hobbes' intelligent subject/inanimate object distinction. Her rejection of mind/body dualism and her vital atomism were consistent with her early atheistic denial of a first cause. Later, she was to admit the possibility of the existence of an eternal, omnipotent author of nature. Most of Cavendish's philosophical writings criticize aspects of empiricism and rationalism. Her *Orations of Diverse Sorts* calls for what Cavendish herself viewed as the masculization of women: the nurturance of body and mind. Cavendish wanted women to have much more than physical and intellectual strength; she wanted that strength to be achievable without sacrificing the "feminine" virtues of modesty, chastity, temperance, humility, patience, and piety. And although she was acutely aware of social impediments to women's intellectual growth, she rarely addressed feminist issues, preferring instead to write metaphysics and epistemology.

The skepticism of Queen Kristina of Sweden (b. 1626) informed her personal and philosophical life, leading her first to consult with the best-known skeptic of the early seventeenth century, Descartes, and, ultimately, to abdicate her throne. She was influenced not only by skepticism but by epicureanism, neostoicism, platonism, and feminism. She was an eclectic philosopher, studying Iamblichus, Lucretius, Sextus Empiricus, Cicero, Machiavelli, and Galileo. She worked closely, sometimes personally, and sometimes through correspondence, with leading philosophers of her day, including Bayle, Descartes, Gassendi, Grotius, La Peyrere, Pascal, Scheffer, van Schurman, Vossius, and others. She left a vast correspondence, including the famous interchange between herself (through the French ambassador, Chanut) and Descartes on epistemological and metaphysical issues. She also left an incomplete autobiography and two anthologies, *Les Sentiments Héroiques* and *L'Ouvrage de Loisir: Les Sentiments Raisonnables*. Together the anthologies contain about 1300 entries discussing (in imitation of Machiavelli) the Prince (a masculine term which she always used to refer to herself), the nature of heroic virtues, honor, and passion. Importantly, she addresses the gender-identification of the female ruler, the subjection of women, and the idea of feminine virtue as represented in the Christian ideal of virginity and the lesbian rejection of heterosexual marriage.

Like most of her contemporaries, Anne Finch, Viscountess Conway (1631–1679), had no formal education and was largely self-taught. In addition to mathematics and philosophy, which she studied with Henry More, Conway learned Greek, Hebrew, Latin, and French. Her philosophical circle included Francis Mercury van Helmont (who introduced her work to Leibniz nearly twenty years after her death), Ralph Cudworth (father of Damaris Cudworth Masham), Glanvill, Rust, and Whichcote. She held critical views of Hobbes, Descartes, and Spinoza and was a strong influence on Leibniz. Her work *The Principles of the Most Ancient and Modern Philosophy* was post-humously published in Latin translation by Francis Mercury van Helmont. The original holographic work has not survived. In her *Principles*, Conway attempts a reconciliation of mechanism and

Platonism, developing a metaphysics in which every created entity is both vital and capable of motion. In this system, God is one of three possible kinds of entities, Christ a second, and created entities a third. It is from God that all created entities, including spirit, mind, and body, emanate. In her view, life is the purest form of motion, and all created entities have life. Since mind and body are two kinds of created entity, they can exert causal influence on, i.e., move, each other. Thus Conway synthesizes the mind-body dualism of the Cartesians with an account of motion as the unifying characteristic of created entities.

Sor Juana Inés de la Cruz de Asbaje y Ramírez (1648–1695) was born near Mexico City. She was an illegitimate child of Spanish and Creole parentage. At age three she charmed her sister's primary-school teacher into teaching her to read. As a young child she expressed a desire to be sent to Mexico City disguised as a boy to study science at the university. Despite punishment for doing so, she read her grandfather's books and at age 12 won a prize for her writing. Although she was briefly tutored in grammar, she was otherwise self-educated. The humanistic ideas of Erasmus had been banned by the Inquisition. However, a century before Sor Juana's birth the philosopher Bishop Juan de Zumarraga had summarized Erasmus' views and published them unattributed in his *Doctrina Breve*. The humanist philosopher Alonso de la Vera Cruz had introduced the Aristotelian *corpus* to Mexico and had written books on metaphysics, logic, and dialectic. The Mexico in which Sor Juana grew up boasted a century-old Royal and Pontifical University in which humanism, scholasticism, and mysticism had continued to thrive beyond the time of their European zenith. As a young adult, she entered a religious order which encouraged study. Known primarily as a poet and playwright, she studied Plato, Augustine, Chrysostom, Aquinas, Machiavelli, and others.

Her works include more than 200 poems and twenty plays as well as prose writings. The chief sources of our knowledge of her philosophical views are two prose works, *Carta atenagórica* and *Respuesta a Sor Filotéa de la Cruz*, and a long poem, *Primero Sueño*. Sor Juana developed an architectural representation of the nature of human knowledge which is reminiscent of some descriptions of ways of knowing offered by Hildegard, Mechtild, Hadewych, Julian, and other medieval philosophers (see Volume 2 of this series). In distinction to some medieval mystics, however, Sor Juana sees discursive reasoning, rather than intuition or revelation, as the way to illumination. Her philosophic orientation is predominantly that of late scholasticism. However, she fits no single school of philosophy. The emphasis on the value of reason places her prior to Benito Diaz de Gamarra in the Mexican rationalist response to scholasticism. The central importance of the idea of freedom of the understanding has caused some to consider her a philosopher of the Enlightenment. Her views on personal liberation and the education of women make her a representative of early American feminist philosophy. The sheer volume and literary quality of her works is astonishing, as is her synthesis of past and contemporary philosophic perspectives in the development of a mystical, feminist, and rationalist libertarianism.

Damaris Cudworth Masham (1659–1708) was raised in a climate of philosophical discourse. Her father, Ralph Cudworth, one of the more prominent members of the Cambridge Platonist school, created a home environment in which the views of Calvin and Hobbes were criticized. Damaris Cudworth Masham shared many of the views of the Cambridge Platonist school and also shared many of John Locke's views. Her writings frequently defend both. She and Locke maintained a close friendship, and he lived the final thirteen years of his life at her home. Through her philosophic circle, which included Locke, Leibniz, Newton, van Helmont, and Henry More, Masham had knowledge of other well-respected women philosophers. Through Locke she became acquainted with the works of Catharine Trotter Cockburn. In addition to the connection with Catharine Trotter Cockburn's work, there are several connections between Masham and Anne Finch, Viscountess Conway. In a letter to Masham, Leibniz mentioned Anne Conway. Masham's friend, van Helmont, had edited and translated Conway's *Principles*, and her friend Henry More had been Conway's close friend. Masham's correspondence with Leibniz covered a number of issues, including free will, her father's account of "plastic natures," the relationship between mind and body, and Leibniz' idea of pre-established harmony. Damaris Masham was less interested in metaphysics than Conway had been. Rather, she focussed on epistemology, moral philosophy, and Christian theology, particularly the relationship between faith and reason, and the morality of worldly pursuits. Her *Occasional Thoughts* supported Locke against Stillingfleet on the question of the relative merits of revelation and reason. Masham argued that preferring revelation alone to revelation which stood up to scrutiny by reason would lead people to view Christianity as unreasonable. The consequences would be either fanaticism or skepticism. Although, according to Masham, many principles of Christian morality are derivable from reason and from common sense, religion provides the only support for virtuous action. This is because people are naturally inclined to follow passion unless dissuaded by a rational fear of God.

Masham's writings address the feminist issues of her day. She objected not only to the denial of educational opportunities to most women but to the double standard of morality imposed on women. She also claimed that conventional morality and conventional religious sentiments do not always accord with rational Christianity, according to which virtue is action in accord with "right reason." Masham's *Discourse on the Love of God*, in response to John Norris' *Practical Discourses*, objected to the claim that loving creatures is incompatible with loving God. She argued that love of creatures is a necessary prerequisite for loving God. Similarly, she objected to the austerity of the Calvinist rejection of the world and of material things. Instead, she argued, only inordinate love of the world conflicts with love of God. In her view, there is virtue in social intercourse and in public life, not only in the contemplative life.

Mary Astell (1666–1731) was born in Newcastle, England. She was a self-educated woman whose family was in commerce. She wrote on a number of epistemological issues and was a proponent of women's education. Her anonymously published *A Serious Proposal to the Ladies For the Advancement of their True and greatest Interest* was well received and went through several editions. At the request of John Norris, she published her correspondence with him under the title *Letters Concerning the Love of God*. There followed a series of philosophical pamphlets on religious and political issues, a text on marriage, and a summary of her religious and educational theories, *The Christian Religion as Profess'd by a Daughter of the Church of England*. Another work, *An Essay in Defence of the Female Sex*, is generally attributed to her, but its authorship is sometimes still attributed to Judith Drake. I have examined the second edition of the *Essay*. It contains a poetic tribute to the author written by James Drake. There is also a brief piece which is signed "JD." "JD" notes that the author's work has sometimes been attributed to her, and that she would like to take credit for it but cannot. This disclaimer is followed by Astell's thanks to JD for not taking credit for Astell's work. The disclaimer by JD coupled with Astell's acknowledgement that when the work originally appeared it was sometimes misattributed, should satisfy those few who persist in identifying the work as Drake's.

In the view of John Norris, Astell had succeeded in demonstrating the absurdity of certain aspects of Locke's epistemology. Although she agreed with Locke that intuition was the best source of knowledge, she argued for the existence of innate ideas and for Cartesian skepticism as an appropriate methodology with which to seek knowledge of those innate ideas. She urged women to fulfill their essentially human nature by requiring reason to govern passion and by refraining from exercising judgment in the absence of clear and distinct ideas. Astell intended her critiques of Locke and Descartes to work to women's advantage in recognizing the role of passion, the potential for reason to dominate it, and the need for education to develop not only rational skills, but habits of controlling the emotions. With such education, she felt, women would be prepared to seek alternatives to traditional forms of marriage, and men would be prepared to seek women who were their intellectual equals. But in addition to addressing epistemological issues as they affect women's intellectual and social status, Astell addressed issues of religious epistemology. She examined the nature of revelation and its relationship to reason; whether matter can think; whether God is the efficient cause of pain and pleasure, and other epistemic questions as well.

Catharine Trotter Cockburn's (1679–1749) philosophical writings, like those of Sor Juana Inés de la Cruz, have been included in the *corpus* of her literary writings. In consequence, they have escaped the notice of historians of philosophy. The impoverished and self-taught daughter of a deceased ship's captain, Catharine earned early fame as a young playwright and acclaim as a philosopher. She was among the first to defend John Locke in print. (Samuel Bold and Damaris Cudworth Masham preceded her.) Cockburn published a comprehensive defense of Locke's epistemology in response to Thomas Burnet of the Charterhouse. Burnet had supported the position of Bishop Stillingfleet in the latter's highly politicized controversy with Locke. The fact that Catharine Trotter was a Catholic who ably defended

Locke against Burnet, and implicitly against Stillingfleet, may have played into the hands of those who suggested that Locke's views supported "Romish papists" against the Anglican Church. It is interesting therefore that Cockburn converted to the Anglican Church shortly after her *Defence* appeared. The aged and ailing Locke read and appreciated Cockburn's defense of him and authorized Peter King, his cousin and business manager, to make her a substantial financial gift. Bishop Gilbert Burnet of Salisbury and John Norris both praised her work. From her correspondence we know that George Burnet (brother of Locke's friend and intermediary with Leibniz, Thomas Burnet of Kemnay) had discussed Trotter's work with Leibniz as well as with Princess Sophie. Leibniz wished to consider Trotter's work prior to transcribing his own critique of Locke's *Essay*. Her delivery of text and portrait coincided with Locke's death. From the correspondence it appears that Damaris Masham also acquired a copy of Trotter's *Defence* at about this time.

Thomas Burnet of the Charterhouse had presented three major criticisms of Locke's *Essay*. He had claimed that the *Essay* did not give a firm basis for morality. In response, Trotter showed that Burnet was mistaken in claiming that the perception of good and evil was analogous to sensory perception and, like sensory perception, occurred independently of reason. Burnet had claimed that Locke's principles also undermined religion in that they entailed that God could not make virtue into vice and vice into virtue. Trotter argued against Burnet that unlike natural wonders and catastrophes, which might be considered to be "natural" virtues and vices, moral good and evil is defined exclusively in reference to human nature. Having created us a particular way, God necessarily has defined moral good and evil according to the nature he has given us. Consequently, knowledge of moral good and evil is possible through reflection on human nature. Burnet had also questioned how we could know which moral laws to obey in the absence of revelation and a natural conscience characterized by innate ideas. To this Trotter replied that Burnet had confused the distinction between innate principles and innate or natural abilities to make moral judgments regarding actions. This sort of confusion, Trotter noted, characterized Burnet's criticism of Locke. Catharine Trotter Cockburn gained a reputation as a philosopher and was widely encouraged to publish her collected works, including her correspondence. Thanks to her friend Thomas Birch her biography, her philosophical writings, her plays, and her correspondence have been preserved.

Émilie du Châtelet (1706–1749) was both a scientist and a philosopher. Her philosophical work includes ethics, rhetoric, and philosophy of science; however, her most important work was in metaphysics. In metaphysics, du Châtelet had one very large, well-defined project: to provide a sound metaphysical foundation for Newtonian physics. Du Châtelet was convinced that Newton had accurately described *how* the universe works as it does. Cartesian skepticism had provided a method with which to achieve a degree of certainty about metaphysical and empirical truths. But what Newton did not do, du Châtelet believed, was to explain *why* the universe works as he claimed it did. After a false start, du Châtelet provided the necessary metaphysical underpinning for Newtonian physics by incorporating Leibniz' principle of sufficient reason, his principle of non-contradiction, his principle of the identity of indiscernibles, and a modified version of his monadology.

Du Châtelet understood that much more than mere physics was at stake if Newtonian science lacked a firm metaphysical foundation. At stake too were contemporary concepts of divine nature and human nature, the doctrine of free will and human moral responsibility, and, ultimately, the basis for the authority of the church and the state. Du Châtelet's *Analytical Institutions* presented her account of how selected elements of Leibnizian metaphysics preserved for Newtonian physics the role of an omnipotent, omniscient, and benevolent deity in the creation and maintenance of the universe. Although some prominent Newtonians were initially critical of her work, by the time *Analytical Institutions* appeared du Châtelet had already been widely known as "Lady Newton" for her work with Voltaire on his *Elements of Newton's Philosophy*, as well as for her prize-winning essay on the nature of fire.

Émilie du Châtelet will be known for achieving what the Leibniz-Clarke debates could not, namely an adequate Newtonian response at least to some of Leibniz' criticisms. Importantly, this response was achieved by demonstrating how Leibnizian metaphysics provided badly needed support for Newtonian physics. Du Châtelet showed how the two supplemented and supported rather than contradicted each other. When she was in her forties, and working hard on writing a French translation/analysis of Newton's *Principia*, she became pregnant. Concerned that she would die in childbirth, she reportedly worked twenty hours a day until her delivery. She and her child died shortly after the birth. Incredibly, given the renewed interest in Newton occasioned by Einstein's discoveries nearly two centuries later, Emilie du Châtelet's edition of the *Principia* remains the standard French translation of that work.

Known primarily to historians of feminism as the author of *A Vindication of the Rights of Woman*, Mary Wollstonecraft (1759–1797) was a prolific writer of social and political philosophy and philosophy of education, a contributor of many book reviews to *The Analytical Review*, a translator of works on moral and religious philosophy, a poet, a novelist, and an autobiographer. She was born in England of an Irish mother and an English father of the mercantile class. A violently abusive childhood seems to have greatly affected Wollstonecraft's views on the rights of women. Her alcoholic father, her submissive, suffering mother, and a sister whose marriage replicated that of her parents profoundly influenced Wollstonecraft's views. Her *A Vindication of the Rights of Men* (1790) replied to Edmund Burke's *Reflections on the Revolution*. Two years later Thomas Paine's *Rights of Man* and Mary Wollstonecraft's *A Vindication of the Rights of Woman* followed. Wollstonecraft held that women were the moral and intellectual equals of men and on that account had a moral right to social, economic, and political opportunities equal to those enjoyed by men. She criticized Rousseau's confusion of nature and nurture and insisted that the moral worth of social institutions be assessed by their consequences. In her view, the moral justification for paternalistic institutions which view women as wards of their male relatives fails when one sees that the consequence is that women are deprived of their rights to become full human beings. She also detailed an alternative to Talleyrand's philosophy of education, calling for universal public education which concentrates on teaching intellectual, rather than practical, skills. In calling for liberal education of women, Wollstonecraft followed the tradition of van Schurman, Makin, and Astell. Wollstonecraft differed from them in that she made that demand in the context of arguments from social justice, rather than in the context of arguments from epistemology and religion. After Wollstonecraft, feminist political activism was increasingly characterized not only by arguments that it was morally indefensible to deny full equality to women; it was also characterized by public demonstrations and women's defiance of contemporary social mores.

Although little is known about Clarisse Gauthier Coignet's (b. 1823) early life, we do know that the reform of the French educational system which followed the founding of the Republic was the subject of her earliest publications. Her support of public education and of the teaching of moral values independent of religious values within that system earned early recognition for her philosophy of education. For a five-year period she was editor of a weekly newspaper, *La Morale Indépendante*. Her association with the Saint-Simonians who published that paper and her study of Kantian and neo-Kantian moral philosophy led to several publications of philosophic importance. *La Morale indépendante dans son principe et son object* and *De Kant à Bergson; reconciliation de la religion et de la science dans un spiritualisme nouveau* described her analysis of the connections and dissimilarities between moral philosophy and religion. In addition, Coignet wrote on the histories of philosophical ethics and the practical moralities of social institutions. She also wrote works of jurisprudence and social philosophy, particularly as they concerned the rights of women. She urged careful consideration of the idea that social and political change has historically represented nothing more than a transition from one form of intellectual tyranny to another. She took a radical approach to moral theory and asked that we recognize that freedom is not derived from the laws of nature and does not consist in conformity to a general order of which morality, like physics, is but a part. In contrast, she claimed that freedom is a primitive, a first, irreducible principle of human existence and therefore of moral science. It is not a conclusion that we reach as a consequence of moral theory. Neither God nor constitutions make us free, she said, freedom is constitutive of human nature. It is a human accomplishment. Therefore, morality is created by humans, not by deities or by states. Kantianism makes sense because man is neither an imitation of God nor an imperfect creature in search of perfection. Man *qua* man is an end in himself. Coignet held that the French Revolution did not go far enough in opposing the rule of man to the rule of God and in separating religious and civil law. What France needed to do was to exclude religious values from the foundation of social values and hence eliminate the social benefits of religious affiliation. Such a radically different state would recognize that all people, independent of religious persuasion, are linked in civil contract founded on a morality based in conscience. All this, she held, was completely possible without denying the psychological components of religious belief: hope, inspiration, spiritualism. Coignet's independent morality also sought a renewal of women's dignity and equality so that women could live in a society in which a woman was a sovereign end in herself. She viewed such a society as one which denied that women were to be glorified as useful instruments to their husband's ends. And although Coignet regularly wrote about the suffrage movement in England, she believed that the character of the French people required that equality of women be acquired in a different order. Where British women sought political power as a way of instituting educational and social reform, Coignet believed that the equality of French women was more likely to be successful if reforms of civil law, educational opportunities, and greater equality in marriage preceded political suffrage.

Antoinette Louisa Brown Blackwell (1825–1921) was an American philosopher. She was the first woman minister ordained in the United States, a suffragist, poet, and novelist. She wrote six books of philosophy, the most extensive of which, *The Philosophy of Individuality*, presented an elaborate cosmology of mind and matter as dual aspects of nature. *The Physical Basis of Immortality* paralleled the indestructibility of the self with that of matter, and *The Sexes Throughout Nature* provided a critique of sexism inherent in evolutionary theories. Her philosophical formation was intricately connected to her religious vocation. She synthesized aspects of evolution and a natural philosophy informed by Newtonian physics and inspired by Christian faith. She acted on her philosophical and religious views and took a leadership role in the suffrage, temperance, and abolitionist movements. Struggle characterized her life. After considerable effort to gain ordination and education at Oberlin College, she struggled to find a position as head of a congregation. In a *New York Times* article Horace Greeley memorialized her public-speaking efforts at the World Temperance Convention. She lived ninety-six years, and of the original women suffragists she may have been one of few who survived long enough to actually vote in a presidential election. At age ninety-five, blind and ill, she was escorted to the poll to vote for president for the first time. Antoinette Brown Blackwell made substantial contributions to philosophy and used philosophy and her pulpit as means with which to address the important scientific, social, and political issues of her day.

Julie Velten Favre (1834–1896), born in Wissembourg, France, was a lifelong educator and moral philosopher. Her liberal view on childhood education supported intellectual freedom and the cultivation of individual conscience through the study of the history of moral philosophy. She particularly emphasized those moral theories which analyzed the nature of virtue and the historical connectedness of all people. Her works included *La Morale des Stoicïens, La Morale de Socrate, La Morale d'Aristote, La Morale de Ciceron, La Morale de Plutarque (Préceptes et exemples),* and *Montaigne Moraliste et Pédagogue.* Many of her writings analyzed her views on moral education and moral psychology. She also analyzed the application of particular moral theories to social institutions affecting women. She claimed that women's particular virtue is to inculcate moral virtue in others through precept and example. She acknowledged that the social roles of women as wives, mothers, and teachers provide opportunities for women to enhance the lives of others and the moral quality of society. The opportunities to positively affect society are maximized, she claimed, when women are themselves well-educated. Consistent with her view that the social roles assigned to women can help women develop special abilities to enhance the common good through nurturance is her view that all persons are first citizens of the world and secondly members of their family and state. Positive social justice, she claimed, is inseparable from love of others. Although the social roles assigned to women give them special responsibilities for nurturing the development of the moral emotions in children, she held that there is no particular reason to believe that women are better than men at nurturing children's development of affectionate and hence, justice-giving relationships to others. In Favre's view, moral education has a central role to play in the evolution of a just society. Education that reinforces the idea of human imperfection risks failing to stimulate the desire to improve. Educational focus on compensatory justice, i.e., on balancing rights and wrongs, tends to neglect the idea that it is a natural duty to make individual choices and to take responsibility for developing a commitment to moral ideals and to living a life of virtue.

* * *

A referee of this volume requested that I include in it mention of other women who, in the referee's judgment, were "philosophers." Some of these were subjects whom I had previously researched. I had concluded that it was premature to identify them as philosophers. The difficulty of deciding which women to include and which to exclude from an introductory work such as this arises from a desire to introduce a representative cohort of women of the period who were philosophers, without stretching the criteria for "who counts as a philosopher."

There have always been at least two lists of philosophers. The first is the list of the so-called "greats." Historically, these are those male philosophers whom we dare not omit from the introductory texts. On the second list has been the "less than truly great males." There is a third list, that of women. Most were held in great esteem by their colleagues, only to be later ignored by the historians of philosophy. I am sensitive to the fact that the need for a series such as this has arisen in part because introductory texts typically claim to include only the most important philosophers. "Importance" has turned out to be defined in terms of males influenced. Without commenting on the appropriateness of this criterion, it is clear that women philosophers' thought did influence male philosophers. In my view, the "importance" criterion for inclusion in the philosophical *corpus* has been abused. What we have had until now is a measure of the importance of female historical subjects to male historians, rather than to contemporaries of both sexes. Women philosophers' exclusion from the history texts may reflect an inability of male philosopher-historians to offer a disinterested, unbiased evaluation of women's writings.

What should the inclusionary criteria be? Should a person have made a contribution to philosophy that advanced discussion on a given list of philosophical issues? This criterion too, reintroduces the question of bias. For how are philosophical issues defined, and who are the definers? Most of the subjects of this volume were a part of ongoing philosophical circles that were dominated by men. Others, particularly some feminist philosophers, were known by such exclusionary terms as *salonistes*, "bluestockings," or "suffragettes." They often travelled in woman-centered domains or addressed their writings primarily to other women. The writings of feminist philosophers were certainly well-known to circles of male philosophers, yet they appear to me to have advanced philosophical discussion mostly among women. If this observation is well-founded, then male philosophers, excepting perhaps Leibniz and Mill, ignored, discounted, and suppressed feminist philosophy. This is not surprising, for it accords with women's exclusion from the academy, from the vote, and from most forms of professional life. At bottom, however, the "advancement" criterion also begs the question. That a discussion is or is not advanced may be attributed as much to the capacity of those who hear the arguments to engage in them as to the quality of the arguments that are offered. The following pages will show that the failure of feminist philosophy to advance among male philosophers the discussion of human nature, natural rights, and political justice for women reflects male bias, not shabby philosophizing by women. When we consider the overwhelming success of feminist philosophy in influencing male debates on emancipation we see the bias more clearly. Generally speaking, women engaged the arguments of feminist philosophy to make the case for women and blacks. White men were willing to apply the conclusions of feminist arguments in the case of blacks, but not in the case of women. To exclude women feminist philosophers from the canons of philosophy because of the bias of their male contemporaries not only perpetuates the bias but enshrines bias as an appropriate inclusionary criterion.

The problem of bias brings me to another source of difficulty in developing inclusionary criteria. Most of the women who are considered in this volume fit squarely within the "malestream" tradition of philosophy for the historical period in question. However, as previously mentioned, there are many whom I am less eager to identify as philosophers. In part this diminished enthusiasm stems from the primary identification of this group of authors with other disciplines and genres. Do political activism, religious devotion, literary writing, or scientific experimentation disqualify an author from consideration as a philosopher? Clearly, these have not been grounds for excluding Jefferson, Bernard, Sartre, or Newton from, for example, *The Encyclopedia of Philosophy*. Therefore, they are not grounds for excluding Anna Doyle Wheeler, Sor Juana Inés de la Cruz, Mary Wollstonecraft, or Emilie du Châtelet from this volume. I have therefore included women whose writings in my judgment critically analyzed any recognizably philosophical subject or issue, utilizing any recognizable philosophical methodology which demonstrates knowledgeability of philosophy through mastery of its history, methods and/or problems.

Colleagues and referees have provided names of women to consider as subjects in this volume. I have excluded some of those prospective subjects on the basis of the foregoing criteria. The excluded are Aphra Behn, Mme de Coiçy, Emily Dickinson, Mary Baker Eddy, Eliza Farnham, Margaret Fell Fox, Margaret Fuller, Mme Gaçon-Dufour, Angelina Grimké, Mary Hay, Julia Ward Howe, Lady Mary Wortley Montagu, Lucretia Mott, Etta Palm d'Aelders, Anne Radcliffe, Mary Anne Radcliffe, Elizabeth Cady Stanton, Madeleine de Scudery, Germaine de Staehl, Harriet Beecher Stowe, and Victoria Woodhull. In my judgment, the present state of research indicates that some of the women listed are at best competent students of philosophy. If the case can be made for their inclusion, I would be happy to consider them for future editions of this volume.

A second referee requested that I explain the criteria by which an entire chapter is devoted to a subject, and the criteria by which a subject is relegated to less space in the final chapter. An entire chapter is devoted to a subject if three conditions are met. First, I must be convinced that the subject was a philosopher. Second, there must be sufficient material available about her to interestingly fill twenty to thirty manuscript pages. Third, one of the scholars who are part of the Project on the History of Women in Philosophy must have the background, interest, and opportunity to write the chapter. Since only a few universities have supported research of this nature, we the Project are long on qualified subjects and short on authors. Many of those subjects are, unfortunately, relegated to the final chapter which I write. Subjects are not consigned to the last chapter for lack of merit. The result is a volume which presents a fairly comprehensive history of women philosophers, albeit one which is necessarily incomplete. Certainly Catharine Ward Beecher and Harriet Taylor Mill, among others, merit fuller exposition and analysis than is possible under these circumstances. It is my hope that, as has happened in the case of women who are subjects of the first two volumes of this series, our accounts of each of the subjects of this third volume will stimulate further research by members of the philosophic community.

Women philosophers of the seventeenth, eighteenth, and nineteenth centuries helped shape and in turn were shaped by the social, political, and scientific transformations characterizing the industrial revolution.

This was a period in which women's access to formal education remained sharply restricted. Opportunities for convent education were few, and opportunities for university education were rare. Despite such obstacles, women addressed the full scope of philosophical issues facing the industrial age. They made significant contributions to all areas of philosophy and to the major philosophic discussions of their day. Although many argued for women's existential worth and philosophic potential, they held different views of women's social rights. Most were active participants in a larger philosophic community which was well acquainted with their ideas and which held them in great esteem. Many knew of other women philosophers. Some were honored by major universities, governments, professional societies, and by other eminent scholars. All are worthy subjects of further research and merit inclusion in standard histories of philosophy. It is an honor to be able to introduce them to you.

1. Margaret Cavendish, Duchess of Newcastle

LONDA SCHIEBINGER

> Being a Woman [I] Cannot ... Publickly ...
> Preach, Teach, Declare or Explane [my works]
> by Words of Mouth, as most of the most Famous
> Philosophers have done, who thereby made their
> Philosophical Opinions more Famous, than I fear
> Mine will ever be...[1]

I. BIOGRAPHY

Margaret Cavendish (1623–1673) was one of the few women in seventeenth-century England to write about natural philosophy.[2] How was it possible for a woman to do philosophy at a time when women were excluded from university and academy? Had Margaret Cavendish not been of elevated rank, it is unlikely that she would have been a philosopher. The privileges of rank gave her access to a world of philosophy. Cavendish was born Margaret Lucas, daughter of Thomas Lucas of the lesser gentry of Colchester. As she recorded in her autobiography, she had little formal education, and what education she had was that suited to a lady – singing, dancing, "playing on music," reading, writing, and the like.[3] Though women were not "suffer'd to be instructed in Schools and Universities," as she never tired of reminding her readers, this did not dampen her appetite for ideas, for (as she wrote some years later) "thoughts are free, [and we women] may as well read in our Closets, as Men in their Colleges."[4]

Margaret Lucas recognized that women's greatest access to knowledge at this time was through men. "Most Scholars," she wrote, "marry, and their heads are so full of their School Lectures, that they preach them over to their Wives when they come home, so that they [the wives] know as well what was spoke, as if they had been there."[5]

Mary Ellen Waithe (ed.), A History of Women Philosophers/Volume 3, 1–20.
© 1991 *Kluwer Academic Publishers. Printed in the Netherlands.*

Consequently, Margaret married with care William Cavendish, Duke of Newcastle, in the 1640s. Through marriage she became a member of what Robert Kargon has identified as the "Newcastle circle," consisting of William and Charles Cavendish, Thomas Hobbes, Kenelm Digby, Mersenne and Gassendi, and (while exiled in France in the 1640s and '50s) Descartes and Roberval.[6] Without this private philosophical network, Margaret Lucas Cavendish could not have become a natural philosopher.

Advantages of rank did not, however, outweigh disadvantages of sex. Though the Duchess of Newcastle found a place in the philosophical world, her ties to learned men remained tenuous. The intellectual status of noblewomen was not unlike the legal status of women of all ranks. Legally, married women were *femmes couvertes,* literally under the "cover" of their husbands. Intellectually too, women were under the cover of male mentors.

Although Margaret Cavendish was part of the "Newcastle circle," she suffered from isolation. Her contacts with other philosophers (all male) produced few intellectual rewards. Her relations with Descartes, for example, remained indirect. She may have sent philosophical queries to him through the pen of her husband, but she did not correspond with him herself. When Descartes dined at the Newcastle table, the dinners passed largely in silence. As Margaret Cavendish reported, "he spake no English, and I understand no other language, and those times I saw him, which was twice at dinner with my Lord in Paris, he did appear to me a man of the fewest words I ever heard."[7]

Cavendish's isolation was not voluntary. The breeding grounds of the new science, such as the newly founded Royal Society of London, did not allow women to become members. Membership in the Royal Society was more open and fluid than its counterpart in Paris, the Académie Royale des Sciences, and it would not have gone against the expansive temper of the English Society to have invited qualified women to join. The Duchess of Newcastle in particular was a well-qualified candidate, having written some six books about natural philosophy, along with several other plays and books of poetry. In addition, she had long been a generous patron of Cambridge University and would have been a financial asset to the impoverished society.

Although never invited to join the Royal Society, Cavendish was so bold as to ask to attend a session.[8] One should recall that fellows of noble birth bestowed prestige upon the new society; men above the rank of baron could become members without the scrutiny given other applicants.[9] When the duchess asked for nothing more than to be allowed to visit a working session of the society, however, her request aroused a flood of controversy. Nonetheless, she was allowed to attend one session after some discussion among society fellows. The famous visit took place in 1667. Robert Boyle prepared his "experiments of ... weighing of air in an exhausted receiver; [and] ... dissolving of flesh with a certain liquor."[10] The duchess, accompanied by her ladies, was much impressed by the demonstrations and left (according to one observer) "full of admiration."[11] This single encounter with the men of science, however, could hardly have been satisfying. The duchess never even mentioned this visit in her memoirs.

Although no official record of the discussion of Cavendish's visit remains, Samuel Pepys tells us that there was "much debate, *pro* and *con*, it seems many being against it, and we do believe the town will be full of ballads of it."[12] When no other ballads appeared, Royal Society member John Evelyn wrote one of his own.[13] From Pepys's report it seems many fellows felt that Cavendish's presence would bring ridicule rather than honor. Margaret Cavendish's visit indeed appears to have set a precedent – a negative one. No woman was elected to full membership in the Royal Society until 1945.[14]

Nor did Cavendish benefit from intellectual companionship with other women. Salons did not flourish in England as they did in France, and as a result intellectual women in England suffered from isolation. Apart from a brief membership in Katherine Philips's "Society of Friendship," Cavendish cultivated few intellectual friends among women. Indeed, she often chided the ladies of her day for "playing at cards" and not being "delighted in ... Philosophy."[15] She did not know Anne Conway, for example, a philosopher with whom Cavendish might have had much in common.

Cavendish's chief intellectual companions were within her family. A frontispiece reproduced in several of her philosophical works shows a "semy-circle" of ladies and gentlemen seated amicably around a table, the caption bears the title "The Duke and Dutchess of Newcastle and their Family." By her own account, Cavendish "never had a familiar acquaintance, or constant conversation with any profest Scholar, in my life, or a familiar acquaintance with any man, so as to learn by them, but those that I have neer relation to, as my Husband, and Brothers."[16] Cavendish claimed she had never spent "even an hour" discussing philosophy with those other than her family.

Margaret Cavendish learned a great deal from her brother, Lord John Lucas, one of the original Fellows of the Royal Society; she also claimed to have profited from discussions with Sir Charles Cavendish, brother of William, who had a real interest in science and mathematics and kept abreast of all the latest developments.[17] Yet it was her husband, William, whom Margaret claimed as her "Wits Patron."[18] William Cavendish – a man thirty years her senior – was himself a respectable gentleman *virtuoso*, reputed by William Petty to be a great patron to Gassendi, Descartes, and Hobbes.[19] While exiled in France and Holland from 1644 to 1660, William Cavendish collected seven telescopes – four made by Estacio Divino, two by Torricelli, and one by Fontanus.[20] William was, however, neither deeply scholarly nor profound. His greatest love was the "noble and heroick Art of *Horsemanship* and *Weapons*."[21] If William was not the critic Margaret required, he did serve her well with his moral and financial support. Nearly all of her philosophical works include a laudatory verse from William.[22] In addition, he financed the repeated private publication of her many works.

According to her own account, Margaret Cavendish remained, for most of her life, cloistered in her study working in her own world of philosophy. This she attributed, in part, to her "bashfull" nature and, in part, to her condition as a woman. Excluded by custom and temperament from public life, the Duchess of Newcastle tried to make contact with the learned world through her books. These she dedicated to the "most famously learned" men of the universities. She sent each of her beautifully published volumes to Oxford and to Cambridge, where her husband and two brothers had been educated. This she did for her own glory, to be sure – the duchess was not properly modest for an English woman of the seventeenth century. But she also intended that her works be an example for the "good encouragement" of other women and give "our Sex Courage and Confidence to Write, and to Divulge what they Writ in Print."[23] She also sent a complete set of her philosophical work to Christian Huygens at the University of Leiden, along with a Latin index.[24] In return she received letters of thanks and vapid praise of the type a courtier would offer a lady. Only Joseph Glanvill and Huygens engaged her in serious correspondence: Glanvill discussed with her his work on witchcraft; Huygens discussed with her "Rupert's exploding drops."[25]

II. WORKS

The Duchess of Newcastle was not only one of the first women to produce original natural philosophy, she was also the boldest and most prolific. In addition to literary orations, plays, and poems, Cavendish wrote a number of philosophical works: *Philosophical and Physical Opinions* (1655), *Natures Pictures Drawn by Fancies Pencil to The Life* (1656), *Philosophical Letters: or, Modest Reflections upon some Opinions in Natural Philosophy, Maintained by Several Famous and Learned Authors of this Age* (1664), her fascinating *Observations upon Experimental Philosophy* (1666), to which was added a utopia or science fiction, *The Description of a new World, called The Blazing World,* and her *Grounds of Natural Philosophy* (1668). Margaret Cavendish was an extremely self-conscious writer; to all of her works she appended prefaces which provide a vivid portrayal of her philosophical ambitions and her keen sense of the barriers faced by one of her sex.

Although often addressed to women, Cavendish's natural philosophy was not written as a simplification or popularization for the "weaker sex." Rather, she participated in discussions central to her life and times, taking up debates about matter and motion, the existence of the vacuum, the nature of magnetism, life and generation, color and fire, perception and knowledge, free will and God. Cavendish also entered into (usually one-way) correspondence with key philosophers on these issues. Her *Philosophical Letters* presented a point-by-point critique of Hobbes's *Leviathan,* while her *Elements of Philosophy* attacked Descartes and his vortices, Henry More's proof of God, and van Helmont's "odd and strange Art of Chemistry." Her philosophical boldness remained long unmatched by any other woman.

Cavendish's great purpose in writing was to achieve fame. She was as she put it "as ambitious as ever any of my Sex was, is, or can be."[26] She identified three avenues to fame in the England of her day: leadership in government, military conquest, and innovation in philosophy. As government and military were closed to her by law, she took up natural philosophy. In her *Description of a New World* she wrote:

Though I cannot be Henry the Fifth, or Charles the Second, yet I endeavour to be Margaret the First; and although I have neither power, time nor occasion to conquer the world as Alexander and Caesar did; yet rather then [sic] not to be Mistress of one, since Fortune and the Fates would give me none, I have made a World of my own.[27]

This was not, in her view, such a poor alternative, given that men "hold Books as their Crowne ... by which they rule and governe."[28] Cavendish hoped her books would bring her similar glories. She pleaded with Lady Fortune to

place my Book in Fames high Tow'r, where every Word, like a Cymball, shall make a Tinkling Noise; and the whole Volume, like a Cannon Bullet, shall Eccho from Side to Side of Fames large Brasen Walls, and make so loud a Report, that all the World shall hear it.[29]

Margaret Cavendish based her claim to fame on the originality of her work.[30] Referring to her contemporaries, she wrote,

I found so much difference betwixt their conceptions and my own in Natural Philosophy, that were it allowable or usual for our Sex, I might set up a sect or School for my self, without any prejudice to them; But I, being a woman, do fear they would soon cast me out of their Schools ....[31]

Unable to found her own "sect" of philosophy, Cavendish set forth to "argue with some famous and eminent writers," ancient and modern, whose conceptions of nature did not conform to her own.[32] Though many of Cavendish's views were original, many also reflected those of the Newcastle circle as transmitted through her husband, William, reflecting (especially) the views of Hobbes, who had tutored William in years past.

III. NATURAL PHILOSOPHY

Margaret Cavendish set out her natural philosophy most clearly in three major works: her *Philosophical Letters, Observations upon*

Experimental Philosophy, and her *Grounds of Natural Philosophy.*[33] Cavendish was a thoroughgoing materialist.[34] Yet, she did not contribute to what Carolyn Merchant has described as the "death of nature," the process by which master mechanists of the scientific revolution came to think of nature as a system of dead, inert particles moved by external forces.[35] Central to her conception of nature is that matter is intelligent. For Cavendish, nature is composed of an infinite number of "intelligent" atoms, each with self-knowledge and self-propulsion. In her *Observations on Experimental Philosophy,* Cavendish enumerated her views:

> 1. Matter, Self-motion and Self-knowledge, are inseparable from each other, and make Nature, one Material, self-moving, self-knowing Body.
> 2. Nature being Material, is dividable into parts; being infinite in quantity and bulk, her parts are infinite in number.
> 3. No part can subsist singly ... precised from the rest; but they are all parts of one infinite body ....
> 6. Nature is purely corporeal and material, spiritual beings... are no ways belonging to Nature.[36]

Cavendish denied that there is "any Creature or part of Nature without...Life and Soul."[37] For Cavendish matter is not dead body, devoid of spirit; rather, corporeal nature is both subject and agent. Objecting to Hobbes's distinction between intelligent subject and inanimate object, Cavendish stated that "all things, and therefore outward objects as well as sensitive organs, have both sense and reason."[38] On similar grounds, she criticized Descartes's radical distinction between mind and body. She insisted that a fundamental unity pervaded the world, that nature was composed of one self-moving, intelligent matter.[39]

Cavendish's rejection of mind/body dualism led her into the atheist camp. For Cavendish, only matter exists. This matter being itself "intelligent," there is no need for a first cause. "Self-moving matter, which is sensitive and rational," she wrote, is "the only cause and principle of all natural effects."[40] On this basis, she objected to Descartes's notion of vortices set in motion by God. "I cannot," she wrote, "well apprehend what Des Cartes means, by Matter being at first set a moving by a strong and lively action [God]."[41] Cavendish banished God to the supernatural and relegated things spiritual to a sphere beyond experimental philosophy. Cavendish held that

> Nature has infinite ways of Motions, where of none is prime or principal, but self-motion, which is the producer of all the varities Nature has within herself.[42]

Much like the authors of the Royal Society, Cavendish too struck a compromise with established religion by separating philosophy from theology. In her 1663 *Philosophical and Physical Opinions*, she wrote:

> Thus, Noble Readers, you will find, that this present Work contains Pure Natural Philosophy, without any Mixture of Theology, ... this Work, as aforesaid, is onely natural Philosophy, which will neither Obstruct nor do Harm either to the Church or State, or to the Conscience of Life of Man ....[43]

In one of her earlier works, Cavendish had conceded that knowledge of God might be innate. Unlike Descartes, however, Cavendish made knowledge of God a part of both inanimate and animate matter. "All parts of Nature," she wrote, "even the inanimate, have an innate and fixt self-knowledge, it is probable that they may also have an interior self-knowledge of the existency of the Eternal and Omnipotent God, as the Author of Nature."[44]

Margaret Cavendish's rejection of a sharp distinction between animate and inanimate nature led her to reject the Cartesian imperative that man through science should become "master and possessor" of nature. Such a view, Cavendish held, was impossible. "We have," she insisted, "no power at all over natural causes and effects." Man is merely one part of nature.[45] The whole (nature itself) can know the parts, but the parts (men) cannot know the whole. Consequently, since he is not above nature, man must be content with things as nature is

> ... pleased to order them ... for man is but a small part ... his powers are but particular actions of Nature, and he cannot have a supreme and absolute power.[46]

Nor was Cavendish as quick as Descartes or Henry More to proclaim man the "flower and chief of nature."[47] Cavendish thought that man was in no position to judge such an issue, since he was himself author of the debate. Cavendish thus found man "partial" in this matter where other creatures were given no voice. She argued moreover that "Elemental Creatures" (that is, non humans) are as "excellent and Wise" as man: for what man, she asked, is as clever as a bee and able to build a honeycomb? The much-praised man she deemed not so useful to his fellow-creatures, as his fellow-creatures are to him, for men are not so profitable for use and more apt to make spoil.[48]

Within two years of her critique of the rationalists Hobbes and Descartes, Cavendish penned an equally sharp critique of the experimentalists (though unnamed, most probably) Robert Boyle and Robert Hooke.[49] A firm advocate of contemplative speculation, Cavendish judged reason more reliable than sense: "Neither ought Artists," she wrote, "... prefer the Experimental part [of Philosophy] before [the contemplative] .... Reason must direct first how sense ought to work."[50] Reason, in other words, ought to ground philosophy. Senses, too apt to be deluded, could not serve as a sure foundation for reason. If Cavendish judged the sensory organs unreliable, she judged the new telescopes and microscopes even more unreliable. The glass of these new scientific instruments she found too often cracked, concave, or convex and in danger of distorting the figure. In her view, glasses present a "hermaphroditical" view of things, "partly artificial, partly natural so that a Lowse appears like a Lobster."[51] More important, these impure images go no further than reason in providing true knowledge – what she called "the interior natural motions of any part or creature of Nature."[52] Cavendish also criticized experimental philosophy for being impractical: "The inspection of a Bee, through a Microscope, will bring ... no more honey."[53]

Cavendish argued eloquently for the vitality of matter and the dignity of animals; and, within contemporary discourse, these views were consistent with her anti-Cartesianism. Yet, it is unclear why she held one set of views over another. Never in her writings did Cavendish draw out political or social consequences from her philosophical positions. It may be that isolated in her chamber, as she was, she did not see the connection between one set of views and another.

Cavendish's bold attack on rationalist and empiricist, ancient and modern, was sharply censured by Joseph Glanvill, one of the leading figures in the Royal Society. In explicit reference to her work, Glanvill warned that "he is a bold Man, who dares to attack the Physics of Aristotle himself, or of Democritus ... or Descartes, or Mr. Hobbs."[54] The Duchess of Newcastle did not take criticism lying down. She made clear that her want of learning – for which she repeatedly apologized – was not peculiar to her but was a liability of her sex. "[That] I am not versed in [learning], no body, I hope, will blame me for it, since it is sufficiently known, that our Sex is not bred up to it, as being not suffer'd to be instructed in Schools and Universities."[55] She also recognized some criticism for what it was – pure prejudice: "I as a Woman, cannot be exempted from the malice and aspersions of spiteful tongues, which they cast upon my poor Writings, some denying me to be the true Authress of them; for ... those Books I put out first, to the judgment of this censorious Age, were accounted not to be written by a Woman. ..."[56] Though Cavendish reported "censorious" criticisms of her work, we do not know the source of that criticism or how it was communicated to her. In fact, her work suffered the worst censor of all – neglect. Unlike the work of the entomologist Maria Merian or the philosopher-physicist Émilie du Châtelet, Cavendish's work was not reviewed in major European journals.

IV. FEMINISM

The Duchess of Newcastle was greatly frustrated by the limitations placed upon her because of her sex. And, indeed, she had a great deal to say about women – not all of it favorable. In many ways, Cavendish's life stood at odds with her writings. Though her actions were bold, her views of women were often conventional.

It is important to look in some detail at Cavendish's writings on women because her treatment highlights structural problems in the treatment of the woman question that persist to this day. The first thing to note is that Cavendish's remarks on women appeared in prefaces to her works and in letters; she did not integrate women's issues into mainstream philosophical discourse. More important, as we will see below, Cavendish did not plant her proto-feminist views in new philosophical ground. Though Cavendish prided herself on the uniqueness of her philosophy, she did not ground the "woman question" in the new philosophy. In this Cavendish followed the example of the men she criticized – Descartes, Hobbes, Hooke, and Boyle. Like other philosophers of her day, Cavendish did not meet the woman question head on: women and their distinctive concerns were relegated to the sidelines of official philosophy.

In her early work, Cavendish uncritically accepted the long-standing pronouncements of the ancients on women. Along with Aristotle, she judged the masculine spirit superior to the feminine. "It is not," she wrote, "so great a Fault in Nature for a Woman to be masculine, as for a Man to be Effeminate: for it is a Defect in Nature to decline, as to see Men like Women, but to see a Masculine Woman, is but onely as if Nature had mistook, and had placed a Mans Spirit in a Womans Body."[57] Cavendish also accepted the ancient doctrine of humors which judged women inherently inferior to men: "It cannot be expected I should write so wisely or wittily as Men, being of the Effeminate Sex, whose Brains Nature hath mix'd with the coldest and softest Elements." The "softness" of the female brain (not, surprisingly, women's lack of education) explained, for Cavendish, women's poor showing in philosophy:

> This [the softness of the female brain] is the Reason why we are not Mathematicians; Arithmeticians, Logicians, Geometricians, Cosmographers, and the like; This is the Reason we are not Witty Poets, Eloquent Orators, Subtill Schoolmen, Subtracting Chimists, Rare Musicians, [and the like]. ... What Woman was ever so wise as Solomon, or Aristotle ... so Eloquent as Tully? so demonstrative as Euclid? It was not a Woman that found out the Card, the Needle, and the use of the Loadstone, it was not a Woman that invented Perspective-Glasses to pierce into the Moon; it was not a Woman that found out the invention of writing Letters, and the Art of Printing; it was not a Woman that found out the invention of Gunpowder, and the art of Gunns... or what ever did we do but like Apes, by Imitation?[58]

Like so many of her day, Cavendish judged this supposed inferiority in women's physical and intellectual character consistent with their social disenfranchisement:

> But to speak truth, Men have great Reason not let us in to their Governments, for there is great difference betwixt the Masculine

Brain and the Feminine, the Masculine Strength and the Feminine;
For could we choose out of the World two of the ablest Brain and
strongest Body of each Sex, there would be great difference in the
Understanding and Strength; for Nature hath made Mans Body
more able to endure Labour, and Mans Brain more clear to understand and contrive than Womans; and as great a difference there is
between them, as there is between the longest and strongest
Willow, compared to the strongest and largest Oak ....[59]

Cavendish never contradicted her view that the "wisest woman [is] not
so wise as the wisest of Men." Yet she left a caveat to explain her own
achievement. "Some women," she wrote, "are wiser than some men."
In her view, women of the educated classes were superior in learning
to "Rustick and Rude-bred men."[60]

Cavendish never renounced these views borrowed, for the most
part, from the ancients. In her "Femal Oration" (1662), however,
Cavendish seemed less certain about them. Her "Oration" is composed
of five voices, each presenting a different view of women's character
and social condition. The first voice represents the strongest opponent
of the "Tyrannical Government" of men. Though Cavendish energeti-
cally recorded this view, it was never her own.

Ladies, Gentlewomen, and other Inferiours, but not less Worthy, I
have been Industrious to Assemble you together, and wish I were
so Fortunate, as to persuade you to make a Frequentation, Association, and Combination amongst our Sex, that we may Unite in
Prudent Counsels, to make our Selves as Free, Happy, and Famous
as Men.... Men are so Unconscionable and Cruel against us, as
they Indeavor to Barr us of all Sorts or Kinds of Liberty, as not to
Suffer us Freely to Associate amongst our Sex, but would fain Bury
us in their Houses or Beds, as in a Grave; the truth is, we Live like
Bats or Owls, Labour like Beasts, and Dye like Worms.[61]

A second voice counters with the argument that nature, and not men,
has made women inferior:

But we have more Reason to Murmur against Nature than against
Men, who hath made Men more Ingenious, Witty, and Wise than
Women, more Strong, Industrious, and Laborious than Women.[62]

Voice number three – perhaps Cavendish's own – pleads for a nurturing of women's bodies and minds in order to develop within them a "masculine" strength:

> For Strength is Increased by Exercise, Wit is Lost for want of Conversation... let us Hawk, Hunt, Race, and do like Exercises as Men have, and let us Converse in Camps, Courts, and Cities, in Schools, Colleges, and Courts of Judicature, in Taverns, Brothels [!], and Gaming Houses, all which will make our Strength and Wit known, both to Men, and to our own Selves, for we are as Ignorant of our Selves, as Men are of us .... Wherefore, my Advice is, we should Imitate Men, so will our Bodies and Minds appear more Masculine, and our Power will Increase by our Actions.[63]

Yet another voice (perhaps an undecided Cavendish) warns that *nurture* cannot contradict *nature*. To educate women and to extend to them "liberties of conversation" would be like grafting peach branches onto an apple tree that might then bear the wrong fruit.[64] To contradict nature's will, in other words, is dangerous. A feminine manner becomes a female body; to attach masculine virtues to a feminine body would be unnatural and unwise:

> The former Oration was to Persuade us to Change the Custom of our Sex, which is a Strange and Unwise Persuasion, since we cannot make our selves Men; and to have Femal Bodies, and yet to Act Masculine Parts, will be very Preposterous and Unnatural; In truth, we shall make our Selves like as the Defects of Nature, as to be Hermaphroditical, as neither to be Perfect Women nor Perfect Men, but Corrupt and Imperfect Creatures; Wherefore, let me Persuade you, since we cannot Alter the Nature of our Persons, not to Alter the Course of our Lives, but to Rule our Lives and Be-haviours, as to be Acceptable to God and Men, which is to be Modest, Chast, Temperate, Humble, Patient, and Pious: also to be Huswifely, Cleanly, and of few Words ....[65]

Above all, this fourth speaker warns women against becoming "hermaphroditical," corrupt and imperfect. The hermaphrodite – the "womanish man" or "manly woman" – provoked uneasy feelings in the Europe of her day, and Cavendish used the term degradingly to refer to anything of a mixed nature – as, for example, impure alloys of tin or brass. If metals were to be censured for ambiguous identity (being, as she pointed out, half natural and half artificial), how much more serious was the charge of ambiguous sexual identity. The speaker in this oration (like Cavendish herself) admonishes women to follow their own nature and remain properly "feminine," "huswifely," "cleanly," and "of few words."

A fifth and final voice closed the Oration with the familiar neo-Platonic view that women are different from, and indeed superior to, men:

> Why should we Desire to be Masculine, since our Own Sex and Condition is far the Better? for if Men have more Courage, they have more Danger; and if Men have more Strength, they have more Labour...; if Men are more Eloquent in Speech, Women are more Harmonious in Voice; if Men be more Active, Women are more Gracefull... Wherefore, Women have no Reason to Complain against Nature, or the God of Nature ...[66]

In this "Femal Oration" Cavendish left unresolved the source of women's subordination – tyrannical men, nature, or nurture. She also left unresolved the relative value of masculinity and femininity. Are the strengths and liberties of masculinity the preferred traits, and thus to be cultivated in women as well as in men? Or, are the sexes to strike a bargain, wherein each perfects its own virtues? Or, alternatively, are the beauty and grace of femininity, in fact, culturally superior qualities? As Cavendish later remarked, she spoke freely in these orations – *pro* and *con* – but did not take sides.[67]

After these orations only occasional remarks on women appeared in prefaces to Cavendish's works and in her letters. She abandoned the woman question in her major philosophical works. Though her actions remained bold, she failed to set old questions concerning women on new philosophical foundations. Rather, as Cavendish read deeper into the philosophy of Hobbes and Descartes, she increasingly spoke only of generic "man."[68]

Was there potential (however unfulfilled) within Cavendish's philosophy of nature for a liberal posture toward women? In her later works, consistency alone demanded that Cavendish abandon her earliest notions that feminine weakness – the small arms and tender feet, the soft and moist brain – adequately explained women's subordination, for in these works there is no possibility of stronger or weaker minds: rational matter is homogeneous. Rational matter, being all of the same quality, can have no differences in strength. Cavendish portrayed a kind of democracy among the infinite bits of matter. Harmony in nature required that each bit of matter follow its own inner logos. If the strong dominated the weak, the methodical and regular workings of the weaker parts would be violated and there would be no harmony. Nature's laws would be violated.[69] Though her views on matter might conceivably have been extrapolated to human relations, Cavendish left that potential unfulfilled. A staunch royalist, the good duchess was uncomfortable with any changes which threatened ancient privilege.[70] Though philosophically a modern, she frowned upon those whom she considered "unconscionable Men in Civil Wars," who endeavor "to pull down the hereditary Mansions of Noble-men and Gentlemen to build a Cottage of their own; for so do they pull down the learning of Ancient Authors, to render themselves famous in composing Books of their own."[71] Cavendish followed the moderns who advocated the use of the vernacular over Latin, and philosophy which made "hard things easy so that they might be understood by all."[72] Yet the Duchess of Newcastle did not advocate changes which might have threatened the privilege she herself enjoyed over men of lower rank.

Cavendish's hesitant approach to the woman question was never consistent with her own ambitions. She had refused from her earliest years to follow a traditionally female path. In her youth, she took up the pen and not the needle. In her maturity, she took up philosophy and not housewifery. "I cannot for my Life be so good a Huswife, as to quit Writing ... the truth is, I have somewhat Err'd from good Huswifry, to write nature's Philosophy."[73]

V. CONCLUSIONS

Margaret Cavendish attempted to launch herself into mainstream philosophical debates. Through her station she achieved limited access to a European network of learned men. Yet convention was against her, and for her efforts she was dubbed "Mad Madge" by her contemporaries Samuel Pepys and Mrs. Evelyn. She was not, however, mad, but immodest. Every part of her project – her voluminous publication, her visit to the Royal Society, her autobiography, her criticism of "learned men" – overstepped the bounds of convention. Rather than apologizing for finding fault with Descartes's philosophy (as did Elisabeth, Princess of Bohemia), Cavendish relished her attack. Nevertheless, there were times she was forced to bow to convention. In 1656, she published the first autobiography of an English woman as part of her *Natures Pictures*. When *Natures Pictures* was republished fifteen years later, the autobiography had been removed.[74]

How are we to explain Cavendish's departure from the English custom of quiet, pious feminine deportment? Cavendish never revealed the source of her feminism. She was unaware of her intellectual predecessors – women such as Christine de Pisan or Anna van Schurman. Nor did Cavendish search for feminist forebears: "I have not read much in History to inform me of the past Ages, ... for I fear I should meet with such of my Sex, that have out done all the glory I can aime at ..."[75] The upheaval of the Civil War, and the short-lived toleration of public voices for women may have influenced Cavendish in her youth. Perhaps during her years of exile she took in the feminist air of the Continent. The Restoration, in any case, along with the return of the duke and duchess to England in 1600, served to silence her philosophical voice. Two years after her critique of experimental philosophy and shortly after her visit to the Royal Society in 1667, Margaret Cavendish published a more modest edition of *Grounds of Natural Philosophy* (taking back many of her earlier claims) as her last philosophical work. She died soon thereafter and was buried in Westminster Abbey, where she still lies today.

NOTES

1. Margaret Cavendish, *Philosophical and Physical Opinions* (London, 1663), "An Epistle to the Reader."
2. Between 1475 and 1700, women in England and America published some 600 books, or about half of one percent of the total number of books published (Elaine Hobby, "English Women in Print, 1640–1700," paper delivered at the Sixth Berkshire Conference on the History of Women, June 3, 1984). Twenty-one of these books were published by Margaret Cavendish alone; fifteen were original works which then appeared in various editions to equal twenty-one publications in all.

3. Margaret Cavendish, "A true relation of my Birth, Breeding, and Life," in *Natures Pictures* (London, 1656), p. 370.

4. Cavendish, *Worlds Olio* (London, 1655), "The Preface to the Reader."

5. *Ibid.*

6. Robert Kargon, *Atomism in England from Hariot to Newton* (Oxford, 1966), pp. 68–76.

7. Margaret Cavendish, *Philosophical and Physical Opinions* (London, 1655), "An Epilogue to my Philosophical Opinions."

8. See Samuel Mintz "The Duchess of Newcastle's Visit to the Royal Society," *Journal of English and Germanic Philology* 51, no. 2 (1952), pp. 168–176.

9. Thomas Birch, *History of the Royal Society*, 2 vols. (London, 1756–57), vol. 2, p. 175.

10. Samuel Pepys, *The Diary of Samuel Pepys*, ed. Robert Latham and William Matthews, 11 vols. (London, 1970–1983), vol. 8, p. 243.

11. Michael Hunter, *The Royal Society and its Fellows 1660–1700: The Morphology of an Early Scientific Institution* (Chalfont St. Giles, Bucks, 1982), p. 9.

12. Pepys, *The Diary of Samuel Pepys*, vol. 8, p. 243.

13. Douglas Grant, *Margaret the First: A Biography of Margaret Cavendish, Duchess of Newcastle, 1623–1673* (London, 1957), p. 26. See also Virginia Woolf, "The Duchess of Newcastle," in *The Common Reader* (London, 1929), pp. 98–109.

14. Kathleen Lonsdale and Marjory Stephenson were elected in 1945. *Notes and Records of the Royal Society of London* 4 (1946), pp. 39–40. See also Kathleen Lonsdale's thoughtful article, "Women in Science: Reminiscences and Reflections," *Impact of Science on Society* 20, no. 1 (1970), pp. 45–59.

15. Margaret Cavendish, *CCXI. Sociable Letters* (London, 1664), p. 38.

16. Cavendish, *Worlds Olio*, "Epistle" following p. 26. The best account of Cavendish's intellectual development is in her *Philosophical and Physical Opinions*, "To the Reader." Here Cavendish clearly stated that her education came from the male members of her family. "But let me tell my Readers that what I have learned since I was married, it is from my Lord, and what I had learned before it was from my own familie, as from my own brothers ...."

17. Grant, *Margaret the First*, pp. 23 and 91. For his correspondence with Descartes concerning mathematics, see René Descartes, *Oeuvres de Descartes*, ed. Charles Adam and Paul Tannery (Paris, 1964–1972), vol. 4, pp. 380–389.

18. Cavendish, *Worlds Olio*, "My Lord."

19. Kargon, *Atomism in England from Hariot to Newton*, p. 68. See also Descartes, *Oeuvres de Descartes*, vol. 4, pp. 325–330 and vol. 5, pp. 117–118. Descartes tired of William's queries about the nature of hunger and thirst, the heat of animals, and so forth. In 1648, he wrote to Mersenne, "Ie serois aussy réponse à Monsr. de Neucastel; mais il me propose des questions, ausquelles ie ne puis repondre en moins d'une grande feuille de papier." *Ibid.*, vol. 5, p. 117.

20. Grant, *Margaret the First*, p. 93.

21. Cavendish, *Observations upon Experimental Philosophy* (London, 1666), "To his Grace the Duke of Newcastle."

22. See, for example, William's verse in *Observations upon Experimental*

Philosophy: "This Book is Book of Books, and only fits Great Searching Brains, and Quintessence of Wits; For this will give you an Eternal Fame... And make me famous too in such a Wife ...."

23. Cavendish, *The Philosophical and Physical Opinions* (1655), "To the two Universities. Most Famously learned;" Cavendish, *Sociable Letters*, pp. 225–226.

24. Cavendish also hoped to have her *opus* translated into Latin in order to make her work available to foreign scholars, but to no avail; the idiosyncracies of her terminology baffled the translator. See Grant, *Margaret the First*, p. 218.

25. *Letters and Poems in Honour of the Incomparable princess, Margaret, Dutchess of Newcastle* (London, 1676), pp. 108–119. See also, Grant, *Margaret the First*, pp. 193–194.

26. Margaret Cavendish, *The Description of a New World, called The Blazing World* (London, 1666), Preface.

27. *Ibid.*

28. Margaret Cavendish, *Poems and Fancies*, 2nd ed. (London, 1656), Preface.

29. Margaret Cavendish, *Worlds Olio* (London, 1655), A "Dedication to Fortune."

30. "As for the Ground of this Philosophical work, as Matter, Motion and Figure," she wrote, " 'tis as Old as Eternity it Self, but my Opinions of this Ground are as New as from my First Conception." Margaret Cavendish, *Philosophical and Physical Opinions* (London, 1663), "Epistle to the Reader."

31. Margaret Cavendish, *Observations on Experimental Philosophy*, "Observations Upon the Opinions of some Ancient Philosophers," p. 1–2.

32. *Ibid.*, Preface. Cavendish's critical remarks are sometimes difficult to follow; she often took a rather atomistic approach criticizing particular points rather than entire systems. In addition, her criticism is often addressed to "Some Wise and Learned Men" rather than specific individuals.

33. Her earlier *Philosophical and Physical Opinions*, written before she had studied philosophy, was incoherent and naive, as she admitted in a preface to her *Grounds of Natural Philosophy* (London, 1668).

34. Grant's excellent biography pays little attention to Cavendish's philosophical views and where he does, he incorrectly stresses her agreement with the growing consensus of a dual nature of body and spirit. Grant, *Margaret the First*, p. 196. Only in her last work does Cavendish pay lipservice to the distinction between animate and inanimate nature, and even then inanimate nature is "self-knowing." Cavendish, *Grounds of Natural Philosophy*, p. 3. For an interesting treatment of Cavendish's philosophy, see Lisa Sarasohn, "A Science Turned Upside Down: Feminism and the Natural Philosophy of Margaret Cavendish," *The Huntington Library Quarterly* 47 (1984), pp. 289–307.

35. Carolyn Merchant, *The Death of Nature: Women, Ecology and the Scientific Revolution* (San Francisco, 1980), p. 193.

36. Cavendish, *Observations on Experimental Philosophy*, "Of Knowledge and Perception in General," p. 155.

37. Cavendish, *Philosophical Letters* (London, 1664), "A Preface to the Reader."

38. Cavendish, *Philosophical Letters*, p. 18.

39. *Ibid.*, p. 111. As others of her day, Cavendish was quick to question Descartes's notion of the pineal gland as the meeting point of mind and body. "Neither can I

apprehend," she wrote, "that the mind's or Soul's seat should be the Glandula." *Ibid.*

40. *Ibid.*, "To the Reader."
41. *Ibid.*, part 1, p. 49.
42. *Ibid.*, part 1, p. 50.
43. Cavendish, *Philosophical and Physical Opinions*, "An Epistle to the Reader."
44. *Ibid.*, "To the Reader."
45. Cavendish used "man" in the generic sense. I remain true to her style.
46. Cavendish, *Observations on Experimental Philosophy*, "All powerful God and Servant of Nature."
47. Cavendish, *Philosophical Letters*, p. 147.
48. *Ibid.*
49. Grant, *Margaret the First*, p. 204.
50. Cavendish, *Observations upon Experimental Philosophy*, "Further Observations upon Experimental Philosophy."
51. *Ibid.*, pp. 7–8.
52. *Ibid.*
53. *Ibid.*, "The Preface to the ensuing Treatise."
54. *Letters and Poems in Honour of the Incomparable princess, Margaret, Dutchess of Newcastle*, p. 119.
55. Cavendish, *Observations upon Experimental Philosophy*, "To the Most Famous University of Cambridge."
56. Margaret Cavendish, *The Life of the thrice Noble, High and Puissant Prince William Cavendishe, Duke, Marquess, and Earl of Newcastle* (London, 1667), "To his Grace." Douglas Grant has suggested that Cavendish's critical attitudes arose from her belief that experimental philosophy was undermining the tradition of rational speculation, and with it the legitimacy of her philosophical voice. Grant, *Margaret the First*, pp. 205–209.
57. Cavendish, *Worlds Olio*, p. 84.
58. Cavendish,. *The Worlds Olio*, "The Preface to the Reader." It should be noted that Cavendish's assessment of women's scientific accomplishments differed dramatically from those of someone like Christine de Pizan who emphasized women's innovations in fields such as agriculture and domestic economy. See Christine de Pizan, *The Book of the City of Ladies*, trans. Earl Jeffrey Richards (New York, 1982).
59. *Ibid.*
60. *Ibid.* In this section I quote extensively from Cavendish's works. These passages convey an excellent sense of seventeenth-century debates on the character of woman.
61. Margaret Cavendish, "Femal Orations," in *Orations of Diverse Sorts* (London, 1662), p. 225.
62. *Ibid.*, p. 227.
63. *Ibid.*, p. 228.
64. Cavendish, *The Worlds Olio*, "The Preface to the Reader."
65. Cavendish, "Femal Orations," p. 229.
66. *Ibid.*, p. 231.

67. Cavendish, *Sociable Letters*, "The Preface."
68. Cavendish died in 1673, too early to have known François Poullain de la Barre's radical application of Cartesianism to the woman question, *De l'égalité des deux sexes: Discours physique et moral* (Paris, 1673).
69. Cavendish, *Grounds of Natural Philosophy*, p. 14.
70. The Duke and Duchess of Newcastle were both royalists. William Cavendish was general of all royalist forces in the north of England during the Civil War. Janet Todd has pointed out that at the end of the seventeenth century there was an as-yet unexplained link between feminism and royalism. *A Dictionary of British and American Women Writers 1660–1800* (London, 1984), p. 5. See also Catherine Gallagher, "Embracing the Absolute: The Politics of the Female Subject in Seventeenth Century England," *Genders* 1 (1988), pp. 24–39.
71. Cavendish, *Observations upon Experimental Philosophy*, "The Preface to the Ensuing Treatise."
72. *Ibid.*
73. Cavendish, *Philosophical and Physical Opinions*, "Dedication."
74. See Grant, *Margaret the First*, p. 154 and Hobby, "English Women in Print, 1640–1700."
75. Cavendish, *Natures Pictures*, "An Epistle to my Readers."

2. Kristina Wasa, Queen of Sweden

SUSANNA ÅKERMAN

The irreligious skepticism of Kristina of Sweden (1626–1689) is one of the most interesting forces behind her abdication in 1654. Her doubts, during her transition from Lutheranism to Catholicism, were provisionally resolved by a naturalistic religion with materialistic implications. Instead of behaving outwardly like others while thinking like a skeptic, Kristina explicitly defied traditional expectations of royal manners and language. She seemed to have abandoned her duties by renouncing God's pact with her as an anointed ruler. Through her public actions, Kristina became a symbol of atheism, lesbianism, and other unorthodox, clandestine opinions. Her philosophical skepticism is reflected not only in her actions, but particularly in her religious beliefs as well as in her social, political, and moral philosophy.

I. BIOGRAPHY

Kristina was born in 1626. By 1632, with the death of her father, Gustavus Adolphus (Gustav II, "The Lion of the North and the Bulwark of Protestantism"), Kristina Wasa inherited the leadership of an aspiring and warring nation. Early in her reign, her country triumphed: with the Peace of Westphalia in 1648, the devastating Thirty Years religious war ended. It is important to understand the early years in imperial Sweden in order to understand Kristina's personality. A year after the death of Gustavus Adolphus Kristina was separated from her allegedly insane mother, Maria Eleanore. Kristina recalls that she had a peculiar "respect" for her mother. But she confesses a "deadly aversion" towards the "pack of dwarfs" that always sur-

Mary Ellen Waithe (ed.), A History of Women Philosophers / Volume 3, 21–40.
© 1991 *Kluwer Academic Publishers. Printed in the Netherlands.*

rounded her neurotic mother. Kristina soon developed a contempt for her dolls and other feminine things. She often feared that her mother would interfere with her studies.

> Thus I was relieved when my study hours called me to my rooms ... I dashed to them engulfed by an immense joy and often came much too early. I studied six hours in the morning and six hours in the evening.[1]

As a young ruler Kristina was aware of the threat to her power. Like her father, she endorsed an absolutist theory of monarchy. The Oxenstiern faction of higher nobility had introduced a provisional constitution, the *regeringsform* of 1634, forming a mixed government that intervened with her sovereign rights. However, during the ten years of her rule, Kristina skillfully manoeuvred the factions of the council of state, using tensions between the aristocracy, the peasant, and the bourgeois classes to drive her positions through. Refusing to marry, she decided that her cousin, Charles Gustavus (Charles X), was to become crown heir.

Kristina's academic interests absorbed most of her free time. Her fervor for learned discussions made her gradually less responsible as a ruler. She spent enormous sums on manuscripts, scholars, art, plays, and other intellectual pursuits. At the same time, she began to develop definite neurotic symptoms. Her first thoughts of abdication began to take form. In a long series of state councils she arranged for her own financial support following her abdication.[2] After her nervous break-down in 1652, Kristina's interests weakened. Indeed, some scholars, such as Pierre-Daniel Huet, who worked on a translation of Origen, began thinking that Kristina had lost all interest in learning. One day, the library, normally in the care of Mazarin's former librarian Gabriel Naudé, was turned upside-down in Kristina's frenzy to turn the room into a ballroom. However, sessions were held weekly and scholars were able to continue with their work.[3] On June 16, 1654, Kristina decided to abdicate, to leave Sweden, and to seek a new, more satisfying life. "And it is," she says at age twenty-seven, "somewhat out of self-love, to please my own fancy, that I design my private retirement."[4] Scandalizing everyone, she traveled throughout Europe. Wearing men's clothes and with her hair cut short, she settled for almost a year in Brussels. In Innsbruck in 1655, Kristina publicly converted to Catholicism. In 1521 Gustavus I had made Sweden Lutheran and the throne hereditary. Kristina Wasa abandoned both.

Kristina knew seven languages. She used French and Italian in her correspondence, read Latin and Greek, and had an elementary knowledge of Hebrew and Arabic. She read medical works and began conducting chemical experiments in Fontainebleau in 1657.[5] Well aware of her value as a political instrument for the Papal League, and steeped in ideas of her own greatness, she tried to position herself advantageously for a general peace in Europe. She took the name Kristine Alexandre after her hero. Always insisting on her royal title, but without her throne, she became obsessed with the idea of absolute sovereignty as an expression of divine will. Although doubtful of the nature of the divine, she emulated the role it seemingly sanctioned. In 1657 at Fontainebleau she ordered the execution of her servant Marquise Monaldesco. Her responsibility for this murder made her infamous. She quickly found that political intrigue and worldly power were as influential abroad as they had been at home. Pressed for money, Kristina became involved in European politics. Using her close contact with Jewish bankers, she aspired to become the ruler of Naples in 1657. Unwelcomed, she visited her Swedish estate in 1660 and tried to win the Electoral throne of Poland in 1668.[6]

Simultaneously pursuing knowledge and power, Kristina visited Hamburg in 1660. She became interested in the theory of the philosopher's stone which the alchemist Borri claimed to have discovered. She also studied astronomy with Lubenitz in 1666. When Kristina returned to Rome in 1668 she set up an observatory in her palace with two permanent astronomers and a *distillarium* (chemistry laboratory).[7] Gradually losing her political clout, she turned to the internal politics of Rome: papal elections and cultural projects. She published a letter on tolerance of the French Huguenots in Pierre Bayle's *Nouvelles de la Republique des Lettres*[8] and wrote a manifesto defense of the Jews in Rome's ghetto.[9] She became a patron of the arts and held academies in her Rome *palazzo*. Thus she continued to make a practical contribution to learning. Her *Academia degli Arcadia* continued after her death. Her *Academia Reale* of 1674 included such collaborators as the physiologist Giovanni Borelli and the astronomer-mathematician Cassini. She also held discussions with Palompari (who had a laboratory with the atmospheric scientist Borricelli), with the anatomist Marcello Malpighi, and with other Italian scientists.[10]

Another facet of her Academy was her interest in theatre and music. She contributed to the building of a theatre which presented plays until the death of the liberal Pope Clement X, in 1676. Kristina held musical events, had a vast collection of nude paintings, and supported young musicians, including Corelli and Scarlatti.[11]

At the very end of her life, Kristina turned to Catholic mysticism, trying through quietism to reconcile a daring youth with the demands of a lonely old age. She died in 1689. In violation of her Last Will and Testament, for propagandist purposes she was given a solemn funeral procession through the Vatican to her crypt in the Dome of Peter. Kristina had gained a double-edged reputation: as a bizarre and ruthless intriguer in power politics and as a patron of Baroque art music, theatre, unorthodox opinions, science, and philosophy. Her contemporaries found her androgynous character strange and suspicious. Ironically, she may have understood this. In her autobiography she confesses that she has three regrets:

> I have all too much despised the good manners that belong to my sex, which often make me appear as more faulting than I really am ... and I laugh all too often and all too loud and I walk too fast ... a consequence of my impulsive nature.[12]

The literature on Kristina is vast. The 1751 collection of letters and other materials published by Arckenholz contains hundreds of items. Kristina has been studied from the perspectives of history, biography, theology, the arts, and letters. Poets have sung her praise in panegyrics, verse, and dramatic plays. Stories about Kristina's defiant comments abound, and medical studies have psychoanalyzed her. In what follows, I shall discuss Kristina Wasa, Queen of Sweden, as a philosopher.

II. PHILOSOPHY

Of the manuscripts in Kristina's own hand (and more legibly in the final secretarial drafts) the most important are her collections of maxims and the never-completed autobiography. The maxims, which probably were begun in letter form *circa* 1670, were ultimately collected in two sets: *Les Sentiments Héroiques* and *L'Ouvrage de*

Loisir: Les Sentiments Raisonnables. Together they contain approximately 1300 entries which are carefully worked out in numerous earlier versions. In the spirit of Machiavelli, they speak of the Princly heroic virtue, honor, and passions. Kristina's autobiography is a study of spiritual change, as well as a confession and a self-serving attempt to salvage her early reputation. Some minor works are also of interest, including her biography of Alexander the Great, her reflections on the virtues and vices of Caesar, an homage to Cyrus the Great, and some lyrical verses on love and fate in the style of Petrarch. Kristina made sketches of laboratory equipment and planned a larger work: Paradossi Chimici.

1. *Traditional Assessments of Kristina's Views*

Kristina's skeptical doubts and her practical involvement with philosophy and science are of greatest interest. There have been few attempts to understand the content of her thought or the intellectual climate in which she lived. Even the scholarship of such giants as Ernst Cassirer,[13] René Pintard,[14] Leopold von Ranke,[15] and Sven Stolpe[16] have not given sufficiently detailed accounts of Kristina's words and actions to make her life choices understandable. In general, scholars have toned down the popular contemporary image of Kristina. However, a great deal of controversy remains on how to characterize her. Cassirer, who describes Kristina's relation to Descartes and neostoicism, can be criticized for giving too disinterested an interpretation. (Cassirer also conjectures that Descartes' dialogue *The Search After Truth by the Light of Nature* was written in Stockholm as a pedagogical text for Kristina.) Unaware of the historical facts, he overestimates the internal consistency of her conversion.[17] Pintard treats Kristina as an example of the libertine age, without pursuing Kristina's own reasons for her behavior. The valuable Vatican accounts of the conversion were located by von Ranke, whose attempt to show how the Jesuits caused her conversion underestimates the effect of Kristina's skepticism. Stolpe offers the most comprehensively researched biography, but he interprets Kristina through French and Italian humanism, bypassing material explaining her interests in the connection between science and religion. In reading the confession-like autobiography, the maxims, and other late material, Stolpe sees a gradual transition from stoicism to quietist mysticism.

He treats Kristina's skepticism as transitory, just as her autobiography reinterprets her life to fit Christian ideals.[18] We know that Kristina seriously searched for a satisfactory religion, but we also know that her beliefs embraced so many anomalous elements that the word "catholic" was hardly descriptive.

If one instead takes as one's reference point not the last few years of Kristina's life but the early period in which she was an independent and searching individual, our picture of her alters. Kristina becomes not the saintly figure of her confessions but the free-thinking, autonomous individual who worked for peace, tolerance, and non-interference with Jews; who promoted academies; and who embraced skepticism. The young, daring, and newly abdicated Kristina needs to be evaluated and understood. By reexamining the events from 1648 to 1668, we see the emergence of her philosophical skepticism and the profound effect it had on her religious beliefs and on her social, political, and moral philosophy, as different aspects of her thought were reflected by her actions. Kristina's skepticism played a decisive role during the twenty-year period (1648–1668) preceding the Polish election. To understand how her skepticism affected her life, it is necessary first to consider the years preceding her abdication.

2. *Kristina's Philosophical Development*

Kristina's early introduction to philosophy came through Matthiae and Oxenstierna. Through them she gained an early exposure to classical philosophy and, particularly, to stoicism. Kristina was raised as any other prince would have been, learning to ride, fence, and hunt. At age seven her formal education began under the supervision of Johannes Matthiae, who in 1643 became Bishop of Strangnas and was himself trained in the educational system of Johann Amos Comenius. Matthiae with his strong unionist tendencies is responsible for Kristina's tolerant and critical perspective on religion. Matthiae was a controversial priest who was very concerned with proliferating the pursuit of universal knowledge as a way to prepare for the anticipated end of the world. Comenius' followers had been favored by Gustavus Adolphus, and Matthiae was therefore in a strong position to present new ideas. His 1644 work, *Idea boni in Ecclesia Christi*, argues for the ecclesiastical constitution of the Bohemian brethren and attempts to reconcile Lutheranism and Calvinism. The book was widely criticized by clergy and council; in 1647 he retracted it. Asked not to defend the book, Kristina said that it did not need her defense; it defended itself.[19]

Axel Oxenstierna, who led Sweden during Kristina's minority, taught her the art of politics and warfare. They read Justus Lipsius' *Politica*, a set of quotations from the Stoics which was arranged by subject heading. They discussed possible interpretations of historical events in Tacitus. Kristina had the works of Epictetus and Seneca on her desk and also studied William Camden's history of the reign of Queen Elizabeth.[20] Like many others of her time, Kristina championed neostoic ideals of individual autonomy. "Sometimes," writes the French Ambassador Chanut, "... she likes to talk like the stoics of the preeminence of virtue, which is our sovereign good in life. She is marvelously strong on this theme, and when she speaks on it with those she knows well, and dwells on what should be the true value of human things, it is a pleasure to see her place her crown beneath her feet and proclaim that virtue is the only good, to which all should be firmly attached without consideration of their circumstances."[21]

Raised as a prince, and refusing to marry, Kristina developed into a *literati*, financing publications and attracting scholars to her court. She corresponded with René Descartes and with Hugo Grotius. Both traveled to see her and both died of pneumonia as a consequence. She also corresponded with Pierre Gassendi, whose Epicureanism she admired, and with Blaise Pascal, who sent her his computing machine. In Stockholm, Dutch neostoics and French linguists and so-called libertines formed a Wednesday Academy to divert themselves and the Queen. The word spread: "Kristina has seen all, has read all; she knows all and she gives judicious judgments on it all."[22]

Isaac Vossius came to Stockholm in 1648 to organize the fine war booty from Prague into one of Europe's most comprehensive libraries. At that time, there were few foreign scholars at court. Swedish theological linguists such as Johannes Bureus, Arnold Messenius, and Georg Stiernhielm were setting the stage for Swedish imperialism by exploring the hidden Gothic past. The quest of Gustavus Adolphus had many times been assumed to be analogous to the prophecy of the Lion of the North in Isiah 41:25, Jeremiah 50:9, Daniel 11:5, and Ezekiel 38:15 and 39:2. Sweden was at the end of the earth and, although but a minor European power, it had a mission to fulfill through its purifying wars.[23] It is this atmosphere that led Kristina to doubt that religion was anything but a political invention. Her contacts with foreign ambassadors led Kristina to appreciate Continental ideas, and as a result Kristina invited scholars to her court. The new ideas they brought gradually led Kristina to abandon Swedish imperial intentions and to seek new ideas to inform her role as ruler. By 1648, when the first foreign scholars entered her court, Kristina had already developed a thorough grounding in state government and a firm grasp of classical history and philosophy. Still, she apparently was not content with being a Protestant prince. Between 1648 and 1653 she gathered a circle of the most important Netherlands scholars around her: Nicholas Heinsius, Isaac Vossius, Claudius Salmasius, and Johannes Scheffer. They were all influenced by the neo-stoicism professed at the University of Leiden by Justus Lipsius. The German proponents of neo-stoic politics, Johannes Freinshemsius and Heinrich Boecler, and the orientalist grammarians Samuel Bochart and Christian Ravius also contributed to making Stockholm a center of classical learning.[24]

3. *Kristina and Descartes*

Kristina was a philosopher in her own right, as evidenced by her extensive study of classical and contemporary philosophy and by her attempts to live her life consistently with her political, social, and moral ideas. Yet, her fame in philosophical circles is mistakenly attributed to her relationship with Descartes. She invited René Descartes to Stockholm in 1650 where, after only four months, he contracted pneumonia and died. Kristina has been depicted as an exacting and ruthless student, and she is blamed for requiring Descartes to arrive at five o'clock in the morning to instruct her in his principles. Descartes is to be pitied as he always otherwise slept until eleven o'clock and could not tolerate the early morning cold.[25]

Kristina was at the time of Descartes' arrival deeply involved in Greek studies with several of Europe's leading philologists. One of them, Isaac Vossius, reports that Kristina thought she already had read Descartes' main doctrines in the works of Sextus Empiricus and Plato.[26] That she understood Descartes' mechanistic physics is not to be doubted. In the talks with the Jesuits she showed interest in Galileo's ideas on mathematical hypotheses, and she was generally reported to have a sharp and gifted mind.[27] Pierre-Daniel Huet remarked that of the three most learned women of the time, Kristina,

Madeleine de Scudery, and Anna Maria van Schurman, the Queen had the sharpest intellect.[28] In the *Maxims* Kristina states that the questioning philosophical attitudes of Aristippus, Diogenes, and Socrates are worth admiring.[29] It is probable that she was a more discursive intellect who preferred analyzing the practical applications of philosophy to its purely technical, academic exercise. Her attitude is best illustrated in her maxim "One must know the world morally, not only physically or mathematically."[30] Already in 1646, the French Ambassador Chanut began to correspond with Descartes, transmitting Kristina's questions. She wanted to know what was worse: the ill use of love or hate? Chanut hastened to add that "the term 'love' was used in the sense of the philosophers, not as it so frequently rings in the ears of girls, and the question was general."[31] Descartes reinterpreted the question into three parts and gave it a Catholic tinge in directing the question of love to the theological issue of the relationship between body and mind.[32] Descartes answered the problems: (1) what love is; (2) whether intuition teaches us to love God; (3) which is worse, disordered and misused love, or hate? He displayed his particular version of dualistic mechanism, declaring that although love as a passion is a movement of the nerves, intellectual love occurs when the soul perceives some good to which it willingly decides to join itself. The question of loving God is difficult since the attributes of God are so far beyond our ability to imagine them that we must instead see him as a thinking being. Although we cannot imagine God, we bear some faint resemblance to the infinite power of God and can thereby understand our love for him. We can perceive our love for him and our wish to join him, and we may consider ourselves as a small part of his immense creation. Descartes concludes that love can be put to more misuse if it is disordered, because it blinds us more than does hate.

Through Chanut, Kristina answers that she is unable to judge the problem of love as she never has felt any such emotion. Dismissing the greater part of Descartes' eight-page letter, she instead challenges him with the argument that his ideas of an infinite God and creation conflict with Christian doctrine:

> ... if one once admits the world infinite in its matter and substance, then so much the more must one also believe it infinite in all its parts, and thus the history of Creation, stated very clearly in the

Holy Scripture, would not retain its manifest authority; and at the
other term of duration, the end of the world, it is likewise difficult
to conceive it in a large infinity of a production without limits.[33]

A Christian follows the Scripture and as

> ... we conceive the world as but a small work of an immense power
> which is not entirely depleted, we see the obstacle to its having a
> beginning and an end.[34]

Kristina further thought that in an infinite universe, man cannot be the
end of creation, the one for which all other things have been made

> ... if we conceive the world in that vast extension you give it, it is
> impossible that man conserve himself therein in this honorable
> rank, on the contrary, he shall consider himself along with the
> entire earth he inhabits as in but a small, tiny and in no proportion
> to the enormous size of the rest. He will very likely judge that these
> stars have inhabitants, or even that the earths surrounding them are
> all filled with creatures more intelligent and better than he, cer-
> tainly, he will lose the opinion that this infinite extent of the world
> is made for him or can serve him in any way.[35]

The continued discussion reveals the characters of the correspondents.
Kristina was troubled and sought an answer to her far-reaching
questions. Descartes tried to reconcile and tone down the conflict with
Scripture and doctrine. They moved on to the question of the highest
good, a question temporarily remedied by a stoic ethic consisting of a
firm will to do well and the contentment which that produces. At this
point, it appears that Chanut contributed more to the discussion than
Kristina – maybe because he saw in Descartes a way for France to
flatter the Queen.

   Four years later, Descartes decided to go to Stockholm. Perhaps
Descartes was hoping to attract attention to his latest production, the
mechanistic treatise on the *Passions of the Soul*. In the meantime,
Kristina read his *Principles of Philosophy* and had her Greek tutor
Freinshemsius help her. Descartes was very impressed by Kristina at
first, but only had an audience with her a few times. Bitterly, he
claimed that she seemed to be more interested in other scholars and

doubted that she would ever grant him time. He failed to gain access to the inner circles of the court, complaining that men's minds seem to freeze in the winter.[36] Kristina ordered Descartes to compose a libretto to a ballet on the birth of peace, in honor of her role at the 1648 negotiations in Osnabrück. But apparently she did not find Descartes himself terribly interesting. Instead, she devoted her time to politics and classical studies. Kristina later wrote that if he had attempted to do so Descartes could have extinguished the ideas of all others, and would have dethroned Aristotle to make himself the leader of philosophy. In 1667 Kristina claimed that her conversation with Descartes gave her her first insights into Catholicism.[37] Inventively, but on unstated grounds, Behn sees the Kristina/Descartes meeting as an outcome of Kristina's dynamical mysticism.[38] But as we know, she was already entertaining other religious propositions. Kristina's interest, shortly after Descartes' death, in Pierre Gassendi and his Epicureanism may shed some light on her attitude at that time. That Gassendi was summoned but did not come to Stockholm may have been a great disappointment. Descartes' draft of statutes for the Stockholm academy thus was not put into practice due to lack of a leading scholar. Those who came after 1650 tended to be quarrelsome and spurred by mutual envy. They came and stayed for a few years, but never intended to be a permanent part of the court.

4. *Religious Skepticism*

During the period of the abdication in June 1654, Kristina was considered to be very indifferent to her religion. Strange stories were passed around concerning her demeanor and her cynical remarks. She became a symbol of impiety. One observer, on June 26, 1654, said: "those who have had a very personal and very dear relationship unto her count her a very atheist."[39] Kristina had doubts very early on, doubts that were enforced by her French libertine friends. But she also had doubts of her own. Her evaluation of her disbelief appears in her late confessional autobiography and also in her communications with the Jesuits Malines and Casati, beginning in 1651. But already, her early doubts about what she heard in her Lutheran environment and her questions to Descartes in 1647 on the possibility of a Christian creation in an infinite universe show that she was deeply troubled by Church dogma.

The first doubts that she recalled came when she was ten years old. Following her second hearing of a sermon on the fires of damnation, she asked her tutor whether this was not just a fictional story. She was harshly admonished not to ask such things. The Jesuit Casati wrote that Kristina's doubts about Lutheranism made her inquire into all religions and to weigh the difficulties of each: "She thus employed about five years with a great perturberation of mind, because she could find no place where she could stop."[40] Kristina's well-known inner tension and hysterical frenzy coincided with her religious skepticism. "Estimating," as Casati reports, "all things on merely human principles, she thought that many things might have been mere political inventions to the commoner order of minds."[41] This insight led Kristina to turn the arguments of the religious sects against themselves. She was particularly impressed by Cicero's claim in *De Natura Deorum* that all religions may be false but only one of them can be true. Kristina became convinced that it did not matter whether one followed a particular religion, as long as one did not act contrary to reason. She believed she had never done so, saying that she thought she had never done anything that could make her blush. On the other hand, she found ecclesiastical dogma to be repulsive to reason. She doubted the idea of Providence. She asked questions on the eternal salvation of the soul and admitted to the Jesuits that she had been, as Casati has it, "too profane in seeking to fathom the profoundest mysteries of the Godhead."[42]

At the same time as Kristina was having secret discussions with Jesuits, she began acting increasingly non-conformist, making startling claims such that Moses among the Hebrews was like Mohammed among the Arabs. She even doubted that there was any difference between Good and Evil, apart from the utility of injurious character of actions. She claimed that she had no fear of God and she allegedly said that the fable of Christ was of great use to the Roman Church. In her view, the Incarnation doctrine was wholly unworthy of credence.[43] To reinforce her own skeptical doubts, Casati says, "she read every book treating on matters pertaining to this subject, she lighted upon many things of the ancients, and of the gentiles, and of the atheists." Kristina sought out anti-religious views. She met with Isaac la Peyrere in Antwerp in 1654 and had his *Prae-Adamitae* financed for publication. Thus, she supported the most advanced Bible-criticism and was willing to question the authority of the

Scriptures.[44] In 1656, a year after her conversion, she obtained a banned manuscript of Jean Bodin's *Heptaplomeres*, the colloquium of seven religions in which natural religion and Jewish law is contrasted with the many inexplicable Christian mysteries. She read Pierre Garasse's *La Doctrine Curieuse*, which attacks the claims of the freethinkers and atheists, but in such a suspiciously feeble way as to place its sequel on the Inquisition's Index. Kristina was rumored to have such outrageous skeptical religious views that no one doubted that her search for the book on Jesus, Moses, and Mohammed (*Les Trois Imposteurs*) was not serious. Her readings of such works continued even after her conversion to Catholicism, evidencing that the conversion did not mean a rejection of her religious skepticism.[45]

On the constructive side of her doubts, we find that coupled with acquiring an Iamblichus manuscript, she decided that the world-soul was the only admissible form of immortality. In October 1656, Kristina declared to an interested scholar that her religion was that of the philosophers. It was Lucretius' *De Rerum Natura* that impressed her the most.[46] Lucretius presents a complete system of the universe as governed by immanent material forces. He also describes the psyche and its activities so as to sanction the popular form of Epicureanism that many of Kristina's non-conformist entourage espoused, and which was professed at the University of Leiden as the "new" ancient discovery.

Kristina's doubts were never written down in systematic form, and many of her most interesting opinions are reported by others, recorded in correspondence and memorabilia. We can begin to see how her philosophical skepticism explains and supports her belief that she could stand above law, convention, and behavioral norms. In a society structured around the notion of God's presence on earth, Kristina's unconventionality was not inconsequential: it struck an irritable theological-political nerve.

5. *Philosophy and Linguistics*

Pursuing her interests in linguistics, Kristina had met with scholars Johannes Gronovius and Anna Maria van Schurman outside Utrecht in 1654. In France in 1656 she held an academy where at least twenty-seven different problems on the nature of love were discussed. Her academy was a literary circle with interests in astronomy, cosmology, and philosophy. This was an important activity in an era in which scholars had just begun to identify the many applications of classical science. The reading of texts and the study of nature were assumed to proceed in a uniform way. Textual analysis, with comparative methods for finding the principal parts of speech, was assumed to be similar both to the biochemical analysis upon which modern medicine depended and to the speculative analysis of the nature and origin of the universe.

6. *The Maxims*

Of Kristina's written works, the maxims are the most difficult to interpret. In two collections dating from *circa* 1670, called *Les Sentiments Heroiques* and *L'Ouvrage de Loisir* (subtitled *Les Sentiments Raisonnables*), 1300 entries are worked out. They represent Kristina's views on her relations to God, to the passions, to virtue, to the heroes, to the Church as an institution, to women, and to her role as prince, among other subjects. None of this material was published in her lifetime, but a final secretarial draft called *Les Sentiments* is considered the most authoritative version. This version was not completed until the 1680's and takes on a devout Christian cast. Still, there are many elements of classical stoic morality and biting comments in Kristina's own style that seem not to fit her public appearance of piety.

Anyone who reads the maxims must try to understand Kristina's rhetorical dissimulation; this is necessary for reasons of discounting the influence of her later life on her representation of the earlier period and for striking a balance between her real influence and her professed beliefs. Pierre Bayle calls Kristina's maxims "as beautiful as those of M. La Rochefoucauld."[47] Monica Zetterwall notes that there is a certain comparison to be made with the 1665 maxims of that master of psychological unmasking, la Rochefoucauld.[48] Although the maxims contain a similar play of cynicism and disclosure of human bigotry, Kristina differs from la Rochefoucauld in her work by concealing her own personality. At times, she is a master of suppressed disguise – a theme well exposed in Zetterwall's essay on Kristina's maxim "To be unable to dissimulate, is to be unable to live."[49] Kristina's own marginal comments on La Rochefoucauld's maxims are reprinted by Truchet.[50]

The 499 entries of *Les Sentiments* begin and end with the affirmation of God's presence. The first entry reads, "There is unfailingly a God who is the unique principle, and the last end of all things." The last entry is the signature "These sentiments are from one who imposes nothing on anyone else, and who also fears nothing."[51] In themselves, they do not commit Kristina to any more elaborate a theology than Deism and Stoicism. But several other maxims in the opening sections affirm Catholicism or Quietism. Problematically, all the Quietist material has been struck out. Stolpe has shown that Kristina was drawn to the teachings of the quietist Miguel Molinos, but in the latter's inquisition in 1684, Kristina finally saw her mistake in supporting Molinos. She had 300 penitence letters to him destroyed.

7. Misogyny and Feminism

Kristina's worldly success both before and after the abdication is due to her "male" attributes. She was admired because she managed to assimilate to the dominant, severely patriarchal culture of mid-seventeenth-century Europe. Her life is a good example of how a woman who acts in the political, theological, and judicial spheres came to be treated as an anomaly. Kristina's androgynous manners aroused both surprise and suspicion. In August 1654 an observer wrote:

> We hear strange stories of the Swedish queen with her Amazonian behavior; it being believed, that nature was mistaken in her, and that she was intended for a man, for in her discourse, they say, she talks loud and sweareth notably.[52]

In a sense, Kristina fulfilled the ideal of the Corneillian drama and the rising feminist literature. Through classical imitation they brought forth the image of *la femme forte*: the Warrior Woman who, in a furore, decapitates or cunningly triumphs over weak and helpless men. But Kristina herself refused to be intimidated by such caricatures. She disdained female culture. She gave reasons why women should not rule, thus approving of the Salic law.[53] Kristina understood that the Amazon Queen never existed, and wrote in her maxims:

I can not find anything as stupid and ridiculous as the Amazon republic. This fable is badly invented.[54]

Although Kristina was completely absorbed by the Alexander legend, she refused to believe the only part where women are given an active role. In the same way, she claimed that the woman killer of Cyrus the Great was a fiction. Whether this was a sign of cynical clarity or of Kristina's resigned submission to socially accepted views of women can perhaps be determined by a more extensive analysis of the sections on women in her maxims. Those passages are marked with contempt for irresoluteness among women that makes them enter into marriage. In one passage Kristina exclaims:

The feminine sex is a great embarassment and a great obstacle to virtue and merit. This fault [of nature] is the greatest one can know, it is almost incorrigible and few persons can with honor withdraw from this embarassment.[55]

Kristina reveals her limitations most when she tries to deal with the problem of being a woman. During the election to Poland, for example, she elaborates on reasons why a woman can qualify for the throne.[56] But, she plays on her reputation and emphasizes her male experience. Although she is reported to only seldomly speak with women, she did have contact with them. She is suspected of being in love with the Swedish noblewoman Ebba Sparre. Both before and after Ebba's marriage, Kristina wrote her very devoted, affectionate letters.[57] Kristina in her youth was very affectionate with Magnus Gabriel de la Gardie and with her libertine physician Pierre Bourdelot. In addition, she met with the Spanish Ambassador Pimentel late at night and had a long-lasting (but unrequited) love correspondence with Cardinal Azzolino. Due to these well-known relationships it is sometimes argued that she is "saved" from actually being a lesbian. However, she was publicly viewed as a lesbian. She herself was convinced of her unusually "dry and hot" (i.e., male) temperament. She also rejected marriage.[58] Kristina's lesbianism is therefore unambiguous from the perspective of modern radical feminists who argue that *La Femme Seul* is only one form of lesbian existence. Common to lesbian experience on a continuum ranging from spiritual communion among women on one end to lesbian sexuality on the other is the rejection of heterosexual marriage. The thesis that Kristina was an hermaphrodite was studied by Essen-Moller[59] and is more or less refuted by Carl Hermann Hjortsjö's osteological post-mortem at the opening of Kristina's sarcophagus in 1965.[60]

Kristina personified what was considered deviant sexuality – an image consistent with libertine advances following the religious wars. In the outbreak of the Paris *Frondé* of 1648 women made claims to more active social roles. In the ensuing libertine circles with their ethic of free sexual expression, women like Madeleine de Scudéry began to theorize about women's inferior role in marriage.[61] Kristina also met with the Epicurean Ninon de Lenclos in Paris in 1656 and knew of the humanist scholar Anne Lefèvre-Dacier. Kristina read and corresponded with these women but remained outside the debate which took place in an epicurean aristocratic culture to which she did not belong. Kristina, who wanted to merge with her fictional hero Alexander, also had another symbolic guide: the Catholic ideal of virginity. She points out that it is this symbol of Catholicism that appealed to her most. Kristina saw that in the many female martyrs, saints, and nuns there is an element of strength that derives from the Madonna legend. She did not want to marry and probably embraced values that relieved the pressure to justify her decision. It is important to note that Kristina's rejection of dynastic marriage alone did not make her abdication inevitable.[62]

III. CONCLUSIONS

Kristina's skepticism, her stoicism and quietism, her remarks on marriage and her arguments to avoid marriage, her choice of literature on women, her paintings, and her peculiar imprints on coins celebrating her independence together present a more comprehensive and appealing account of her philosophical views than that found in her maxims alone. After all, Kristina was a woman who acted pragmatically, in accordance with a variety of philosophical, political, theological, and scientific ideas. Even if she did this with a distorted view of her own abilities, her achievements are not diminished.

NOTES

1. [Kristina.] *Drottning Kristinas Självbiografi*. Stockholm, 1967, p. 75. Hereafter as *Autobiography*.
2. Oestreich, Gerhard. *Neostoicism and the Early Modern State*. Cambridge: Cambridge University Press, 1902, p. 116. Weibull, Curt. *Drottning Christina. Studier och Forskningar*. Stockholm: Natur och Kultur, 1931.
3. Huet, Pierre-Daniel. *Commentarius*. Amsterdam 1718. Comp. Lindroth, 1975.
4. Whitelock, Bulstrode. *A journal of the Swedish Embassy in the years 1653–1654*. ed. H. Reeve. 2 vols. London, 1855, p. 371.
5. Cf. Oestreich, 1982.
6. Weibull, *op. cit.*
7. Bildt, Carl. *Christine de Suède et Cardinal Azzolino, Lettres inédites*. Paris, 1899. Stolpe, Sven. *Drottning Kristina*. Stockholm: Askild & Karnekull, 1982, p. 416. Hereafter as *Kristina*.
8. Letter to Terlon. 2 Feb. 1686, reproduced in *La Vie de M. Bayle*.
9. Valentin, Hugo. "Drottning Kristinas av Sveriges Judiska forbindelser," in *Festskrife ... David Simonsens*, ed. J. Fischer et al. København: 1923, p. 234 n. 2.
10. Stephan, Ruth. "A Note on Christina and her Academies," in *Queen Christina of Sweden – Documents and Studies*. ed. Magnus von Pleten. Stockholm: 1966, pp. 365–371.
11. Bjurstrom, Per. *Feast and Theatre in Queen Christina's Rome*. Stockholm, 1966.
12. *Autobiography, op cit.*, p. 65.
13. Cassirer, Ernst. *Descartes-Lehre-Personlichkeit-Wirkung*. Stockholm: Behrmann Fischer Verlag, 1939.
14. Pintard, René. *Le Libertinage Érudit dans la première moitié du XVIIe Siècle*. 2 vols. Paris: Boivin, 1943, pp. 315–320, 388–403.
15. von Ranke, Leopold. *The history of the Popes – Their Church and State – and especially of their conflicts with Protestantism in the sixteenth and seventeenth centuries*. 3 vols. London: George Bell & Sons, 1906, pp. 351–367.
16. Stolpe, *Kristina*.
17. Nordström, Johan. "Cartesius och Drottning Kristinas omvandelse." *Lychnos*: 1940.
18. Stolpe, Sven. *Fran Stoicism till Mystik – Studier i Drottning Kristinas maximer*. Stockholm: Bonniers, 1959. Hereafter as *Stoicism*. Stople, Sven. "Kristina-studier," *Credo, Katolsk tidskrift* 40 (1959): 4, pp. 203–315.
19. Stolpe, *Kristina*, p. 136.
20. Clark, M.L. "The making of a Queen: The education of Christina of Sweden," *History Today*: 28 (1978), pp. 228–235.
21. Chanut, Pierre-Hector. Letter to Brienne. 1 Feb. 1648.
22. Gabriel Naude to Gassendi. 19 Oct. 1652.
23. Lindroth, Sten. *Svensk Lardomshistoria. Stormaktstiden*. Stockholm, 1975.
24. Oestreich, *op. cit.*, p. 109.
25. Cf. Baillet, Adrien. *La Vie de M. Des-Cartes*. 2 vols. 1691.

26. Wieselgren, H. *Drottning Kristinas Bibliotek och Bibliotekarier före hennes bosättning i Rom. Vitterhetsakademiens Handlingar.* Stockholm: Norstedt (1901): 33:2.

27. Galeazzo, Gualdo Priorato. *Historia della Sacra Real Maesta di Christina Alessandra Regina di Svezia.* Venedig, 1656.

28. Arckenholtz, Johan. *Mémoires concernant Christine, reine de Suède...* 4 vols. Amsterdam & Leipzig, 1751–1760, V. 1, p. 261, quoting Huet.

29. Stolpe, Sven, ed. *Drottning Kristina Maximer Les Sentiments Heroiques.* Stockholm: Bonniers, 1959. Maxim 495. Translation mine. Hereafter as *Maxims*.

30. *Ibid.*, p. 99, translation mine.

31. Chanut to Descartes, 1 Dec. 1646, in Blom, John J. *Descartes – His Moral Philosophy and Psychology.* New York: New York University Press, 1978, p. 200.

32. Descartes to Chanut, 1 Feb. 1647, in Blom, *op. cit.*, p. 201ff.

33. Chanut to Descartes, 11 May 1647, in Blom, *op. cit.*, p. 215.

34. *Op. cit.*, pp. 215–216.

35. Descartes to Christina of Sweden, 20 Nov. 1647, *op. cit.*, p. 228ff.

36. Descartes to Bregy, 15 Jan. 1650.

37. Letter to Salmasius quoted in Behn, Irene. *Der Philosoph und die Königin.* Freiburg/Munchen: Albers, 1957, p. 73. Cf. Stolpe, *Kristina*, pp. 182–189.

38. *Ibid.*

39. Thurloe, John. *Thurloe State Papers.* 6 vols, 1648–1667, Vol. IV, 26 June 1654, p. 377.

40. Casati in von Ranke, *op. cit.*, app. 131.

41. *Ibid.*

42. *Ibid.*

43. Casati, *ibid.*; Pintard, *op. cit.*, p. 391; Stolpe, *Kristina*, p. 207.

44. Pintard, *op. cit.*, p. 420. Popkin, Richard H. "Menasseh Ben Israel and Isaac La Peyrere II," *Studia Rosenthaliana* XVII: 1 (January, 1984), pp. 12–20.

45. Communication to Morisot, 1656. Cf. Pintard, *op. cit.*, p. 395.

46. Pintard, *op. cit.*, p. 391ff; Stolpe, *Kristina*, pp. 204–205.

47. Bayle, Pierre, letter to M. L'Abbe Bos, Jan. 3, 1697. Tr. ed.

48. Zetterwall, Monica. "Role playing in maxim form – a comment on Queen Christina's maxims," *Scandinavian Studies* 2 (1985).

49. [Kristina]. *Maxim L'Ouvrage de Loisir.* Kungliga Biblioteket, Stockholm, D 682, p. 38.

50. Truchet, J., ed. *La Rochefoucauld Maximes.* Paris: Editions Garniers, 1967, pp. 599–621.

51. Stolpe, *Maxims*. Maxim 1, Maxim 499. Translation mine.

52. Thurloe, *op. cit.*, 28/18 Aug. 1654, vol. V., p. 451.

53. Stolpe, *Maxims*. The Salic Law Maxim 356.

54. Stolpe, *Maxims*. Amazons note 67 to Maxim 358. Thomiris Maxim 427.

55. Stolpe, *Maxims*. Maxim 357. Bracketed materials have been crossed out. Translation mine.

56. André, Louis. "La Candidature de Christine de Suède au Trone de Pologne (1688)," *Revue Historique* 2 (1908), pp. 209–243.

57. Kristina's letters to Ebba Sparre in Stolpe, *Maxims*, cf. Stolpe, *Kristina*, pp. 77–88.

58. Rich, Adrienne. "Compulsory Heterosexuality and Lesbian Existence," *Signs, Journal of Women in Culture and Society* 5 (1980): 41, pp. 631–660.

59. Essen-Möller, Elis. "La Reine Christine. Étude Médicale et Biologique," *Hippocrate*, Paris, 1937.

60. Carl Hermann Hjortsjö in von Platen, Magnus, *op. cit.*, pp. 138–158.

61. Madeleine de Scudéry. *Discours pour et contre l'amitié tendre*, 1653. *Astrée, ou le Grand Cyrus*, 1649–1653. Cf. Stolpe, *Maxims*, p. 78.

62. Cf. Stolpe, *Maxims*, pp. 83–85.

3. Anne Finch, Viscountess Conway

LOIS FRANKEL

I. BIOGRAPHY

Anne Finch, Viscountess Conway, was born in London in 1631 and died in 1679. She had no formal education, but was an avid reader and studied French, Greek, Hebrew, Latin, mathematics, and philosophy. She is best known outside philosophical circles for her incapacitating headaches, which brought her into contact with some of the better-known physicians of the day, including William Harvey and Robert Boyle.[1] Late in life, she became a Quaker, much to the consternation of many of her friends.

Conway was exceptionally close to her brother, John, and through him became acquainted with Henry More. One of the more prolific Cambridge Platonists, More started out as a Cartesian but later rejected the Cartesian philosophy as an enemy of religious belief in his *Enchiridon Metaphysicum*. More became Conway's teacher and later her close friend. In addition to More, her philosophical circle included the Kabbalist Francis Mercury van Helmont and Cambridge Platonists Ralph Cudworth, author of *The True Intellectual System of the Universe*, a critique of atheism; Joseph Glanvill; George Rust, whose works included *A Discourse of Truth*, a summary of some of Cudworth's work; and Benjamin Whichcote, who wrote nothing but is considered the inspiration behind the Cambridge Platonists.[2] These and other philosophers and churchmen were frequent guests at the Conway home. In addition, Conway was familiar with and critical of the work of Descartes, Hobbes, and Spinoza, and is credited with being a major influence on Leibniz, who was made acquainted with her work by van Helmont in 1696, nearly twenty years after Conway's death.[3]

Mary Ellen Waithe (ed.), A History of Women Philosophers / Volume 3, 41–58.
© 1991 *Kluwer Academic Publishers. Printed in the Netherlands.*

II. INFLUENCE ON LEIBNIZ

Leibniz was strongly influenced by Conway's work and even, according to Carolyn Merchant, owes his use of the term *monad* to her.[4] While Leibnizian monads are purely spiritual, for Conway monads are both physical and living (i.e. have both physical and spiritual qualities), as are all creatures.[5]

> [E]very Body is a certain Spirit or Life in its own Nature, ... the same is a certain intelligent Principle, having Knowledge, Sense, Love, Desire, Joy, and Grief; as it is this or that way affected; and by consequence hath Activity and Motion, *per se*; so that it can remove itself whithersoever it desires to be: I say, in its own Nature, wherein it was originally created, and as it shall be again, when it shall be reduced to its primitive State, and delivered from that Confusion and Vanity, to which it is subject by reason of Sin.[6]

There is also perhaps a preview of Leibniz's doctrine that monads "have no windows" – i.e. do not interact causally – in Conway's statement that the least parts of a creature, its "atoms," "cannot have internal Motion; because every Motion hath at least two Terms or Extreams," nor can it receive anything, motion or perception (a type of motion) from without.[7] Nevertheless, in Conway's system all creatures are composite and do interact:

> [God] is One, and this is his Perfection, that he hath need of nothing without him: But a Creature, because it needs the assistance of its Fellow-Creatures, ought to be manifold, that it may receive this assistance: for that which receives something is nourished by the same, and so becomes a part of it, and therefore it is no more one but many, and so many indeed as there are Things received, and yet of a greater multiplicity; therefore there is a certain Society of Fellowship among Creatures in giving and receiving, whereby they mutually subsist one by another ... by consequence every Creature which hath Life, Sense, or Motion, ought to be a number or, a Multiplicity.[8]

For Leibniz, while composite beings can be said to interact, such beings and their interactions exist on the level of phenomena, less 'real' than that of the purely spiritual monads. Leibniz's concept of monadic hierarchies and of a dominant monad is also found in Conway's thought, although she holds the dominant monad itself to be a multitude.[9]

> And so every Spirit hath its Body, and every Body its Spirit; and as the Body, *sc.* of a Man or Beast, is nothing else but an inumerable multitude of Bodies, compacted together into one, and disposed into a certain order; so likewise the Spirit of a man, or Beast, is a certain innumerable multitude of Spirits united together in the said Body, which have their Order and Government so, that there is one Captain, or Chief Governor, another a Lieutenant, and another hath a certain kind of Government under him, and so through the whole, as it is wont to be in an Army of Soldiers; wherefore the Creatures are called Armies, and God the God of Hosts.[10]

> [T]hough the Spirit of Man is commonly spoken in the Singular, as though it were but one Thing; yet the said Spirit is a certain composition of more, yea innumerable Spirits; as the Body is a composition of more Bodies, and hath a certain Order and Government in all its Parts, much more the Spirit which is a great Army of Spirits, wherein there are distinct Offices under one governing Spirit.[11]

In addition, Leibniz shares Conway's passion for harmony and reconciliation of opposing principles and philosophical systems. While there are several interesting comparisons to be drawn between Conway and Leibniz,[12] it is no less important to examine her work on its own.

III. PHILOSOPHICAL WRITING

The Principles of the Most Ancient and Modern Philosophy, Conway's only published philosophical work, is dated by Nicolson at 1671–1674 and at 1677–1679 by Lopston. It was written, not very legibly, in a notebook, and left unfinished and unrevised at Conway's death. Van Helmont had the work translated into Latin and published in 1690. It was retranslated into English in 1692 by one identified only as "J.C.," but thought to be either Jacobus Crull or John Clark.[13] The original is no longer in existence, but the Latin translation is published along with the English retranslation in Lopston's edition. We can only hope that the content of the work was not greatly distorted by its passage through so many hands.

Conway is committed to reconciling opposing forces: the emanationistic and vitalistic tenets of the ancients (primarily the Greeks, the Kabbalists, and Philo of Alexandria) with the mechanistic philosophy of the moderns and with Christian theology. Conway, like all of her time, found herself confronted with the new science and the resultant popularity of mechanistic explanation – the explanation of all events through motion and impact. She desired to reconcile mechanism with Platonism, and the result is a system in which every created being is both alive and capable of motion and in which motion is a central explanatory device. In keeping with her Christian background, the existence of God, a perfect being, is central to Conway's system and is asserted without proof in the beginning of her treatise:

> God is a Spirit, Light, and Life, infinitely Wise, Good, Just, Mighty, Omniscient, omnipresent, Omnipotent, Creator and Maker of all things visible and invisible.[14]

According to Conway, God is one of three kinds of beings (the others being Christ and creatures), each with a different essence, though not necessarily without some common attributes. For there to be *more* than these three kinds would, she argues, be contrary to the divine wisdom. A consequence of assigning a single essence to all creatures is that creatures are interconvertible, e.g., a horse can turn into a bird. Of greater philosophical interest is the consequence that spirits can turn into bodies, and vice versa.[15] Thus, spirit or mind and body are not essentially different, not 'really distinct.' The importance of this result will become clear in the course of this chapter.

Conway might best be described as a Cambridge Platonist, for she is Platonistic in her imagery and, as we shall see later on, in her background assumptions. Her language abounds with neo-Platonistic and Kabbalistic imagery; for example, in the passage below she speaks of God as a complete, self-sufficient "fountain" from which all creatures "emanate" necessarily. God's emanative creativity is one of its essential attributes.[16] Because God's creativity is emanative, rather than deliberate, God does not 'decide' to create the world. Rather, creatures flow from God's very nature.

> For God is definitely Good, Loving and Bountiful; yea, Goodness and Charity it self; an infinite Fountain, and Father of Goodness, Charity, and Bounty. Now how can it be, that this Fountain shall not always plentifully flow, and send from it self Living Waters? And shall not this Ocean perpetually abound with its own Efflux to the Production of Creatures, and that with a certain continual Stream? For the Goodness of God in its own proper nature is Communicative, and Multiplicative, and seeing in him nothing is wanting, neither can any thing be added to him, by reason of his absolute fullness, and transcendent fertility ... This Communicative Goodness of God ... is his Essential Attribute.[17]

In general, not only God's creation, but all of its actions flow automatically from its very nature. Thus, God does whatever it can do (i.e. is a necessary agent).[18] Because its nature involves perfection, Conway's God can do everything conceivable (non-contradictory).[19]

> Indifference of Will hath no place in God, by reason it is an Imperfection; who thought he be the most free Agent, yet he is also above all the most necessary Agent; so that it is impossible that he should not do, whatsoever he doth in or for his Creatures; Seeing his Infinite Wisdom, Goodness, and Justice, is a Law unto him, which he cannot Transgress.[20]

Because God's supreme wisdom is a part of its nature, and it would be inconceivable for God to fail to act in accordance with that nature, it follows that necessarily God acts always based on its supreme wisdom. "God cannot do that which is contrary to his Wisdom and Goodness, or any of his Attributes."[21] That is, for Conway the principle of sufficient reason, commonly associated with Leibniz, is a *necessary* truth.[22]

Like all Platonists, Conway was influenced by the Pythagorean column of opposites, which dominates Platonist and neo-Platonist thought:

the unlimited (undifferentiated, matter)	form
plurality	unity
left	right
female	male
motion (change)	rest (permanence)
curved	straight
dark	light
oblong	square
even	odd
evil	good

Conway and her rationalist contemporaries perpetuate the dualism of the column, along with the Platonistic emphasis on its right side. Perhaps Conway takes to heart the statement in the Kabbalah that in the first *Sephira*, an aspect of God portraying it [Conway refers to God as "He." – ed.] as the great unchangeable Father of all,[23] "all is right side."[24] Thus, unity, spirit, God, male, and light are more highly regarded than plurality, matter, creatures, female, and darkness.

> In every visible Creature there is a Body and a Spirit, or *Principium magis Activum, & magis Passivum*, or *more Active and more Passive Principle*, which may fitly be termed Male and Female, by reason of that Analogy a Husband hath with his Wife. For as the ordinary Generation of Men requires a Conjunction and Co-operation of Male and Female; so also all Generations and Productions whatsoever they be, require an Union, and conformable Operation of those Two principles, to wit, Spirit and Body; but the spirit is an Eye or Light beholding its own proper Image, and the Body is a Tenebrosity or Darkness receiving that Image, when the Spirit looks thereinto, as when one sees himself in a Looking-Glass.[25]

Perfection is associated with the right side and imperfection with the left. Thus Conway's God is entirely spiritual (always associated with the right side) and incorporeal,[26] eternal, simple, and immutable.

> In God there is neither Time nor Change, nor Composition, nor Division of Parts: He is wholly and universally one in himself and of himself, without any manner of variety of Mixture: He hath no

manner of Darkness, or Corporeity in him, and so consequently no kind of Form of Figure whatsoever.[27]

The divine creation is timeless with respect to the deity, but successive with respect to creatures. God creates all things together, in the sense that it created the

> Universals, Seeds, and Principles of all Things which (in subordination to God, who is the Principle Beginning of all Things) are, as it were Springs and Fountains from whence Creatures did flow in the order of their succession.[28]

But this continual Action or Operation of God, as it is in him, or proceeds from him, or hath respect unto him, is one only continual Act or Command of his Will, neither hath Time or Succession in it; nor first; nor latter; but is together, and always present with God; so that nothing of him is either past or to come, because he hath not parts: But so far as he appears or terminates in Creatures, he hath Time and Succession of parts ... Suppose a great Circle or Wheel to be moved by a Centre, whereas the Centre always remains in one place, even as some do think the Sun after this manner to be moved about his Centre (by some Angel or Spirit remaining in the Centre) within the space of so many days. Now albeit the Centre moves the whole Wheel, and causes a great and continual Motion in the same; yet that always resteth, neither is it in the least moved: How much more then is the same in God, who is the First Mover in all his Creatures, according to all their true and appointed Motions, yet he is not moved of them?[29]

Indeed, the concept of time is not appropriate to the deity. In this respect, Conway's position is very much like Leibniz's: Time is relative to succession and motion, both of which belong only to creatures. They are the inferior analogues of eternity and of the will whereby God creates.

> Time is nothing else but the successive Motion or Operation of Creatures; which Motion or Operation, if it should cease, Time would also cease, and the Creatures themselves would cease with Time: Wherefore such is the Nature of every Creature, that it is in

Motion, or hath a certain Motion, by means of which it advances forward, and grows to a farther perfection. And seeing in God there is no successive Motion or Operation to a farther perfection; because he is most absolutely perfect. Hence there are not Times in God or his Eternity.[30]

While God does not move, strictly speaking, its will is analogous to motion. Furthermore, as the ultimate spirit and source of life, it is also the ultimate source of motion, including vital motion,[31] though itself unmoved.

Motion it self is of God, by whose Will all Motion happens: For as a Creature cannot give Being to it self, so neither can it move it self; for in him we Live, Move and have our Being; so that Motion and Essence come from the same cause, *sc*, God the Creator, who remains immoveable in himself; neither is he carried from place to place, because he is equally present everywhere, and gives Being to Creatures.[32]

But that in him which hath an Analogy or Agreement with the Motions or Operations of Creatures, is the Government of his Will, which (to speak properly) is not Motion, because every Motion is successive, and cannot have place in God, as is above demonstrated.[33]

In addition, because emanative creation is creation 'out of' God, rather than 'out of' nothing, there is at least some sense in which creatures have a share of the divine nature. God, in creating, *gives* something of itself to its creatures without being thereby diminished – the divine fountain is an endless one. Henry More felt that this way of thinking about creation did not maintain a proper separation between God and creatures, and led to pantheism. These concerns led him eventually to reject Conway's Kabbalistic thought.[34] For Conway, however, the close relationship between the divine and created natures is desirable because it conduces to the harmony of her system.

God's emanative creativity (i.e. God's will) is, as we have seen, the divine analogue of motion. Motion, in turn, is the emanative product and the inferior analogue of the divine will. Note also Conway's use, in the following passage, of the term 'emanation', which clearly shows that emanation and motion are closely linked in her mind.

Moreover the consideration of this Infinite Divisibility of every thing ... is ... a thing of very great moment; *viz.* that thereby may be understood the Reasons and Causes of Things; and how all Creatures from the highest to the lowest are inseparably united one with another, by means of Subtiler Parts interceding or coming in between, which are the Emanations of one Creature into another, by which also they act one upon another at the greatest distance; and this is the Foundation of all Sympathy and Antipathy which happens in Creatures: And if these things be well understood of any one, he may easily see into the most secret and hidden Causes of Things, which ignorant Men call occult Qualities.[35]

Divine emanative causation and causation by motion in creatures are respectively the superior and inferior manifestations of causation: Among creatures, some sort of motion, whether vital or merely mechanical, must be involved in any causal interaction. Note in the passage above the *physical* nature of the linkage Conway describes among creatures. Given the close relation between motion and divine emanation, even one who believes spirit to be superior to body, or one who believes spirit to be more real than body, can be a mechanist, by interpreting mechanism (mere, as opposed to vital motion) as the means of causal interaction of less perfect beings.

This notion of a physical link accounting for causation among creatures suggests that there must be a similar, analogous link between creatures and their creator. For Conway, Christ, sharing some qualities, including mutability and bodily nature, with creatures, but sharing divinity, immutability and spirituality with God,[36] is the link or 'medium' between God and Creatures.

[Christ] is a natural *Medium* between [God and creatures] by which the Extreams are united, and this *Medium* partakes of both Extreams, and therefore is the most convenient and proper *Medium*; for it partakes of the one Extream, *viz.* Mutability, to wit, from Good to a greater degree or measure of Goodness, and of the other Extream, *viz.* that it is altogether unchangeable from Good into Evil; and such a *Medium* was necessarily required in the very Nature of Things; for otherwise there would remain a Chasm or Gap.[37]

Christ, who participates in the divine perfection, is begotten, or emanated immediately, rather than created. Creatures are emanated through the medium of Christ, "by whom all Things are said to be made."[38] Conway's point here is Kabbalistic in origin. The Kabbalah refers to the *Sephiroth* as the medium between the *Ain Soph* (the absolute) and the real world. Like Christ's relation to God, the *Sephiroth* are emanations, not creations of the *Ain Soph*.[39]

Just as bodies exert causal influence by giving off portions of themselves (a theory of sensation popular during the early modern period held that the objects of sense give off small particles which are received by the sense organ), an emanative creator 'gives off' (but without being thereby reduced) images or reflections of itself. In keeping with the Platonic tradition, the images arc naturally less perfect than the original. Thus, some of God's attributes are communicable (though in lesser form) to creatures (and with respect to these attributes the creatures resemble the creator), but others are not (and thus there are some intrinsic differences between creatures and creator).

> The Divine Attributes are commonly and rightly distinguished, into communicable, and incommunicable; the incommunicable are, that God is a Being, subsisting by himself, Independent, Unchangeable, absolutely Infinite, and most Perfect: The communicable are, that he is a Spirit, Life, and Light, that he is Good, Holy, Just, Wise, & c. But now there are none of these communicable Attributes, which are not living, yea Life itself.[40]

While creatures can and must differ from the creator in some ways (they are mutable, while the creator is immutable), it appears that they must all have at least some attributes communicated from God. This requirement enables Conway to argue that everything which exists is alive. She points out that matter in itself has no divinely communicated attributes.

> Now what Attributes or Perfections can be attributed to dead Matter, which do analogically Answer to those which are in God? If we diligently enquire thereinto, we shall find none at all; for all his Attributes are living; yea, Life it self. Moreover, seeing the Creatures of God, so far as they are Creatures, ought necessarily in some

things to resemble their Creator; now I demand, in what dead matter is like unto God? If they say again in naked Entity, I answer, There is none such in God or his Creatures: And so it is a mere *non ens*, or nothing.

But as touching the other Attributes of Matter, *viz*, Impenetrability, Figurability, and Mobility; certainly none of these have any place in God, and so are not of his communicable Attributes; but rather Essential Differences or Attributes of Diversity, whereby the Creature, as such, is distinguished from God ... And seeing dead Matter doth not partake of any of the communicable Attributes of God, we must certainly conclude, that the same is a mere *non ens* or nothing ... a thing impossible.[41]

Only if matter is also *alive* can it be a divine product, for life is a communicable and essential attribute of God.

[S]eeing the Goodness of God is a living Goodness, which hath Life, Power, Love, and Knowledge in it, which he communicates to his Creatures, How can it be, that any dead Thing should proceed from him, or be created by Him, such as mere Body or Matter, according to their Hypothesis, who affirm, that the same is wholly incontrovertible, to any degree of Life or Knowledge? It is truly said of one that God made not Death, and it is as true, that he made no dead Thing ... And because every Creature hath a Communication with God in some of his Attributes, now I demand, In what Attribute dead Matter hath it, or a Body that is uncapable of Life and Sense for ever?[42]

Conway's claim that there is no such thing as 'dead' matter must not be taken as a denial of the existence of matter *per se*. Furthermore, to say that matter for Conway is 'nothing but congealed spirit'[43] is misleadingly reductionistic: Because matter and spirit are distinguished only by their relative "subtlety" or "grossness,"[44] and are interconvertible, one could just as well call spirit 'rarified matter'. Conway's claim is rather that matter and spirit are essentially the same, and differ from one another only modally, that is, in their *manner* of existence. Unlike God, who is pure spirit, creatures are a mixture of body and spirit, and their relative imperfection, or sinfulness, is related to their share of corporeity.[45]

Although Conway is not a dualist in the Cartesian sense of holding mind and body to be really, essentially distinct, nor in the sense of taking one to be more 'real' than the other, she places them on a continuum, on which spirit is more favorably placed than matter.

> Creature is but one Essence or Substance, as to Nature or Essence, as is above demonstrated, so that it only differs *secundum modos existendi*; or, *according to the manners of existence*; among which one is a Corporeity; whereof also there are many degrees; so that a Thing may more or less approach to, or recede from the State and Condition of a body or a Spirit; but because a Spirit (between these two) is more excellent in the Natural Order of Things, and by how much the more a Creature is a Spirit ... so much the nearer it approaches to God, who is the chiefest Spirit.[46]

Certainly, the desire for a unified, harmonious ontology is one motivation for the unification of principles which others (i.e. the Cartesians) have considered opposites. Such a system has the additional advantage of providing a solution to a problem plaguing the Cartesian dualists (though not considered a problem by Descartes himself): how two substances, mind and body, considered to be essentially different, 'really distinct', and to have nothing in common, can interact. This is a problem if one shares, as we have seen that Conway does, the view that like causes like – that the cause must have something in common with the effect.[47] Deny an essential difference between mind and body, then, and the problem vanishes. It is solved by allowing both spirit and body to be in motion, indeed, constantly so,[48] *and thus alive*, motion being a property which in creatures implies life and spirit.[49]

> But if it be granted that the Soul is of one Nature and Substance with the Body, although it is many degrees more excellent in regard of Life and Spirituality, as also in swiftness of Motion, and Penetrability, and diverse other Perfections; then ... it will be easily conceived, how the Body and Soul are united together, and how the Soul moves the Body, and suffers by it or with it.[50]

Just as every body is living, and thus has spiritual characteristics, every created spirit has material characteristics, such as motion and figure. As the above passage makes clear, all creatures are both spiritual and corporeal, and have qualities usually restricted to either matter or spirit, life being for Conway equivalent to spirit.[51] Every body has a spirit, and vice-versa.[52]

> For we may easily understand how one Body is united with another, by that true agreement that one hath with another in its own Nature; and so the most subtile and Spiritual Body may be united with a Body that is very gross and thick, *sc.* by means of certain Bodies, partaking of subtilty and grossness, according to diverse degrees, consisting between two Extreams, and these middle Bodies are indeed the Links and Chains, by which the Soul, which is so subtile and Spiritual, is conjoined with a Body so gross; which middle Spirits (if they cease, or are absent) the Union is broken or dissolved; so from the same Foundation we may easily understand, how the Soul moves the Body, *viz.* as noe subtile Body can move another gross and thick Body: And seeing body it self is a sensible Life, or an Intellectual Substance, it is no less clearly conspicuous, how one Body can wound, or grieve, or gratifie, or please another; because Things of one, or alike Nature, can easily affect each other: And to this Argument may be reduced the like difficulties, *viz.* how Spirits move Spirits; and how some Spirits strive and contend with other Spirits; also concerning the Unity, Concord, and Friendship, which good Spirits reverence among themselves; for if all Spirits could be intrinsically present one with another, How could they dispute or contend about place? And how can one expel or drive out another? and yet that there is such an expulsion and conflict of Spirits, and especially of the Good against the Evil, some few who have been acquainted with their own Hearts have experimentally known.[53]

This passage shows that both bodily and spiritual characteristics must be present in creatures. Note also the similarity to Conway's account of Christ as medium.

We stated before that according to Conway all causation among creatures is capable of being explained in terms of some kind of motion. Motion includes local or internal, and mechanical motion ("the carrying of Body from place to place")[54] and vital motion, which is superior:

Wherefore *Hobbs*, and all others who side with him, greviously erre, whilst they teach that Sense and Knowledge is no other than a reaction of Corporeal particles one upon another, where, by reaction, he means no other than Local and Mechanical Motion. But indeed Sense and Knowledge is a Thing far more Noble and Divine, than any Local or Mechanical Motion of any Particles whatsoever; for it is the Motion or Action of Life, which uses the other as its Instrument ... and can like Local Motion be transmitted through divers Bodies, although very far distant asunder, which therefore are united, and that without any new Transition of Body or Matter. *ex. gr.* a Beam of Wood of an exceeding great length, is moved by one Extream from the North to the South, the other Extream will necessarily be moved also; and the Action is transmitted through the whole Beam, without any Particles of Matter sent hither to promote Motion, from one Extream to the other; because the Beam it self is sufficient to transmit the said Motion: After the same manner also, a Vital Action can proceed together with Local Motion from one thing to another, and that too at a great distance, where there is an apt and fit *Medium* to transmit it, and here we may observe a kind of Divine Spirituality or Subtilty in every Motion, and so in every Action of Life, which no created Body or Substance is capable of, *viz.* by Intrinsical Presence, which (as before proved) agrees to no created Substance; and yet agrees to every Motion or Action whatsoever: For Motion or Action is not a certain Matter or Substance, but only a manner of its Being; and therefore is intrinsically present in the Subject, whereof there is a *Modus*, or Manner, and can pass from Body to Body, at a great distance, if it finds a fit *Medium* to transmit it.[55]

Here Conway expresses her differences with those who advocate purely mechanistic explanations. Yes, life and thought are bound up with motion, but it is *vital* motion, not mere mechanical motion.

IV. SUMMARY

We have seen that Conway incorporates the mechanistic account of causation through motion, and the neo-Platonic account of causation through emanation, into a single account of causation. Motion, especially vital motion (reminiscent of the Platonic world-soul), and divine emanation are not intrinsically different forms of causation; rather they are variations on a theme. Conway differs from the pure mechanists in that rather than taking motion to be the source of life, she takes life to be the source of motion. Indeed, "Sense and Knowledge is a Thing far more Noble and Divine, than any Local or Mechanical Motion of any Particles whatsoever; for it is the Motion or Action of Life, which uses the other as its Instrument."[56] Even sin is explained in terms of motion: It is *ataxia* – improper motion.[57]

The universality of motion puts an end to the mind-body problem of the Cartesians. Because all creatures have life and motion (indeed the motion of life is the most noble kind), there is no reason why the mind and body cannot exert causal influence upon (or move) one another.

It was noted earlier that Conway's system shares many features with Leibniz's. Both philosophers are interested in reconciliation of opposing principles. Which reconciliation is more successful? It seems that Leibniz needs to do much more 'hand-waving' to make his system fit together than does Conway: For Leibniz, God *somehow or other* sees to it that phenomena and reality, mind and body, efficient and final causes, are all harmonized. Conway's treatment of every creature as having life and motion makes their interaction real (for Leibniz, it is merely phenomenal) and understandable. On the other hand, Conway's system is much less complete and comprehensive than Leibniz's (here it must be pointed out that Leibniz enjoyed substantially longer life, better health, and greater opportunity for study than did Conway). In many respects, Leibniz's system is more 'modern' in that it begins to incorporate logic into metaphysics. Conway says little of deduction and necessary connections, which play important roles in the Leibnizian account of causation, making use instead of the analogous concept of emanation. Both are committed to the primacy of intellect or soul, and to a God-centered system.

Although Conway, on the basis of one short work, is unlikely ever to be considered a major philosopher, her work is important and worthy of study. I have chosen to concentrate on her accounts of motion and emanation; others have and, I hope, will examine other aspects of her work.

NOTES

References to Conway's *The Principles of the Most Ancient and Modern Philosophy*
consist of chapter and section numbers, followed by a page reference to the English
portion of Lopston reprint edition (The Hague: Martinus Nijhoff, 1982). Ex: VII.4 210
refers to chapter VII, section 4, p. 210.

1. Marjorie Hope Nicolson, *Conway Letters*, New Haven, Yale, 1930, p. 114.
2. Nicolson 6, 49.
3. Carolyn Merchant, "The Vitalism of Anne Conway: Its Impact on Leibniz's
   Concept of the Monad," *J. Hist. Phil.* XVII.3 (July 1979), p. 256.
4. He began to use the term during the same period in which Van Helmont
   introduced him to Conway's work (Merchant 255f).
5. III.9 163.
6. VII 191.
7. VII.4 208–209.
8. VII.4 209–210.
9. VII.4 210.
10. VI.11 190.
11. VII.4 207–208.
12. See the works of Merchant listed in the bibliography, and Lopston's introduction
    to Conway's *Principles*.
13. Lopston 25 n. 33, quoting Nicolson 453, n. 6.
14. I.1 149.
15. VI.3–4 176–179; for a discussion of Conway's essentialism, see Lopston 52–59.
16. II.5 155.
17. II.4 154–55.
18. III.3 158.
19. In this context, she sounds much like Spinoza, although Conway's God, unlike
    Spinoza's, is pure spirit, without extension.
20. III.2 158.
21. III.9 163.
22. III.1 157.
23. S.L. Macgregor Mathers, *The Kabbalah Unveiled*, London: Routledge & Kegan
    Paul, 1888, p. 22.
24. Mathers 24.
25. VI.11 188–189.
26. Conway makes a point of expressing disagreement with Hobbes on this point
    (IX.3 222).
27. I.2 149, see also VII.1 192.
28. IV.1 165.
29. III.8 161.
30. II.6 155. See also II.2 153, VII.4 204; cf. Leibniz: "time is the order of existence
    of things possible successively" (C.I. Gerhardt, *Die philosophischen Schriften von
    G.W. Leibniz*, Berlin, 1875–90, vol. II, p. 269; Leroy E. Loemker, *Leibniz,
    Philosophical Papers and Letters*, 2nd ed., Dordrecht: D. Reidel, 1969, p. 536).

31. VIII.2 213, IX.9 230.
32. VIII.2 213.
33. III.8 161.
34. Allison Coudart, "A Cambridge Platonist's Kabbalist Nightmare," *Journal of the History of Ideas* XXXVI.4 (Oct.–Jan. 1975), p. 650.
35. III.10 164.
36. IV.1–2 165; V.2–5 167–171.
37. V.3 169.
38. IV.1 165.
39. Kab. Unv. 38–39, from Jellinek's *Beitrage zu Geschichte der Kabbalah, Erstes Heft*, Leipzig, 1852.
40. VII.2 196.
41. VII.2 197.
42. VII.2 196.
43. As Coudart does, p. 650.
44. VII.2–4 200–208.
45. VII.1 193–194.
46. VII.1 192.
47. VIII.3 215.
48. VI.6 180.
49. VII.4 205.
50. VII.2 214.
51. VII 191.
52. IX.7 225.

As to those Creatures which are Spirits, and can penetrate each other, in every created Spirit, there may be some infinity of Spirits, all which Spirits may be of equal extension, as well with the aforesaid Spirit, as they are one with another; for in this case those Spirits are more Subtile and Aethereal, which penetrate the Gross and more Corporeal, whence here can be no want of Room, that one must be constrained to give place to another. (III.5 159–160)

Every Man, yea, every Creature, consists of many Spirits and Bodies ... and indeed every Body is a Spirit, and nothing else, neither differs any thing from a Spirit, but in that it is more dark; therefore by how much the thicker and grosser it is become, so much the more remote it is from the degree of a Spirit, so that this distinction is only modal and gradual, not essential or substantial. (VI.11 190)

[Thoughts] have Body and Spirit; for if they had not a Body, they could not be retained, nor could we reflect on our own proper Thoughts. (VI.11 189–190)

A Thing may more or less approach to, or recede from the State and Condition of a body or a Spirit. (VII.1 192)

A Spirit is capable of Corporeity, *Secundum majus & minus*, or more and less; although not infinitely, yet in many degrees. (VII.1 194)

> And thus Life and Figure are distinct, but not contrary Attributes of one and the same Substance, and Figure serves the Operations of Life ... Life and Figure consist very well together in one Body, or Substance, where Figure is an Instrument of Life, without which no Vital Operation can be performed. (IX.8 226)

53. VII.3 214–215.
54. IX.9 226.
55. IX.9 227–228. By "intrinsical presence" Conway means the ability of one substance to enter into another of equal dimensions, without increase in bulk, i.e. the ability to occupy the same spatiotemporal region (VII.4 203).
56. IX.9 227.
57. VIII.2 214.

4. Sor Juana Inés de la Cruz

MARY CHRISTINE MORKOVSKY, CDP

Sor Juana Inés de la Cruz de Asbaje y Ramírez (1648–1695) is a major Baroque literary figure of the New World who accepted the classical/medieval philosophy prevalent in Spain until the sixteenth century and transplanted to Mexico largely through priests who were professors. Two disquietudes or mysteries of her own experience for which philosophy gave her no answer appear often in her writings. The first, an insatiable desire to understand everything thoroughly, could be considered a predominantly personal or psychological problem. The second, the widespread opinion that women are inferior to men, is a social or cultural one as well. In writing about both of them, Sor Juana transcends her individuality as well as her epoch, for she does intimate they are universal human problems.

Sor Juana maintained that women as well as the native peoples of the New World had the right to education. In her own search for wisdom, Sor Juana experienced the perils of being a female explorer and became convinced that the difficulties of her pursuit did not come from her sex but largely from obstacles raised by men. The philosophy implicit as well as explicit in her works is basically late Scholasticism, and she makes no original contributions to this school. The central theme of freedom of the understanding has caused her to be considered a precursor of the Enlightenment while the theme of liberation and education of women has endeared her to contemporary feminists.

I. BIOGRAPHY

Juana, illegitimate daughter of a Spaniard from Vizcaya, Pedro Manuel de Asbaje, and a Creole, Isabel Ramírez de Santillana, was baptized December 2, 1648,[1] in the village of San Miguel de Nepantla

Mary Ellen Waithe (ed.), A History of Women Philosophers / Volume 3, 59–72.
© 1991 *Kluwer Academic Publishers. Printed in the Netherlands.*

near Mexico City. When she was about three she followed an older sister to class in one of the "Amigas" schools first founded for native girls by Fray Juan de Zumárraga. There she cajoled the teacher into teaching her to read. A few years later she begged her mother to send her to the capital city disguised as a boy so she could study the sciences in a university. Her mother refused, so Juana tried to satiate her desire for learning by reading her grandfather's books even though she was punished for doing so. At the age of twelve she composed a *"Loa en honor del Santísimo Sacramento"* which won a prize, a book. She received about twenty grammar lessons and encouraged herself to learn by trimming her hair whenever she had not met her goals. When she came to Mexico City about the age of eighteen to live in the palace of the Viceroy, the Marquis of Mancera, as a lady-in-waiting to his wife, her well-stocked memory was much admired; and she astounded interlocutors in a public test of her learning arranged by the Viceroy.

Because of her natural desire for study, Juana would have preferred to live alone and be free to study her books, but she made the rational decision to enter religious life to secure her salvation and find refuge and solitude. After a short stay with the Carmelites, whose way of life was too hard for her health, she entered the Order of St. Jerome, making her vows in 1669. She discovered that her desire for learning, whether prize or punishment, was the chief enemy she took with her into the convent.[2] She claims this desire was almost irresistible in her. The Jeromites, a Benedictine Order, encouraged study. Contact with laypersons was not forbidden, and each nun was permitted to acquire study aids such as books and musical instruments. She maintained close ties with her family and helped them when they were in financial need. For years she had a personal slave, Juana. One of her friends was Carlos de Sigüenza y Góngora (1645–1700), ex-Jesuit, astronomer, mathematician, cosmographer, and historian. His poetry is mediocre compared with hers, but his constant searching for scientific proof of his hypotheses is similar to her care to bolster her conclusions with examples or logical reasoning.

In the convent she continued to study in every spare moment, having no teachers or student companions except her books. She pursued the human arts and sciences – logic, rhetoric, physics, music, arithmetic, geometry, architecture, history, law, astrology, and mechanics in general without specializing in any one. All of these led to the peak of sacred theology and were useful for understanding the Holy Scriptures.

The nobility frequently sought her company and asked her to write verses for birthdays and special occasions as well as plays and pageants for solemn celebrations in the viceregal court. Jealousies and petty persecutions accompanied her popularity, but she found strength in the example of Socrates, in the maxim of Machiavelli to despise the braggart because he distinguishes himself by discrediting others, and in the fact that the Pharisees hated Christ. A superior who considered studies a matter for the Inquisition once forbade her to study for three months, and Sor Juana obeyed. However, she found herself continuing to learn in every corner – psychology in people, geometry in the architecture of the dormitory, physics in children's toys, chemistry as well as philosophy in the kitchen.

Sor Juana remarks that the studiousness which is considered meritorious in men is not merit in her since it is a driving need. However, she does not consider her learning to be a fault since she never trusts herself but always submits to others' judgments. Two years before her death, she decided to renounce literature, sold her library, and gave the proceeds to the poor. This renunciation has been viewed as the result of the influence of her strict confessor, Antonio Nuñez de Miranda, or of a personal conversion. Octavio Paz links it to the social unrest of the last decades of the sixteenth century in Mexico.[3] French corsairs threatened in the Gulf of Mexico, epidemics broke out in the cities, viceroys were changed in quick succession, and finally in 1692 the native population of Mexico City staged riots and demanded food. They stoned the Viceroy's palace and set it on fire. Processions with the Blessed Sacrament as well as public punishment of the instigators of the rebellion followed. It was a period of disillusionment with the dream of uniting different peoples in one harmonious empire, and Paz relates it to Sor Juana's inability to move out of literary forms that were confining even though she employed them so gracefully. To destroy them would have been to destroy herself. Personal and social conflict could not be resolved without demolishing the presuppositions on which the colonial world was based. When dissent is impossible and the prevalent attitude is that there is nothing more to discover, add, or propose then to renounce rational speech and to burn government buildings are similar responses.

Nursing her Sisters during a bubonic plague epidemic, Sor Juana died on April 17, 1695. The Tenth Muse of Mexico wrote more than 200 lyric poems of various lengths, most of them sonnets, and almost a hundred short *"villancicos"* for church feast days are attributed to her. Lengthy religious plays and spectacles such as *"El Divino Narciso"* and secular comedies such as *"Los Empeños de una Casa"* number over 20. Her prose works include *"Neptuno Alegórico,"* *"Carta atenagórica,"* and *"Respuesta a Sor Filotéa de la Cruz,"* as well as devotional works. Two volumes of her works went through several editions in Spain during her lifetime.

II. PROSE PHILOSOPHICAL WORKS

The chief sources that reveal Sor Juana's philosophical ideas are the *"Carta"* and *"Respuesta"* just mentioned, the long poem she titled *"Primero Sueño,"* and about a dozen sonnets. The late Medieval view of philosophy as predominantly training in reasoning was brought from Spain to the New World and propagated in universities and monasteries. Adhering to what she was taught, Sor Juana viewed reality as essentially orderly, ruled gently by God and progressing to even greater harmony with the help of the morally good actions of human beings.

1. *Carta Atenagórica*

Sor Juana shows her mastery of logical argument in her critique of a sermon by the Portuguese Jesuit, Antonio de Vieyra, confessor to Queen Kristina of Sweden, that came to be called the *"Carta Atenagórica."* In 1690 the bishop of Puebla, Don Manuel Fernández de Santa Cruz, asked her to comment on a Maundy Thursday sermon preached by the Jesuit in Lisbon. Although the *"Súmulas"* she authored have been lost,[4] this treatise shows her skill in logic and ability to defend her views with abundant reasons. The question proposed is: What was the greatest kindness of Christ? Vieyra presents and rejects the views of three saintly authorities and then defends his own choice. Sor Juana comes to the support of the three scholars he attacks and then offers her own opinion as to what was the greatest expression of Christ's love.

St. Augustine claimed the finest action of Christ was to die for humankind; Vieyra claims it was to absent himself. Defending Augustine's view, Sor Juana carefully distinguishes *terminus ad quo* from *terminus ad quem*, the being of God from the being of Christ, soul from body, means from end, and creation from conservation. Besides these fine distinctions, she points out that death implies absence. Moreover, it is false to say Christ absented Himself since before His death He perpetuated His presence on earth by instituting the Eucharist.

The second authority, St. Thomas Aquinas, said Christ's greatest kindness was to remain with us in the Eucharistic sacrament; Vieyra counters that it was to remain in the sacrament without the use of His senses. Sor Juana says the Jesuit's argument is invalid because Aquinas proposes in general while Vieyra responds in specifics. Moreover, not to sense at all is better than to feel offenses and insults.

The third saint, John Chrysostom, singled out as Christ's finest gesture the washing of the feet of the disciples, while Vieyra says that the cause which moved Him to wash them is greater. Sor Juana defends Chrysostom, saying that such a prodigious effect actually had many causes. Love was Christ's motive; however, the saint was not talking about love but about the courtesy which is its exterior sign. To Vieyra's own view that the greatest kindness of Christ was to love without proportionate response, Sor Juana brings a whole arsenal of counter-arguments, from showing that Christ does want humankind's love to proving that the greatest good of human beings is to be God-like, which is impossible unless they love God. Finally, she proposes her own subtle view: the greatest kindnesses of Christ are the benefits He does *not* grant humankind because He knows the evil and in-gratitude with which they will be repaid. Withholding favors is a favor of God-as-God and a kindness that continues forever. God restrains His natural goodness so people will not harm themselves by being ungrateful.

2. *Respuesta*

As Octavio Paz points out, Sor Juana's view that God's gifts are negative suggests a divine indifference and leaves too much up to human free will. Perhaps the bishop who believed that divine grace is humankind's very life and freedom is its reflection was aware of these implications even though he had the letter published without her knowledge. Then, under the pen name of Sor Filotéa, he wrote her a letter admonishing her to abandon worldly studies and devote herself to the study of Sacred Scripture. Her reply, published posthumously, pleads eloquently for intellectual freedom and for the rights of women to education. In the *"Respuesta"* dated March 1, 1691, Sor Juana insists that she avoids writing about sacred things out of fear and reverence. To write about such subjects would go against what is considered proper for her sex and age. In her own life she studies not to write or to teach but only because by studying she becomes less ignorant. She regards sacred theology as the highest and best learning but claims no expertise in that holy field. Moreover, she experiences a dread of it which she does not feel when writing about secular subjects since a heresy against art is not punishable by the Inquisition. The narrative of her labors and triumphs in which she both defends and mocks her love of learning continues in this vein. The autobiographical details about her voracious desire for learning, the self-discipline she practiced to achieve it, and the authorities she quotes are all designed to appeal to the reason of her accuser. She cites Doctor Arce, an authority on Scripture, who says that although women should not preach or read in public, it would be very beneficial and useful for them to study, write, and teach privately. How much damage would have been avoided in her own country, she laments, if women of old had been educated.

"Women should be silent in church" is indeed a quote from Scripture, but Sor Juana gives numerous examples to support her claim that to grasp the import of the Bible requires knowledge of much history, customs, ceremonies, proverbs, and ways of speaking in bygone times. A more thought-provoking Scriptural passage is "Let a woman learn in silence." If women were to be uneducated, why, she asks, did the Church approve the writings of Saints Gertrude, Theresa, and Bridget? For that matter, did the prohibition apply to Martha and Mary, Marcella, Mary the mother of James, and Salome in the early Church?

The discipline in Sor Juana's convent gave her more leisure for scholarly pursuits than was enjoyed by women in other walks of life and more freedom from investigations of orthodoxy than was enjoyed by her contemporary male religious who had the duty of instructing the faithful. She claims that her own inclinations were in the direction of pleasing others rather than blazing new trails. Without bitterness or militancy she states that she was persecuted. For what? For using every means available to make herself less ignorant. By whom? By persons whom she threatened, especially her superiors. While erudition is praised in learned men, Sor Juana found herself as a woman blamed for her learning. But she was animated to persevere in her scholarship by the example of wise women of whom she had read. In the "*Respuesta*" she names and provides thumbnail sketches of thirty-one distinguished women ranging from Deborah in the Old Testament, New Testament heroines, pagan scholars, Christian scholars, to royal women including the Countess of Villaumbrosa.

Toward the end of her reply she asks whether her crime was to write the "*Carta.*" But if she is being considered insolent to voice opinions contrary to Father Vieyra, why was not he considered insolent to disagree with three holy Fathers of the Church? She demands, "Isn't my understanding as free as his since it springs from the same ground?"[5] Are his personal opinions principles of faith to be believed blindly? If her critique was heretical, why did not the censor denounce it?

III. PHILOSOPHICAL POETRY

1. *Sueño*

In addition to finesse in argument, Sor Juana's writings reveal a fairly coherent worldview. Since verse came more naturally to her than did prose, it is not surprising that her views of God, humanity, and the world are best seen in her poem of almost a thousand hendecasyllables, the "*Sueño.*" Written in imitation of Luis de Góngora y Argote, (1561–1627), it is nevertheless a reliable source for her own thoughts and feelings, for she says, "I have never written a single thing of my own volition but only in response to the requests and commands of others. This is so much the case that I don't recall having written anything for my own pleasure except the little paper called 'The Dream.' "[6]

The opening word, "*Piramidal,*" is a rich symbol. As the pyramid points to heaven, so the human mind strives to mount to the First Cause. Although the five human senses and imagination are the corporeal foundation for knowledge, human beings have three interior faculties which enable them to touch heaven though they are dust. Humankind's high lowliness allows it to participate in the nature of angels, plants, and animals. In sleep the living human clock slows down its well-regulated movement. Breathing continues and the brain receives clear exhalations alternately from the four humors. These do not obscure the images which the estimative sense presents to the imagination which, to preserve them more surely and clearly, entrusts them to memory. Sleep allows the phantasy room to form a variety of images of earthly creatures as well as to try to picture invisible realities. Almost separated from her corporeal chain, the soul soars like an eagle to the top of the high mental pyramid where she is elevated to a part of her own mind so sublime that she believes herself to be in a new region.

Suspended, joyful, content yet amazed, the soul finds that neither distance nor obstacles impede her vision of all creation. Instead of being overwhelmed by the excess and greatness of things to be known, the soul considers comprehension to be possible. However, just as the sun causes tears to form in the eyes of the one who attempts to gaze directly at it, so the understanding is overcome by the immensity and variety of the universe. Attempting to see everything, it misses both the whole and its integral parts. The soul before whom these immense vistas open out is so astounded that she can form only a confused concept and formless assemblage of ideas without order or unity. The human mind is too small to encircle so diffuse an object. Discursive reasoning, not intuition, is the proper procedure for a rational animal. A human mind that tries to grasp all reality in a glance is headed for shipwreck and will find that one must stick to one subject or investigate one by one the things that fit into the ten categories. Soaring so high in dream and exalting the mental powers, Sor Juana's thought remains anchored in Aristotelian philosophy. She does, however, call the ten categories "*artificiosas*," ingenious, a word needed for the rhyme but probably also showing that she did not consider those categories to be eternal or self-evident.

The human mind in non-dreaming reality cannot encompass all creation in a single intuition. Its procedure is to abstract and form universals, to reduce complexity to simplicity, to make up for this defect. It also forms an ascending order of concepts, disciplining its weak forces so as to attain the summit. This is not the Cartesian method, according to which one becomes indubitably certain of God before one is sure of the world. Sor Juana is describing the classical method of proceeding from inanimate beings of the lowest class and secondary causes, reaching that noble creature with whom God was pleased as the ultimate perfection of creation.

To judge that humankind can comprehend everything is very daring since experience teaches that we do not understand even the smallest and easiest part of the most evident natural effects. Some people give up and refuse to use their reason. Others instead of acknowledging defeat attempt to eternalize their own name, even stooping to cajolery and flattery. The conclusion of this exploration of human understanding is poignant awareness of its limitations, but not skepticism or a call for universal doubt.

Through the interior pyramids of consciousness, Sor Juana has been seeking the First Cause, God Himself, central point from which everything can be understood. She dreams of going from here to everything contained in the circumference of her geocentric system. This is definitely not a report on the dark night of the soul described by mystics. Light comes from the human mind rather than from divine illumination or the beatific vision. Although this ascent promotes intellectual delight, it is accompanied by moral uneasiness due to awareness of one's daring in the face of the danger that on these heights one can get lost or lead others astray.

Sor Juana next describes the understanding as foundering on reefs or lost in pathless quicksand, lacking material to maintain its ardor. She describes the slackening involved in physiological aspects of dreaming, showing more than a surface acquaintance with the human body and the functioning of its main organs. The food that fed the body's fire caused by the union of moisture and heat has been consumed, and the chains of sleep are loosening. The brain is emptied; phantasies evaporate; the morning star heralds the sun; the birds begin to sing. The sun rises brilliantly, imparting color to visible things and restoring to the external senses their operations. Now that the light is more constant and the world is illuminated, Sor Juana awakens.

She seems to put her mind to sleep as she describes the increasing activity of the bodily members and the loveliness of earth and sky at dawn. How different are her last four stanzas from the morning prayers she and her Sisters recited daily as soon as possible after rising. The theme of these morning hymns is praise of the Lord of creation, thanks for all His gifts, and requests for grace for the day ahead. In the morning of her poem, Sor Juana paints the beauty of stars, planets, birds, sun, sky, and light without mention of their cause, purpose, or future. Her restless mind has forgotten about pyramids and seems to be watching and enjoying the beauty of the world.

In spite of its abstractness and lack of expressions of personal emotion, the "Dream" may be a revealing personal testament. Dreams are not communal; a dreamer is necessarily solitary. Her active mind, constrained by convention but apparently not unduly harried by demands made on her during the day, enjoys the freedom of solitude at night. In that rich personality which could never give itself fully to the life of the viceroy's court or the Jeromite cloister there was always a part of her mind which watched, reflected, judged, ordered, and set limits to evade excesses. Factors contributing to this questioning stance included a natural reserve and reluctance to abandon herself entirely as well as her knowledge of scholastic philosophy. Pfandl's Freudian interpretation of the "Dream" as linked with frustrated motherhood seems groundless.[7] More than likely Sor Juana was hungry for wider intellectual horizons and greater freedom in investigating them.

2. *Sonnets*

In addition to the "Dream," eight of Sor Juana's sonnets are classified as philosophical poems. One points out the deceptions of a flattering painting of herself. Another[8] on the vanities of the world contains her personal morality captured in noteworthy antimetaboles: "I try to set beauty in my understanding and not set my understanding on beauty." "I am happier placing riches in my mind than placing my mind on riches." "I consider it better to waste the vanities of life than to waste life in vanities." One poem to a rose examines how it is both a happy cradle and a sad grave. Another has the rose teaching that it is better to die while one is young and beautiful. A poem extols those who undertake grand projects in spite of danger while another considers undeserved applause to be as nefarious as insults. Hope as a precarious balancing scale and as a shadow sought by those who view everything in delightful shades of green are other themes.

The effort to penetrate reality in the "Dream" is complemented by her views of God, humankind, knowledge, and values interwoven in the rest of her poetry. In contrast to the views of God appearing in devotional writings by nuns of her period, Sor Juana's portrayal of the divinity is abstract and metaphysical. She refers to God as First Cause and divine center, the origin and end of all things. Her characteristic manner of finding Him is through nature rather than ideas.

Nature for her is comprised of species and individuals and is hylemorphic. She treats matter and form, soul and body, the alternation of generation and corruption, the four elements, and the continuation of species despite the death of individuals in a very exact Scholastic/Aristotelian manner. She also found meaning in the Augustinian/Platonic view of the tripartite soul. Memory, understanding, and will are the parts. In one birthday poem she pictures them as a noblewoman, a doctor, and a queen concerned with the past, future, and present, respectively.[9]

Sor Juana speaks more frequently of the understanding than of any other human power. In it the divine being as well as abstracts or summaries of creation can be contained. A very important characteristic of this noble faculty is its freedom, a trait Scholastics prefer to attribute to will, although both intellect and will participate in free choice. Since understanding is superior to the senses and definitely individual, she wonders why she finds it so slow to mitigate pain and so ready to cause it. Deft in argument as she herself is, she warns that wisdom does not consist in inventing subtle discourses but in choosing what is most sound.

Right moral choices are for Sor Juana the key to good human life. The law of nature is part of the law of grace, which gives divine precepts. Natural law is limited and imperfect, needing grace for illumination. Various virtues are personified and praised in her works, and she sometimes preaches a bit to the people to whom she writes her occasional poems. The highest values for her personally were wisdom, truth, reason, and beauty.

An example of Sor Juana's reasoning about moral values can be found in the *"decima"* which begins *"Al amor, cualquier curioso"* (Number 104). One kind of love is born of choice and is rational while the other kind originates in domineering influence and is sensible, tender, natural, and affectionate. While rational love has one sovereign object, the other kind has a thousand divisions, depending on its objects. Only the love coming from understanding is worthy of reciprocation since it is of a more noble essence than love seeking to discharge an obligation. She then proves this by reasoning about the logical implications of how lovers behave and justify their behavior. The conclusion is that love without thought cannot be a love of the whole soul, for understanding is a part of that very soul.

Woman as temptress of man is a fruitful literary inspiration as exposed in Genesis as well as in the literature of every epoch. Man as tempter of woman is less frequently portrayed. Sor Juana accuses men fearlessly though not stridently in her most quoted poem which her editors classify as her only philosophical satire. It begins:

> You are foolish, men, who unjustifiably accuse
> A woman without realizing you
> Are the cause of the very thing you blame.[10]

In the tradition of romantic poetry, she continues. Men are like children who invoke a goblin but are terrified when it appears, or like persons who tarnish a mirror and then are sorry it is not clear. Men work industriously to overcome a woman's resistance to their advances, and when they achieve their purpose they call it frivolity. A woman is never right, for if she treats a man badly he complains; and if she loves him dearly, he makes fun of her. If she shuns him, she is cruel; if she accepts him, she is unchaste. How can a woman love truly if her disdain causes displeasure while her docility causes anger? Caught between anger and grief, a woman does well not to love and to censure. Who is more blameworthy, she who fell because of entreaty or the one who entreated her to fall? She who sins for pay or he who pays for sin? Men should either love women as they have made them or make them the way they desire them to be. Her parting words are:

> I establish with good ammunition
> What your pride does contest,
> For in promise and petition
> You join the devil, the world, and the flesh.

IV. CONCLUSIONS

Sor Juana does not experience grave difficulty in reconciling human limitations and failures with divine goodness and generosity in an overall way, with the help of faith and the divine law. But her outlook exemplifies late Baroque thought. Neither the attribution of disharmony to personal sinful choice that was St. Augustine's solution nor the serene confidence in the will's ability to be guided by intellect that characterized St. Thomas' thought nor even the exhilirating idea that humankind can control the world that appeared in Renaissance speculation predominates in Sor Juana's writings. Rather, one senses tension between the conceptual framework to which she acquiesces and the data supplied by life. The Scholastic method did not seem to work in every case, and there is a suspicion that the reason for its inadequacy is neither an individual's weakness nor a basic human impotence. Is there not a way of proceeding, are there not some ways of thinking, that would better satisfy a human being's voracious desire to understand? Is she really exceptional in her need to learn and experience *for herself*? Without foreshadowing the Enlightenment tenet that understanding has no limits provided it follows a certain method, she emphasizes both the freedom of reason and the fruitfulness of orderly investigation. Her own acute powers of observation and ability to use Latin as well as Nahuatl and black dialect with precision are exceptional in a person of any period.

Although she is not a philosopher of the highest rank, Sor Juana habitually viewed matters from a philosophical perspective. This bright, passionate, ironic woman assimilated rather than merely memorized the philosophies she studied, and her erudition permeates even her religious poetry without pretense or apology. Her formidable analytical powers are evident in her prose and poetry, which mirror as well as try to embellish and elevate the life of her day. Consciousness of complexities of every kind disturbed her but did not lead her to skeptical doubt or to search for a non-rational epistemological foundation. For her,

Reasoning is clouded over
With fearful darkness;
But who will be able to enlighten me
If reason be blinded?[11]

NOTES

1. See the detailed biography by Alfonso Méndez Plancarte in *Obras Completas de Sor Juana Inés de la Cruz* (México: Fondo de Cultúra Economica, 1951), especially Vol. I, pp. lii and liii.
2. "Confessions" like these are found in her *"Respuesta a Sor Filotéa de la Cruz,"* which is also her intellectual biography.
3. *Las Peras del Olmo* (Barcelona: Editorial Seix Barral, 1971), especially pp. 17–19, 34–48.
4. Moreno, Rafael, "Modern Philosophy in New Spain," in *Major Trends in Mexican Philosophy* (Notre Dame, Indiana: University of Notre Dame Press, 1966), p. 134.
5. *"Respuesta a Sor Filotéa de la Cruz,"* p. 844 in *Obras Completas*, third edition (Mexico: Porrúa, 1975). All translations in this article are my own.
6. *Ibid.*, p. 845.
7. See Ludwig Pfandl, *Sor Juana Inés de la Cruz* (México: Universidad Nacional Autónoma, 1963).
8. Number 146, *"En perseguirme, Mundo ¿que interesas?"*
9. *"Loa a los años de la Reina Nuestra Senora Doña Maria Luisa de Borbon."*
10. *"Hombres necios que acusáis,"* Number 92.
11. *"Mientras la Gracia me excita,"* Number 57.

5. Damaris Cudworth Masham

LOIS FRANKEL

This chapter begins with a brief examination of the life of Damaris Cudworth Masham. Section II focuses on her philosophical writing including her correspondence, her ideas on the relationship of faith and reason, her views on reason and women's education and possible feminist aspects of her views on morality and epistemology.

I. BIOGRAPHY

Damaris Cudworth lived from January 18, 1659, to April 20, 1708, the daughter of Ralph Cudworth. Ralph Cudworth, a prominent member of the Cambridge Platonist school, was the author of the lengthy but unfinished treatise, *The True Intellectual System of the Universe*, a criticism of atheistic determinism. He had intended, but never accomplished, the addition of a criticism of Calvinism. This opposition to Calvinism was a central tenet of the Cambridge Platonist school. They also considered Hobbes to be a primary philosophical opponent. In addition, they held that God is essentially rational and true Christians ought to share in that rationality. They held also (as did Leibniz) that God is adjudged good based on its* works; God's works are not considered good just because God performed them. Though denied access to higher education, as were all women of her time, Damaris Cudworth grew up accustomed to philosophical discourse. She shared many philosophical views with her father and many with Locke (indeed, often their views were compatible), and frequently wrote in defense of both their views.[1] She married Sir Francis Masham in

---

* Masham used the pronoun 'He' when referring to God. – ed.

Mary Ellen Waithe (ed.), A History of Women Philosophers / Volume 3, 73–85.
© 1991 *Kluwer Academic Publishers. Printed in the Netherlands.*

1685, and employed with their son some of Locke's educational methods, apparently with great success. Replying to Molyneux, who wrote in praise of Locke's educational methods on Molyneux's son, Locke writes:

> the child above mentioned [Masham's son], but nine years old in June last, has learnt to read and write very well, is now reading Quintus Curtius with his mother, understands geography and chronology very well and the Copernican system of our vortex, is able to multiply well and divide a little, and all this without ever having had one blow for his book.[2]

II. WORKS

Masham's works include *A Discourse Concerning the Love of God* (1696, a reply to John Norris's *Practical Discourses*), *Occasional Thoughts in reference to a Virtuous or Christian Life* (1705), and correspondence with Locke and Leibniz. Locke wrote admiringly of Masham:

> The lady herself is so well versed in theological and philosophical studies, and of such an original mind, that you will not find many men to whom she is not superior in wealth of knowledge and ability to profit by it. Her judgment is excellent, and I know few who can bring such clearness of thought to bear upon the most abstruse subjects, or such capacity for searching through and solving the difficulties of questions beyond the range, I do not say of most women, but even of most learned men. From reading, to which she once devoted herself with much assiduity, she is now to a great extent debarred by the weakness of her eyes, but this defect is abundantly supplied by the keenness of her intellect.[3]

1. *Correspondence*

Masham wrote to Locke on April 7, 1688, in praise of an abridgement of Locke's *Essay*, which he had recently published in order to elicit criticism and interest in the full work. Masham apologized for her limited knowledge of philosophy, mentioning her poor eyesight and that she had been discouraged from reading philosophical books. It is unclear whether this discouragement was on the grounds of her failing sight, or because those who discouraged her considered such reading unsuitable for her. Nevertheless, in accord with her father, Ralph Cudworth's position on the issue, she challenged Locke's denial of innate ideas, suggesting that his difference with those who believed in such ideas was not 'really so great as it seems', because the proponents of innate ideas had not claimed that specific ideas were innate, but only that there was 'an active sagacity in the soul'.[4]

Masham's correspondence with Leibniz was primarily of a philosophical nature. She had sent him a copy of her father's *The True Intellectual System of the Universe*, and wrote that "The esteem you express for that work pleases me very much ... and ... it is a new confirmation to me of the worth of that performance."[5] Her correspondence with Leibniz ranged over several topics, including Leibniz's Pre-Established Harmony, the relationship between mind and body, free will, Cudworth's account of "plastic natures," and her affection for Locke, whose "direction" she credits for the successful upbringing of her son.[6]

More central than her acquaintance with Leibniz was the close friendship – both philosophical and personal – which she maintained with Locke. They had enjoyed a romantic attachment prior to her marriage to Sir Francis Masham and continued a close friendship thereafter. It was at the Masham home, Oates, that Locke ended his days in 1704, having been a resident beginning in 1691.

During Locke's residency, the household was visited by Isaac Newton,[7] with whom Masham and Locke discussed the Bible, and Francis Mercury van Helmont,[8] the latter a close friend of Anne Conway, about whom I have written elsewhere in this volume. While there is no direct evidence that Conway's work was discussed in van Helmont's visit, it is not unlikely that it was. Masham had at least a passing acquaintance with Conway's work through Leibniz, who mentions Conway in passing to Masham in a letter of December 14/25, 1703.[9] Additionally, Ralph Cudworth's fellow Cambridge Platonist Henry More was a close friend of Conway's.

2. *Faith and Reason*

While Anne Conway concentrated on metaphysical issues, Masham, though not without interest in metaphysics,[10] emphasized Christian theology, epistemology, and moral philosophy. On this score, her interests included the relationship between faith and reason, and the question of the morality of worldly pursuits. In particular, Masham wished in *Occasional Thoughts* to support Locke against Stilling-fleet[11] on the relative merits of reason and revelation. Stillingfleet had claimed that Locke upheld reason at the expense of revelation:

> Your answer is, That your Method of Certainty by Ideas, shakes not at all, nor in the least concerns the Assurance of Faith. Against this I have pleaded. 1. That your Method of Certainty shakes the Belief of Revelation in general. 2. That it shakes the Belief of Particular Propositions or Articles of Faith, which depend upon the Sense of Words contained in Scripture.[12]

Masham argues that preferring revelation alone to revelation scrutinized by reason will lead people to consider Christianity to be unreasonable, resulting either in fanaticism ("enthusiasm") or skepticism. Nevertheless, she argues in *Occasional Thoughts* that religion provides the only sufficient support for virtue, based on divine reward and punishment.[13] Although many of the Christian rules of morality are, she thinks, derivable from reason and the "light of nature," our passions will tend to overwhelm us without the steadying influence of religion and a "rational fear of God," "experience showing us that natural light, unassisted by revelation, is insufficient to the ends of natural religion."[14]

> Religion has, I think, been rightly defined to be *the knowledge how to please God*, and thus taken, does necessarily include virtue, that is to say *Moral Rectitude*.[15]

> ... a farther impediment to men's obeying the law of nature, by virtue of the mere light of nature; which is, that they cannot, in all circumstances, without revelation, make always a just estimate in reference to their happiness.[16]

However, in order to believe in divinely based results of our actions, we must[17] have solid *evidence* for religious beliefs. Therefore, Masham objects, perhaps following her father's opposition to dogmatism,[18] to mere rote teaching of catechism.[19] If studied only by rote, she argues, the pronouncements of religion often seem contrary to common sense.[20] But Christianity should not seem to be teaching doctrines contrary to reason, for the discovery of seeming absurdity leads people to doubt the reasonableness of religion. Women are especially susceptible to this doubt, not having the advantage of education to overcome the "ignorance or errors of their childhood."[21]

In his chapter "Of Enthusiasm" (*Essay* IV.xix), added in the fourth edition, Locke decries "enthusiasm," the rejection of reason in favor of revelation, as an attitude which

> takes away both reason and revelation, and substitutes in the room of them the ungrounded fancies of a man's own brain, and assumes them for a foundation both of opinion and conduct.[22]

Locke adds that reason and revelation are not so opposed as the enthusiasts believe, but are instead closely related, reason being "natural revelation" and revelation "natural reason enlarged by a new set of discoveries communicated by God immediately."[23] While genuine revelation is absolutely true and certain, we must first be certain of having received a revelation, and such certainty must be more than "ungrounded persuasion" of our own minds.[24] It must at least "be conformable to the principles of reason" or be attended with outward signs, such as miracles, of revelation.[25]

In support of Locke, Masham reiterates his claims that revelation may provide rational grounds for belief,[26] but that reason must be employed in order to determine whether a revelation has indeed occurred. No revelation could be contrary to reason.[27] In this position, she is in accord with the Cambridge Platonist view that God is essentially rational and good Christians ought to share in that rationality.

3. *Women, Education and Reason*

When examining the works of long-ignored women philosophers, particularly those women who lived during times when philosophy was considered an inappropriate occupation for women, one is moved to look for evidence of feminist attitudes. One first looks for such fairly obvious indications as protests about women's lot in life. These abound in Masham's work, as we shall see in this section. In addition, more subtle manifestations of feminism might be found, depending on one's interpretation of feminism: Is it meaningful, for example, to speak of epistemology, ethics, theology, or metaphysics as capable of being informed by feminism? We will consider this possibility in section 4.

Explicit feminist claims are found in several of Masham's arguments: First, she objects to the inferior education accorded women, but primarily on the grounds that such inferior education (a) makes them unfit to educate their children properly, and (b) conduces to impiety in women and their children, because those not properly educated will believe in Christianity out of habit, or rote, rather than out of understanding, and therefore will be unable to defend their faith against any doubts with which they may be confronted. Before condemning the weakness (by late twentieth-century standards) of the feminism expressed in her arguments, however, we ought to consider her times and audience.

> For if Christianity be a religion from God, and women have souls to be saved as well as men; to know what this religion consists in, and to understand the grounds on which it is to be received, can be no more than necessary knowledge to a woman, as well as to a man: Which necessary knowledge is sufficient to enable any one so far to answer to the opposers or corrupters of Christianity ....[28]

Masham laments the fact that women of her time were discouraged from intellectual endeavors. Being barred from formal higher education was a major impediment which she herself must have felt. Young women of the upper classes were kept busy with social diversions, so that they had no time to spend on the improvement of their understanding.[29] Masham has nothing to say of women of other classes, but they were obviously barred from intellectual activity also. Even though Masham herself was encouraged in her studies by her father, Locke, and Leibniz, it appears to be a somewhat indulgent, paternalistic encouragement given by learned men to an exceptional woman of leisure. In general, however, she notes that women are dependent on the good opinions of men, and blames the attitudes of men who, for the most part, were not over fond of learning themselves, and thus threatened by educated women, for this sorry state of affairs:

> The improvements of reason, however requisite to ladies for their accomplishment, as rational creatures; and however needful to them for the well educating of their children, and to their being useful in their families, yet are rarely any recommendation of them to men; who foolishly thinking, that money will answer to all things, do, for the most part, regard nothing else in the woman they would marry: and not often finding what they do not look for, it would be no wonder if their offspring should inherit no more sense than themselves... girls, betwixt silly fathers and ignorant mothers, are generally so brought up, that traditionary opinions are to them, all their lives long, instead of reason.[30]

> Thus wretchedly destitute of all that knowledge which they ought to have, are (generally speaking) our English gentlemen: And being so, what wonder can it be, if they like not that women should have knowledge; for this is a quality that will give some sort of superiority even to those who care not to have it?[31]

> As for other science, it is believed so improper for, and is indeed so little allowed them, that it is not to be expected from them: but the cause of this is only the ignorance of men.[32]

Second, Masham objects to the double standard of morality imposed on men and women, and especially to the claim that women's 'virtue' consists primarily in chastity.[33] Masham objects to this as insufficient, seeing chastity as a low-level necessary condition, without which a woman would be "contemptible,"[34] and opposes its being considered "the chief merit [women] are capable of having."[35] To regard chastity in this way, she argues, lowers women's self-esteem or makes them think men unjust. She also points out that being over-proud of one's chastity leads to being conceited.

> To bring out but one instance more of the commands of Christ being complied with but so far only, as they do comply with some other rule preferred thereto by such as yet pretend to be Christians;

chastity (for example) is, according to the Gospel, a duty to both sexes, yet a transgression herein, even with the aggravation of wronging another man, and possibly a whole family thereby, is ordinarily talked as lightly of, as if it was but a peccadillo in a young man, although a far less criminal offense against duty in a maid shall in the opinion of the same persons brand her with perpetual infamy: The nearest relations often times are hardly brought to look upon her after such a dishonor done by her to their family; whilst the fault of her more guilty brother finds but a very moderate reproof from them; and in a little while, it may be, becomes the subject of their mirth and raillery. And why still is this wrong placed distinction made, but because there are measures of living established by men themselves according to a conformity, or disconformity with which, and not with the precepts of Jesus Christ, their actions are measured, and judged of?[36]

Here Masham has reminded the reader that conventional moral and religious teaching is not always in accord with rational Christianity. True virtue is action in accord with "right reason" or the gospel, which are "one and the same, differently promulged,"[37] not the exact observance of custom or civil institutions.[38] Virtue is not just following the rules, as religion is not just reciting the catechism. Both require the proper employment of the understanding.

4. *Epistemology, Feminism and Moral Philosophy*

It has been argued recently by Nancy Chodorow[39] and Carol Gilligan[40] that the 'male experience' resulting from child-rearing practices in our society conduces to males defining their masculinity in terms of separation and detachment, while the same practices provide a 'female experience' leading females to define themselves in terms of relation and connection. These self-definitions, Gilligan argues, shape our moral life, females making decisions in terms of relationships, males making them in terms of rules and abstractions.[41] Nancy Holland[42] has extended these theories to epistemology, pointing out the atomistic structure of Locke's epistemology, where simple ideas are combined to form all other ideas, including ideas of substance and of relations, and abstract general ideas. Holland sees this as exemplifying the "repression of relation and connection that

Chodorow describes as characteristic of male experience."[43] While I am not entirely convinced of the Chodorow/Gilligan thesis – the claim of a universal 'female experience' and 'male experience' is supported primarily by anecdotal evidence and psychoanalytic theory – it nevertheless suggests criteria for identifying 'feminine', if not necessarily feminist, approaches to philosophy: We look for appeals to relation and rejection of atomism, and find some in Masham's work.

The *Discourse on the Love of God*, Masham's other published book, is a response to John Norris's *Practical Discourses*, the latter based on the *Principles* of Malebranche. Masham particularly objects to Norris's claim that we ought not to love creatures at all, because doing so is incompatible with loving God. She argues that love of creatures is a necessary prerequisite to the love of God, that Norris's and Malebranche's arguments are insufficient and even injurious to piety, and that one can love creatures and God without any incompatibility. In this passage, Masham responds to Norris's claims (indicated by Masham's italics):

> But another reason, besides the narrowness of our capacities, Why *we cannot divide our love* between God and the creature, is, *because we cannot love either of them, but upon such a principle as must utterly exclude the love of the other*; which is thus offered to be made out: *We must not love any thing but what is our true Good: There can be but one thing that is so: And that must be either God, or the creature,*

> What is our *True Good*, he tells us is that which can both *deserve and reward our love*. But certainly whatever is a good to us, is a *true good*; once whatever pleases us, pleases us: And our love, which he says is to be *deserved and rewarded*, is nothing else but that disposition of mind, which we find in our selves towards any thing with which we are pleased. So that to tell us, that we must not love any thing but what is our *True [Good]*; Is as much as to say, that we must not be pleased with anything but what pleases us; which it is likely we are not in danger of.[44]

Here we see Masham objecting to Norris's dualistic and atomistic thinking with regard to the sharing of love between God and creatures. Such an objection could, by the criteria discussed above, be considered feminist.

Male philosophers have traditionally associated women with nature, the earth, the body, and everyday or 'worldly' things in general, while associating men with God, the spirit, and 'other-worldly' things. One form of feminist response might be to reject such dualistic stereotypes; another, which Masham embraces to a limited extent, is to rehabilitate the female side of the dichotomy, rejecting some of the more austere values embedded in patriarchal systems. Masham objects to any strong proscriptions against loving 'the world', arguing that only 'inordinate' love of the world conflicts with our duty to God. Here she is in accord with her father's emphasis on the virtues of "the good of the system" and "public-spiritedness" – the social life, as opposed to the contemplative life advocated by Norris.[45]

> [S]uch declamations as are sometimes made against pleasure absolutely (not the irregular pursuit of it) as if pleasure was in its own nature, a false, and deceitful, not a real and solid good, have produced this ill effect, that many from the absurdity hereof are confirmed in an evil indulgence of their appetites, as if to gratify these was indeed the truest wisdom of a rational creature ....[46]
> That happiness consisting in pleasure, we are so much the happier as we enjoy more pleasure must unquestionably be found true; but that the gratification of men's desires and appetites cannot therefore be that which should always, as they are rational agents, determine, or regulate their actions in pursuit of happiness, is no less evident; in that we perceive our selves, and the things to which we have relation, to be so framed, and constituted in respect one of another, that the gratification of our present desires and appetites, does sometimes for a short, or small pleasure, procure to us a greater and more durable pain.[47]

> [T]he love of pleasure implanted in us (if we faithfully pursue it in preferring always that which will, on the whole, procure to us the most pleasure) can never mislead us from the observance of the law of reason: and that this law enjoins only a right regulation of our natural desire of pleasure, to the end of our obtaining the greatest happiness that we are capable of: so that there is an inseparable connection, or relation of moral good and evil, with our natural good, and evil.[48]

Finally, rejecting the patriarchal preference for pure power (activity is preferred to passivity, existence to nonexistence, strength to weakness, rigidity to flexibility), Masham argues that God is not to be loved simply because it is our creator, and more powerful than we, but because God is good and the source of our happiness. Mere existence is not necessarily a good thing, for the damned and many unhappy people in this world do not consider it so. We should worship not just the author of our existence, but the author of our happiness.[49] Thus, things in this world must be worthy of love in order that their creator, which must be more perfect than its creations,[50] may be worthy of our greatest love.[51] In other words, worship and love are due only to a being deemed worthy of it, not to a being which is merely powerful and our creator:

> For God as powerful (which is all we should know of him, considered barely as a creator) is no more an object of love than of hate, or fear; and is truly an object only of admiration. It seems therefore plain, that if any could be without the love of the creatures, they would be without the love of God also: For as by the existence of the creatures, we come to know there is a creator; so by their loveliness it is that we come to know that of their author, and to love him.[52]

The claim that the positions discussed in this section constitute a feminist approach to the issues involved, or represent a particularly 'feminine' perspective, depends on accepting something like the Chodorow/Gilligan thesis, which requires more discussion than is possible here. Nevertheless, it is clear that Masham's calls for improved education for women and an end to the double standard regarding chastity represent at least a limited feminist orientation. And perhaps that is the most that we can expect from a woman of her times.

III. CONCLUSIONS

In her writings, Masham analyzed the relationship between faith and reason, and the question of the morality of worldly pursuits. She supported Locke against Stillingfleet on the relative merits of reason and revelation. Masham objected to the inferior education accorded women and the double standard of morality imposed on men and women. She rejected certain aspects of patriarchal metaphysical systems by urging that love of God be grounded in love of that which is the source of our happiness, rather than in love of the powerfulness of a creator. Damaris Cudworth Masham lived her life in a philosophically rich environment in which she and other noted philosophers discussed metaphysics, theology, epistemology, and moral philosophy. Her contributions to these subject areas of philosophy merit considerable additional discussion.

NOTES

1. Passmore, 91. Passmore comments in a footnote that Masham wrote to Bayle to defend her father against the claim that his views led to atheism. Passmore adds that the belief that Masham abandoned her father's theories to take up those of Locke is a result of ignorance of Cudworth's unpublished work.
2. Bourne II 267, citing 'Familiar Letters,' p. 57, Locke to William Molyneux, August 28, 1693.
3. Bourne II 213, citing MSS in the Remonstrants' Library: Locke to Limborch, March 13, 1690–91.
4. Cranston 300, citing B.L. MSS. Locke, c.17, f. 154.
5. To Leibniz, March 29, 1704, Gerhardt III 337.
6. To Leibniz, November 24, 1704, Gerhardt III 365.
7. Bourne II 219.
8. Cranston 374.
9. Gerhardt III 337.
10. See her correspondence with Leibniz, Gerhardt III 333–375.
11. See Christophersen 41–42.
12. "Answer to Mr. Locke's second Letter; wherein his Notion of Ideas is prov'd to be Inconsistent with it self, and with the Articles of the Christian Faith." London, printed by J.H. for Henry Mortlock, etc. MDCXCVIII, pp. 178 in 8vo, p. 65; quoted in Christophersen 41–42.
13. *Occasional Thoughts* 14–15.
14. *Occasional Thoughts* 55–56.
15. *Occasional Thoughts* 84.
16. *Occasional Thoughts* 103.
17. *Occasional Thoughts* 16.
18. Passmore 81.
19. *Occasional Thoughts* 18ff.
20. *Occasional Thoughts* 20.
21. *Occasional Thoughts* 21.

22. *Essay* VI.xix.3.
23. *Essay* IV.xix.4.
24. *Essay* IV.xix.11.
25. *Essay* IV.xix.14.
26. *Occasional Thoughts* 34.
27. *Occasional Thoughts* 35.
28. *Occasional Thoughts* 166.
29. *Occasional Thoughts* 151.
30. *Occasional Thoughts* 162.
31. *Occasional Thoughts* 174.
32. *Occasional Thoughts* 169.
33. *Occasional Thoughts* 21.
34. *Occasional Thoughts* 22.
35. *Occasional Thoughts* 22.
36. *Occasional Thoughts* 155.
37. *Occasional Thoughts* 97–98.
38. *Occasional Thoughts* 96.
39. Nancy Chodorow, *The Reproduction of Mothering*, Berkeley: University of California Press, 1978.
40. Carol Gilligan, *In a Different Voice*, Cambridge: Harvard University Press, 1982.
41. Gilligan 100, cited by Nancy Holland, "Gender and the Generic in Locke," presented at the Pacific Division meeting of the American Philosophical Association, March, 1986, p. 3.
42. *Ibid.*
43. Holland 4.
44. *Discourse* 89–90.
45. Passmore 79.
46. *Occasional Thoughts* 79.
47. *Occasional Thoughts* 75.
48. *Occasional Thoughts* 77–78.
49. *Discourse* 62–63.
50. Masham shares this principle with the Platonists.
51. *Discourse* 64.
52. *Discourse* 64–65.

6. Mary Astell

KATHLEEN M. SQUADRITO

I. BIOGRAPHY

Mary Astell, seventeenth-century English philosopher, was born in Newcastle on November 12, 1666. Although she was a well-known Platonist during her time, the facts about her life and works are relatively obscure. A short account of her life and influence is recorded by Ballard in his *Memoirs of Several Ladies of Great Britain* (1752).[1] The only major biography was written by Florence Smith in 1916.[2] According to Smith, the material presented by Ballard is often based on rumor. Many of the conclusions which Smith draws in contradiction to Ballard are based solely upon single ambiguous statements made by Astell. The accuracy of information about Mary Astell's early education is therefore questionable.

Astell's family was prominent in commercial affairs. Her father, Peter Astell, was hostman of Newcastle and was assigned the duty of entertaining merchants and supervising their sales. Her uncle, Ralph Astell, curate of St. Nicholas in 1667, is credited with her early education. Since he died when Mary Astell was thirteen, it is assumed that a good deal of her education can be attributed to a wide range of reading. The Astell family maintained a strong tradition of loyalty to both the church and the King. They also upheld a tradition of loyalty to educational ideals.

Astell's father died in 1678 and her mother, Mary Errington, in 1684. After the breakup of her home Mary Astell left for London. According to a letter from Thomas Birch to Ballard, she settled with Lady Catherine Jones in Chelsea. Lady Catherine was prominent in court circles and introduced Mary Astell to a number of influential and well-educated women who shared an interest in changing the status of

Mary Ellen Waithe (ed.), A History of Women Philosophers / Volume 3, 87–99.
© 1991 *Kluwer Academic Publishers. Printed in the Netherlands.*

women. The traditional view that Mary Astell was a recluse was probably based on her later ill health. She took an intimate part in the life of Chelsea. As her reputation grew, her home took on the character of a salon. Discussions usually concerned philosophy, religious controversies and education for women. As Smith reports, the

> 'great Mr. Locke' she knew and respected, however much she might refuse to accept his opinions. She had dared to oppose Swift, Steele, Defoe, but she commented only on their political writings and activities.[3]

Among Astell's circle of friends was Elizabeth Elstob, the Anglo-Saxon scholar, and Lady Mary Wortley Montagu. A first edition of the *Serious Proposal To The Ladies* was autographed and presented to Lady Mary by Astell. Lady Anne Coventry of Smithfield, author of *Meditations and Reflections Moral and Divine*, was interested in Astell's plans for a woman's college.

II. WORKS

Mary Astell's first published work, *A Serious Proposal To The Ladies For the Advancement of their True and greatest Interest* (1694), was followed by part two in 1697. The work was well-received and went through several editions. In 1695, at the request of John Norris, Astell's correspondence with Norris was published as a text entitled *Letters Concerning the Love of God*. In 1700 she published *Some Reflections Upon Marriage*. From 1704 to 1705 several of Astell's pamphlets dealing with political and religious controversy appeared in print. In 1705 she published a summary of her religious and educational theories in *The Christian Religion As Profess'd by a Daughter of the Church of England*. In 1729 her health began to decline. Shortly before her death she refused to see friends and spent her days in religious meditation. Mary Astell died from cancer on May 11, 1731. She was buried in the churchyard at Chelsea on May 14.

The authorship of *An Essay In Defence of the Female Sex* (1696), a work generally attributed to Mary Astell until 1913, is still a subject of controversy. In 1913 Professor A.H. Upham contended that the subject matter of the essay was inconsistent with ideas expressed in

Astell's other works. The essay appeared to be more consistent with a group of French pamphlets that were popular in England at the time. In the 1738 edition of Bayle's *Dictionary*, three pamphlets are listed as among Astell's "other works"; the *Essay* is not mentioned. According to Smith, even though the publication of one edition in Newcastle would tend toward the ascription to Mary Astell, a copy mentioned in a list of publications of E. Curll, a bookseller, ascribes the work to Mrs. Drake. The ascription is confirmed by a note in the British Museum copy "By Mrs. Drake." However, since no relation between the *Essay* and any of the French pamphlets has been established, the work is still to be found listed among the writings of Mary Astell.

Given the disrespect with which women were held in the seventeenth century, Astell preferred to remain obscure. Her works were published anonymously. Ballard notes that "Notwithstanding her great care to conceal herself, her name was soon discovered and made known to several learned persons."[4] Her work was generally respected by most scholars. In his preface to the *Letters*, Norris comments:

> … so great and noble is the subject, and so admirable both your thoughts and expressions upon it; such choiceness of matter, such weight of sense, such art and order of contrivance, such clearness and strength of reasoning, such beauty of language, such address of stile.

Norris shared the opinion of many other theologians and philosophers that

> … the learned authoress hath with great dexterity and success retorted Mr. Locke's metaphysical artillery against himself, confuted his Whimsical Idea of Thinking matter, and given him a genteel foil.[5]

Astell was usually referred to as the "Philosophical Lady." But in spite of her philosophical reputation, her suggestion for a woman's college made her the subject of the leading satirists of the day.

Astell's reputation in philosophy did not survive the particular metaphysical and religious controversies of the seventeenth century. Historically, she has been recognized for her educational and feminist theory. The first reference to her work is found in John Evelyn's

Numismata, 1697. A subsequent biographical reference appears in one of the supplemental volumes to Bayle's *Historical Dictionary*. The 1738 reference appears in a note to a discussion of John Norris. Given Ballard's difficulty in obtaining material for his biography of 1752, it is reasonable to conclude that Astell's reputation had died out. Although Ballard found a widespread lack of interest in his *Memoirs*, his text did revive some interest in the writings of women. By 1766 Mary Astell's name appeared regularly in biographies that were devoted to the works of women. Her reputation continued to grow as the feminist movement developed in the nineteenth century.

III. RELIGIOUS EPISTEMOLOGY AND WOMEN

1. *Condition of Women*

According to Smith, "it may not be entirely unfair to lay claim to Mary Astell, with Ballard, as the first defender of 'the rights and privileges of her sex.' "[6] Although she fully supported the New Testament and defended the Christian religion, she argued for the conn of Ciaitical and educational rights of women. In the *Christian Religion* she complains,

> ... the sphere alloted to us women, who are subjects, allows us no room to serve our country either with our Council or our lives. We have no authority to Preach vertue or to Punish vice, as we have not the guilt of Establishing Iniquity by Law, neither can we execute Judgment and Justice.[7]

Astell attributes this oppressive condition to male arrogance and pride. In order to combat oppression and to be true Christians, women need to be educated and instructed in proper methods of reasoning. A Christian woman, she says,

> ... must not be a *Child in Understanding*; she must serve GOD with *Understanding* as well as with *Affection*.[8]

Contrary to the popular opinion that women should not question religious propositions, Astell asserts:

If God had not intended that Women shou'd use their Reason, He wou'd not have given them any, for He does nothing in vain.[9]

She points out that she is a Christian and member of the Church of England not because of custom or conformity to her parents' ideology, but because she has examined the doctrines of Christianity. Astell urges women to avoid being overly concerned with matters relating to the body. The good of the mind, she contends, is

> infinitly preferable to the good of the body; Spiritual Advantages to Temporal; and Temporal are to be valued among themselves in proportion as they contribute to Spiritual and Eternal.[10]

Astell shared Lady Mary's opinion that in no part of the world were women treated with so much contempt as in England. In the seventeenth century schools for women were limited in number and the curriculum confined to music, dancing, embroidery and singing. Women were encouraged to exhibit obedience to authority, to keep silent in church and to study only the art of household management. The tradition of denying educational opportunities to women and of stifling their intelligence prompted Mary Astell to write *A Serious Proposal To The Ladies*. In the first part of this work Astell argues that women are just as capable of education as men. Her proposal was to erect a monastery, a religious retirement for women. "For here," says Astell, "those who are sick of the vanity of the world and its impertinencies, may find more substantial and satisfying entertainments and need not be confin'd to what they justly loath." Astell's proposed school would have given women a curriculum similar to that offered to men, *viz.*, the study of science, philosophy, religion and languages. She points out that one great end of this institution would be "to influence the rest of the Sex, that Women may no longer pass for those little useless and impertinent animals," to

> expel that cloud of ignorance which custom has involv'd us in, to furnish our minds with a stock of solid and useful knowledge.[11]

Astell complains that most women quit the substance for the shadow, reality for appearance, and embrace those things which if understood they should hate. They become less than human simply because they desire to be admired by men. According to Astell, women should seek virtue and seek the admiration of God rather than that of humans.

2. *Women, Epistemology and Reason*

The second part of the *Serious Proposal* addresses the philosophical methodology necessary for achieving intellectual goals. Astell employs Platonic and Cartesian theory in addition to Locke's view of simple ideas and judgment. She contends that the most noble pleasure is the search for truth. The method of seeking truth is Cartesian:

> not to judge of anything which we don't Apprehend; to suspend our assent till we see just Cause to gie it, and to determine nothing till the Strength and Clearness of the Evidence oblige us to it. To withdraw our selves as much as may be from Corporeal things, that pure Reason may be heard the better; to make use of our Senses for which they are designed and fitted, the preservation of the body, but not to depend on their Testimony in our Enquiries after Truth.[12]

According to Astell, all truth is "Antient, as being from Eternity in the Divine Ideas" and is only new with respect to our discoveries.[13] Athough she was greatly influenced by Locke, she nonetheless argued for the existence of innate ideas as well as the equal capacity of men and women to understand such ideas. Like Descartes and Locke, she argues that intuition is the best source of her knowledge. She finds that the difference in reasoning ability between one person and another lies in the accumulation or the number of simple ideas and the disposition of such ideas in terms of order. Among the rules Astell suggests that women follow in the search for knowledge is to begin with simple ideas and simple objects and to ascend by degrees to knowledge of more complex things. Like Locke, she also insists that we judge no further than we perceive and not accept anything as true which is not evidently known to be so.[14] In some cases it is proper to be content with probability rather than certainty. She contends that ideas may be considered wrong or false when they have no conformity to the real nature of things. Properly speaking, it is not the idea but the judgment that is false. Astell does not bother to address arguments concerning the epistemological or ontological status of ideas. She tells us simply that by the term 'idea' "we sometimes understand in general all that which is the immediate Object of the Mind, whatever it Perceives; and in this large Sense it may take in all thought, all that we are any ways capable of Discerning."[15] She holds a representative theory of knowledge in which the term 'idea' is "more strictly taken for that which represents to the Mind some Object distinct from it, whether Clearly or Confusedly."[16]

Astell cautions women to regulate the will and govern the passions. She contends that the true and proper pleasure of human nature consists in exercising dominion over the body and governing passion according to right reason. The principal cause of error is judgement prior to obtaining clear and distinct ideas: "The First and Principal thing therefore to be observed in all Operations of the Mind is, That we determine nothing about those things of which we have not a Clear Idea, and as Distinct as the Nature of the Subject will permit, for we cannot properly be said to Know any thing which does not Clearly and Evidently appear to us."[17] Astell accepts Descartes' definition of clarity and distinctness.[18] Given this definition she argues that we have a clear, but not a distinct, idea of God and of our own souls. She agrees with Locke that not all truths are equally evident because of the limitations of the human mind.

3. *Marriage and Subjection of Women*

Astell's proposal was intended to provide women with a viable option to marriage. In *Some Reflections Upon Marriage* she contends that if better care were taken than usual in women's education,

> ... marriage might recover the Dignity and Felicity of its original Institution; and Men be very happy in a married State.[19]

Marriage fails because most men do not seek the proper qualifications in a spouse. She points out that it makes no difference if a man marries for money or for the love of beauty. In either case, the man does not act according to reason, but is governed by irregular appetites. Women should not marry because they think that it is their duty, nor should they marry to please friends or to escape the hardships of life. A woman must distinguish between truth and appearance, between solid and apparent good. If she does so she

... has found out the Instability of all earthly Things, and won't any more be deceived by relying on them; can discern who are the Flatterers of her Fortune, and who the Admirers and Encouragers of her Vertue; accounting it no little Blessing to be rid of those Leeches, who hung upon her only for their own Advantage.[20]

Men must choose qualities in a woman that relate to the soul and spiritual values. Astell appeals for as much equality in marriage as possible. She finds subjection to have no end or purpose other than to enhance the pride and vanity of those who have power. If all men are born free, how is it, she says,

... that all Women are born Slaves? As they must be, if the being subjected to the *inconstant, uncertain, arbitrary Will* of Men, be the *perfect Condition* of *Slavery?*

According to Astell, men practice the type of arbitrary dominion in their families which they abhor and exclaim against in the state. If arbitrary power is an improper method of governing people it "ought not to be practis'd any where."[21]

Astell construes the biblical curse on women as a prediction rather than a command from God. With regard to Paul's argument for women's subjection from the reason of things (1 Tim. 2:13), Astell retorts:

... it must be confess'd, that this (according to the vulgar Interpretation) is a very obscure Place, and I should be glad to see a Natural, and not a Forc'd Interpretation given of it by those who take it Literally: Whereas if it be taken allegorically, with respect to the Mystical Union between Christ and his Church ... the Difficulties vanish. For the Earthly *Adam's* being *form'd* before *Eve*, seems as little to prove her Natural Subjection to him, as the living Creatures, Fishes, Birds, Beasts being form'd before them both, proves that Mankind must be subject to these Animals.[22]

She goes on to point out that female prophets and strong women are often mentioned and admired in scripture.

IV. EPISTEMOLOGY AND RELIGIOUS KNOWLEDGE

1. *Reason and Revelation*

In *The Christian Religion*, Astell presents versions of the ontological, cosmological and teleological arguments for the existence of God. She argues that since God is the most perfect being it would be contradictory to assume that He does not exist. Self-existence, she contends, "is such a Perfection as necessarily includes all other Perfections."[23] She goes on to address questions concerning the mysteries of Christianity. Astell agrees with those who claim that the Bible contains many mysteries, but concludes that the Christian religion is very "far from being *Dark* and *affectedly Mysterious*; its revelations are as clear and as plain as the sublimity of the matter will admit."[24] She points out that no one would suggest that mathematics is an obscure and mysterious science, yet some of its theorems appear as abstruse and mysterious as some doctrines in the Gospel. According to Astell, the reasonableness of Christianity consists in two "great truths," (1) that there is not anything so reasonable as to believe all that God has revealed and to practice his commandments, (2) that God has given such proofs and evidences as are sufficient to satisfy any reasonable person that the Christian religion is a divine revelation.[25]

2. *Whether Matter Can Think*

Although Astell seems to think that Locke aligned himself with the Socinians, she prefers not to accuse him of this, but rather, to refute his claims that appear to support Socinianism. She criticizes his lack of interest in supporting the doctrine of the Trinity, a truth, she says, "which is absolutely requir'd to be believed to make any one a Christian."[26] Locke's claim that God could give matter the power of thinking was subject to ridicule by many seventeenth-century theologians and philosophers. A good deal of the *Christian Religion* is devoted to showing that Locke's claim involves logical inconsistencies.

Astell claims that given the incongruity between thought and extension, it is evident that body cannot think. The ideas of thought and extension, she argues, are two completely different ideas and have different properties and affections. They may be considered without any relation to, or dependence, on each other. To be distinct from a thing, she says,

> ... is all one as not to be this Thing, so that since Thought and Extension are Distinct and Different in their own Natures, as we have seen, 'tis evident that a Thinking Being can't be Extended, and that an Extended Being does not, cannot Think any more than a Circle can have the Properties of a Triangle, or a Triangle those of a Circle.[27]

According to Astell, there cannot be anything in a being that is not contained in the idea of this being. Since thought is not contained in the idea of body, she concludes that matter cannot think.

Astell cites certain passages from Locke's *Essay* and his letters to Bishop Stillingfleet as being inconsistent with his contention that it is *not impossible* for God to give parcels of matter the power of thinking. "This Judicious Writer," she says, "tells us 'That in some of our Ideas there are certain Relations, Habitudes, and Connexions so visibly included in the nature of the Ideas themselves, that we cannot conceive them separable from them, by *any power whatsoever*." She takes Locke's example of a triangle as analogous to the case of thinking matter. According to Locke, the idea of a triangle necessarily includes an equality of its angles to two right ones. Astell asserts:

> But now shou'd I with *weak Reason* and *Strong Imagination* affirm, That *God* may give to this Triangle the Property of including no Space, or of being equal to a Square; say, that He may *according to the good Pleasure of His* Omnipotency, *give it a speaking*, a *walking*, or a *dancing Faculty*, and make it able to Eat and Drink; shou'd I tell our Ingenious Author That to deny *God's Power* in this case, only because he can't Conceive the manner how, is no less than an Insolent Absurdity; and a limiting the Power of the Omnipotent Creator.[28]

She concludes that to say that a square is a triangle, or that an extended Substance is a Thinking substance, is as contradictory as to say that motion is rest.

If Locke had considered the essence of body to be extension and the essence of mind to be thought, Astell's criticisms would have been valid. However, Locke regards thinking and extension as modes of substance and not their defining properties. Given Locke's view, matter and thought are not incompatible. Astell apparently holds a Cartesian view of thought and extension as defining properties or the essence of substance. On that view, which Astell does not question, the two *are* incompatible.

3. *Whether God Is the Efficient Cause of Pain and Pleasure*

Astell tends to be critical of any philosophy such as Locke's that does not recognize the Ideal. Although she praises Norris, her *Letters* are primarily critical and address the specific issue of efficient causality. Astell agrees with Norris that God is the only efficient cause of all our sensations and that God is the sole object of our love. However, she contends that unacceptable conclusions follow from his principles. If God is the object of love because He is the only efficient cause of our pleasure, as Norris contends, it will follow, she says,

> … either that the being the Cause of our Pleasure is not the true and proper Reason why that Cause should be the Object of our Love, (for the Author of our Pain has as good a Title to our Love as the Author of our Pleasure;) or else, if nothing be the Object of our Love but what does us Good, then something else does us Good, besides what causes Pleasure.[29]

Norris replies that pain is an effect of God, "yet it is not after the same manner the Effect of *God* as Pleasure is. Pleasure is the natural, genuine and direct Effect of *God*, but Pain comes from him only indirectly and by Accident." According to Norris, God wills our pleasure as we are "Creatures, and our Pain only as we are Sinners."[30] Astell considers this reply a resolution to the difficulty. She goes on to explain her philosophy of sensation to Norris. When the understanding and will deviates from the order and perfection of their nature and are "destitute of their proper good," mental pain results.

According to Astell, mental pain is the only proper evil of a person,

> … both because the Mind being the Man, nothing is truly and properly his Good or Evil, but as it respects his Mind; as also because so long as he is under it, 'tis impossible for him to enjoy any degree of real Happiness.'

God is not regarded as the author of this pain. It is due to human folly. Astell goes on to distinguish the inferior part of the soul from the superior part, explaining that disagreeable modifications (pain) exist in the inferior part, "that which is exercis'd about objects of sense" and not in the superior part, "the Understanding and Will."[31] Given this distinction, pain is not considered to be a real evil to that which is properly the person.

V. CONCLUSIONS

Since Astell was unable to arouse a wide enough interest in her proposal for a woman's college, she attempted to establish a charity school for girls in Chelsea. The school was established in 1729 by Lady Catherine Jones and other friends. Astell's ultimate educational goal was to train women to have logical grounds for religious belief and practice. She was critical of custom only insofar as it stood in the way of this goal.

As Smith points out, it is difficult to determine Astell's influence on the next generation, since the influence was not exactly that of one individual, but of the developing ideology of an age. Astell most certainly contributed to the goal of women's intellectual and economic independence. Her philosophical works are an important part of seventeenth-century debate.

NOTES

1. George Ballard, *Memoirs of Several Ladies of Great Britain* (printed by W. Jackson), 1752.
2. Florence M. Smith, *Mary Astell* (New York: Columbia University Press), 1916.
3. Smith, p. 164.
4. Ballard, p. 447.
5. *Ibid.*, p. 456
6. Smith, p. 164.
7. *Ibid.*
8. Mary Astell, *The Christian Religion As Profess'd by a Daughter Of The Church of England* (London), 1705, p. 6.
9. *Ibid.*
10. *Ibid.*, p. 100.
11. Mary Astell, *A Serious Proposal to the Ladies for the Advancement of their True and Greatest Interest* (London: Fourth Edition), 1694, p. 17.

12. *Ibid.*, p. 95.

13. *Ibid.*, p. 71.

14. *Ibid.*, p. 107.

15. *Ibid.*, p. 18.

16. *Ibid.*, p. 98.

17. *Ibid.*, p. 102.

18. That may be said to be "Clear which is Present and Manifest to an attentive Mind; so as we say we see Objects Clearly, when being present to our Eyes they sufficiently Act on 'em, and our Eyes are dispos'd to regard 'em. And that Distinct, which is so Clear, Particular, and Different from all other things, that it contains not any thing in it self which appears not manifestly to him who considers it as ought" (Part I, par. 45).

19. Mary Astell, *Some Reflections Upon Marriage* (London: Fourth Edition), 1700, p. 15.

20. *Ibid.*, p. 24.

21. *Ibid.*, p. 107.

22. *Ibid.*, pp. 110–111.

23. Astell, *The Christian Religion*, p. 8.

24. *Ibid.*, p. 49.

25. *Ibid.*, p. 65.

26. *Ibid.*, p. 75.

27. *Ibid.*, p. 250.

28. *Ibid.*, pp. 253–255.

29. Mary Astell, *Letters Concerning the Love of God* (London: Norris), 1695, p. 4.

30. *Ibid.*, p. 12.

31. *Ibid.*, p. 30.

7. Catharine Trotter Cockburn[1]

MARY ELLEN WAITHE

I. BIOGRAPHY

Catharine Trotter was born August 16, 1679, of Scots parentage. Her father, a sea captain, died when Catharine was young. Although not raised in favorable circumstances, she was, according to Edmund Gosse, a child prodigy, who learned French, Latin, Greek, and logic.[2] An early student of works of great literature and philosophy, Trotter was mostly self-taught. She was forced to support herself since adolescence and earned early fame as a playwright. So popular was she that clergy and aristocracy alike subscribed in advance to her plays. When she read Thomas Burnet's anonymously published criticism of Locke's *Essay*, she wrote a systematic defense of Locke's epistemology. She was only twenty years old at the time. One gets the impression of a tremendously talented intellect, analytical as a philosopher, yet creative as a playwright. Though she is gifted, so also is she brave in publicly defending her choices, whether that choice be to convert, to marry a poor clergyman, or to produce a play about political intrigues in Sweden. She did not seek conflict, yet in defending Locke's epistemology, she came on the receiving end of public criticism and mockery. Someone even made her the insincere, feather-headed major character in a farcical play.

Catharine Trotter Cockburn was the author of five dramatic works. Her first play, *Agnes de Castro*, was produced at Drury Lane in 1695–6, when she was only seventeen years old. Agnes de Castro was based on a legendary character who appeared in the theatre of Spain's "Golden Age."[3] According to Kendall,

Trotter's main source was, without question, the 1688 novel by

> Aphra Behn. *The History of Agnes de Castro* by Behn seems to be a
> faithful translation of a French novel by Mlle. de Brillac.

Agnes de Castro, like her *Fatal Friendship*, which appeared in 1698,
deals with love and friendship. According to Kendall[4] *Olinda's
Adventures* is a thinly fictionalized autobiography. Published in 1718,
this work depicts Trotter as a young, adventurous woman, aware and
proud of her intellect and wit, who is given to passionate relationships
with men and women alike. Trotter's self-portrait ends at age sixteen,
two years prior to Burnet's publication of his first attack on Locke.
Her enormously successful play, *Fatal Friendship*, was produced in
1698. In 1700 Trotter's *Love at a Loss* was produced, followed by the
production of her *Unhappy Penitent* and the completion of her defense
of Locke in 1701. Several years later, when Trotter could no longer
reconcile Locke's epistemology with her Catholic faith, she converted
to the Church of England and published *A Discourse concerning a
guide in Controversies; in two letters: Written to one of the Church of
Rome, by a person lately converted from that communion.* Her friend
Gilbert Burnet, Bishop of Salisbury, anonymously wrote the preface to
the 1707 and the 1728 editions of the *Discourse*. The main topic of
that work is the infallibility of the Catholic church and the authority of
the Scriptures.

In 1739, Trotter Cockburn began writing *Remarks upon some
Writers in the Controversy concerning the Foundation of Moral Duty
and Moral Obligation*, which appeared in 1743 in an anthology, *The
History of the Works of the Learned*. In 1747, three years after
Rutherforth's *Essay on the Nature and Obligations of Virtue*, she
published *Remarks on Rutherforth's Essay, in Vindication of the
contrary Principles and Reasonings introduced in the writings of the
late Dr. Samuel Clarke*. By this time Trotter Cockburn had gained a
reputation as a philosopher and was widely encouraged to publish her
collected works. But she was old and ailing, although mentally still
very sharp. She died in May 1749 at the age of 71.

A Catholic who later converted to the Church of England,
Catharine Trotter had been the third person to defend Locke in print
(Samuel Bold was the first, Damaris Cudworth Masham the second),
and was Locke's first defendant against Thomas Burnet. (This is
Thomas Burnet of the Charterhouse, not to be confused with Thomas
Burnet of Kemnay, the latter sometimes spelled "Burnett," nor with

his brother, George Burnet of Kemnay, Trotter's friend and her intermediary with Leibniz, nor with Dr. Gilbert Burnet, the Bishop of Salisbury, who wrote an introduction to one of Trotter's works and who was the second husband of Elizabeth Berkeley.) Trotter was one of several women defenders and admirers of Locke, including Damaris Cudworth Masham, with whom she corresponded (see Chapter 5) and Mary Astell (see Chapter 6).

II. PHILOSOPHICAL WRITINGS

In an age when few persons understood Locke's *Essay on Human Understanding*, and at a time when most commentators disputed its principles, young Catharine Trotter published a defense of Locke against the 1697 criticisms of the then-anonymous Thomas Burnet. Burnet had supported Stillingfleet's criticism of the consequences of Locke's *Essay* for religion and morality. Burnet anonymously wrote three sets of *Remarks* on Locke's *Essay*. His first *Remarks* appeared in 1697. Burnet's polite, even genteel, queries concerning Locke's views generally supported Stillingfleet against Locke. Locke wrote a two-and-a-half-page nasty reply to Burnet, in which he attacked Burnet's personal integrity, rather than the substance of Burnet's queries. Locke appended his brief retort to his reply to Stillingfleet's answer to Locke's first letter.[5] Angry at being so rudely dismissed by Locke, Burnet wrote a second set of *Remarks* that same year. Locke ignored them completely, and in 1699 Burnet wrote his third *Remarks*, to which Locke did not reply. In the third attack he claimed that not only had Locke undermined the authority of religion, but the very good of government and society. Although Locke did not respond to Burnet this time either, he did make some marginal notes to Burnet's last *Remarks*.[6] The fourth edition of Locke's *Essay* appeared at the end of 1699, although bearing a publication date of 1700. Catharine Trotter completed her defense of Locke against Burnet in 1701.[7] Trotter considered Burnet's third *Remarks* to be little more than a restatement of those he had made in his second remarks, but her footnotes show that she had studied Burnet's final remarks and had also compared the fourth edition of the *Essay*[8] to the third.

From Locke's correspondence with Elizabeth Berkeley Burnet, it is apparent that he had heard of Trotter's *Defence* prior to receiving Mrs. Burnet's appraisal of it. He had probably purchased it through Trotter's bookseller. Locke read and appreciated her defense of him and took great pains to locate her (see correspondence between Locke and Elizabeth Burnet and Locke and Peter King) and make a monetary gift to the impoverished Trotter. His letter to Trotter in appreciation of her *Defence* is reprinted with her works as well as in his correspondence.

Trotter's *Defence* of Locke focuses on Burnet's second *Remarks* (although there are many references to the third) and cites numerous references to the third and fourth editions of the *Essay*. Trotter's correspondence with her friend George Burnet of Kemnay[9] (near Aberdeen) indicates that she completed her *Defence* by early December 1701, i.e., within a year of the publication of the fourth edition of the *Essay*. In that letter, Trotter indicated that she was apprehensive that the appearance of a defense of Locke written by a woman would have the effect of further prejudicing the Stillingfleet imbroglio against Locke. Yet, she decided to publish anonymously in May of 1702. It is probably through this connection that Elizabeth Burnet (formerly Elizabeth Berkeley) heard that Trotter had written something that was not a literary work and requested a copy of it from her. Writing on June 19, 1702, Elizabeth Burnet thanks Trotter for providing her with a copy of her *Defence*. In her letter, Mrs. Burnet cites that both Bishop Gilbert Burnet (Bishop of Salisbury) and "Mr. Norris" (John Norris) of Bemerton thought highly of Trotter's defense of Locke. That John Norris should concede the merit of Trotter's *Defence* of Locke is itself interesting. Norris was the primary English defender of Malbranche in opposition to Locke's theory of the origin of ideas and had been the first to publish a criticism of Locke. (In 1696, Damaris Cudworth Masham had defended Locke against Norris.)[10]

On June 20, the day after she wrote to thank Trotter for the copy of the *Defence*, Elizabeth Burnet wrote to Locke about Trotter's work, but without naming her. From the time Locke heard of Trotter from Mrs. Burnet, he showed an intense interest in locating her. On July 2, Locke responded to Elizabeth Burnet, asking her to strike up a friendship with Catharine Trotter, possibly to make Trotter a present of books. On July 15, Elizabeth Burnet wrote Locke, confirming his letter of July 2 and giving Catharine Trotter's name and address. In this letter, Mrs. Burnet agreed to make contact with Trotter in order to make gifts on Locke's behalf, but cited difficulties owing to Catharine Trotter's religion. There was no further correspondence until November 10, when Elizabeth Burnet wrote to Locke that Trotter was impoverished and asked him to authorize her to give Trotter, or to give her directly, the sum of four or five guineas. Burnet mentioned that she had previously assisted Trotter. On November 15, Locke wrote to Peter King, enclosing his response to Burnet's letter of the tenth and asking King to discuss with Elizabeth Burnet a matter which he and King had previously discussed as the best way of making a gift to Catharine Trotter. Then on November 24 Peter King responded to Locke, reporting his discussion with Elizabeth Burnet concerning the gift to Trotter. The following day Locke directed King to give five guineas (1987 value approximately US$500.00) to Trotter. He repeated this directive in his letter to King of December 14, when he also told King to explain to Trotter that the press of business had delayed King in executing the order which Locke had given him a long time ago. Then, on December 30, Locke sent Trotter the following letter from Oates, the home of Damaris Masham.

Madam, There was nothing more public, than the obligation I received from you, nor anything more concealed, than the person I was obliged to. This is a generosity above the strain of this groveling age, and like that of superior spirits, who assist without showing themselves. I used my best endeavours to draw from you, by your Bookseller, the confession of your name, the want whereof made me, that I could whist you kept yourself under that reserve, no more address myself directly to you with good manners, than I could without rudeness have pulled off your mask by force, in a place where you were resolved to conceal yourself. Had not this been so, the bearer hereof had not the first time have come to you, without a letter from me, to acknowledge the favour you had done me. You not affording me an opportunity for that, I designed to make you some small acknowledgement, in a way, that chance had opened to me, without your consent. But this gentleman transgressed my order in two main points of it. The one was, in delaying it so long: the other was, in naming me to you, and talking of matters, which he had no commission from me to mention. What he deserves from you for it, must be left to your mercy. For I cannot in earnest be angry with him for procuring me, without any guilt of mine, an opportunity to own you for my protectress, which is the greatest honour my Essay could have procured me. Give me leave therefore to assure you, that as the rest of the world take notice of the strength and clearness of your reasoning, so I cannot but be extremely sensible, that it was employed in my defence. You have herein not only vanquished my adversary, but reduced me also absolutely under your power, and left no desires more strong in me, than those of meeting with some opportunity, to assure you, with what respect and submission I am, Madam,

Your most humble, and most obedient servant,

J. Locke.

There are two minor discrepancies in the account of the Locke-Trotter relationship. The first concerns how Locke learned Trotter's name. Although Locke's letter to Trotter and his correspondence with his cousin Peter King suggests that he asked King to learn Trotter's identity and to locate her, Locke had actually learned her identity from Elizabeth Burnet, but kept the confidence. The second discrepancy concerns the nature of Locke's gift to Trotter. The correspondence with Burnet initially suggested a gift of books, but the later correspondence and that with King indicates that cash was given. The introduction to Trotter's *Defence* includes Locke's letter to her and a statement that she received a gift of books. Most likely, both were given, and the books were merely a publicly acknowledgeable vehicle for delivering the cash.

In addition to Trotter's *Defence* of Locke, her critical works include responses to published sermons by Holdsworth against Locke, *A Letter to Dr. Holdsworth: occasioned by his Sermon preached before the University of Oxford on Easter Monday, concerning the Resurrection of the same Body* and *A Vindication of Mr. Locke's Christian Principles, from the injurious Imputations of Dr. Holdsworth*. She also refuted criticisms of Locke by other religious leaders, including Rutherford and Seed in her *Remarks upon some Writers in the Controversy concerning the Foundation of Moral Virtue and Moral Obligation. With some thoughts concerning Necessary Existence; the Reality and Infinity of Space; the Extension and Place of Spirits; and on Dr. Watts's Notion of Substance*.[11] In addition to these published works, Trotter maintained a lengthy correspondence with Thomas Burke, who in 1751, two years after Trotter Cockburn's death, published her collected works.

Thomas Burnet (of the Charterhouse), author of *Theoria Telluris Sacra*, wrote in defense of Stillingfleet against Locke. Although Trotter claims only recently to have acquired a copy of Locke's *Essay*,[12] her defense of Locke against Burnet's anonymous letter *Remarks upon an Essay concerning Humane Understanding*,[13] shows a firm grasp of the issues. In addition she has a clear understanding of the issues in the Locke-Stillingfleet debate. (Stillingfleet was a subscriber to her works.)[14] Trotter's comments are primarily directed towards Burnet's second remarks, those which drew comment from Locke in print. Burnet's third remarks drew little attention from either Locke or Trotter. She argues frequently from analogies showing the absurdity or inconsistency of Burnet's three primary criticisms: (1) that Locke's *Essay* does not give a firm and full basis for morality; (2) that it does not secure the certainty of revealed religion; and (3) that it does not provide a philosophical foundation for the immortality of the soul.[15] Although Burnet, and Trotter, in her criticism of him, enunciates these as separate issues, arguments employed in their discussions show that Burnet, Trotter, and Locke all considered the issues to be closely related. I shall briefly discuss Trotter's response to each of Burnet's criticisms of Locke, with particular emphasis on the last.

III. EPISTEMOLOGICAL FOUNDATIONS OF MORAL LAW

Trotter begins her defense of Locke against the still-anonymous Burnet by considering Burnet's initial suggestion that when Locke's Principles, as expressed in the *Essay*, are considered together, they cannot give us a sure foundation for morality and revealed religion. She says it is clear to her that whatever can be known at all must be discoverable by Mr. Locke's principles.

> ... for I cannot find any other way to knowledge, or that we have any one idea not derived from sensation and reflection.[16]

1. *Knowledge of Virtue and Vice*

Trotter takes up Burnet's claim that the perception of the morality and immorality of particular acts, called virtues and vices, is as immediate and independent of any reasoning process as is the perception of the scent of a rose.

> I do not know what it is, to perceive the morality and immorality of these things without any ratiocination. Justice and injustice, I think, depend upon the rights of men, whether natural, or established by particular societies, and therefore to know what they are, it is necessary to know what right is, which, requires some reflection.[17]

She claims that to know independently of any reflection that injustice is evil is nothing more than to know that the term "injustice" stands for something that we do not know, which is evil. Trotter tries to grant Burnet some ground by saying that she understands him, but what he is saying cannot be construed as an objection to Locke. She explains that Burnet has a perception of the disagreement of two ideas: of one man's having a right to something and another having a right to take it away. And as soon as Burnet knows what it is to have a right to a thing, he perceives that preventing someone from having that which they have a right to is evil. He can understand this without any further reflection. But knowing what a right is and what evil is, on the one hand, and knowing through reflection what the relationship is between the denial of someone's rights and doing evil, requires rational reflection. It cannot be directly perceived. The process of recognizing the agreement or disagreement of particular ideas (such as those of good and evil) with the understanding of the idea that resulted from reflection (e.g., understanding why it is wrong to deny rights) is a different cognitive process than the process of immediate sensory perception, like smelling a rose.

Trotter then turns to analyzing Burnet's purpose in claiming that the distinction between moral good and evil is in the nature of things themselves and requires no reference to any other thing. She claims to be stymied as to how the goodness of the moral virtues or the evil of the moral vices can be known independent of any reference to human beings or to society. She says:

> I desire any one, to try, whether he can conceive it to be an eternal truth, that it is a wicked thing for a man to kill his father ... though there had never been, or designed to be, such a thing as father, or man. But whether he can or not, it will still be a truth as *certain and*

immutable, as any proposition in mathematics. No mathematician, that I know of, thinks it necessary to establish the immutability of this truth, that the three angles of a triangle are equal to two right ones; to affirm, that it is true, without any relation to angles or triangles. Either of these propositions are sufficiently established, if it is, and always must be true, supposing those things, to which it relates, to exist.[18]

Trotter says that these remarks constitute only a partial consideration of moral truths. They are related only to what she calls "the present constitution of things." She is not referring to the original source of such truths in the mind of God.

Burnet had criticized Locke's views on natural morality:

As to Morality, we think that the great Foundation of it is, the Distinction of Good and Evil, Virtue and Vice, Turpis & Honestis, as they are usually call'd: And I do not find that my Eyes, Ears, Nostrils, or any other outward Senses, make any distinction of these Things, as they do of Sounds, Colours, Scents, or other outward Objects; nor from any Idea's taken in from them, or from their Reports, am I conscious that I do conclude, or can conclude, that there is such a Distinction on the Nature of Things; or that it consists only in Pleasure and Pain, Conveniency and Inconveniency.[19]

And further

You allow, I think Moral Good and Evil to be such antecedently to all Human Laws: but you suppose them to be such (if I understand you right) by the Divine Law. To know your Mind farther, give me leave to ask, What is the Reason or Ground of that Divine Law? Whether the Arbitrary Will of God, the Good of Men, or the intrinsick Nature of the Things themselves: If I know upon which of these Grounds you woul'd build your Demonstration of Morality, I could make a better judgement of it.[20]

Trotter argues against Burnet that Locke's epistemology enables us, through reflection on our own nature, to know that God exists and that human nature is a reflection of the will of God. Through introspection into that nature we come to recognize that there must be a supreme being. Therefore Lockean principles provide a foundation for natural religion, including a view of the soul as an immaterial, immortal substance capable of thought. Similarly, Trotter shows that Lockean principles show that we have a natural foundation for the moral law: God requires us to seek our happiness through the fulfillment of those capacities that he has designed us to develop. These capacities include the ability to fulfill that which we, as a consequence of our nature, have come to call the virtues. Chief among these is the capacity for justice: to respect those rights that all humans have by virtue of their God-given human nature.[21] Therefore, Trotter concludes, rather than destroying religion, society, and government, Locke's principles enable us to identify their natural philosophical foundations.

2. *Natural Conscience*

Trotter notes[22] that Burnet's Third Remarks focus on one aspect of the question of whether on Locke's principles there is an epistemological basis for natural morality and revealed religion. It is useful here to compare Locke's marginal reply to Burnet on this point with Trotter's.

Burnet had said, referring to Locke's *Essay*

Conscience you say is nothing else but our own opinion of our own actions. But of what sort of actions, I pray, in reference to what rule or distinction of our actions? Whether good or evil or as profitable or unprofitable or as perfect or imperfect.[23]

Locke's marginal note to this is that

An ingenuous and fair reader cannot doubt but that I there meant *opinion* of their morality.

Burnet queried which laws are to be obeyed, and how they can be known without divine revelation and without a natural conscience with the innate knowledge of good or evil.[24] To this Locke noted that conscience doesn't determine the principles of morality, it merely judges whether actions are in accord with moral principles:

It is not conscience yt makes the distinction of good & evil conscience only judging of an action by yt wch it takes to be ye rule of good & evil, acquits or condemns it.[25]

Trotter's comment is similar, but far more analytical than Locke's marginal note. She says[26] that part of Burnet's problem with Locke is that Burnet employs more than one sense of natural conscience. What Burnet has confused, Trotter says, is the difference between innate principles and an innate or natural power to make moral distinctions regarding actions. The former Locke denies, the latter he concedes.[27] She makes what she says is a

> ...very material observation, which is, that, throughout this whole discourse, the Remarker uses indifferently, as terms of the same signification, *law of nature, natural conscience, innate principles, innate powers, and natural principles,* which all signify very different things; and of thich Mr. *Locke* has only denied *innate principles*...[28]

Yet Burnet claimed that the innate power of judging the morality of actions consists of a power to make non-rational judgments, i.e., judgments which do not require the use of reason. From the undisputed claim that there is a natural non-rational ability to judge whether one likes or dislikes particular sensory perceptions, Burnet infers that there is an analogous, non-rational power to perceive and judge the morality of actions, i.e., there is a natural ability to perceive the good or evil of actions. Trotter responds to Burnet's claims with the sarcasm of a professional writer:

> He might every whit as well have told us, that since we have a power of distinguishing *moral relations,* without the use of our eye-sight, we may distinguish red, and yellow, without eyes; they being no more the proper and only inlets of our ideas of colours, than reflection is of moral distinctions; which the Remarker says we may have without reflection, since we can distinguish colours, and other sensible qualities without reflection.[29]

Trotter says that Locke's *Essay* had anticipated most of Burnet's remarks on natural conscience, and she reiterates a number of places in the *Essay* in which Locke had anticipated such criticisms.[30]

Returning to Burnet's claim that there is an ability to make moral distinctions without reason, Trotter urges[31] Burnet to consider whether he means that moral judgment can occur independent of awareness that any rational action has taken place, or whether it actually precedes rationality. She proposes two, non-exclusive explanations of moral judgment-making which might make moral judgment *appear* to occur independently of reason itself. *First*, she suggests that a moral judgment can be a consequence of previous moral reasoning, for example, as when having received prior moral education or instruction, one acquires some confused concept of good and evil, so that the act of reaching a moral judgment is often really the consequence of recalling, reconsidering, and improving upon previous judgments. *Second*, she suggests that reaching a particular moral judgment is the consequence of combining a series of related prior judgments in an informal reasoning process which occurs so quickly that one barely takes note of the fact that one has made complex logical inferences.

IV. EPISTEMOLOGICAL FOUNDATION OF RELIGION

1. *The Role of Rewards and Punishments*

Trotter's comments are primarily directed towards Burnet's second remarks, those which drew comment from Locke in print. Burnet's third comments drew little attention from Locke or from Trotter. Locke's comments on Burnet's third *Remarks* are published by Porter in his "Marginalia Locke-a-na."[32] (There is no indication whether Locke's marginal comments were made before or after reading Trotter's *Defence*, the absence of a receipt date on the letter, or of mention of Burnet in Locke's correspondence suggests that the marginalia precede Trotter's *Defence*.) There, Locke responded to Burnet's claim that if we admit that God has specific moral attributes, which are deducible from knowledge of God's nature, then we have an innate ability (that of "natural conscience") to know that God will reward compliance with moral law and punish transgressions of it. Related to Burnet's charge that Locke's philosophy provides no basis for the moral law is his claim that Locke

…seems to ground his demonstration upon future punishments and rewards, and upon the arbitrary will of the law-giver; and he does not think these the first grounds of good and evil.[33]

Trotter is fully aware that in a work as lengthy as the *Essay*, a work which has already seen some revision, careless remarks might remain in the text. She tries to save Locke from criticism by saying that it matters less what Locke thinks, than what may be proven from his principles. According to Trotter, on Locke's principles God's arbitrary will and God's use of rewards and punishments affects humans by giving morality the force of law. Our expectation of reward for living in accord with the moral law, and our fear of punishment for its violation, has a deterrent effect on humans, she says. That doesn't mean that on Locke's principles, the expectation and fear themselves become the philosophical basis of the moral law:

> ...the Remarker cannot deny, whatever he thinks, the first grounds of good and evil; or however clearly we may see the nature of these things, we may approve or condemn them; but they can only have the force of a *law* to us, considered as *the will of the Supreme Being*, who can, and certainly will, reward the compliance with, and punish the deviation from that rule, which he has made knowable to us by the light of nature.[34]

Burnet claims that just as children naturally seek sweet-tasting things and have an innate, natural aversion for bitter, they can have innate ideas that God rewards some behaviors and punishes others and that innate ideas together with revelations about God's moral qualities, form the basis of "natural conscience" or natural morality, rather than, as Locke claims, reasoning about sensory perceptions and about our own nature. It is striking to note, in their independent responses to Burnet's analogy, how similarly Locke and Trotter think. To Burnet's comment Locke responds:

> Shew such an aversion in children to all immorality as soon as they are capable of moral actions and yt will be something to yr purpose. Are Rewards and punishmts deducible from the nature of god by any one without Ratiotination. But tis without Ratiotination yt yu contend Natural conscience works.[35]

Trotter says:

> But if this were so, Mr. *Locke* may very well say, what the
> Remarker believes he will not, that then children would be able to
> distinguish moral good and evil, for they very clearly distinguish all
> the objects of sensation, that come in their way; and this principle
> could never be *improved*, or *corrupted*, as no one can be persuaded,
> that any sensation he has is more or less agreeable, or that a
> disagreeable sensation is an agreeable one; which if we could, it is
> evident, that our senses would not be sufficient to their end, to give
> us notice of what is convenient or inconvenient to the body. And it
> is reasonable to think, if there were such an inward sensation
> designed, as the Remarker says, to direct us as to what is good or
> hurtful to the soul, it would operate as constantly as those others do:
> no man could prefer vice to virtue, any more than he can pain to
> pleasure; othewise it would not answer the end it was designed
> for.[36]

Sterling Power Lampecht,[37] referring to the implications of Locke's
appeal to God's punishment and rewards, notes that this part of
Trotter's defense of Locke against Burnet incorporates positions
similar to those taken by Nathanael Culverwel[38] before Locke wrote
the *Essay* and by Samuel Pufendorf[39] after Trotter published her
Defence.

> But that we can only know these things to be his will by their
> conformity to our nature, and that therefore they cannot be ar-
> bitrary, I have before shewn; and that he will punish or reward us
> according to our obedience or disobedience to it, is a consequence
> of his nature.[40]

Trotter also discusses Burnet's connection of the punishment/reward
issue with his criticism of Locke's claim that the soul does not always
think. She says:

> The Remarker on another occasion tells Mr. *Locke*, the grounds of
> our expectation of *future punishments and rewards* are, that *there is
> a presage of them from natural conscience*; and that *they are
> deducible from the nature of God, if we allow him moral attributes.*

She continues:

> Now it is evident, that neither of these two grounds can lose any of their force upon this supposition, that the soul does not think in sound sleep, and will not they [the two premises] secure us, that we shall not continue in this sleep after death? If not, why does the Remarker mention them as proofs of a future state? [i.e., of the immortality of the soul] But if they do prove it, why does he say, he *could make out no certain proof of the immortality of the soul, upon this supposition, that it is somtimes without thoughts?* Since those proofs he mentions remain in their full force, notwithstanding this supposition. Thus having shown, that all the consequences the Remarker draws from Mr. *Locke's* supposition are without grounds, I may with assurance conclude, that it is of no consequence to the immortality of the soul, nor does at all weaken any proof of it.[41]

Burnet had also claimed that had God so pleased, he might have made virtue vice, and vice, virtue.[42] To this, Trotter says, given that God created human nature as it is, and created us in his image, moral good and evil cannot be other than they are. Like pain and pleasure, virtue and vice do not exist independently of human capacity for them. Trotter says if Burnet carefully considered the difference between moral good and evil, on the one hand, and natural good and evil, on the other, he would not find fault with Locke's views on moral good and evil. Trotter says that Burnet ought not confuse the moral law as a source of law for humans with the idea of natural good and evil – natural wonders and catastrophes that exist independent of human action. She also says that our knowledge of moral good and evil are products of reflection on our own natures, which imperfectly reflect God's nature. In her view, our only source of ideas of God's moral attributes is consideration of our own attributes and consideration of ourselves as imperfectly made in God's image. We would have no idea of God's moral attributes without reflection on ourselves. In contrast to our knowledge of moral good and evil, we have no notion of what the original standard of natural good and evil is, we only know that some things are agreeable and some repugnant to our nature. Therefore, what human nature causes us to perceive as morally or as naturally good we ascribe to God. By reflecting on our own nature, and on the operations of our minds we can come to know the nature of God.

From whence it will follow, that the nature of man, and the good of society, are to us the reason and rule of moral good and evil; and there is no danger of their being less immutable on this foundation than any other, whilst man continues a rational and sociable creature. If the [moral] law of [human] nature is the product of human nature itself, it must subsist as long as human nature; nor will this foundation make it the less sacred, since it cannot be doubted that it is originally the will of God, whilst we own him the author of that nature, of which this law is a consequence.[43]

Knowledge of the nature of the moral law comes from our knowledge of human nature. But God created human nature in his image and according to his will. Therefore, the moral law is a consequence of God's willing us to have a particular nature. Knowledge of the moral law is therefore a consequence of God's willing us to know our own nature and thereby know his attributes.

2. *On Revelation*

Burnet could not understand how Locke's principles could demonstrate the truth of divine revelation. Burnet complained that Locke talked much of God's perfections, but failed to give an account of the idea of perfection itself.

'Tis not enough (as I judge) for our satisfaction, and to establish the certainty of Revealed Religion, that we know the Physical or Metaphysical Attributes of the Divine Nature: we must also know its Moral Attributes, as I may so call them; such as Goodness, Justice, Holiness, and particularly Veracity. Now these I am not abel to deduce or make out from your Principles. You have prov'd very well an Eternal, All-powerful, and All knowing Being: but how this supreme Being will treat us, we cannot be assur'd from these attributes.[44]

Trotter takes a shot at Locke's critics generally, urging readers to take notice of

...the folly of those men, who think [that the effect of Locke's principles is] to weaken the authority of religion, by calling it a politic contrivance, established for the good of government or society.[45]

According to Trotter, Locke's principles have shown that it is our indispensable duty from God, but independent of any revelation of God's will, to accept the authority of religion, because human nature is the product of divine workmanship. Through Locke's principles we can reflect on the idea of perfection of the Supreme Being and arrive at the original concept of intrinsic holiness. Locke's critics' mistakes lie in having learned truths after their discovery by others. Finding the truths agreeable, Trotter says, those critics assent unreflectingly and without asking how those ideas were first known. They are likely to conclude that those things which they come to know first as revelations are themselves the first principles of knowledge, even though the ideas embodied in those revelations are the product of others' comparison of ideas about God's nature and will.

V. THE IMMORTALITY OF THE SOUL

Burnet believes that Locke's principles do not support the immortality of the soul because Locke has claimed (a) that the soul does not always think; and (b) that God may add the capacity for thought to matter. According to Christophersen, on Burnet's view it is impossible to observe that one does not think, for observation is in itself thinking.[46] Further, Burnet claims if the soul is not always thinking what causes the soul to resume thinking? (a) Trotter addresses Burnet's criticism of consequences of Locke's theory for the prevailing view of the immortality of the soul.[47] She first reminds Burnet that no theory can provide certainty of the immortality of the soul independent of divine revelation, and that consequently it is no argument against Locke's theory that it provides no greater certainty of the soul's immortality than do other philosophies. However, for Burnet, the idea that the soul is not always engaged in thought, as Locke claims, threatens the basis of belief in its immortality. Trotter claims that Burnet's comments are irrelevant.[48] As Christophersen notes, Burnet, as Leibniz, points to the insensible motions in the soul:

the unconscious life, etc., even in daytime.[49] Burnet had questioned how Locke might observe that the soul does not always think, because the act of observing would itself be a form of thought. To this Trotter responds that if Burnet is really claiming that Locke meant that the person knows when and that his soul does not think, Burnet is imputing to Locke a different concept of personal identity than Locke enunciated in the *Essay*.[50] Rather, Trotter says, Burnet is stumbling over semantics. For Locke, the terms *soul, man,* and *person* are not synonymous. According to Trotter, Locke understands *soul* to be a permanent metaphysical entity capable of thought, *man* to be the soul and body united, and *person* to be self-consciousness. Trotter, quoting Locke's *Essay* at pp. 44 and 45, says that

> ...if the *soul* can, whilst the body is sleeping, have its thinking and enjoyments apart which *the man* is not at all conscious of; his *soul,* when he sleeps, and the *man consisting of body and soul,* when he is waking, are two *persons.*[51]

Since by *person* Locke means *self-consciousness,* Locke is rejecting the account Burnet defends, that the soul of the sleeping man and the wakeful man are two self-consciousnesses or two persons. However, they are not the same permanent substances. For Locke, personal identity consists in the same consciousness and not in the same substance; he may therefore hold that the soul is a permanent substance, but that the man, consisting of body and soul, is not a permanent substance. Criticizing Burnet for this attack on Locke, Trotter says:

> But the Remarker is to be excused for making an inference so inconsistent with the design of that discourse, since he confesses he does not understand what it tends to, and perhaps only ventured at a shrewd guess to provoke a clearer account.[52]

(b) Trotter addresses Burnet's First Remarks (at page 9) where he discusses how thought might be generated if the soul is not always thinking. If thoughts die when we sleep, Trotter says, why not die every time they are considered? If we can remember ideas not continually being thought, why not be able to recall ideas after awakening? She says:

The force of which argument lies thus: *cogitation* in the soul answering to *motion* in the body; as the same motion cannot be restored, but a new *motion* may be produced; so the same *cogitations* cannot be restored, but new *cogitations* must be produced. *Ergo*, we seem to have a new *soul* every morning. This may be a good consequence, when the Remarker has proved, that every *new motion* makes, or seems to make a *new body*. In the mean time, all I can infer from this parallel, is, that my thoughts to-day are not the same numerical thoughts I had yesterday; which, I believe no body supposes they are, though they did not suspect that they had a *new soul* with every *new thought*.[53]

Burnet's atomistic criticism of Locke, Trotter says, cannot support the doctrine of innate ideas. Referring to Locke, Burnet had said:

If you say the ideas remain in the soul, and need only a new excitation; why then, say I, may not infants have *innate ideas* (which you so much oppose) that want only objects and occasions to excite and actuate them, with a fit disposition of the brain?[54]

Trotter criticizes[55] Burnet for believing that he has shown the doctrine of recollection to be analogous to the theory of innate ideas and thus trapped Locke into admitting the existence of innate ideas. The two examples are disanalogous, Trotter claims, because we readily distinguish new ideas, on the one hand, and recollected, previously known ideas on the other. We recognize when an idea is new to us and recognize also as ideas we had previously considered those which we recollect. Furthermore, she claims that the fact that we easily distinguish between previously considered and new ideas argues against innate ideas. If ideas are innate, they should all be recognized as recollections; none should appear to us to be new. Trotter says that her comment that if ideas are innate all ideas should be recognized as recollections is relevant to Burnet's suggestion that innate ideas needed objects to excite them. Trotter questions why innate ideas need objects to jog them to our consciousness. We know we recollect ideas without directly perceiving the objects which first stimulated those ideas. If ideas are innate, we should be able to recollect them without being stimulated by the objects the ideas represent.

1. *Whether God May Add Thought to Matter*

Burnet remarks that if the soul is not

> distinct from the Matter of the Body, when that is corrupted and
> dissolved, 'tis manifest she must be dissolved also. And if she be a
> Substance, distinct from Matter, however you say she is sometimes
> without Thoughts, or any manner of Operation; why then may she
> not be so (according to this Doctrine) after Death thoughtless and
> senseless, and so without life.[56]

Burnet is concerned that Lockean epistemology threatens received
religious doctrines on the immateriality of souls and the existence of
spiritual entities like souls and angels. If the capacity for thought can
be added to matter, how do we know that our souls are necessarily not
matter? If matter is capable of thought, why did God create immaterial
spirits? According to Burnet, it is impossible to conceive how the
capacity for thought could be a property of matter. He says:

> But there is still a farther Doubt or Difficulty in this Case, even as
> to the Nature of God and his Immateriality. I'm afraid the
> Materialists will profit too much from that Notion or Concession,
> that Matter may think: For, say they, if Matter be capable of
> Thinking, it may have Will and Understanding, and any other
> Faculty of a thinking Substance, and in any Degree of spiritual
> Perfection, and consequently may be God.[57]

Clearly, Burnet saw a great danger in Locke's view that the soul
sometimes does not think and that God may add to matter the capacity
for thought; that danger was that any matter might be capable of
thought, or of any other power or quality, and hence, there is a danger
of materialistic denial of the existence of spiritual entities. There is
also a danger of pantheism, of all matter being God.

Christophersen quotes Burnet further:

> They will further argue with you thus. You say you have no Idea of
> the Substance of Matter, nor know what Properties may flow from
> it: you do not know then, whether it includes Cogitation, or ex-
> cludes it?[58]

Trotter addresses Burnet's assumption that God may add the capacity of thought to matter, but she is careful to address this supposition in the context in which Burnet offers it, i.e., as a claim which undermines belief in the immortality of the soul. Trotter notes that rather than show why such a hypothesis would weaken the proofs of the immortality of the soul, Burnet instead attempts to undermine Locke's hypothesis. Trotter poses her own hypothetical:

> For suppose to convince an intelligent heathen, who thought the soul material, and doubted of a future state of rewards and punishments [i.e., of an eternal life], arguments were used to prove the soul in its own nature undissolvable, and that therefore it must remain after death; he might then reasonably enquire in what state it remains, how he may be sure, that it is in a state of rewards and punishments, and that it does not return to the universal soul of which it may be an effluence; or inform the next parcel of matter it finds fitted for it, as some philosophers have thought.[59]

A primitive person who was convinced by arguments that there is an eternal life might still not be able to conceive of an immaterial soul because "he has no notion of a substance without any extension." But the lack of proof of the immateriality of the soul would not weaken such a person's belief in its immortality. Similarly, she says, Locke's assumption that God may have given to some kinds of matter the power to perceive and to think does not entail that we abandon belief in the immortality of the soul.

VI. SUMMARY

Catharine Trotter Cockburn's *Defence* capably addressed Burnet's three major criticisms of Locke's *Essay*. Burnet had claimed that Locke's *Essay* did not give a firm basis for morality. Trotter showed that Burnet was mistaken in claiming that the perception of good and evil was analogous to sensory perception and, like sensory perception, took place independent of reason. According to Trotter, Burnet's alleged "perception" of good and evil was nothing more than awareness that the definitions of actions known to be morally good are inconsistent with those of actions we know to be morally evil. On her view, Burnet merely perceived the agreement or disagreement of two ideas. Burnet had also claimed that Locke's principles undermined religion in part because they entailed that God was prevented from making virtue vice and vice virtue. Trotter argued that unlike natural wonders and catastrophes, which might be considered to be the natural virtues and vices, moral good and evil is defined exclusively in reference to human nature. Having created human nature in a particular way, God necessarily defined moral good and evil according to that nature. Consequently, knowledge of virtue and vice (moral good and evil) was possible through reflection on human nature. According to Trotter, revelation confirmed Locke's epistemology in that it informed us that human nature was but an imperfect mirror image of divine nature; therefore, we could come to know about the nature of God through reflection on our own nature and on the operations of our own mind. Burnet had also questioned how we could know which moral laws to obey without the aid of divine revelation and a natural conscience characterized by innate ideas. To this Trotter says that Burnet has confused the distinction between innate principles and innate or natural abilities to make moral judgments regarding actions. This sort of confusion, she claims, characterizes Burnet's *Remarks*, including his criticism of Locke's claim that the soul does not always think. Trotter defends Locke's position on two grounds. First, she shows that Burnet is imputing to Locke a concept of personal identity which is not Locke's. Second, she shows that Burnet's criticism cannot accomplish his goal of showing that he has involved Locke in an inconsistency which Locke can escape only by embracing the doctrine of innate ideas. Lastly, Trotter shows that Burnet is throwing a red herring into the Locke-Stillingfleet debate by alleging that Locke is committed to a view which permits the soul (and by implication, God) to be material substance. Such a view, Burnet claimed, undermines the doctrine of the immortality of the soul, a conclusion Trotter shows to be absurd.

VII. CONCLUSIONS

A self-taught intellectual, Catharine Trotter achieved early, if not financially rewarding, success as a playwright. The sole support of her widowed mother, she spent much of her life in poverty, marrying a clergyman solely for financial security. Yet the list of subscribers to her works show that influential academicians and theologians, as well as the social and political *intelligentia*, respected her creative and analytical abilities. She had a clear understanding of the most controversial philosophical and religious issues of her day and marshalled her witty articulateness to defend Locke against his critics. She confronted her own personal religious beliefs in light of her assessment of the consequences of Lockean epistemology for prevailing theories of the nature of the soul, the nature and source of religious and secular knowledge, and the nature and source of the moral law. As a result of this process of living the philosophical life, she felt compelled to sever her affiliation with the Catholic church. Her views were respected by philosophers and theologians including Locke, Bishop Gilbert Burnet of Salisbury, and Locke's critic, John Norris. Locke's friend Thomas Burnet[60] of Kemnay was Locke's intermediary with Leibniz. Burnet's brother George discussed Trotter's *Defence* with Leibniz, with Princess Sophie Charlotte, and probably her mother Sophie the Electress and Queen Caroline of Anspach.[61] Indeed, Leibniz repeatedly inquired about Trotter's defense of Locke, particularly because Burnet conveyed Locke's approval of it. Leibniz was completing his own critique of Locke and did not want to begin to transcribe it until after he had had the opportunity to study Trotter's work. Trotter delayed providing Leibniz with a copy of her work until a miniature of her which Leibniz had requested could be completed. The delivery of her text and portrait coincided with Locke's death. It is also likely that by that time Trotter's defense of Locke had been seen by Damaris Masham.

Although Catharine Trotter Cockburn received initial fame as a playwright, her adult life was spent in the pursuit of philosophy. The *Defence* of Locke was but her first philosophical work. Her knowledgeable discussions of the epistemological issues and their consequences for religious doctrines continued throughout her lifetime. Those discussions would often involve public criticism of the views of eminent philosopher-theologians affiliated with powerful religious and academic institutions. Thanks to Thomas Birch, her biography as well as her philosophical essays and correspondence have been preserved. Unfortunately for historians and students of philosophy, and particularly for students of modern epistemological theory and theory of religious knowledge, those philosophical writings have been long overlooked, buried in the corpus of her literary works.

NOTES

1. I am indebted to Kathryn M. Kendall, Ph.D., who while a graduate student in Dramatic Arts, University of Texas, Austin, brought Trotter to my attention.
2. Gosse, Edmund, "Catharine Trotter, the Precursor of the Bluestockings," *Transactions of the Royal Society of Literature of the U.K.*: XXXIV (1916): 90.
3. Kendall, Kathryn McQueen, "Friends or Rivals? Two Versions of the Same Tale," p. 7 of unpublished 1984 draft of doctoral dissertation, "Theatre, Society and Women Playwrights in London from 1695 through the Queen Anne Era," University of Texas at Austin, 1986.
4. Kendall, *op. cit.*, p. 28.
5. *Mr. Locke's Reply to the Right Reverend the Lord Bishop of Worcester's Answer to his Letter, concerning some Passages Relating to Mr. Locke's Essay of Humane Understanding: in a Late Discourse of his Lordships, in Vindication of the Trinity*, 1697.
6. Porter, Noah, "Marginalia *Locke*-a-na," *The New Englander and Yale Review*, Vol. XI, new series, Vol. XLVII, complete series: July 1887: 33–49.
7. Birch, Thomas, ed., *The Works of Mrs. Catharine Cockburn, Theological, Moral, Dramatic, and Poetical*, 2 vols., with an account of the author's life. London: 1751. Hereafter as *Works*.
8. *Defence*, in *Works*, Vol. I, pp. 87, 88.
9. See *Works*, Vol. I, p. 155.
10. See Chapter 5 by Lois Frankel.
11. *Works*, Vol. I.
12. *Defence*, in *Works*, Vol. I, p. 87, p. 89.
13. Burnet, Thomas, *Remarks upon an Essay concerning Humane Understanding*. In a Letter address'd to the Author. London, Printed for M. Wotton, at the Three Daggers in Fleetstreet. 1697, pp. 15 in 8vo.
14. Hundreds of subscribers are listed in Volume I of her *Works*.
15. For an assessment of Burnet's criticisms see Christophersen, H.O., *A Bibliographical Introduction to the Study of John Locke*, New York: Burt Franklin, 1968 reprint of 1930 edition.
16. *Defence*, in *Works*, Vol. I, p. 53.
17. *Defence*, in *Works*, Vol. I, p. 54.
18. *Op. cit.*, Vol. I, pp. 55–56.
19. Quoted from Christophersen, *op. cit.* at note 2, quoting Burnet at pp. 4–5.
20. Christophersen *op. cit.* quoting Burnet at p. 6.
21. *Defence*, in *Works*, Vol. I, p. 54.
22. *Defence*, p. 92.
23. Porter, *op. cit.*, p. 35.
24. Porter, in *ibid*.
25. Porter, in *ibid*.

26. *Defence*, p. 93.
27. Porter, *op. cit.*, p. 38.
28. *Defence*, p. 97.
29. *Defence*, pp. 93–94.
30. *Defence*, pp. 95–99.
31. *Defence*, p. 100ff.
32. *Op. cit.*
33. Burnet's Second Remarks, p. 2, quoted in Trotter, *op. cit.*, Vol. I, p. 60.
34. *Op. cit.*, Vol. I, pp. 61–62, especially note n, p. 61.
35. Porter, *op. cit.*, p. 42.
36. *Defence*, p. 94.
37. *The Moral and Political Philosophy of John Locke*, New York: Columbia University Press (1918 reprint from *Archives of Philosophy* No. 11), pp. 108–109.
38. Culverwel, Nathanael, *On the Light of Nature*, Edinburgh, 1857.
39. Pufendorf, Samuel, *On the Law of Nature and Nations*, Oxford, 1703.
40. Lamprecht's bibliography lists Trotter's work under "Deckburn, Mrs. Catharine Trotter" although other references to her in the text are under "Cockburn."
41. *Defence*, in *Works*, p. 82, referring to Burnet's Third Remarks, p. 13.
42. *Op. cit.*, p. 56.
43. *Defence*, in *Works*, pp. 56–58, material in square brackets mine.
44. Christophersen, *op. cit.*, pp. 44–45, citing Burnet at p. 7.
45. *Op. cit.*
46. Christophersen, *op. cit.* at note 2, quoting Burnet at p. 10.
47. *Defence*, p. 69ff.
48. *Op. cit.*, p. 69.
49. Christophersen, *op. cit.*, p. 45.
50. *Op. cit.*, p. 71.
51. *Ibid.*
52. *Op. cit.*, p. 74.
53. *Defence*, *Works*, Vol. I, p. 76.
54. *Op. cit.*, p. 77.
55. *Op. cit.*, p. 78.
56. Cited from Christophersen, *op. cit.*, note 3, quoting Burnet, p. 12.
57. *Ibid.* at note 4, quoting Burnet at pp. 13–14.
58. *Ibid.* at note 4, quoting Burnet at pp. 13–14.
59. *Defence*, *Works*, Vol. I, p. 89ff.
60. Spelled "Burnett" in E.S. De Beer, ed., *The Correspondence of John Locke* Volume VII. New York: Oxford University Press (1982), elsewhere as Burnet.
61. *Works*, Vol. II, p. 164ff.

8. Gabrielle Émilie le Tonnelier de Breteuil du Châtelet-Lomont

MARY ELLEN WAITHE*

I. BIOGRAPHY

Émilie du Châtelet, as she is known, was the daughter of Louis-Nicolas Baron de Breteuil and Alexandra-Elisabeth de Froulay. The Baron was a minor noble at the court of Louis XIV; however, due to the size of the family, Émilie was raised in Paris rather than at the apartment which would have been allocated to the Baron at the Palace of Versailles. At age nineteen in a ceremony at Nôtre Dame she married a military leader who was ten years her senior, the Marquis Florent-Claude du Châtelet-Lomont. Émilie du Châtelet had three children by the Marquis; the last was born in 1734 and died in infancy. In 1730 the Marquise Émilie du Châtelet and the Duc de Richelieu became lovers. The Duc de Richelieu was a grand-nephew of Cardinal Richelieu. He had long been a friend of the Châtelet family and of Voltaire. It is through the Duc that she became reaquainted with Voltaire,[1] whom, coincidentally, she had also known through her father.

Émilie du Châtelet was a true Enlightenment woman. She was educated by tutors and by the time she was twelve she read, wrote, and spoke English, Italian, Spanish, and German and was busy translating Aristotle's *Politics* and *Aesthetics* from the classical Greek, as well as Virgil's *Aeneid* from the Latin. Although she had an excellent early education, Émilie du Châtelet did not have access to a higher education comparable to that which men of her rank and wealth had access to. Women were excluded from the Sorbonne. Women (except prostitutes, who were confined to the back rooms) were also excluded from the new "cafés" where intellectuals met to sip the exotic Turkish brew. In 1733 Émilie du Châtelet set out to overcome both barriers to higher education. At first, she simply appeared at the Café Gradot and joined her friend, the Académie des Sciences member Maupertuis, and others at his table. Maupertuis' just-published Newtonian *Discours sur les différentes figures des astres* (1732) was of major interest to the Marquise. The café management firmly but politely told her to leave. Undaunted, du Châtelet had a suit of men's clothes made for her and a week later she rejoined the philosophers and poets at the tables, obvious in "drag."[2] Émilie continued to participate in daily discussions of poetry and philosophy with the assembled young *savants* at Maupertuis' table. The Sorbonne was a more formidable barrier to education, but the wealthy Marquise du Châtelet simply hired its mathematics and physics professors to come to the Palace du Châtelet-Lomont several times each week. By spending several days each week in tutoring sessions and afternoons at the Café Gradot, Émilie du Châtelet was able to pursue advanced studies in physics and mathematics.

In 1733 Émilie du Châtelet began a close analysis of Newton's *Mathematical Principles of Natural Philosophy*.[3] That same year, she and her new lover, Voltaire, retired to Cirey, an estate belonging to her husband, the Marquis du Châtelet-Lomont. Voltaire refurbished the estate at his own expense. He and Mme du Châtelet filled it with 20,000 volumes of philosophy, history, mathematics, literature, and physics. There, Mme du Châtelet read Newton, Locke, and Pope and began her study of Leibniz. To the remote Cirey came authors such as Maupertuis and Algarotti, who arrived in 1735 to work with Voltaire and du Châtelet while completing his *Neutonianismo per le Dame*. Newtonian physics proved to be Émilie du Châtelet's primary and enduring philosophical and scientific interest. She spent the rest of her life with Voltaire at Cirey. There, she collaborated with Voltaire on his *Elements of Newtonian Philosophy* (and perhaps his *Treatise on Metaphysics* and other works), conducted physics and chemistry experiments, undertook an extensive philosophical and scientific correspondence, and wrote philosophy. Her thematically related investigations of metaphysics, physics, and philosophy of science do not reveal the full scope of her philosophical interests. She also wrote on ethics, religion, and philosophy of language.

During her fifteen years with Voltaire at Cirey, Mme du Châtelet simultaneously pursued a number of projects. She undertook an unending series of physics experiments. She turned the large main corridor of the mansion into a labrynthine passage of tables and equipment constituting one of Cirey's two state-of-the-art physics laboratories. There, she replicated Newton's experiments. She simultaneously (and surreptitiously) prepared her *Essai sur... feu* (Essay on the nature and propagation of fire). Her *Institutions de Physique* (Institutions of Physics), an analysis of theories of physics originally intended as a textbook for her son, was also in progress during this period.[4] So were her commentaries and analyses, which later would be incorporated into her translation of Newton's *Principia* and her *Examen de la Genèse* (Examination of Genesis).

Voltaire lived with the Marquise du Châtelet until her death. However, by age forty-two Émilie du Châtelet had taken a new, younger lover, with whom she had her fourth child. Her correspondence indicated that she expected to die in childbirth:

> ... I saw that I must resign myself... to the loss of the entire fruit of my efforts should I die in childbirth...[5]

With that fear, she had worked an incredible twenty hours a day throughout her pregnancy to complete her translation analysis of Newton's *Principia*.[6] Both she and the child died shortly after the birth, in September 1749.

II. ETHICS, RELIGION AND PHILOSOPHY OF LANGUAGE

Émilie du Châtelet's primary philosophical interests were in metaphysics. Yet her writings on ethics, religion, and philosophy of language show that she also had an interest in the major philosophical issues of her time and was familiar with views on these subjects held by philosophers of the late seventeenth century and earlier.

1. *Ethics*

The Marquise du Châtelet condensed and translated Mandeville's *The Fable of the Bees; Or Private Vices, Public Benefits*. Her *La Fable des abeilles* (1735)[7] demonstrates du Châtelet's familiarity with seventeenth-century arguments about the nature of vice and virtue and the role of morality in political society. Mandeville's view was that without the existence of vice, there would be no need (and no moral justification) for the creation of a political state, nor would much of the economic infrastructure of the society survive.[8] According to Mandeville, the survival of an economically strong social state depends upon the survival of criminal and morally offensive behavior by some of its members. Were morally offensive behavior to be eliminated, there would be no need for institutions and occupations including the military, the police, courts, attorneys, locksmiths, gunsmiths, accountants, and others. Mme du Châtelet's completion in 1735 of her condensed translation of Mandeville's *Fable* appears to have heavily influenced Voltaire's *Défense du Mondain* (1737), although, according to Wade, as a work-in-progress it may as well have influenced his *Traité de Métaphysique* (1734).[9]

There is disagreement concerning the authorship of an essay on free will. Wade[10] argues that the work is Voltaire's. Janik argues that du Châtelet is the author of the "Chapitre 5 de la liberté," a work which I have not seen. It survives only in the collection of du Châtelet's works in the Leningrad public library. Janik cites physical, textual, and anecdotal evidence in support of her conclusion. The chapter is included in du Châtelet's papers. In addition, corrections to the manuscript are in du Châtelet's own hand and the ink color and pen nib is the same. Internal evidence includes pagination, section numbering, and subject matters which are consistent with references in the published version of *Institutions*. As "anecdotal" evidence, Janik cites Voltaire's handwritten notes on the manuscript identifying it as du Châtelet's. Further, Voltaire included an adaptation of the chapter in *Éléments de la philosophie du Neuton*, which he acknowledged to be their joint production.[11]

Du Châtelet's *Réflexions sur le Bonheur*[12] (Reflections on Happiness) is a vaguely Epicurean, autobiographical spoof of then-popular discussions of the nature of happiness. Much of it is devoted to explaining how gambling, study, passion, and common sense could contribute to the happiness of women.

2. *Philosophy of Religion*

Wade attributes *Examen de la Genèse* (Examination of Genesis) to Mme du Châtelet.[13] According to Wade, *Examen de la Genèse* was composed over an extended period, possibly beginning as early as

1736, and was not completed until perhaps as late as 1749, the year of du Châtelet's death. This five-volume work is an acerbic refutation of the major arguments of the Bible. According to Besterman, the original survives only in the library of Troyes.[14] Wade reproduces in *précis* a portion refuting the arguments of the Book of Genesis. The *Examen* shows that Mme du Châtelet had studied Spinoza's *Theologico-Political Treatise*[15] In it, du Châtelet follows Spinoza's method of Bible criticism, rather than his specific conclusions.[16] Her interest in the idea of Genesis even led her to read Newton's *Chronology of Ancient Kingdoms Amended.*[17] Given the close conceptual relationship between metaphysical questions about the nature of the universe and religious doctrines about its origin, it is not unexpected that a philosopher like du Châtelet, whose primary interests were in metaphysics, would investigate religious as well as scientific claims about the origins of the universe.

3. *Philosophy of Language*

Émilie du Châtelet also contributed to the development of a philosophy of language at a time when French authorities (the Académie Française) were convinced that French was the most perfect language, and one whose rules every "good" language must imitate. Émilie du Châtelet sought to provide an epistemic and logical foundation for ordinary language which took into account philosophic advances in analyzing the mind/body problem, particularly regarding the nature of perception. Du Châtelet's philosophy of language is set out in *La Grammaire Raisonnée*, of which only parts survive.[18] According to Wade[19] among the topics which the lost opening chapters apparently dealt with are perception, judging, and reasoning as three operations of the mind upon objects. In those discussions, Wade surmises, du Châtelet closely followed Book III of Locke's *Essay concerning human understanding*. She says:

> We say, in Chapter 2 that our mind performs three operations on objects, perceiving, judging and reasoning. It is always the second of these operations which men reveal when speaking, and that is because, not only can one not disclose simple perceptions, but similarly because one cannot do so without forming a judgment. ...
> If I say to others "I see a man" I judge that the object that I perceive

has the identifying marks of that which I am accustomed to giving the name "man." Therefore whatever men reveal by words is always formulated by words which indicate a judgment of the mind.[20]

The surviving later chapters in part explore the relationship between language and logic. In du Châtelet's view, rules of language are rules of rhetorical logic. However, they function not only in a regulatory way, but also as reminders of the ways in which language reveals thought processes. When the logical, regulatory aspects of linguistic rules coincide with public usage rhetorical elegance is the result.

III. COLLABORATIVE WORKS

In addition to her solely authored works, Émilie du Châtelet collaborated with Voltaire on one or two works, and apparently influenced his thinking in a way that became evident in some of his other writings.

1. *Collaboration on Voltaire's* Éléments

According to Voltaire, du Châtelet collaborated on his *Éléments de la philosophie de Neuton*[21] (Elements of Newton's philosophy). *Éléments* offered a systematic analysis of the relationship of Newton's philosophical, mathematical, and scientific works. As part of the process of preparing this volume, du Châtelet and Voltaire immersed themselves in all the relevant philosophical writings. According to Voltaire's correspondence, he and Mme du Châtelet were reading the Leibniz-Clarke correspondence,[22] Locke's *Essay*, the works of Descartes and the prominent Cartesians including Malebranche, Fontenelle, and Mairan, as well as the writings of Newtonians Algarotti, Maupertuis, and others. Du Châtelet's immersion in Leibniz' metaphysics convinced her to delete some of the metaphysical material from Voltaire's *Éléments* and to develop her own account of a metaphysical basis for Newtonian physics. Leibniz' principle of sufficient reason had been incorporated by du Châtelet into some parts of Voltaire's *Éléments*[23] but Voltaire clearly had the final word here: the application is tentative. Du Châtelet's role (if not her authority) in the composition of Voltaire's *Éléments de la Philosophie de Neuton* is apparently not overstated by Voltaire, who in a document which predates the publication of the book says:

> ...madame Du Châtelet had her part in the work. Minerva dictated and I wrote.[24]

The attribution of joint authorship of the work to Mme du Châtelet is elaborated upon in the *avant propos* (foreword) to the first edition, and also in the *épitre dédicatoire* (letter of dedication) to the 1748 edition of *Éléments*. With the publication of the first edition of Voltaire's *Éléments* in 1738, du Châtelet became known as "Lady Newton."

After the publication of the *Éléments* du Châtelet apparently revised her discussion on optics which appeared in that work. All that survives of this revision is a portion in which she analyzes color formation. The revision was found by Wade in the Voltaire collection at the Leningrad public library. It is reproduced in Wade's *Studies on Voltaire*.[25]

2. *Collaboration with Voltaire on* Traité de Métaphysique

Wade summarizes Émilie du Châtelet's contributions to Voltaire's *Traité de Métaphysique* (Treatise on Metaphysics). The title of this 1734 book is misleading: it is primarily about moral philosophy. According to Wade,

> ...we are now in a position to see more clearly the relationship of Voltaire and Mme du Châtelet in the confection of the *Traité de métaphysique*... Mme du Châtelet suggested the writing of the treatise. But it now appears that she also presented problems for consideration and debated them with Voltaire. Moreover, Voltaire gave her the finished sections for comment and in one case at least she added a comment. ...On the other hand... she talked over with him her translation of Mandeville and handed to him her finished sections for comment. This explains how so much of Mandeville and so much more of Mme du Châtelet's additions to Mandeville entered into the composition of Chapters VIII and IX of the *Traité*.[26]

Some commentators have speculated that the concept of literary ownership of ideas was not strictly applied by Voltaire and du Châtelet to the matter of their publications. One gets the impression of an environment at Cirey in which insights and counterarguments were freely exchanged in verbal and sometimes written form, only to appear in whichever author's work in progress had occasioned the discussion.

IV. METAPHYSICS

Gabrielle Émilie du Châtelet achieved renown for her work in philosophy of science and metaphysics. The works in this group are each properly considered to include both metaphysics and philosophy of science. In what follows I shall (1) briefly describe her writings in this hybrid area; (2) outline the chronology of the development of Émilie du Châtelet's metaphysics; (3) briefly describe the nature of the metaphysical issues which, in du Châtelet's view, were left unresolved by Newtonian physics; (4) briefly describe the nature of the solutions to these problems offered by du Châtelet; and (5) summarize the reaction to du Châtelet's metaphysical writings.

1. *Writings on Metaphysics and Philosophy of Science*

Émilie du Châtelet's fame as a philosopher began with her collaboration on Voltaire's *Éléments de la philosophie de Neuton*. Her synopsis of *Éléments ...* was published in *Journal des Sçavans*.[27] Other works on metaphysics and philosophy of science by the Marquise du Châtelet include the mostly lost *L'Essai sur l'optique*[28] (Essay on Optics), the *Dissertation sur la nature et la propagation du feu*[29] (Dissertation on the nature and propagation of fire), the *Institutions de Physique*[30] (Institutions of Physics), the *Principes Mathématiques de la Philosophie Naturelle*[31] (a translation commentary on Newton's *Principia*), and a response to a critic,[32] "Response of Madame *** to the letter which M. de Mairan, Perpetual Secretary of the Royal Academy of Science, wrote her on February 18 on the question of *forces vives*."[33]

Émilie du Châtelet's posthumously published commentary/French translation of Newton's *Principia Mathematica* made that work widely available to French audiences for the first time. However, to

call her work a translation obscures the fact that she added considerable commentary and analyses of her own. Margaret Alic
explains:

> Châtelet's two-volume translation of Newton's *Principia* was the
> culmination of her life's work. It included her commentaries, the
> first part of which was purely mathematical and the second, a 6-
> chapter revision of, and vast improvement over the *Éléments*. Her
> work remains the only French translation of Newton. With its
> publication, Newtonian scientific method became an integral part of
> French Enlightenment philosophy of science for the first time.[34]

It is uncertain exactly when Émilie du Châtelet began her work on the
translation of Newton's *Principia*. However, it is clear from her letters
during the last year of her life that she considered her edition of the
Principia to be her most important work. She remained firmly
convinced that Newtonian physics presented an accurate account of
how the universe worked. Her prior work, *Institutions de Physique*,
had been developed to set the stage, as it were, for *Principia*. *Institutions* provided the metaphysical account of *why* the universe is as
Principia explains it to be. Her translation is perfectly truthful to
Newton; her explanations and analyses are intended to demonstrate
the probative force of his theories. Her corrections and addenda are
clearly labelled as such. It is clear to the reader where Newton leaves
off and du Châtelet begins.

2. *The Development of du Châtelet's Views on Metaphysics*

Frederick of Prussia was a man whom Voltaire was flattered to be
courted by, and whom du Châtelet loathed and mistrusted. According
to Iltis[35] Mme du Châtelet's introduction to Leibniz came during the
period 1736–1737. This was when Frederick sent to Cirey the first
French translation of Wolff's Leibnizian metaphysics, *Vernunsstige
Gedancken von Gott, der Weld und der Seele des Menschen, aus allen
Dingen überhaupt*.[36] Du Châtelet apparently read it in March of 1737.
Du Châtelet also read Mairan's anti-Leibnizian *Dissertation*[37] and the
Leibniz-Clarke correspondence in the Desmaizeaux anthology.[38]

In December 1737 Émilie du Châtelet wrote to Maupertuis about
force vive. At about this time she also read Leibniz's *Acta Eruditorum*

article of March 1686, the "Brevis demonstratio,"[39] on *vis viva*, and Johann Bernoulli's *Discours sur les lois de la communication du mouvement*[40] (Discourse on the laws of communication of motion). Bernoulli's *Discours* had won the *Académie Royale des Sciences* 1730 essay contest. In that essay he demonstrated the consistency between Kepler's third law of motion (on planetary revolution) and Descartes' theory of vortices. These readings set off a chain of events which convinced du Châtelet that Newtonian science needed, as a philosophical underpinning, Leibnizian metaphysics. In February 1738 du Châtelet wrote to Maupertuis concerning Bernoulli's *Discourse*.[41] Maupertuis' response favored Bernoulli over Mairan's criticism of Leibniz.[42] That is to say, Maupertuis favored Descartes and Leibniz over Mairan's defense of Newton and Locke.

In April 1738 Émilie du Châtelet asked Maupertuis whether he concurred that Newton's law of conservation precluded the possibility of free will and whether Leibniz avoided that problem.[43] A week later, she indicated that she was intrigued with the possibility that philosophy and science could demonstrate the synthetic *a priori* character of physics.[44] Her suspicion grew that there was a possibility of firmly grounding the impressive Newtonian physics in Leibnizian metaphysics in a way which would not require (as she argued Newtonianism seemed to) an abandonment of some basic theological positions concerning divine and human nature.

Unknown to Voltaire and to Maupertuis, at this time Mme du Châtelet was preparing for submission to the censor Pitot her incomplete manuscript of the *Institutions de Physique*. Janik[45] suggests that du Châtelet needed to obtain an objective review of *Institutions* prior to revising it. However, du Châtelet's identity would become known and once that happened, refereeing would follow political lines. Voltaire's enemies would dismiss the work while supporters would be uncritically favorable. In order to secure an objective review, the manuscript was submitted anonymously through her friend Mme Champbonin in September 1738. By November it had passed censorship and was ready for printing.[46] However, the first version of *Institutions* did not explore the theological problems which du Châtelet was just then coming to realize were posed by an acceptance of Newtonianism.

The arrival of Maupertuis in January of 1739 began a period in which du Châtelet clarified her understanding of Leibniz' philosophy and its relevance to Newtonian physics. Mme du Châtelet immediately began revising the already-submitted manuscript of *Institutions de Physique*. By February 1739, she had sent some proof corrections to the printer Prault. That same month, at Maupertuis' insistence, she hired Wolff's disciple Koenig to tutor her in mathematics. Koenig arrived on April 27. According to Janik,

> Between May and August of 1739, Koenig – unwittingly, as he was unaware until September of the forthcoming book – induced mme Du Châtelet to carry out a massive rewriting of the earlier chapters of the *Institutions*, in order to bring her so far rather eclectic metaphysical views directly into line with some of the major doctrines of Wolff and Leibniz. Printing began again in September – which meant, incidentally, that mme Du Châtelet had had approximately four months, during the crucial and extremely busy period of the family lawsuit in Brussels, to rewrite entirely about a quarter of her text and substantially revise the mathematical and other details in the remaining chapters – with, unavoidably, Koenig at last admitted to the secret of the forthcoming publication.[47]

3. *Free Will: Problems for Newtonian Science*

During the 1720s and 1730s some members of the *Académie des Sciences* began to abandon Cartesian metaphysics in favor of Newtonian physics. In general, Émilie du Châtelet was convinced by Newtonian physics. However, she felt that until the question "why these laws of physics and not some others?" could be answered, scientists could not know with confidence that the laws of physics with which the world *appeared* to be in accord would remain those with which it was in accord. Newton (and Voltaire) had a quick answer to the question "why these laws and not some others?" They cited God's omnipotence as the source of the truth of the laws of physics. But, du Châtelet wondered, did God create the universe as an expression of his omnipotent will, or as an expression of his omniscient reason? Iltis notes:

> For Newton and Clarke the world could have been otherwise, for it depended on the free exercise of God's will.[48]

If that were the case, du Châtelet realized, Newtonian physics had no predictive power. God could change his mind.

Cartesian metaphysics and mechanics had dominated the *Académie Royale des Sciences*, although some members were willing to abandon speculative metaphysics in favor of the impressive experimental Newtonian physics. Descartes had held the position that a valid mechanical explanation of motion must involve the contact of forces in motion with forces at rest. Newtonian science left unidentified the causes of "forces at a distance" (e.g., gravitational and magnetic attraction). Thus Newtonian "forces at a distance" failed to satisfy an important basic requirement of Cartesian mechanics. Du Châtelet's September 1738 article "Lettre sur les elements de la philosophie de Newton" in *Journal des Sçavans* had explained and defended Newton's theory of attraction. Du Châtelet had been a pure Newtonian, at least at first, but with Koenig's arrival she became convinced that Leibnizian metaphysics provided a philosophical foundation for Newtonian physics. Or perhaps of greater importance, she saw Leibnizian metaphysics as a way of preserving essential theological judgments including the concept of human free agency, and the concept of an omniscient, omnipotent deity.

According to Newton the universe was a giant perfect machine created by God. Everything in the universe was fixed and merely in one state of motion or rest. Newton's position was that God maintains as constant the amount of movement in the universe. This created two metaphysical problems: first, if the machine is perfect, why isn't it self-correcting? Second, there is the ancient problem of apparent retrograde planetary motion and of otherwise unexplained erratic motions of "heavenly bodies." It would be easy to remedy the second problem by faulting the quality of the observers' reports; but this remedy would appear to cast doubt on the rigor of Newtonian empirical science. For a Newtonian, the first problem is even more intractable. On Leibniz' interpretation, the claim that God must continually act to maintain the constant motion in the universe represents God as an inefficient creator who must regularly intervene in planetary motion, necessitating, as it were, perpetual miracles.[49] This interpretation of Newton was bolstered by remarks made by Clarke (in his lectures) that gravity was caused by the continually exerted force of a superior immaterial being. In Leibniz' view this meant that gravity was either some occult force or was a perpetual miracle.

In the revision of *Institutions* du Châtelet reasoned that all motion, all action in a Newtonian universe would be predetermined reaction; and human initiative would be impossible. No individual would be capable of causing action. This meant that the concept of free will would become meaningless, precluding the possibility of virtue as well as sin. As Mandeville previously noted, the absence of vice posed grave consequences for recent and emerging philosophical justifications for the existence of political society. More importantly, perhaps, it made moot Reformation and Counter-Reformation theories of salvation and moral responsibility. These were the consequences of Newtonianism which Mme du Châtelet knew European society could not readily accept.

4. Solving the Problems of Newtonianism

Émilie du Châtelet was a scientist as well as a philosopher. She was convinced that Newtonian physics provided a sound, statistically valid scientific account of the universe. She recognized the distinction between prediction that is grounded in statistical probability and prediction that is grounded in metaphysical necessity. The former was always susceptible to disconfirming data. The latter was not. While writing the first version of the *Institutions*, Émilie du Châtelet became increasingly convinced that Newtonian physics, although impressive for its fit with empirical data, did not fit philosophical expectations concerning the predictive power of science. Even worse, perhaps, it did not fit with theological judgments about divine nature, nor about human nature. It could not substitute for Cartesian metaphysics and still achieve the desired fit with some of our most basic considered judgments. Once the philosophical and theological consequences of Newtonianism were understood by the intellectual community, they would become untenable. It was important to du Châtelet that, in a manner of speaking, the baby not be thrown out with the bath water. In du Châtelet's view, if Newtonianism were modified or perhaps merely supplemented by Leibnizian metaphysics it would fit with the cherished philosophical and theological views. As a philosopher, she could make it possible for scientists to retain Newtonianism and for theologians to retain the doctrine that an omnipotent, omniscient deity created humans and endowed them with free will. The desire to show the consistency of Newtonian science with Christian theology appears to have provided Mme du Châtelet with the motive for seeking a sounder metaphysical grounding for Newton.

The sounder metaphysical foundation for physics sought by Mme du Châtelet consisted of a Leibnizian ontology, a Leibnizian metaphysics including the doctrine of the identity of indiscernibles, and the principles of non-contradiction and of sufficient reason. Émilie du Châtelet was convinced that Newton had answered the question "how does the universe work?" She set out to answer the question "why is the universe as it is?" Du Châtelet's solution was that Leibniz' principle of non-contradiction explains the logical possibility of the existence of the natural world.[50] A world is a possible world if and only if God understands it.[51] The actual existence of the world is explained by the principle of sufficient reason.[52] That which is possible, i.e. that which is understood by God, becomes that which actually exists if and only if God wills its existence.[53] In du Châtelet's view, Leibniz had argued convincingly that that which God wills must be the best of all possible worlds. In du Châtelet's view when Leibniz' metaphysics was added to Newton's physics, the resulting system did not preclude belief in God's perfection as Creator. Her explanation went beyond the limits of mechanical explanation without requiring an abandonment of Newtonian mechanistic physics.

The development of an ontology was crucial to the development of du Châtelet's view. Émilie du Châtelet offered a Leibnizian account of *vis viva*: the dynamics of bodies in motion. Her account reduced to ridicule arguments offered by Cartesians Mairan and Jurin.[54] Iltis[55] and Schiebinger[56] note that Mme du Châtelet came to the conclusion that Leibniz' concept of *force vives* or vital "monad" together with his principle of sufficient reason would provide the necessary foundation for Newtonian physics. Leibniz' concept of "monad" was of a primitive active force (entelechy) inseparably combined with a primitive passive (material) force: a true substance. In *Institutions...*[57] du Châtelet describes Wolff's adaptation of Leibniz' monadolgy. In it, ontological primitives are non-material, non-extended simple beings. She postulated that Newtonian-style atoms are material, extended aggregates of those simple beings, and visible objects are aggregates of atoms. Janik summarizes du Châtelet's argument:

...if one accepts Newtonian ontology in which everything real is in principle observable, because composed of extended atoms in motion, mechanistically related by discoverable laws, then the laws, once discovered, must so to speak exhaust the explanation-space. In a perfectly literal sense, nothing *remains over* as explanandum or explanans.[58]

Du Châtelet's adaptation of Leibnizian ontology to Newtonian atomism also resolved the problem of the predictive power of physics. According to du Châtelet, Leibniz' principle of sufficient reason explained why merely possible events actually occurred according to Newton's laws of physics rather than remaining merely possible. Possible events become actual events because they are willed by God.

> But in mme Du Châtelet's eyes, the result of accepting Leibniz's and Wolff's claim that the material world is not the only one, nor the most fundamental one, is that the distinction between mechanistic and rational explanation, between cause and sufficient reason, neatly matches that between material and immaterial, phenomenal and real, *être composés* and *êtres simples*. And the conclusion implicit in the structure of the 1740 [revised] text of the *Institutions* is that a re-evaluation of the foundations of scientific knowledge needs to be worked out in the light of this new ontology.[59]

That new ontology identifies the actual world as that which is willed by God because it is the best of all possible worlds. And, du Châtelet reasoned, if it is the best of all possible worlds, God will not change the way it works because it already must reflect his perfection. Conceptually speaking, God cannot change the way this best of all possible worlds works. Since, as du Châtelet assumed, Newtonian physics provides a sound, valid explanation of the way the actual world works, it provides a sound, valid explanation of the way in which the best of all possible worlds will *continue* to work. By adapting Leibnizian metaphysics to Newtonian physics, Émilie du Châtelet was able to establish the predictability of Newtonian science.

If the laws of logic and of physics can themselves be viewed as expressions of God's perfect omniscience, then the principle of non-contradiction would explain the logical possibility of free will, just as the principle of sufficient reason would explain the actual existence of beings with free will. The existence of humans who are endowed with free will is possible because it is a product of God's understanding.

Our actual existence is a consequence of God's willing our existence. What God wills is the best of all possible worlds, therefore human free will is describable as the freedom to will to act within the constraints of human possibilities as those possibilities have been determined by God. Du Châtelet's applications of Leibnizian metaphysics to Newtonian physics imply that a better fit is possible between Newtonian mechanistic accounts of the universe and our considered judgments about divine and human natures. No longer are humans reduced to being a cog in the machine. Human initiative is possible, human action is not necessarily reduced to mere mechanical reaction. Free will is restored to the canon and, along with it, virtue, vice, and the warrant for the establishment of political society.

5. *Reaction to du Châtelet's Metaphysics*

Émilie du Châtelet did not want to discard Newtonian physics, rather she considered it circumscribed: limited to explanations of empirical physical phenomena.[60] The revised *Institutions de Physique* went beyond synthesizing the philosophies of Newton and Leibniz. It directly addressed theological questions raised by the new science as well as questions of scientific method and of the limitations of experimental science. Nevertheless, du Châtelet's three-volume *Institutions de Physique* was considered treasonous amongst Newton's disciples. Voltaire apparently did not recognize the need for a metaphysical foundation for physics, believing instead that Newton's experiments were so conclusive that speculative metaphysics was an amusing waste of time. Voltaire publicly granted that du Châtelet's analysis and explanation of Leibniz showed greater clarity, precision, and relevance to Newtonian physics than did Leibniz' correspondence with Clarke. Following the publication of the *Institutions* members of the *Académie* began corresponding with du Châtelet on her adaptation of Leibniz' theories to Newton's physics. The dispute solidified du Châtelet's reputation as a metaphysician; her reputation as an experimental physicist had become widely recognized with the publication of Voltaire's *Éléments*. Her writings in metaphysics and philosophy of science apparently became widely known rather quickly. In 1747, the *Gedanken von der wahren Schatzung der lebendigen Kräfte* (Thoughts on the True Estimation of Living Forces) by the previously unpublished Immanuel Kant acknowledged the merits of du Châtelet's criticism of Newton and her polite rejoinder to Mairan. However, Kant ridiculed her failure to treat the "great" Mairan with sufficient deference.[61]

V. PHILOSOPHY OF SCIENCE

As part of her refurbishing of the estate at Cirey, Émilie du Châtelet had converted the huge main hall into a physics and chemistry laboratory where she performed experiments on heat, light, elasticity, and magnetism. Newtonian explanation of these and other phenomena was founded on what was considered by the scientific and philosophic community to be a very high quality empirical science. In experimental science, du Châtelet's interests ranged from empirical studies of fire, light, and color to mechanical properties of physical objects including magnetism, elasticity, and resistance. This interest in experimentation had been sparked by a desire to evaluate Newtonian physics by replicating some of his results in preparation for translating the *Principia*. This desire, in turn, had led her to examine critically questions of scientific method. In what follows I shall (1) describe du Châtelet's writings on the nature of fire, light, and color and (2) describe her views on scientific method.

1. *Fire, Light and Color*

A subject of intense scientific interest in the early eighteenth century was the question whether heat was a material substance or was a form of energy. Scientific inquiry into the nature of heat (and light and color as entities associated with heat) greatly interested du Châtelet. In 1737 the *Académie des Sciences* sponsored a physics essay contest. Voltaire spent months discussing with Mme du Châtelet the development of an essay in which he claimed that light and fire were separate material entities which exerted pressure, divided, and propagated. Voltaire and du Châtelet jointly conducted experiments, but their results did not support Voltaire's thesis.

At the last minute Émilie du Châtelet decided to secretly perform her own experiments and to submit her own entry. In "Dissertation sur la nature et la propagation du feu"[62] (Dissertation on the nature and propagation of fire) she claimed that light and heat were a singular entity. This entity emitted (and was perceived as) light to the extent that its particles moved in a straight line. It emitted (and was perceived as) heat to the degree that the particles moved irregularly. Different colored rays emitted different degrees of heat, she claimed.[63] Although this last conclusion was later experimentally validated, du Châtelet failed to recognize that the movement was vibration, with light and heat caused by vibrations at different speeds.[64] Boyle was believed to have shown that fire was extended, particulate matter (having mass and weight). When metals are calcinated, it was thought that the penetration of fire into the metal increased the weight of the metal. Mme du Châtelet repeated Boyle's experiments with metals of varying weights. Du Châtelet's essay demonstrated that fire was not composed of heavy particles which entered into metal during the calcination process; rather, calcination entailed a fixation of one or more of the elements of which air was composed. Lavoisier (1743–1794) would later identify oxygen as the material which chemically combined with metal during calcination to increase the weight of the metal. Although neither Voltaire nor du Châtelet won the academy's prize, both essays were published by the academy together with the prizewinning essay. After submitting this essay du Châtelet began her intense consultations with Maupertuis and Koenig and began to see the relevance of Leibniz' philosophy to physics. She pleaded with the *Académie* to permit her to make changes to her *Essai sur... feu*. The *Académie* reluctantly agreed to permit her to append two pages of *errata*, but refused to permit du Châtelet to make the major revisions she wanted.

Another essay-length work by du Châtelet is the surviving fourth chapter of the otherwise lost *L'Essay sur L'Optique* (Essay on Optics). That chapter, "De la Formation des Couleurs par Mme du Châtelet" (On the Formation of Colors by Madame du Châtelet) appears to be a straightforward rendering of Newton's views on color formation from the *Optics*. The chapter is reproduced in full by Wade in *Studies on Voltaire With Some Unpublished Papers of Mme du Châtelet*.[65]

2. Scientific Method

Émilie du Châtelet understood that much of the disagreement between the Newtonians and the Cartesians centered on an as-yet unclear account of scientific method. The debate was not merely over whether experimental physics or theoretical metaphysics provided a more accurate account of how the universe functioned. Some issues could be settled if physicists employed sound methods of scientific research. Du Châtelet recognized that some of the disputes over, for example, gravity and planetary revolution were as much methodological as metaphysical. Voltaire sided with Clarke in the debates against Leibniz and with Locke against the metaphysics of Descartes. Descartes had explained planetary movement around the sun in terms of vortices, an explanation adopted by Leibniz. Newton on the other hand, explained planetary revolution phenomenologically: we observe the phenomenal effect; a force must cause this effect; the name of the force is gravity. There had been insufficient data for Newton publicly to hypothesize the cause of gravity, so he framed no hypotheses.[66] According to Newton, the empirical evidence provided sufficient proof of gravity as an explanation for planetary revolution in the solar system. Only God could have created such a perfect system; "blind metaphysical necessity...could produce no variety of things."[67] Newton's convincing account of gravity and planetary revolution may have prompted Voltaire to dismiss the need for metaphysics as a foundation for science. As early as 1737 Voltaire claimed:

> To my mind, all of metaphysics contains two things, the first, that which all sensible men know, the second, that which they can never know.[68]

Émilie du Châtelet disagreed. Metaphysics *was* relevant to science, especially at the level of theory-building. It could not be understood at the level of common sense; it could be understood only through careful philosophical analysis. In her introduction to *Institutions* she pointedly paraphrased:

> Metaphysics contains two types of things: the first, that which all who put their minds to good use would be able to know; and the second, and greater, that which they will never know.[69]

As early as the original draft of *Institutions* du Châtelet had argued against Newtonian tendencies to dismiss the use of metaphysical hypotheses in scientific methodology, particularly at the most abstract level, that of theory-building. Newtonians favored instead theory construction by statistical generalization from repeated controlled observations of empirical data. But, du Châtelet reasoned, empirical hypotheses could be demonstrated only to be contingently true. Disconfirming data could appear at any time. After studying Leibniz, du Châtelet became convinced that the principle of sufficient reason had a central role in philosophy of science. In the revised (published) version of *Institutions*, the principle of sufficient reason provides a basis for distinguishing between actualized and non-actualized metaphysical hypotheses. This meant that true scientific hypotheses (i.e., sound or actualized valid metaphysical hypotheses) could be proven to be more than contingently true.[70]

Newton's famous statement *"hypotheses non fingo"* (I frame no hypotheses) had seemingly set the criteria for hypothesis formulation in science. Unable empirically to confirm the cause of gravity, Newton insisted that no hypothesis as to its cause be advanced.[71] Du Châtelet criticized Newton's dictum. In her view, the principle of sufficient reason had proved to be quite serviceable in demonstrating the consistency between Newtonian physics on the one hand and philosophical and theological judgments about human and divine nature on the other. It was therefore essential that a scientific account of the physical universe be constructed in terms of the principle of sufficient reason. In du Châtelet's view, it is inevitable that we formulate some suppositions as part of the accounting process. When we develop a mechanistic and rational explanation of phenomena, she said, we are, in fact, introducing hypotheses. When we conclude that the causes of phenomena are not directly observable, *de facto* hypotheses are being formulated; among them, the negative hypothesis that the observable data are not among the causes. There may be errors in our observation, or faults in our analysis of the data.[72]

Du Châtelet urged the acceptance of guidelines for hypothesis-formulation to assist scientists in distinguishing good from bad hypotheses. Among the things she proposed was that scientists more thoroughly gather and document data; that they be willing to revise hypotheses in light of disconfirming data; and that scientists be willing to consider whether apparent wholesale falsification of a hypothesis by the data requires refutation of the entire hypothesis, or only parts of it. The fact that some hypotheses have been "fantastic," she says, is not sufficient cause for claiming (as Baconian ideology seemed to) that "pure" scientific observation is always possible and can replace metaphysical hypotheses. We must develop an understanding of the limits of scientific hypothesis construction. She says:

> ...in distinguishing between good and bad use of hypotheses, one must avoid both extremes, and without embracing fictions, one need not strip the sciences of a method [e.g. metaphysics] which is essential to the art of inventing and which is the only one that can be used in difficult research which needs many centuries to correct, and the work of many men before reaching a certain [state of] perfection.[73]

Our ability to recognize particular metaphysical hypotheses as false does not prove that no metaphysical hypotheses are true. Rather, it proves that without being able to articulate it, we have acquired the metaphysical knowledge and have developed the scientific methodology to distinguish false from true. On du Châtelet's account, this understanding of the role of metaphysics in scientific theory-formation provides the foundation for scientific progress.

The kinds of distinctions which philosophers of the twentieth century are comfortable making between metaphysics, philosophy of science, scientific theory, and scientific experimentations were less comfortably made three centuries ago. Hence, the distinction which I have made between Émilie du Châtelet's metaphysics and philosophy of science, and between Newtonian physics and accounts of scientific experimentation, are at best contrived and artificial. Nevertheless, such distinctions help to illustrate to the contemporary reader the breadth and depth of du Châtelet's insights. In point of fact, du Châtelet and her contemporaries considered these subjects to be inseparable from each other as well as from larger theological and moral issues.

VI. CONCLUSIONS

Émilie du Châtelet enjoyed all of the prerogatives of an aristocratic woman of the eighteenth century, including that of living openly with her lover, Voltaire, so long as she fulfilled her social obligations as wife of the Marquis du Châtelet-Lomont. This privileged status enabled her to overcome what may otherwise have been insurmountable obstacles to obtaining an advanced education. She hired professors from the Sorbonne to teach her physics and mathematics. She spent a fortune on books and scientific equipment and converted her husband's abandoned, run-down estate into an intellectual sanctuary for herself and Voltaire. Her rank and wealth gave her access to some of the most gifted *philosophes* on the European continent. Her intellect and her talent for philosophy and science gained her the admiration and respect of leaders in both fields.

In du Châtelet's view, the failure of science to inquire *why* was a serious philosophical shortcoming. Du Châtelet's major project was to provide a philosophical foundation for modern physics, to explain *why* the universe must operate according to Newtonian laws of physics. She did that in part by seeking a purely rational explanation of the truths of Newtonian physics. This led to her adaptation of Wolff's Leibnizianism and her application of Leibnizian metaphysics to Newtonian physics. In the process, she found that Newtonian science was needlessly mistaken in its wholesale rejection of Cartesian metaphysics. Elements of modified Cartesian and fairly intact Leibnizian metaphysics could put physics on firm philosophical footings. It could do this without requiring the abandonment of a conception of human nature as endowed with free will and with it, all the advances of Enlightenment theology and moral, social, and political philosophy. As Janik notes, du Châtelet's aim in the *Institutions* was "to demonstrate the complementarity of what to others appeared to be diametrically opposed systems and modes of thought."[74]

As a philosopher and physicist Émilie du Châtelet had the respect of leading thinkers in both fields. She immediately preceded the age of the great French Newtonian-influenced mathematician-scientists Laplace, Fourier, and Lavoisier. Kant's familiarity with her works indicates that her influence quickly extended beyond France. In the twentieth century, Einstein's discoveries rekindled philosophical and scientific interest in Newtonian physics. Yet, for two and a half centuries, Émilie du Châtelet remains the sole French translator of Newton's *Mathematical Principles of Natural Philosophy*. This simple fact indicates the depth and clarity of her analysis of Newtonian physics. Her work to provide a metaphysical foundation for the new physics had crucial implications for the survival of Enlightenment moral, religious, social, and political institutions. She recognized that the survival of theological doctrines of free will and of divine omnipotence and omniscience was largely dependent upon the resolution of related issues in metaphysics and physics. In strikingly different ways, her translation of Newton's *Principia* and her own works *Institutions de Physique* and *Examen de la Genèse* analyzed these issues. Clearly, the importance for Enlightenment philosophy of the contributions made by Gabrielle-Émilie le Tonnelier de Breteuil du Châtelet-Lomont merit additional consideration by contemporary philosophers.

NOTES

* I wish to thank Professor Louise Salstad (University of North Carolina, Raleigh) and Anne Robertson (New York University) for their assistance with bibliographical research. Professor Douglas Lewis (University of Minnesota) shared with me his insights, expertise, and enthusiasm for Leibnizian metaphysics.

1. Samuel Edwards (pseud. for Noel Bertram Gerson), *The Divine Mistress*. New York: McKay (1970), p. 65.
2. Edwards, *op. cit.*, pp. 62–64.
3. William H. Barber, "Mme du Châtelet and Leibnizianism: the genesis of the 'Institutions de Physique,'" in W.H. Barber, J.H. Brumfitt, H.A. Leigh, R. Shackleton, and S.S.B. Taylor, *The Age of the Enlightenment*. Edinburgh and London: Oliver and Boyd (1967), p. 204.
4. Ira Wade, *Voltaire and Madame du Châtelet*. Princeton: Princeton University Press (1941).
5. Theodore Besterman, *Les Lettres de la Marquise du Châtelet*. 2 Vols. Genève: Institut et musée Voltaire (1958), Vol. II, no. 476. My translation.
6. Besterman, *op. cit.*, Vol. II, no. 477.
7. Émilie du Châtelet, *La Fable des abeilles*.
   In Ira Wade, *Studies On Voltaire With Some Unpublished Papers of Mme du Châtelet*. New York: Russell & Russell (1947), pp. 131–187. Hereafter as Wade, *Papers*.
8. Bernard Mandeville, *The Fable of the Bees: Or Private Vices, Public Benefits*. Sixth edition, London: 1729.
9. Wade, *Papers*, p. 47ff., p. 56ff.
10. Wade, *Voltaire and Madame du Châtelet*, pp. 20–21.
11. Linda Gardiner Janik, "Searching for the metaphysics of science: the structure and composition of madame Du Châtelet's *Institutions de Physique*, 1737–1740." *Studies on Voltaire and the Eighteenth Century*: 201 (1982), pp. 85–113.
12. Émilie du Châtelet, *Réflexions sur le Bonheur*, in *Opuscules philosophiques et littéraires, la plupart posthumes ou inédits*. Paris: Suard et Bourlet de Vauxcelles (1796).

13. Ira O. Wade, *Voltaire and Madame du Châtelet*, p. 48ff.
14. Besterman, *op. cit.*, Vol. 1, p. 21.
15. Benedict (Baruch) Spinoza, *Tractatus Theologico-Politicus*. Amsterdam: 1670.
16. Ira O. Wade, *Voltaire and Madame du Châtelet*, p. 106.
17. William H. Barber, "Mme du Châtelet and Leibnizianism: the genesis of the 'Institutions de Physique,'" in Barber, *op. cit.*, p. 204.
18. Émilie du Châtelet, *La Grammaire Raisonnée*, in Wade, *Papers, op. cit.*
19. Wade, *Papers*, p. 125.
20. Émilie du Châtelet, *La Grammaire Raisonnée*, in Wade, *Papers, op. cit.*, p. 209. Translation mine.
21. Voltaire, *Éléments de la philosophie de Neuton*. 1738.
22. Th. Besterman, ed., *Voltaire, Correspondence and related documents*. Genève, Banbury and Oxford: 1968–1977, Documents 764, 911, 978.
23. Wade, *Voltaire and Madame du Châtelet*, p. 7.
24. Besterman, ed., *Voltaire, Correspondence and related documents*, Document 1255 (*circa* January 15, 1737), my translation.
25. Wade, *Papers*, pp. 188–208.
26. Wade, *Voltaire and Madame du Châtelet*, pp. 17–24.
27. [Émilie du Châtelet], "Lettre sur les Éléments de la Philosophie de Newton," *Journal des Sçavans* (September 1738), pp. 534–541.
28. Émilie du Châtelet, *L'Essay sur l'optique*, in Wade, *Papers*, pp. 188–208.
29. Émilie du Châtelet, *Dissertation sur la Nature et la Propagation du Feu*. Paris: Prault, fils (1744).
30. Émilie du Châtelet, *Institutions de Physique*. Paris: Prault, fils (1740).
31. Émilie du Châtelet, *Principes Mathématiques de la Philosophie Naturelle*. Paris: Desaint & Saillant (1759).
32. M.D. de Mairan, *Lettre à Madame *** sur la question des forces vives, ou Response aux objections...dans ses Institutions de physique*. Paris: 1741.
33. [Émilie du Châtelet], *Résponse de Madame *** à la lettre que M. de Mairan, Secrétaire perpétuel de l'Académie Royale des Sciences, lui a écrite le 18 février sur la question des forces vives*. Brussels: 1741.
34. Margaret Alic, *Hypatia's Heritage*. Boston: Beacon (1986), p. 144.
35. Carolyn Iltis [Merchant], "Madame du Châtelet's Metaphysics and Mechanics," *Studies in History and Philosophy of Science*: 8 (1977), p. 30.
36. C.F. von Wolff, *Vernunsstige Gedancken von Gott, der Weld und der Seele des Menschen, aus allen Dingen überhaupt* (1720). U. v. Suhm, translator. 1736.
37. M.D. de Mairan, *Dissertation sur l'estimation et la mesure des forces motrices du corps. Mémoires de l'Académie des Sciences (1728)*, 1730.
38. Pierre Desmaizeaux. *Receuil de diverses pièces sur la philosophie*. 2 vols. Amsterdam: 1720.
39. Iltis, *op. cit.*, p. 30, n. 7.
40. Johann Bernoulli, *Discours sur les lois de la communication du mouvement*. Paris: 1727.
41. T. Besterman, ed., *Les Lettres de la Marquise du Châtelet* Vol. I. Genève: Institut et musée Voltaire (1958), Letter 118 to Maupertuis (2 Feb. 1738). Hereafter as Besterman, *Letters*.

42. Iltis, *op. cit.*, p. 30.
43. Besterman, ed., *Letters*, No. 122, 30 April 1738.
44. Janik, *op. cit.*, p. 102.
45. Janik, *op. cit.*, p. 95.
46. Besterman, ed., *Letters*, No. 241 to Bernoulli (June 1740).
47. Janik, *op. cit.*, p. 97.
48. Iltis, *op. cit.*, p. 32.
49. G.W. Leibniz, "Mr. Leibniz's Second Paper Being an Answer to Dr. Clarke's First Reply," in S. Clarke, *The Leibniz-Clarke Correspondence*, H.G. Alexander, ed., Manchester: Manchester University Press (1956).
50. du Châtelet, *Institutions*, Section 8.
51. du Châtelet, *Institutions*, Section 49.
52. du Châtelet, *Institutions*, Section 34.
53. du Châtelet, *Institutions*, Section 48.
54. For a detailed analysis, including reproduction of du Châtelet's diagrams, see Iltis, *op. cit.*, p. 39ff.
55. Iltis, *op. cit.*, pp. 29–48.
56. Londa Schiebinger, *The Mind Has No Sex? Women in the Origins of Modern Science*. Cambridge, MA and London: 1989, pp. 59–64.
57. du Châtelet, *Institutions*, Sections 102ff.
58. Janik, *op. cit.*, p. 106.
59. Janik, *op. cit.*, p. 107. Bracketed material supplied.
60. Margaret Alic, *Hypatia's Heritage*. Boston: Beacon (1986), p. 144.
61. Immanuel Kant, *Gedanken von der wahren Schatzung der lebendigen Kräfte*, in *Immanuel Kants Werke* Vol. 1. Ernst Cassirer, ed. Berlin: 1922, pp. 1–187.
62. Émilie du Châtelet, *Dissertation sur la nature et la propagation du feu*. Paris: Prault fils (1744).
63. Theodore Besterman, ed., *Voltaire, Correspondence and Related Documents*. Genève: 1968–1977, D1528, 21 June 1738.
64. Edwards, *op. cit.*, p. 264.
65. Émilie du Châtelet, *L'Essay sur l'optique*, in Wade, *Papers*, pp. 188–208.
66. This is the famous "*Hypotheses non fingo.*" Isaac Newton, *Principles of Mathematical Philosophy*. 2nd ed. (General Scholium). London: 1713.
67. Isaac Newton, *Principles of Mathematical Philosophy*, 3rd ed. (General Scholium). London: 1726.
68. Theodore Besterman, ed., *Voltaire, Correspondence and Related Documents*. Genève: 1968–1977, Doc. 1320, translation mine.
69. du Châtelet, *Institutions*, p. 14, translation mine.
70. du Châtelet, *Institutions*, sections 61–62.
71. Isaac Newton, *Principles of Mathematical Philosophy*, 2nd ed. (General Scholium), London: 1713.
72. du Châtelet, *Institutions, op. cit.*, p. 88.
73. du Châtelet, *Institutions*, p. 88. Translation mine, bracketed material supplied.
74. Janik, *op. cit.*, p. 109.

9. Mary Wollstonecraft

KATE LINDEMANN

While it is understandable that not everyone is familiar with Mary Wollstonecraft's novels or book reviews, it is astonishing that some omit her philosophical works from courses in eighteenth-century thought, social philosophy, philosophical psychology or philosophy of education. She offers clear, well-argued theories concerning human nature, the nature of society and the right forms of education, and these theories are significantly different from those of Rousseau and other eighteenth-century philosophers. To omit her work is to omit both a strong proponent of women's equality and a major thinker in the "British radical tradition."

I. BIOGRAPHY

Mary Wollstonecraft was born April 27, 1759, the second child but eldest daughter in a family fraught with difficulties. Her mother, Elizabeth Dickson Wollstonecraft, bore seven children.[1] She was submissive to her husband but overdemanding of these children.[2] Edward John Wollstonecraft never developed enough discipline to "settle down or persevere in the face of difficulties."[3] After receiving his inheritance he quit his job in his father's weaving business and led the family down the social scale through a series of failed farming ventures. He drank a great deal and became increasing violent and brutal at home.[4]

The children developed specific family roles. Mary became "helper and protector" not only for her brothers and sisters but for her mother also.[5]

Mary Ellen Waithe (ed.), A History of Women Philosophers / Volume 3, 153–170.
© 1991 *Kluwer Academic Publishers. Printed in the Netherlands.*

She would often throw herself between the despot and his victim, with the purpose to receive upon her own person the blows that might be directed against her mother. She had even laid [sic] whole nights upon the landing-place near their chamber-door, when, mistakenly, or with reason, she apprehended that her father might break out into paroxysms of violence.[6]

In 1770 the family moved to Beverly and Mary met Jane Arden, whose friendship provided "another family" full of warmth as well as the intellectual influence of Jane's father, John Arden, a teacher and philosopher. In 1774 the family moved to Huxton, and Mary again sought mentors outside her home.[7] The Clares, a retired couple, introduced her to Fanny Blood who became:

...a friend, whom I love better than all the world beside, a friend to whom I am bound by every tie of gratitude and inclination: to live with this friend is the height of my ambition, as her conversation is not more agreeable than improving. I could dwell forever on her praises, and you wo(uld) not wonder at it, if you knew the many favors she has conferred on me, and the many valuable qualifications she possesses; she has a masculine understanding, and sound judgement, yet she has every feminine virtue... .[8]

As she matured Wollstonecraft decided to make her own way in the world and progressed through a series of positions as companion, governess and founder of a day school. At the same time she continued to "rescue" brothers and sisters, nursed her dying mother and suffered the loss of her closest friend, Fanny Blood, in childbirth.[9] In 1785 she took the suggestion of John Hewett and began to write. She composed *Thought on the Education of Daughters: with Reflections on Female Conduct, in the More Important Duties of Life*. In April of 1786 Hewett's publisher, Joseph Johnson, accepted the work with payment of ten guineas.[10] Within a year she joined Johnson's publishing house as a writer and reviewer. In Joseph Johnson she found a caring 'father figure' who offered sound and careful criticism of her writing. Wollstonecraft blossomed and soon produced a sizable corpus of translations and original works.[11]

She proceeded through a series of attachments and love affairs. These are not detailed here since they did not provide the material for her writing to the same degree as her earlier experiences. Of her last attachment and eventual marriage to William Godwin, something should be said because it did provide a new tone to her work and because Godwin compiled the four-volume *Posthumous Works of the Author of a Vindication of the Rights of Woman* and composed his *Memoirs of the Author of a Vindication of the Rights of Woman*, which has been such a remarkable source for biographers.[12]

> Godwin understood much of what drove Mary. He not only loved her, he marveled at her mind, her taste, the assurance that welled up out of the currents of her conflicts, and he recognized she had reached a compelling amalgamation of heart and head he could neither match nor resist. Mary's capacity for tenderness, previously more spoken of than sustained, increased with Godwin, as did her humor, for she could make fun of her own egotism and Godwin's pedantry.[13]

They married but did "not entirely cohabit."[14] They took nearby lodgings. Godwin went to his apartment "every morning and remained sometimes for meals...often returning...for dinner. Mary's study was her own, as were her ideas."[15]

In 1797 while she was pregnant with their second child she worked on a book of reading lessons. She planned another on pregnancy and the care of infants but never wrote it. Mary Wollstonecraft died of pueperal fever ten days after giving birth.[16]

During her lifetime Wollstonecraft's ideas and actions aroused so much ire that at one point her siblings thought to "escape to America" to avoid notoriety.[17] She often acted boldly, even risking imprisonment as when she rescued her seriously depressed sister from a damaging domestic situation.[18] Yet she acted out of reasoned argument and a sense of justice for all. Her essays have outlasted those of her critics.

II. WORKS

After Joseph Johnson bought her *Thoughts on the Education of Daughters* and her autobiographical novel *Mary*, he suggested that she try translations, children's books and the newly developed market for literate, wealthy women. The works flowed:

- 1787: *Original Stories from Real Life; with Conversations, Calculated to Regulate the Affections, and Form the Mind to Truth and Goodness.*
- 1788: First book reviews for Johnson and Christie's new publication, *The Analytical Review.* This was a task she continued for many years.
- 1789: Translation of *De L'Importance des Opinions Religieuses* by Necker. Soon after she translated *Young Grandison* from the French and compiled *Female Reader*, a collection of poetry and prose to which she also contributed.
- 1790: Translation of *Elements of Morality* by Salzmann.
- *A Vindication of the Rights of Men* in answer to Burke's *Reflections on the Revolution.*
- 1792: *A Vindication of the Rights of Woman.*
- 1794: *Historical and Moral View of the Origin and Progress of the French Revolution.*
- 1797: "On Poetry, and Our Relish of the Beauties of Nature." Her first article in another journal, *Monthly Magazine.*[19]

In addition, she composed two unpublished works of fiction, the *Cave of Fancy* and *Maria, or the Wrongs of Women.*[20]

III. PHILOSOPHY

All Wollstonecraft's writings are marked by spirited prose and careful observation. Several employ strong criticism and rigorous logic. What is most remarkable about these works, however, is that their author was without significant formal schooling. Oxford and Cambridge were first-rate universities but, like all institutions of higher education, they were closed to women. Indeed Wollstonecraft lacked more than a few months of day school. What she knew came from reading, from conversation with every person of first-rate mind she met and by careful attention to sound criticism of her own work. Her philosophical essays are especially representative of these modalities.

1. *Human Nature*

A theory about the nature of human beings forms the central core of all Wollstonecraft's philosophy. A succinct statement of this theory occurs in the early part of *A Vindication of the Rights of Woman*:

> In what does man's pre-eminence over the brute consist? The answer is as clear as that a half is less than the whole; in Reason.
> What acquirement exalts one being above another? Virtue; we spontaneously reply.
> For what purpose were the passions implanted?
> That man by struggling with them might attain a degree of knowledge denied to the brutes; whispers experience.[21]

Reason is the distinguishing characteristic of humankind and it is common to all human beings. If there are human beings who do not exhibit cultivated reason, this can only be ascribed to neglect or wrongful socialization perpertrated by society and its institutions.[22] Wollstonecraft is convinced that neither sex nor class are relevant to the initial birthright of human beings as reasonable. To believe otherwise would be to believe either that human beings are not made in the image of God or that God is unreasonable.[23]

This view of human beings is contained in the earlier *A Vindication of the Rights of Men*, which was one of many replies to Edmund Burke's *Reflections on the Revolution in France*.

> But I was not with an individual when I contend for the *rights of men* and the liberty of reason. You see I do not condescend to cull my words to avoid the invidious phrase, nor shall I be prevented from giving a manly definition of it, by the flimsy ridicule which a lively fancy has interwoven with the present acceptation of the term. Reverencing the rights of humanity, I shall dare to assert them...[24]

Burke's essay has asserted "that the hereditary principle of succession was sacred and had never been broken, that the alliance between civil government and an established church was necessary for the maintenance of social order, that civil authority and all careers related to it should be restricted to men 'of permanent property.'"[25]

Wollstonecraft attacked each of these assertions and although the essay as a whole is more specific and contains fewer substantial arguments than *A Vindication of the Rights of Woman*, it reveals most of the assertions and many of the exact phrases used in the later work.

In her second *Vindication* Wollstonecraft elaborates on her theme of a universal human nature and examines its application to sexual differences. Wollstonecraft may not use the vocabulary of sex *vs.* gender distinctions but she clearly employs the concept. The only distinction between the sexes is that "it is observable that the female in point of strength is, in general, inferior to the male. This is the law of nature and it does not appear to be suspended or abrogated in favor of woman."[26] All other distinctions are the result of education and socialization. She consistently asserts that if women do not think for themselves, if they are weak-willed and vacillating or if they are preoccupied by externals of clothing and manners, this is solely the result of their training.

In an important passage she notes that such traits are not the result of sexual distinction because males who receive similarly defective socialization exhibit the same traits. This can be seen by anyone who observes military men:

A standing army, for instance, is incompatible with freedom; because subordination and rigour are the very sinews of military discipline; and despotism is necessary to give vigour to enterprises that one will directs.

...Every corps is a chain of despots, who, submitting and tyranniz-ing without exercising their reason, become dead weights of vice and folly on the community. A man of rank or fortune, sure of rising by interest, has nothing to do but to pursue some extravagant freak; whilst the needy gentleman, who is to rise, as the phrase turns, by his merit, becomes a servile parasite or vile pander.

Sailors, the naval gentlemen, come under the same description, only their vices assume a different and a grosser cast. They are more positively indolent, when not discharging the ceremonials of their station; whilst the insignificant fluttering of soldiers may be termed active idleness. More confined to the society of men, the former acquire a fondness for humour and mischievous tricks; whilst the latter, mixing frequently with well-bred women, catch a sentimental cant. – But mind is equally out of the question, whether they indulge the horse-laugh, or polite simper.[27]

2. *Ethics*

Given that both sexes are equal in everything but physical strength; given that human nature is distinguished by reason and that the daily struggle with passion results in truly human knowledge, both men and women ought to strive for the same human virtues.

> ...from every quarter have I heard exclamations against masculine women; but where are they to be found? If by this appellation men mean to inveigh against their ardour in hunting, shooting and gaming, I shall most cordially join in the cry; but it be against the imitation of manly virtues... the attainment of those talents and virtues... which enables the human character, and which raise females in the scale of animal being, when they are comprehensively termed mankind... (I wish) that they may every day grow more and more masculine.[28]

And what are those virtues? They can be summarized: To act reasonably, to use one's own freedom and respect the freedom of others, to do productive work and to parent wisely. To fail in these virtues is to fail one's duty as a human being.

Wollstonecraft critiques both groups and individuals for their failure to meet these human duties. She criticises men as a group and specific thinkers individually for employing "their reason to justify prejudices" and for avoiding "close investigation" of their vices or the partiality of European civilization.[29] She criticizes all rulers who set themselves above and limit the freedom of common citizens.[30] She criticizes the upper classes, ladies and gentlemen, as unproductive parasites and she criticizes parent(s) who fail "to form the heart and enlarge the understanding of his child" or who fail(s) to raise children as independent, productive citizens.[31] In this last case she argues that the duty of adult children to care for their aging parents is abrogated in those cases where parents failed to meet their duties when the children were young.[32]

3. *Social and Political Philosophy*

"That the society is formed in the wisest manner, whose constitution is founded on the nature of man" is the basis of Wollstonecraft's social and political thought.[33] Thus it is not surprising that she favors an egalitarian society and is critical of every institutionalization of privilege.

Elissa S. Guralnick notes that it is a social/political theory that drives much of Wollstonecraft's work:

...the feminism that animates the *Rights of Woman* is merely a special instance of the political radicalism that animates the *Rights of Men*. To ignore this fact is to misconstrue much of the basic character of *A Vindication of the Rights of Woman*. It is to fail, as Wollstonecraft's critics have usually done to understand the propriety of the work's apparent digressions into such tenuously related material as the tyrannical abuse of power by kings on the effect[ive]ness of their courts, or the detrimental effects upon society of the existence of a standing army and navy, or the mistakes of educators who would lead boys too early into an understanding of the vices of the world. And it is to underestimate as well the full extent of the social reform that Wollstonecraft envisions as necessary to ameliorate the condition of women in her society.[34]

The social critique in *A Vindication of the Rights of Woman* is wideranging. Wollstonecraft critiques the monarchy: "... regal power, in a few generations introduces idiotism into the nobel stem..."[35]

It is impossible for any man, when the most favorable circumstances concur, to acquire sufficient knowledge and strength of mind to discharge the duties of a king, entrusted with uncontrolled power; how then must they be violated when his very elevation is an insuperable bar to the attainment of either wisdom or virtue; when all the feelings of a man are stiffled by flattery, and reflection shut out by pleasure.[36]

She criticizes the army. "A standing army, for instance, is incompatible with freedom; because subordination and rigour are the very sinews of military discipline; and despotism is necessary to give vigor to enterprises that one will directs."[37] She criticizes upper classes, ladies and gentlemen as parasitical. Indeed, she criticizes every non-egalitarian social form. "After attacking the sacred majesty of Kings, I shall scarcely excite surprise by adding my firm persuasion that every profession in which great subordination of rank constitutes its power, is highly injurious to morality."[38] A *Vindication of the Rights of Woman* is a work of feminism, but it is also a cogent exposition of radical social philosophy, and as such it belongs in all presentations of the British radical tradition.

4. *Philosophy of Education*

While some thinkers portray Wollstonecraft as only a reformer for women's education, it is apparent that her proposals for educational reform are far wider in scope. Like much of Western educational theory, Wollstonecraft's proposals for reform are grounded in a clear philosophical psychology, ethics and social philosophy. In addition they benefit from Wollstonecraft's experience as founder and teacher of a children's day school and from her first-hand acquaintance with the tasks and daily preoccupations of the varied classes in eighteenth-century England.

Her criticism of both British and European schools is direct and sharp. "I still, however, think schools, as they are now regulated, the hot-beds of vice and folly, and the knowledge of human nature, supposed to be attained there, merely cunning selfishness."[39] She attacks both public and private schools for their subversion of children's inquisitive minds and the corruption of moral character.[40] She critiques dogmatism and the classism endemic to the system.[41]

So far, however, from thinking of the morals of boys, I have heard several masters of schools argue, that they only undertook to teach Latin and Greek; and they had fulfilled their duty, by sending some good scholars to college.

A few good scholars, I grant, may have been formed by *emulation and discipline*; but, to bring forward these clever boys, the health and morals of a number have been sacrificed.... .

It is not for the benefit of society that a few brilliant men should be brought forward at the expence of the multitude.[42]

Wollstonecraft argues for national, co-educational schools.

> ...day schools, for particular ages, should be established by
> government, in which boys and girls might be educated together.
> The school for the younger children, from five to nine years of age,
> ought to be absolutely free and open to all classes.[43]

Teachers should be chosen by a committee and held accountable for
the performance of their duties.[44] Children should "dress alike" and be
subject to the same discipline so as to root out unnatural distinctions
by class.[45]

The school should be surrounded by open property and children be
granted "gymnastic play" after each hour of sedentary occupation.
They should be encouraged in every form of peer inquiry, and nature
should be the occasion for theoretical learnings.[46] Above all, the
curriculum should emphasize thinking and the formation of character
so that graduates will be good citizens.[47]

Wollstonecraft does not eliminate all remnants of class or gender
distinctions, however, since after the age of nine, separate curricula
are proposed. Vocational students should be separated from those
destined for the liberal arts. All vocational students should continue to
share co-education in the morning but separate training in "women's
trades" and "men's trades" in the afternoon.[48] As for those who by
superior ability or family wealth are destined for the liberal arts, they
should study "the dead and living languages, the elements of science,
...history and politics...polite literature" in co-educational settings.[49]
At all levels of education, the formation of values and the reasoned
training of the passions should be of utmost concern so character, and
not merely intellect, can develop.[50]

A Vindication of the Rights of Woman was written in response to
Talleyrand's report on public education in France, so it focuses its
argumentation on co-equal education for women. The topic is
addressed in every chapter. Wollstonecraft utilizes two separate
frameworks. The first stems from her rational psychology: human
beings are rational by nature and the sexes are equal in all things but
physical strength. Thus, both sexes are called to the same perfection
and unless they receive the same education they will not be able to
fulfill their human destiny. The second framework is more pragmatic,
"Contending for the rights of woman... if she be not prepared by

education to become the companion of man, she will stop the progress of knowledge and virtue; for truth must be common to all, or it will be ineficasious with respect to its influence on general practice."[51] In addition she contends that uneducated women are unable to meet the new social requirements of changing economic conditions.

5. *Influences on Wollstonecraft's Philosophy*

While some think of Wollstonecraft as a "lone rebel," her unique contribution of substance and style is better appreciated when she is seen in the context of eighteenth-century thought. It is not possible, in so short an article, to review all the swirling currents of thought on the Continent and in the British Isles. It is important to note, however, the specific influences of the British "dissenting movement" and some women writers.

Wollstonecraft was long acquainted with the leading thinkers of the Dissenting interest. Newington Green, where she established her day school, was an intellectual center of the Dissenters.[52] Joseph Johnson, her employer and publisher, was a Dissenter and "the publisher of Joel Barlow, Thomas Christie, Joseph Priestly, William Blake, Thomas Paine, the young Wordsworth, and such non-political writers as William Cowper."[53] She would have known the resolutions of 1788 which stated:

1) that civil and political authority were derived from the people; 2) that the abuse of power justifies resistance; and 3) that the right of private judgement, liberty of conscience, trial by jury, freedom of the press and of election – ought ever to be held sacred and inviolable![54]

She reviewed Dr. Richard Price's *A Discourse on the Love of Our Country... to the Society Commemorating the Revolution in Great Britain* for *The Analytical* in December of 1789.[55] Thus, when Edmund Burke attacked the dissenting principles through a reply to Price, she was ready to answer Burke's conservative position and *A Vindication of the Rights of Men* was composed in less than a month.[56]

What Wollstonecraft "had seen and what in her own life had troubled and perplexed her had been given focus and more generalized meaning by the philosophical concepts she had learned from Price ..."[57] Further, the Dissenters around Joseph Johnson taught her to "turn experience to polemical use."[58] Her acquaintance with English Dissenters helped shape both the substance and style of her writing.

A second major influence on Wollstonecraft was the work of a small group of women writers who argued for women's rights and education. *A Serious Proposal to the Ladies* by Mary Astell is one such work, but the *Letters on Education* by Catharine Macaulay is even more significant.[59]

Wollstonecraft neither met nor corresponded with Catharine Macaulay, but she much admired Macaulay's work.[60] Not only is Macaulay one of the several women noted with admiration in Chapter V of *A Vindication of the Rights of Woman*, but Wollstonecraft repeats and develops many points from Macaulay's *Letters on Education*.

For example, Macaulay argues for co-education on these grounds:

First, That there is but one rule of right for the conduct of all rational beings; consequently that true virtue in one sex must be equally so in the other, whenever a proper opportunity calls for its exertion; and vice versa, what is vice in one sex, cannot have a different property when found in the other.

Second, That true wisdom, which is never found at variance with rectitude, is as useful to women as to men; because it is necessary to the highest degree of happiness, which can never exist with ignorance.

Lastly, That as on our first entrance into another world, our state of happiness may possibly depend on the degree of perfection we have attained in this, we cannot justly lessen, in one sex or the other, the means by which perfection, that is another word for wisdom, is acquired.[61]

In another letter Macaulay states:

The social duties in the interesting characters of daughter, wife, and mother, will be but ill performed by ignorance and levity, and in the domestic converse of husband and wife... Be no longer niggards, then, O ye parents, in bestowing on your offspring, every blessing which nature and fortune renders them capable of enjoying!

Confine not the education of your daughters to what is regarded as the ornamental parts of it, nor deny the graces to your sons... Let your children be brought up together, let their sports and studies be the same; ... By the uninterrupted intercourse which you will thus establish, both sexes will find, that friendship may be enjoyed between them without passion. The wisdom of your daughters will preserve them from the bane of coquetry... Your sons will look for something more solid in women... They will become the constant benefactors of that part of their family who stand in need of their assistance; and in regard to all matters of domestic concern, the unjust distinction of primogeniture will be deprived of its sting.[62]

Further, Macaulay claims that there is no characteristic difference between the sexes, and she launches a critique of Rousseau, "the most conspicuous" of those who assert sexual differences in character.[63] In *A Vindication of the Rights of Woman* Wollstonecraft acknowledges her indebtedness. She states that she expected Macaulay's "approbation" and the "Coinciding in opinion with Mrs. Macaulay relative to many branches of education, I refer to her valuable work, instead of quoting her sentiments to support my own."[64]

Wollstonecraft's unique contributions can be fully appreciated when the ideas and styles that influenced her are recognized. She utilized ideas about God, human nature and the state gained from Dissenters and her feminism must be seen against the rising critique of society's partiality. Ralph Wardle notes that Mary's genius was to juxtapose the oppression of men (class oppression) and the oppression of women. Thus, she saw their similarity. Yet her insight was more profound, for she recognized that the liberation of women would engender the liberation of all humankind.[65]

6. *Critique of Rousseau*

While Wollstonecraft is but one of a series of feminists who offers a critique of Rousseau, and while there is similarity in word patterns as well as arguments from Macaulay to Wollstonecraft, the latter offers a far more extensive and documented critique than that of *Letters on Education*. From the first chapter of *A Vindication of the Rights of Woman* Wollstonecraft is at pains to point out the errors in Rousseau's philosophy. Her analysis states:

> Impressed by this view of the misery and disorder which pervaded
> society, and fatigued with jostling against artificial fools, Rousseau
> became enamoured of solitude, and, being at the same time an
> optimist, he labours with uncommon eloquence to prove that man
> was naturally a solitary animal.[66]

She continues in like vein, noting that his disgust "with artificial
manners and virtues" coupled with indiscriminate thought, led him to
blame civilization for the vestiges from barbarism.[67]

In Chapter II, after noting Milton's contribution to the prevailing
opinion concerning sexual character, she states her task and method.
She then focuses on Rousseau:

> I now principally allude to Rousseau, for his character of Sophia is,
> undoubtedly, a captivating one, though it appears to me grossly
> unnatural; however it is not the superstructure, but the foundation
> of her character, the principles on which her education was built,
> that I mean to attack; nay, warmly as I admire the genius of that
> able writer, whose opinions I shall often have occasion to cite.[68]

She continues:

> Rousseau declares that a woman should never, for a moment, feel
> herself independent, that she should be governed by fear to exercise
> her natural cunning, and made a coquetish slave in order to render
> her a more alluring object of desire, a sweeter companion to man,
> whenever he chooses to relax himself.
> What nonsense! when will a great man arise with sufficient strength
> of mind to puff away the fumes which pride and sensuality have
> thus spread over the subject! If women are by nature inferior to
> men, their virtues must be the same in quality, if not in degree, or
> virtue is a relative idea; consequently, their conduct should be
> founded on the same principles, and have the same aim.[69]

A more detailed and systematic set of criticism are found in Chapter
V, *Animadversions on some of the Writers Who Have Rendered
Women Objects of Pity, Bordering on Contempt*, where she cites
passage after passage from *Émile* and shows how each is either based
on false assumptions or leads to logical contradiction or detrimental
social practice.

In addition to this paragraph-by-paragraph critique of *Émile*, Wollstonecraft charges Rousseau with inadequate experience on which to base his claims:

> I have probably, had an opportunity of observing more girls in their infancy than J.J. Rousseau – I can recollect my own feelings, and I have looked steadily around me... .[70]

She also speculates that the psychological basis of Rousseau's consistent denigration of women is "to justify to himself the affection which weakness and virtue had made him cherish for that fool Theresa. He could not raise her to the common level of her sex; and therefore he laboured to bring woman down to hers."[71]

IV. CONCLUSIONS

Mary Wollstonecraft conceived her philosophy out of her own experience. She joined the results of her own history and observations of society of her time with ideas gained from conversation and the critical reading necessary to a professional book reviewer. Although she believed in the importance and power of reason, she subjected every idea to the test of everyday experience. Having felt the force of paternal oppression, the might of the established Church, the monarchy and the non-productive upper classes, she writes with a passion and a logic typical of reformers and revolutionaries on both sides of the Atlantic. Some might find her advocacy of motherhood as the norm for women or her statement "that, from the constitution of their bodies, men seem to be designated by Providence to attain a greater degree of virtue"[72] too conservative for contemporary times, but for the eighteenth century she offered a vision of an egalitarian, democratic, productive society. One of her last letters contains her own assessment:

> Those who are bold enough to advance before the age they live in, and to throw off, by the force of their minds, the prejudices which the maturing reason of the world will in time disavow, must learn to brave censure. We ought not to be too anxious respecting the

opinions of others – I am not too fond of vindications. – Those who know me will suppose that I acted from principle. Nay, as we in general give others credit for worth, in proportion as we possess it – I am easy with regard to the opinions of the best part of mankind. – I rest on my own.[73]

NOTES

1. Emily W. Sunstein, *A Different Fact, The Life of Mary Wollstonecraft* (New York: Harper and Row, 1975), pp. 6–7.
2. Eleanor Flexner, *Mary Wollstonecraft, A Biography* (New York: Coward, McCann & Geoghegan, Inc., 1972), p. 23.
3. *Ibid.*, p. 21.
4. *Ibid.*, pp. 22–24.
5. Sunstein, p. 13.
6. William Godwin, *Memoirs of Mary Wollstonecraft*, p. 11, quoted in Flexner, p. 23.
7. Flexner, pp. 23–27.
8. Ralph M. Wardle, *The Collected Letters of Mary Wollstonecraft* (Ithaca: Cornell University Press, 1979), p. 67.
9. Sunstein, p. 54ff.
10. *Ibid.*, p. 114.
11. *Ibid.*, pp. 150–153.
12. Those interested in an assessment of the effect of this relationship on Wollstonecraft's work should consult: Alison Ravetz, "The Trivialization of Mary Wollstonecraft: a Personal and Professional Career Re-vindicated," *Women's Studies International Forum* 6 (1983), pp. 491–499.
13. *Ibid.*, pp. 339–340.
14. *Ibid.*, p. 334.
15. *Ibid.*
16. *Ibid.*, p. 436.
17. *Ibid.*, pp. 350–353.
18. *Ibid.*, pp. 81–88.
19. Claire Tomlin, *The Life and Death of Mary Wollstonecraft* (New York: Harcourt Brace Jovanovich, 1974), pp. 301–304. Flexner, p. 246.
20. Sunstein, p. 165, Tomlin, p. 202.
21. Mary Wollstonecraft, *A Vindication of the Rights of Woman: An Authoritative Text, Backgrounds, The Wollstonecraft Debate, Criticism*, 2nd ed., ed. by Carol H. Poston (New York: W.W. Norton and Company, 1988), p. 12.
22. *Ibid.*, pp. 12–13.
23. *Ibid.*, pp. 36–37.
24. Mary Wollstonecraft, *A Vindication of the Rights of Men*, Introduction by Eleanor Louise Nicholes (Gainesville: Scholars Facsimiles and Reprints, 1960), p. 2.
25. Eleanor Louise Nicholes, Introduction to Wollstonecraft, *Rights of Men*, p. XVI.

26. Wollstonecraft, *Rights of Woman*, p. 8.

27. *Ibid.*, p. 17.

28. *Ibid.*, p. 8.

29. *Ibid.*, pp. 12–13.

30. Wollstonecraft, *Rights of Woman*, pp. 15–16; *Rights of Men*, pp. 12–17.

31. *Ibid.*, Ch. IX; pp. 19–28.

32. Wollstonecraft, *Rights of Woman*, pp. 152–153.

33. *Ibid.*, p. 12.

34. Elissa S. Guralnick, "Radical Politics in Mary Wollstonecraft's *A Vindication of the Rights of Woman*" in *A Vindication of Woman; Criticism*, p. 308.

35. Wollstonecraft, *Rights of Woman* p. 16. It should be noted that these same sorts of criticisms are made in *Rights of Men*.

36. *Ibid.*

37. *Ibid.*, p. 17.

38. *Ibid.*

39. *Ibid.*, p. 158.

40. *Ibid.*, pp. 157–161.

41. *Ibid.*

42. *Ibid.*, pp. 161–162.

43. *Ibid.*, p. 167.

44. *Ibid.*

45. *Ibid.*, p. 168.

46. *Ibid.*

47. *Ibid.*, throughout chapter XII.

48. *Ibid.*, p. 168.

49. *Ibid.*

50. *Ibid.*, pp. 169–174.

51. *Ibid.*, p. 4.

52. Nicholes, pp. XI–XII.

53. *Ibid.*, p. XI.

54. *Ibid.*, p. XIII.

55. *Ibid.*, p. XIV.

56. *Ibid.*, p. XV. See also Godwin, *Memoirs*.

57. *Ibid.*, p. XVIII.

58. *Ibid.*

59. See, for example, Ralph Wardle, *Mary Wollstonecraft*, pp. 143–145, for enumeration of some women writers who advocated women's rights.

60. "Catharine Macaulay" in *Rights of Woman; Backgrounds*, footnote 1.

61. *Ibid.*, Letter XXI.

62. *Ibid.*, Letter IV.

63. *Ibid.*, Letter XXI.

64. *Rights of Woman*, p. 106, footnote 5.

65. Guralnick, p. 311.

66. *Rights of Woman*, pp. 12–13.

67. *Ibid.*, p. 15.

68. *Ibid.*, p. 24.

69. *Ibid.*, pp. 25–26.
70. *Ibid.*, p. 56.
71. *Ibid.*, p. 82.
72. *Ibid.*, p. 26.
73. Ralph M. Wardle, *The Collected Letters of Mary Wollstonecraft* (Ithaca: Cornell University Press, 1979), p. 473.

10. Clarisse Coignet

JEFFNER ALLEN

I. INTRODUCTION

Clarisse Coignet (1823–?), moral philosopher, educator, and historian, was an active leader of *La Morale indépendante*, a political and social movement that sought to establish the independence of morality from science and religion.

The reform of the French educational system, which followed the proclamation of the Republic, sparked Clarisse Coignet's earliest published writings. Her first defense of public education appeared in 1856; her biography of Elisa Grimailh Lemonnier, a Saint-Simonian who founded professional schools for young women, was published in 1866; two tracts in support of free education in primary schools followed in 1870 and 1871. Coignet's textbook for moral education in secular schools, published in 1874, was widely recognized and debated. Her studies on education in a democracy and morality in education were published in 1881 and 1883. A critical examination of reforms that attempted to reintroduce religion into moral education was completed in 1905.

Of considerable philosophical significance is Clarisse Coignet's *La Morale indépendante dans son principe et son objet*, 1869, a Kantian-inspired work that arose from her editorship of the weekly newspaper, *La Morale indépendante*, 1865–1870. *De Kant à Bergson: réconciliation de la religion et de la science dans un spiritualisme nouveau*, 1911, is an important supplement to her earlier work, for it clarifies and expands her position on the relation between moral philosophy and religion.

Coignet's voluminous writings on the history of morals and culture trace the independent morality from the origins of humanity to the institutions and social practices of the nineteenth century. Primary sources are used, whenever possible, to give a solid historical foundation to these works, beginning with Coignet's articles, published in 1875, on the British women's suffrage movement and the history of jurisprudence, and continuing in her book-length historical studies of the sixteenth-century figures, Francis I and Francis of Scepeau, published in 1885 and 1886. Her research on the French institutional reforms of 1512–1559 appeared in 1890, and her studies of the Fourierist, Victor Considerant, and of Catherine de Médici and François de Guise, were published in 1895. Coignet's analysis of the evolution of French Protestantism in the nineteenth century was published in 1908. Writes Clarisse Coignet in the opening lines of *La Morale indépendante dans son principe et dans son objet*,

> Perhaps no philosophical question in the nineteenth century has given rise to more animated controversy than that of the independent morality; none has had a more popular interest, or has seemed to some more fruitful and to others more threatening,[1]

La Morale indépendante had existed in France since the end of the eighteenth century, primarily as a political movement. One of its leading exponents was Jules Favre, husband of the moral philosopher and progressive educator, Julie Velten Favre.[2] In the early 1860's, *La Morale indépendante* was transformed into a dynamic social movement by a diverse group of individuals who sought a conception of morality that would correspond to the political ideals of the French Republic and who set out to discover that morality by clarifying the domain and goals of practical reason.

The platform of *La Morale indépendante*, which was first presented to the public by the Saint-Simonian, M. Massol, declared:

> The independent morality is a law in conformity with reason, which dictates to us, with an absolute authority, our rights and our duties, and which is drawn from the freedom that endows man with a unique dignity.[3]

The independent morality was, above all else, autonomous. The platform recognized the absolute right of science in the physical domain, but not in human life. Although the movement was not against religious belief, it argued that religion could not guide humans in their individual actions and social organization. The autonomy of the new morality, grounded neither in science nor in religion, was constituted by the irreducible and exclusively human fact: freedom.

The first issue of the new weekly paper, *La Morale indépendante*, edited by C. Coignet, appeared August 6, 1865, and continued with great success until 1870, when the members of the movement were dispersed by the oncoming war.[4] Public interest in the independent morality elicited a flurry of new journals and newspapers that debated the proper relation between morality, science, and religion, and which included *Le Courrier du dimanche, Revue des deux mondes, Les Débats, Le Temps, Le Siècle, La Liberté*, and *L'Avenir national*.[5] At the Cathedral of Notre-Dame, Père Hyacinthe delivered a series of public lectures critical of the independent morality.[6] A lively correspondence arose between Clarisse Coignet, who often wrote as C. Coignet, and Frédéric Morin, Taine, Sainte-Beuve, and Théodule Ribot. The correspondents seem to have assumed that C. Coignet was a man, for their letters, dated 1867 to 1870, open with, "Monsieur Coignet," a confusion that Théodule Ribot later rectified in his review, 1875, of Clarisse Coignet's early writings.[7]

II. METAETHICS AND MORAL PHILOSOPHY

1. *The New Science of Morality*

Clarisse Coignet's major philosophical work, *La Morale indépendante dans son principe et son objet*, 1869, claims to establish a science of morality that is to become "the true philosophy."[8] Moral science, Coignet argues, is independent in its origin and sovereign in human life. The goal of moral science is not to destroy, but to construct, through the equality of rights and the reciprocity of obligations, a new individual and a new society.[9]

The science of morality offers a solution, Coignet suggests, to the crisis of her time. The French Revolution, she maintains, had not completely overturned the feudal society which, founded on transcendence and constituting a series of abuses and privileges based on theological principles that subordinated human authority to divine authority, led morality into a state of subjugation. When the new society of the revolution proclaimed the rule of man and the end of the institutions of the old world, it was, therefore, unable to establish its victory. Amid the confusion of principles and anarchy of facts that had arisen during this transitional period, Coignet observes, it had become much easier for humanity to pass from one intellectual tyranny to another than to withdraw from all the claims of the past in order to posit anew the problem of its destiny.[10] To change this situation, she proposes to take the revolutionary proclamation of the rights of man to its origin and to give those rights a new foundation, elevating human right over divine right in a more radical manner than any theory ever had done.

The methods of metaphysics are rejected by the "critical method" of the independent morality.[11] Criticism, the method of doubt and inquiry, seeks to destroy everything in order to review everything. Unlike metaphysics, the critical method immediately places universals in question. It distinguishes between the thinking subject and the object thought, between a point of view on things and the things themselves. Two domains are thereby recognized: the subjective and the objective, the abstract and the concrete.

The independence of all branches of human knowledge is a direct consequence of the critical method. Because criticism recognizes plurality, it can grant a role and domain for each science. Like Aristotle, the founder of the critical method,[12] the modern practitioner of the critical method can recognize the independence of the natural sciences, moral science, metaphysics, and religion. These sciences are not isolated, but their relationship must be determined anew by observation.

2. *Freedom, a Fact of Human Nature*

The independent morality is founded in the freedom of the individual, writes Coignet.[13] Freedom, as understood by metaphysics and by the natural sciences, exceeds the individual and is imposed either by a speculative order that is conceived *a priori* by reason or by a physical order that is to be recognized in the laws of nature. Freedom, in either instance, is not a primitive fact, but is derivative. It represents not an active faculty but a passive means. Such conceptions of freedom refuse morality an autonomous domain. Freedom is thereby reduced to conformity to a general order, of which morality is but a part.

Coignet's own position claims, in marked contrast, that morality is an autonomous science and that morality, like every science, must depart from a fact. The point of departure for moral science is freedom: a primitive fact of human nature that is perceived directly by man's conscience.[14] Freedom is a primitive fact, that is, an origin or principle. It is irreducible and, at the same time, the generator of a series. The beginning of freedom escapes us, like the beginnings of all the sciences. Yet, because freedom is an active cause that contains its end in itself, it is worthy of the highest respect.

Moral freedom constitutes in itself the human order, independently of metaphysics and the natural sciences. The law of freedom that gives each individual the source of sovereignty and right is found in each person's conscience. From this Coignet deduces the code of virtue by which we should govern ourselves and the world. Freedom is not derived from a principle that transcends the individual, but is brought forth as a human accomplishment and is inseparable from the human milieu in which it is produced.

3. *Man, the Creator of Morality*

The independent morality makes of man the end and true creator of morality. The foundation of morality, Coignet asserts, lies in man, and in man alone.[15] When the critical method has reduced all theories to a blank slate, and when, as if in a great shipwreck, everything has disappeared in its falsehood, man, nevertheless, remains standing.[16]

Counter to the dominant theories of natural science and metaphysics, Coignet argues, man is not a passage on the way to something higher – he is a zenith, an end in himself. With man there begins a series of new phenomena which, rather than developing beyond him and into "higher" species, stop with man, opening before him an unlimited field to be perfected by his work.[17]

The description that Coignet gives of man's creation of the moral order is noteworthy. The moral man is free, Coignet states, because even while locked in the system of forces and laws that constitute nature, he sees a goal that nature does not give him. Man posits this goal and brings it into existence. Man, the cause, end, and agent of his own goals, laboriously draws a plan from himself and fulfills it by his own efforts. He thereby initiates a new order, the order of the individual, freedom, and responsibility. Amid a string of dependent conditions he erects a new system of relations, a string of free causes.[18] The moral world, inseparable from the elements that preceded it, emerges in its independence and develops according to the principle of freedom.

4. *Duty, a Law of Conscience*

Whenever morality is derived from a source outside man, Coignet observes, rights and responsibilities disappear and duty alone remains. She asks the metaphysician, who would ground morality in a code of commandments imposed by an authority higher than man, "If we do not have the credit for our good actions, why do we have the complete responsibility for our misdeeds?"[19] A moral act is every act whose merit, or lack of merit, can be imputed to the individual who does it. We are not responsible for the purely passive and instinctual part of ourselves, for the nature and energy of our passions or the capacity of our rational faculties, all of which are outside the moral domain. We are responsible, however, for our willful activity.

The natural instincts and the faculty of intelligence are neither moral nor immoral in themselves; they become moral by the intervention of conscience. When man reaches into his conscience he experiences in himself duty, rights, and responsibility.

Coignet appeals to a state of nature, an uneducated tribal chief and his wife, to demonstrate the discovery in the conscience of the law of duty and the transformation of the instincts that accompanies that act.[20] The husband beats the wife. She regards him with reproach and he stops. At this point, Coignet writes, "The moral conscience has awakened the sentiment, still obscure, of law and duty, which opens before him new perspectives."[21] The woman, too, has been awakened to a new existence, the right of humanity. "An entire revolution, of which she is not aware, has taken place in her,"[22] Coignet states. Now the woman has become something other than an instrument in the hands of a master. She possesses in her conscience a sanctuary, inaccessible to force, in which her outraged dignity takes refuge. Despite the desire for reconciliation, the husband repeats his action. The woman looks at him as though she feared him no longer. The man wavers between instinct and moral obligation, but he recognizes in himself, at last, the law of duty. With joy and respect, the husband and wife are reconciled.

III. POLITICAL AND SOCIAL PHILOSOPHY

1. *The State, an Extension of Individual Morality*

The antithesis between freedom and authority in the political sphere is resolved, according to Coignet's independent morality, by taking away from the state its traditional prestige as an entity with distinct and superior rights. Whereas metaphysical and naturalist theories condemn the individual's freedom, Coignet claims that the independent morality, by recognizing the individual and reducing the state to a neutral entity, guarantees that freedom.[23] The unity of moral law does not preclude that each act has a double consequence: an individual morality and a collective morality, the latter being a social force which is but a new form of the individual morality.[24] The state is, thus, merely an extension of the individual life, the guarantor of the freedom that is expressed by its citizens. From the state are deduced the family and collective justice.

Justice, like all the elements of the independent morality, is attached neither to a first principle nor to a creator. The foundation of justice is in man. Law, duty, and ideal justice constitute the dignity of the human person and the equality of all persons, for they are identical in each individual. Justice, individual and collective, is the goal of freedom, a goal that comes from the principle of freedom and that is elevated to an ideal when it is perfected by reason.[25]

2. *The Social Contract*

Coignet takes issue with Rousseau's claim, "Man is born free, and everywhere he is in chains." Reversing Rousseau's formula, she says, "Man is born in chains, he must make himself free."[26] From the moment of his appearance on the earth, man is subjected to a double slavery: an external slavery to the force of nature and the world, and an inner slavery to the instincts and his own passions. Freedom, the faculty characteristic of humanity, founds in the natural order an essentially different series of plans and goals. It opposes justice to force and gives to man a law of duty that is unknown in nature. Humanity is thereby awakened from its initial sleep and, from that time on, moral liberty develops by man's own efforts.

The philosophy of morality in history that Coignet sets forth shows that moral science, the subjective science that determines human destiny, develops by the juxtaposition of truths. Natural science contributes to the realization of moral science, but progresses by revolution, for it establishes new theory on the ruins of ancient theory.[27] The study of law that Coignet undertakes in her review of M. Sumner Maine's *L'Ancient doit* argues that "primitive humanity," governed by pure instinct, arrived at the current state of jurisprudence and social legislation solely as the result of man's efforts over time.[28]

The highest level of moral development, Coignet states, is achieved after a long work of civilization. At that point, moral freedom ripens in the conscience and reason disengages it theoretically and posits it as a science.[29] The society that follows from this morality will be a real contract: the contract of wills, reflective and conscious of themselves, bringing about justice by means of freedom.

3. *The Separation of Religion and Morality*

The initial promise made by *La Morale indépendante dans son principe et dans son objet*, to elevate human right above divine right in a more radical manner than any theory ever had done, is carried out by its complete separation of religion and morality. To the law of God, the French Revolution of 1789 opposed the rule of man, which, Coignet states, is the most radical thesis that could be proclaimed.[30] The revolution was mistaken, however, in one of its most important points: the relation between religion and morality. By founding human rights not on the separation of civil law and religious institutions, but on the transformation of religion into the cult of the state as the Supreme Being, and the cult of Reason, the revolutionaries instituted another form of despotism.[31] The true solution to the revolutionary thesis, Coignet maintains, is neither the creation of a new religion nor an accommodation of the religion of the past, but a radical separation: the separation of metaphysics and life, religion and morality, church and state. Such a separation is fruitful and possible only if there is a human morality that is truly independent.

The solution proposed by the independent morality is anti-clerical, but not anti-religious. It excludes religion from society, as an element of public power, but it does not exclude religion from the human soul. The independent morality attacks the metaphysical and social character of religion, but not its psychological foundation. Religion, thus limited, is no longer opposed to morality.[32] Religion recognizes the source of the independent morality, which links all people independently of all religions, and solely on the basis of conscience.

The independent morality does not prevent man from keeping hope and from building, even on that fragile foundation, an individual invisible world. Coignet notes that religion corresponds to a deep feeling in us, the desire to live forever. But man should not be mistaken about the entirely individual nature of his belief.[33] For the pious soul, the consciousness brought forth by inner revelation may be elevated from morality to religion.

De Kant à Bergson; réconciliation de la religion et de la science dans un spiritualisme nouveau offers a significant addition to Coignet's analysis of religion. In an extensive study of Bergson's work, Coignet argues that his philosophy offers a new spiritualism that goes beyond previous religious theory.[34] The weakness of earlier spiritualism was that it turned aside from science; the weakness of previous science was that it turned aside from the invisible world of the spirit. Bergson, in contrast, realized that science could not be avoided, and he recognized, as well, the intuitive faculty of divination. Bergson showed that science, religion, and morality each have a distinct form and he foresaw how the inner life, the moral life, can be a step on the path of religious inspiration.

4. *Women's Suffrage and Women's Destiny*

The British women's suffrage movement was of particular interest to Clarisse Coignet and of direct relevance to her goal of a new world founded on human rights, liberty, and the quality of individuals.[35] The independent morality sought a renewal of women's dignity. "Nothing is destroyed, but everything is renewed. The mother will remain the mother, the husband will remain the husband, and the wife will remain the wife," writes Coignet.[36] The concept of an independent morality was to transform women's role, so that women would no longer be sold or put to death at the arbitrary decision of their husbands.[37] Women were no longer to be glorified as useful instruments, but were to be considered sovereign ends in themselves. Equality with dignity, and without destroying the family, was envisaged by Coignet as the cornerstone of the democratic nation.[38]

Coignet takes issue with "the false poetry that makes of man and

woman two beings so different they cannot understand each other."[39]
There are moral differences between the sexes, she argues, but these
are differences of degree which leave intact a common base. Education, instead of separating men and women by exaggerating the
differences, should bring men and women together by improving their
"weak points: fortifying woman's reason and improving her ideas, and
developing man's heart and delicacy of feeling."[40]

The suffrage meetings in England and the work of John Stuart Mill
were the subjects of several reports that Coignet made to readers of *La
Revue politique et littéraire*.[41] Coignet herself attended some of the
meetings, of which she writes, "I was struck by the respect and
courtesy that is shown to the women orators, and also by the favor
with which the public greets them."[42] The British women's situation is
attributed by Coignet to the superiority of Protestant education over
Catholic education in the development of character. The Protestant
practice of reading and analyzing the Bible and of drawing from that
either a personal faith or a well-justified doubt, instead of merely
following the opinions of others, was thought by Coignet to instill
habits of reflection and independence at an early age. There is no
better culture than this return to self, writes Coignet, this intimate
questioning that places the conscience constantly in action: "Women
brought up in such a regime, marrying late or not at all, will acquire
exceptional qualities: practical knowledge, the use of observation and
reasoning, a firm will that is followed, independence... ."[43] Coignet
predicts the eventual success of the suffrage movement because the
women of England understood that "all rights imply a duty, all power
implies an obligation, and political freedom is the heaviest of responsibilities."[44]

Women's suffrage was considered by Coignet to be beneficial to
the liberal party of England, but not to be preferable in a country such
as France. The English suffragists, she writes, might not immediately
support the liberal party, especially when the privileges of the church
were threatened, but they would be favorable to most of that party's
philanthropic measures. Yet, Coignet declares, "If the rights of men
are ever sufficiently secured in France, so that one can be occupied
with the rights of women, we will think it preferable to begin in
another manner."[45] She proposes beginning with reforms in civil law,
education, and greater equality in the conditions of marriage. Coignet
does not offer a complete explanation for her objection to women's

suffrage in France. She suggests that her mixed evaluation of women's suffrage is due to the fact that in England the right to vote was limited to those who owned property, whereas in France there was already a "universal suffrage," that is, the right of males to vote was not based on property ownership.[46] This rationale is ambiguous, however, for Coignet remarks, with regard to England, that the vote would improve the lives of women, rich and poor, who owned property, and she mentions in particular poor and working class British women who were single and the owners of property.

No matter what form women's future may take, Coignet argues, women's nature will remain the same: "When one has suppressed all the exclusionary laws, obstacles, barriers... when one has granted woman all the freedoms, opened to her all careers, one still will not have changed her nature."[47] Legislative reform will not change women's "great function," the reproduction of the species, which implies, in and of itself, "an entire network of indestructible things."[48] Because woman is "destined" to bring children into the world, her body will be weaker, her preferences less adventuresome, her will less strong, her heart more timid and delicate.[49] Work which has more social value, which has more power and influence, always will escape women. The new rule of freedom will demonstrate conclusively that woman can take her "true place in work" only by that task which is "first in dignity and value," and which is given especially to her: motherhood.[50]

In the face of her own accomplishments, Clarisse Coignet expresses a wariness toward women that might be unexpected:

Of course there will be exceptions. There will be women endowed with rare abilities and who aspire to escape communal life, others who will lack qualities of the heart and who will draw back before the task of motherhood, and others struck in their youth by an inconsolable sorrow. Why should they not be able to ask for work on their own, be it for glory and independence or for strength and forgetfulness? If they miscalculate their strength, if they are ridiculous or pretentious, they will suffer the consequences of their folly, they will suffer the disappointments. So be it: is not disappointment the great lesson of life, and virtue the fruit of freedom?[51]

IV. CONCLUSIONS

Saint-Simonian utopianism and Kantian rationalism led Clarisse Coignet to a new view of the nature of ethics as not merely distinct from, but independent of, religion. In her view, ethics was a product of human introspection, and freedom was a necessary condition of human existence. In her writings Coignet argues that the state is an extension of individual morality, functioning as a guarantor of the freedom that marks human moral maturity. Organized religion is antithetical to that freedom and therefore must be excluded as a political influence on the state. However, religion need not be excluded from the human soul, where it functions as an aspect of the natural human desire for immortality. Coignet's view that moral law is not only grounded in human reason but is of human origin forms the foundation for her social, political, and legal philosophy. The comprehensive system which she describes warrants a closer examination and fuller analysis than can be offered here.

NOTES

1. Clarisse Coignet, *La Morale indépendante dans son principe et dans son objet* (Paris: Baillière, 1869), p. 1.
2. Clarisse Coignet, *De Kant à Bergson; réconciliation de la religion et de la science dans un spiritualisme nouveau* (Paris: Alcan, 1911), p. 4.
3. *Ibid.*, pp. 9, 10.
4. *Ibid.*, p. 31.
5. *Ibid.*, p. 11.
6. *Ibid.*, pp. 11, 12.
7. *Ibid.*, pp. 12–27. See also, Th. Ribot, "Cours de morale à l'usage des écoles laïques," *Revue politique et littéraire*, 15 (1875), pp. 759–760.
8. *La Morale indépendante*, p. 175.
9. *Ibid.*
10. *Ibid.*, pp. 2–5.
11. *Ibid.*, pp. 11–24.
12. *Ibid.*, p. 17.
13. *Ibid.*, pp. 6, 69.
14. *Ibid.*, pp. 7, 8.
15. *Ibid.*, p. 29.
16. *Ibid.*, pp. 189, 190.
17. *Ibid.*, p. 30.
18. *Ibid.*, pp. 58, 59.

19. *Ibid.*, p. 42.
20. *Ibid.*, pp. 107–111.
21. *Ibid.*, p. 109.
22. *Ibid.*
23. *Ibid.*, p. 174.
24. *Ibid.*, pp. 62, 69, 70.
25. *Ibid.*, pp. 61, 62.
26. *Ibid.*, pp. 181, 191.
27. *Ibid.*, p. 125.
28. "Le Droit dans l'antiquité," *Revue politique et littéraire* 15 (1875), pp. 1107–1108.
29. *La Morale indépendante*, p. 189.
30. *Ibid.*, p. 170.
31. *Ibid.*, pp. 171, 172.
32. *Ibid.*, pp. 173–179; "Le Père Hyacinthe et la morale indépendante," *Revue politique et littéraire* 19 (1877), pp. 1092–1095.
33. *La Morale indépendante*, pp. 175, 176.
34. *De Kant à Bergson*, pp. 150–155.
35. *De l'affranchissement des femmes en Angleterre* (Paris, 1874). Excerpted from *Revue politique et littéraire* 13 (1874), p. 1043.
36. *La Morale indépendante*, p. 96.
37. *Ibid.*, p. 138.
38. *Ibid.*, p. 139.
39. "Le Père Hyacinthe et la morale indépendante," *Revue politique et littéraire* 19 (1877), p. 1094.
40. *Ibid.*
41. *De l'affranchissement des femmes en Angleterre* (Paris, 1874). Excerpted from *Revue politique et littéraire* 13 (1874), pp. 1066–1073, 1043–1049. "Le Mouvement des femmes en Angleterre: le suffrage politique," *Revue politique et littéraire* 13 (1874), pp. 251–255, 274–280.
42. "De l'affranchissement des femmes en Angleterre," p. 1068.
43. *Ibid.*, p. 1066.
44. "Le Mouvement des femmes en Angleterre: le suffrage politique," p. 280.
45. "De l'affranchissement des femmes en Angleterre," p. 1071.
46. *Ibid.*
47. *Ibid.*, p. 1072.
48. *Ibid.*
49. *Ibid.*
50. *Ibid.*
51. *Ibid.*, pp. 1072–1073.

11. Antoinette Brown Blackwell

JULIEN S. MURPHY*

Antoinette Louisa Brown Blackwell (1825–1921) was an American philosopher of the late nineteenth century; she was also the first woman minister to be ordained in America and preach before the Civil War, a suffragist, poet, and novelist. Blackwell's philosophy comprises six books. The most extensive, *The Philosophy of Individuality*, presented an elaborate cosmology of mind and matter as dual aspects of Nature. Also of interest are her works *The Physical Basis of Immortality*, which parallels the indestructibility of selfhood with the indestructibility of matter, and *The Sexes Throughout Nature*, her critique of sexism in theories of evolution. In her philosophy, Blackwell brought together strands of evolution with a natural philosophy shaped by Newtonian physics and inspired by the Christian faith. Besides being deeply engaged in writing philosophy, her life was also that of a preacher, a public speaker active in the suffrage, temperance, and abolition movements. Three moments frame Blackwell's public life. First, her fight for ordination, which began in childhood, peaked at Oberlin, and achieved success in a small New York Congregationalist parish. Second, her fight, with others, for the right of public speaking for women, immortalized by Horace Greeley, who wrote in the New York Tribune describing her efforts at the World Temperance Convention: "First day – Crowding a woman off the platform; Second day – gagging her; Third day – Voting that she shall stay gagged."[1] The third moment framed the end of her life, when, after years of involvement in the suffrage movement, and because of her long life, she was able to vote for president. In 1920, blind, ninety-five years old, and in poor health she cast her ballot, loudly declaring for all the polling place to hear, "I wish to vote the Republican ticket, all things considered, at the present time. It seems to me the wisest

Mary Ellen Waithe (ed.), A History of Women Philosophers/Volume 3, 185–196.
© 1991 *Kluwer Academic Publishers. Printed in the Netherlands.*

plan."[2] Her love of philosophy sustained her throughout her ministry and well into old age. She continued writing philosophy in her eighties, and preached her last sermon at ninety.

I. BIOGRAPHY

Antoinette Brown Blackwell was born in 1825 in Henrietta, New York, the seventh of ten children of Joseph and Abby (Morse) Brown. Although sex-segregated education was popular, Antoinette received co-education at the district elementary school, finishing in 1838, and then studied at Monroe County Academy with her brother. In 1846, she was admitted to Oberlin College and studied the Literary Curriculum, which was especially designed for women and granted a diploma, not a degree. Nonetheless, her diploma essay of 1847, "Mind Adapted to Originality of Thought in Investigation," already reflected her philosophical interests. Blackwell was deeply religious and even as a small child had been earnest about a vocation in ministry. Although women were not ordained, she was accepted into the Oberlin Theology Program and completed her studies in 1850. However, although Oberlin was quite liberal on abolition and other political issues, it remained conservative on public-speaking rights for women and awarding women ministerial licenses. Despite Blackwell's outstanding academic performance (for instance, her essay "Exegesis of I Corinthians, IXV, 34, 335; and II Timothy 11, 12" was published in the *Oberlin Quarterly Review* in 1849), Oberlin refused her a ministerial license strictly on the grounds of sex. Yet, Blackwell knew the fight for ordination would not be easy and persevered until she found an Orthodox Congregationalist Church in Southern Butler, New York, that would approve her ordination. In this parish, in 1852, she became the first woman to be ordained as a minister of a major religious denomination in America.

Along with developing her interests in philosophy and her religious vocation at Oberlin, Blackwell was also politicized, in part, through her companionship with the suffragist Lucy Stone. Stone and Blackwell were close friends with many political differences. Stone, for instance, had left the Congregationalist Church because of its opposition to abolition and to public speaking for women. She was less than supportive of Blackwell's interest in ordination, believing that religious indoctrination might dampen Blackwell's political positions and finding theology counterproductive to social change. On one occasion after leaving Oberlin, she wrote Antoinette:

> I wonder if you have any idea how dreadfully I felt about your studying that old musty theology, which already has its grave clothes on, and is about to be buried in so deep a grave that no resurrection trumpet can call it into being... .[3]

Both Stone and Blackwell supported the Married Women's Property Act, abolition, and suffrage, yet Stone was more radical, a Garrison in the abolitionist movement, a major leader in the suffrage movement, an advocate of divorce for women, a bloomer wearer, and, when she married, requiring her husband to devote his life to suffrage and keeping her own name. Blackwell was not a Garrison, was not a major figure in the suffrage movement, opposed divorce and bloomers (admitting long dresses were unhygienic, but believing dress was not a significant political issue), and took her husband's name upon marriage. The predominant political issue for Blackwell was the right for women to have paid work outside the home. She also was committed to reconciling feminism with Christianity by reinterpreting the Bible. She went so far as to propose that prayer be part of the National Women's Rights Convention meetings, and sponsored a resolution declaring that the Bible did not mandate female oppression. Stone and Elizabeth Cady Stanton fought against a blending of religion and feminism, and Blackwell's proposals were not adopted.

The friendship between Stone and Blackwell, which may have grown thin following Antoinette's religious quest in the early 1850's, was strengthened for life when, in 1856, shortly after Stone married Henry Blackwell, founder of the *Woman's Journal*, Antoinette married Henry's brother, Samuel, also the brother of Elizabeth Blackwell, the first woman physician in America. Antoinette's marriage to Samuel lasted forty-five years. Together they had seven children, two of whom died early in infancy, leaving five surviving daughters: Florence, Edith, Grace, Agnes, and Ethel.

Antoinette's philosophical interests began deepening in the 1850's. Shortly after her ordination in 1852, she suffered a major crisis of faith, which she described as

... an ordeal not uncommon in modern days, in which the faith of one's fathers is shaken to the foundations, and ... my health was seriously impaired.[4]

In fact, Blackwell's parish practice brought into sharp conflict her own Calvinist beliefs with the orthodox beliefs of her congregation. In particular, she was regarded as scandalous for not believing in infant damnation and for preaching of a merciful rather than punishing God. Suffering a nervous breakdown, she quit the parish, left South Butler, and took up reading philosophy, with particular emphasis on metaphysics.

Blackwell's first book, *Shadows of Our Social System* (1856), was largely a collection of her newspaper essays written for the New York Tribune about her volunteer work in the slums and prisons of New York City following her religious crisis. After she married in 1856, she began writing philosophy because the raising of her children kept her confined to the home and made preaching difficult. Her first philosophical work, *Studies in General Science* (1875), presented the beginning of her broad metaphysical view that would explain mind and matter in a universe created by God. A year later, she published her argumentative treatise on immortality, *The Physical Basis of Immortality*. Her largest and most expansive philosophical work, *The Philosophy of Individuality* (1893), described the harmony between the particular and the absolute. Believing that women could be productive long into their nineties, Blackwell published late in her eighties two compilations of earlier essays, *The Making of the Universe* (1914) and *The Social Side of Mind and Action* (1915). Both continued refining the metaphysical vision found in her first work.

Blackwell also continued her ministry, changing to the Unitarian Church, while publishing philosophical books. Her preaching at Antioch College inspired Olympia Brown to enter the ministry. She ordained two women ministers herself, Marian Murdock in 1885 and Florence Buck in 1893. As more women were ordained, Oberlin finally bestowed the degrees on Blackwell that she had earned years before. In 1878, Oberlin granted her an honorary A.M., and in 1908 an honorary D.D. The Unitarian Church freed her to develop philosophically as well as theologically. She preached far into old age, with her last sermon in 1915 at the age of ninety, at All Souls' Unitarian Church in New York City, which she helped to found in 1901 and where she was pastor emeritus from 1908 until her death. After a long life of avid mental productivity, Blackwell died peacefully in her sleep in 1921 at the age of 97.

II. PHILOSOPHY

Blackwell constructed a metaphysical theory which allowed for mind and matter to be explained in terms of natural laws within a God-created universe. The breadth of her work is revealed through discussion of her views of metaphysics, truth, perception, time, God, immortality, the mind/body problem, and the nature of the sexes.

1. *Metaphysics*

Of all the branches of philosophy, it was metaphysics that interested Blackwell most. She remarked once about her love of metaphysics, "I am taking a fresh dip into metaphysics so that when I do get an hour to spare it is so fascinating to go up there into the clouds, that everything else is sent adrift."[5] She held that metaphysics, with its emphasis on the nature of Being, ought to be the center of philosophizing. Yet, Blackwell believed that metaphysics was threatened by logic, which she had little use for and compared to a seamstress who "interferes arrogantly in the production of the raw material."[6] Logic tears a philosophical system down, she believed: "logic patches and patches, until at last, some vital breach is made, and the system drops in pieces."[7] The worst training for metaphysicians is logical philosophy, for it teaches only how to compare, reason, and draw inferences without directing one to true insight. "Nature's facts are not strung like beads on a cable of logic, and liable to be disarranged or entangled."[8] The method of philosophy ought to be one of intuition and observation, not logic.

The purpose of metaphysics, for Blackwell, is to study nature, in particular the balance between processes in the universe. Metaphysics ought to provide a unified body of truths, a philosophy of existence that could account for all substances, properties, and change. Hence, philosophy ought to be a science that could develop to an all-comprehensive unanimity, that would correspond with the truths of science. Current disagreements between philosophies are indicative of the stage of philosophical development. Blackwell believed that one day it would be possible to have an internally consistent metaphysical system that would be beyond refutation, for since metaphysics ought to study nature, and since she held there was no disagreement in nature, a true philosophy will be unanimously acceptable.

2. *Truth*

Blackwell believed that truth was an inseparable property of things, either a quality of or applicable to substance. Truth is not abstract or complicated, but simple and self-evident. Truth is inherent in nature, and "the philosopher needs to be sharp-eyed and simple-tongued, that is all."[9] With a method of direct observation, truth could be intuited in the nature of things. Nature's truths are written on natural events, and can be read through careful perception. Bit by bit, humans could accumulate the truths of nature, until nature was wholly known.

3. *Perception*

The Kantian distinction between phenomena and noumena had been dissolved by Thomas Reid, according to Blackwell. Hence, the objects of perception were in fact the objects themselves, and appearances that were mistaken were not falsehoods but simple errors of observation in which the full relations of a thing were not fully comprehended. Through perception, one has "direct insight into the existing facts of nature – observation pure, simple, and immediate."[10] The product of perception was philosophy, while philosophizing was the product of conception, and she insisted that there could only be one true philosophy, since perception was the fundamental tool for knowledge. Truth is not merely represented in perception, but is actually fully presented to the perceiving mind. The true philosophy would be held by scientists, metaphysicians, and theologians alike, for all three disciplines would be pursuing the same reality, Being.

4. *Time*

Blackwell also took issue with Kant on the nature of time. Time, for her, was not merely a subjective category of apperception, but rather a quality of substance. She believed that time was both in the mind and in substance, a property of all Being, infinite and finite, that not only allowed for change but also ensured personal immortality. She believed that a view of time as purely subjective was inconsistent with a notion of Infinite Being and a concept of selfhood as indestructible.

5. *God*

Blackwell believed in God as a Rational Designer, Establisher of the universe, and often used the cosmological argument for God's existence in her work, arguing essentially that we know God best through creation. Her deism viewed the universe as mechanized, a grand, intricately engineered mechanism in which all the forces and parts were compatible. Moreover, the mechanized universe was continually evolving, but evolution was not exactly as Darwin has suggested. Rather, the evolving universe continued to seek balance and harmony at each stage of development and was guided by Absolute Being, not merely blind adaptation of the most suitable qualities. All processes of change in nature reflected the unity and harmony indicative of an omnipotent, omniscient, and omnipresent God. Further, God had designed consciousness in nature at nearly every level. Blackwell believed that plants and animals in addition to humans were capable of consciousness. Plant-mind was wholly subjective consciousness, animal-mind could be both subjective and objective consciousness, and higher animals and humans were capable of volition and social behavior. Every change in the evolution of organic and inorganic substance was an advance in the development of the entity, and any change in one area of nature produced changes in the development of other areas. Hence, God designed a world that was engineered for progress, as evidenced by the social progress of telegraphs and railroads and the advances in science. In fact, the human being was continually advancing and through eugenics, humans could, in theory, eliminate every undesirable trait. Blackwell's views on eugenics, which came at a point in history when it was commonly held that behavior could be transmitted from one generation to the next through breeding, were uncritical of the oppressive potential of eugenic programs and even found eugenics, in its highest aspirations, compatible with her religious views. Even more than improvement of the human species was the possibility of immortality that was afforded by belief in God.

6. *Immortality*

Blackwell's interest in arguing for immortality was great enough to form a book-length study, *The Physical Basis of Immortality*. She believed that belief in immortality could be established on scientific grounds and not merely on religious faith alone, hence science, religion, and philosophy could be reconciled through careful study of nature. She claimed that the desire for immortality seemed wholly natural, in fact, because it is a yearning so deeply embedded in human consciousness and so widespread as to be part of the very constitution of the human mind. The scientific basis for immortality is found by arguments from analogy in the realm of physics. If, as Blackwell believed, psychical and physical reality were dual aspects of Being, and if the smallest unit of physical reality, the atom, could not be destroyed, then it was possible to assume that the smallest unit of psychical reality, selfhood, similarly could not perish. She argued that "if it is granted that neither substance nor force are ever annihilated, then the annihilation of a sentient existence would be the most utterly monstrous anomally which could occur in the universe!"[11] Hence, just as nature endured surface changes while its basic underlying structure, the atom, did not change, so human beings grow and develop while the self remains immortal. She claimed that consciousness was the sentient aspect of the atom, and hence must be indivisible and indestructible, even if self-consciousness need not be a constant in life (i.e. lapses of consciousness in dreams or by amnesia). "Matter and mind when unharnessed by death, ...can be again separated and the conscious soul may retain its personality; the matter and the mind going apart may both continue in being forever."[12]

7. *Mind/Body Problem*

Disagreeing with Descartes, who held that mind and body were two different substances, Blackwell believed mind and body were distinct aspects of the same reality. Mind and matter did not have completely opposing qualities, for though the mind works intensively while the body works extensively, both undergo change and are eternal. "Mind and body are closely associated," she claimed, "in a sense are literally one organism, one more or less temporary unit − nevertheless the Psychic and its 'common carrier', its docile servitor, belong to distinctly differentiated depths of Nature."[13] Nature is double-sided, which accounts for mind and body. Similarly, its dual nature has dual forces: the feelings of the mind and the motions of the body. Rarely do mind and matter cooperate without an intermediary. One such rare instance is thought and brain, which are relational and require judgments about perceptions. The cooperation between mind and matter is evidenced by the physical changes in the brain that result when the mind changes its moods. Mind is as much a part of nature as is matter. Both too are individual. Mind is not related to the body, like Descartes' metaphor of a captain to a ship, but more like a tenant to her home. Human life is the result of the cooperative action of the body, which is a key expression of the cooperation in the universe as a whole. The mind moves the body in action, and the two compose a mind-matter individual or a motion-feeling unity. Blackwell described the form of the mind as the soma, and saw the activities of the mind as a "stream of consciousness" long before William James and the phenomenologists coined the phrase. She wrote that personal mind is "the stream of consciousness produced by cooperations of the body... every endless stream of modes – of merely formal changes, material and mental is structurally, constitutionally a stream of atomic changes."[14] Hence, mind and matter work together in harmony through consistent principles of force and interaction that regulate all of nature.

8. *Nature of the Sexes*

Blackwell's sharpest criticisms of Darwinian evolution concern the nature of the sexes. As a feminist, Blackwell believed that the sexes are equal but distinct, with the differences found in comparable traits for males and females. She supported the work of John Stuart Mill on the woman question and was highly critical of Darwin and Spencer, who, she believed, used the new scientific reasoning to argue for a reactionary hypothesis, namely, that males are mentally and physically superior to females. "Science has no right to announce as physiological truth," she wrote, "that because women exhale smaller quantities of carbonic acid relative to their weights than men do, therefore the evolution of energy is relatively less as well as absolutely less... ."[15] Instead, she drew up a table of qualities that showed for every "advance" in a male trait, there was an equal advance in a female trait.

This approach was meant to counter Darwin's assumption that men were superior by his omission of female traits, as well as Spencer's assumption of female inferiority by his argument that women were physically and mentally arrested in development in order to serve the needs of reproduction. She cited that women excel in endurance while men excel in size and strength; that women excel in direct nurturance while men excel in indirect nurturance, that women excel in making biological products while men excel in sexual love, and that both sexes are identical in parental love, feeling, and thought, though women excel in intuition while males proceed by reasoning.

Blackwell found the thesis that women are inferior to men to be inconsistent with the harmony of natural processes elsewhere, and she claimed that given the assumption of male superiority there was no reason to assume that the gap beween men and women would do nothing but widen, leading to a time in the future when reproduction would not be possible, and the species would become extinct – a highly implausible conclusion. Hence, despite the current bias of science and evolutionists, she argued for the equality of the sexes. To prove that women might be equal to men, Blackwell challenged her contemporaries to no longer waste women's intelligence, but to allow for the full education and participation of women in social life. Women should be educated along with men, in fact, girls would learn faster than boys in the early stages. A life of mental work would in fact not be harmful to women, contrary to the views of her opponents. For instance, she cited the health of older productive women of her time, such as Mrs. Somerville, who wrote science and philosophy in her nineties, Catharine Beecher, and Drs. Elizabeth and Emily Blackwell, all of whom continued productive mental work late in life. Further, she claimed that she herself was educated alongside boys and was not inferior in the rate of learning or in specific learning skills such as recitation.

In fact, she claimed to average three hours of mental work in addition to newspapers and light reading per day, and expected her mental activities to last far into old age without impinging on her health. Yet, at the same time as Blackwell argued for women to assume equal status in education and in social life, she granted part of Spencer's thesis, claiming that women's energies were somewhat arrested during child-bearing years: "In woman, maximum mental power should be reached at a considerably later period than in man, because the greater cost of reproduction though related chiefly to the physical economy, is indirectly psychical; tending to diminish intellectual action also, and to retard its evolution."[16] Yet, once the child-bearing years were completed, women's reserve force will enable them to function long into old age. Blackwell believed that women had a duty to serve reproductive and domestic interests, but that justice demanded that men also be responsible providers, and that monogamy was dictated by the laws of nature and was a sign of human advancement.

III. CONCLUSIONS

The metaphysics of Antoinette Blackwell, like her feminism, favored a view of the universe in which harmony, balance, and cooperation prevailed over competition, strife, and aggression. The purpose of the individual, for Blackwell, was to become nobler, to find better ways of co-working for the good of all, so that humanity could evolve past the need for injustices, oppression would disappear and all life would be glorified.

NOTES

* My thanks to Alison Deming for her helpful comments on earlier drafts of this manuscript.

1. Horace Greeley, New York Tribune, September 1–15, 1853.
2. Handwritten account presumably by Agnes Blackwell Jones, in the Collected Letters, Schlesinger Library, cited in Elizabeth Cazden, *Antoinette Brown Blackwell, A Biography* (New York: The Feminist Press, 1983), p. 267.
3. Lucy Stone to Antoinette Brown Blackwell, 1849, Blackwell Letters, Library of Congress, Washington, D.C.
4. Antoinette Brown Blackwell, *The Sexes Throughout Nature* (New York: Hyperion Press, 1976), p. 166.
5. Antoinette Brown Blackwell to Mary Louise Booth, August 25, 1871, Alma Lutz Collection, Schlesinger Library, Radcliffe College.
6. Antoinette Brown Blackwell, *Studies in General Science* (New York: G.P. Putnam, 1869), p. 32.
7. *Ibid.*
8. *Ibid.*, p. 34.
9. *Ibid.*

10. *Ibid.*, p. 20.
11. Antoinette Brown Blackwell, *The Philosophy of Individuality* (New York: G.P. Putnam, 1893), p. 299.
12. *Ibid.*, p. 263.
13. *General Science*, p. 29.
14. *Philosophy of Individuality*, p. 274.
15. *Sexes Throughout Nature*, p. 240.
16. *Ibid.*, p. 146.

12. Julie Velten Favre

JEFFNER ALLEN

Julie Velten Favre, who sometimes wrote under the name Mme. Jules Favre (1834–1896), was a progressive educator and moral philosopher. Contrary to the prevailing sentiment of her time, which considered punishment and external constraint necessary elements of education, Julie Velten Favre encouraged freedom of the mind and cultivation of the individual conscience. Her moral philosophy emphasizes the practice of the virtuous life and affirms as its guiding motif the unity of all moral theory and the connectedness of all people.

I. BIOGRAPHY

Born in Wissembourg, France, November 5, 1834, Julie Velten's father was a pastor and an official in the Lutheran church, and her mother had primary care of Julie, her three sisters, and two brothers. At an early age she revolted strongly against the external imposition of religious practices. She completed her studies and received her teacher's degree in Wissembourg.[1] During the uprising of 1848 and the establishment of the Second Republic, her belief in freedom and self-determination led her to become a Republican. Soon thereafter, Julie Velten went to Paris as head assistant of the boarding school for young women that was founded and directed by Mme. Frère-jean, an intelligent and generous woman with far-reaching liberal ideas. Julie Velten maintained a close friendship with Mme. Frère-jean, who was thirty-eight years her senior, until Mme. Frère-jean's death in 1860.

The character of the Protestant institution influenced significantly Julie Velten's ideas of education. The institution's approach to education was a forerunner of the liberal ideals that were to appear in

Mary Ellen Waithe (ed.), A History of Women Philosophers/Volume 3, 197–207.
© 1991 *Kluwer Academic Publishers. Printed in the Netherlands.*

the public secondary schools in the 1890's, and went even further. There was no regimentation of the students and no strict surveillance. The will, personal effort, and good habits of the mind were emphasized, instead, as vital to a strong moral education. A similar openness was shown in the studies, which centered around the reading and discussion of well-known texts. In contrast to traditional methods, which began with rules, this view started with examples and from the example it made the rule appear by direct personal observation.

Julie Velten took over the position of director of the school at Mme. Frère-jean's death.[2] She was well liked by the students and known never to punish them. She concerned herself with the students' health, as well as their minds and morals, and every day she had them take a two-hour walk in the park at Versailles where, while walking, the students reviewed their lessons.

During the war and occupation of 1870, Julie Velten stayed at the school and took care of those students who could not leave. In 1871 she married Jules Favre, who was active in the Republican cause and who later became a public official. Throughout their frequent travels, she translated German and Swiss books into French, including Daendliker's *Introduction à l'histoire du peuple Suisse*.[3] At the death of her husband in 1880, Julie Velten Favre went into a period of solitude and mourning in which she compiled the *Discours parlementaires de Jules Favre*, a four-volume series, his *Plaidoyers et discours du Bâtonnat*, a two-volume work, and *La Verité sur les désastres de l'Armée de l'Est*.[4] Julie Velten Favre's completion of these works reflects not only her close collaboration with her husband, a fact which he himself had recognized from the first and for which he had wanted to make her a joint author, but also her strong belief in the growth of democracy.

The directorship of the new Ecole Normale Superieure de Sevres was offered to Julie Velten Favre in 1881.[5] The French government's new organization of the education of young women made it possible, from that time on, for French women to receive a broad secondary education. In addition, whereas in Switzerland and other European countries men taught the advanced classes in the all female secondary schools, in France it was mandated that women, especially, were to teach those courses.

The opening of the school met with great enthusiasm by the students, who came from every region of France, but with considerable ill will and prejudice by the community in which the school was located. As the director, Julie Velten Favre had notable success in the difficult job of increasing the freedom of the students while, at the same time, combating community and administrative misunderstanding and resentment. Among her many innovations was a proposal for a retirement home for students who might find themselves isolated in their old age or whose health might necessitate rest.[6] She continued to teach and write until her death in January 1896. The life-long friendships between the students and Julie Velten Favre have left a legacy of correspondence in which the secret of her influence is attributed to the perfect accord between her convictions and her life.

II. WORKS

Julie Velten's writings on moral philosophy, all but one of which were compiled by her in their final form between April 1887 and June 1891, offer a series of reflections which take as their point of departure classical texts in ethics. Her books, listed according to the date of their completion, are *La Morale des Stoïciens* (April 1887), *La Morale de Socrate* (August 24, 1887), *Montaigne moraliste et pédagogue* (no later than 1887), *La Morale d'Aristotle* (September 1888), and *La Morale de Ciceron* (June 23, 1889). *La Morale de Plutarque (Préceptes et exemples)*, accompanied by the comments delivered at Julie Velten Favre's funeral by MM. Chantavoine, Lemonnier, and Joseph Fabre, and a "Notice sur Mme. Jules Favre" by Mademoiselle L. Belugou, the new director of the school, was edited posthumously by Mademoiselle L. Belugou.

The manner in which Julie Velten Favre's books on moral philosophy were composed illustrates both how she anticipated they might later be read and the moral philosophy they set forth. On Wednesdays after dinner there was the custom, special to the school, according to which students gathered in Julie Velten Favre's dining room while she read to them books from philosophy, literature, and moral conduct, from Emerson and the Stoics, and sometimes from Molière or Corneille, stopping at striking passages to ask the students what they thought. From these philosophical and literary discussions there arose the idea of her books. She decided to collect for the students her reflections and experiences concerning the great task of life upon which they were soon to embark. Beginning in 1886, each student received at graduation a book, the first of which was a French translation, by Julie Velten Favre, of the writings on education by the German author J.P. Richter.

Julie Velten Favre's books on moral philosophy consist of her own reflections on the moral life, discussion of other moral philosophers from her own perspective, and an extensive collection of excerpts from the writings of the philosophers under consideration. *La Morale de Ciceron* and *La Morale de Plutarque* are composed primarily of passages from the works of those philosophers. Each book begins with the topic of God and proceeds to study the soul and moral culture. *La Morale de Socrate*, for instance, commences with reflections on Socratic piety and duties to God and then comments on duties to the soul, which include strengthening the will, love, justice, and education. *La Morale des Stoïciens* starts with an account of the relation of the soul to God, continues with a discussion of moral culture and the means for its realization through knowledge, meditation, philosophy, the good use of time, mastery of the passions, etc., and concludes with duties to one's fellow men and comments on women, education, and punishment.

III. PHILOSOPHY

1. *The Unity of Moral Law*

The moral philosophy set forth by Julie Velten Favre has as its central theme the unity of moral law.[7] She writes in *La Morale d'Aristotle*, with reference to Socrates, Plato, and Aristotle, "the identical conclusions at which these very different minds arrived, even by different paths, demonstrates with evidence the unity of moral law." Because all moral law is, Julie Velten Favre claims, an expression of divine truth, it is possible to exercise freedom of thought in the study of non-Christian moral teachings.[8] She justifies her love of Stoic moral philosophy on the grounds that there is always an intimate relation between divine law and human law, for in all historical epochs God has made some revelation of moral truth.[9] Each text is separated from the academic disputes of the time in order that the basic ideas and the exemplary life of each philosopher can be the principal object of reflection.

Socrates, thus, is considered a precursor of Christ,[10] for his moral philosophy is thought by Favre to lead to the same principle that informs Christian doctrine: the awareness of moral decay and the necessity of perfecting the divine nature of the soul, in which life and happiness are attainable only by resemblance to God. Favre finds Aristotle's moral philosophy "deprived of a marvelous force"[11] because it does not affirm the Platonic belief in the immortality of the soul, but she claims that this lack is overcome by the feeling Aristotle's ethics gives of a bond between the visible world and the invisible world, between the present life and the life to come. The more personal nature of Socrates' God, which reveals itself to the individual conscience and speaks unceasingly to the human soul, is rendered inaccessible by Aristotle's god of pure thought. Nevertheless, Favre argues, reason leads Aristotle to the same goal as Socrates.[12] Aristotle, more human and practical than Plato, better understands man in his complexity. Although Aristotle may have insisted too much on a utilitarian point of view, Favre remarks, he seems always to have concluded by affirming higher principles.

The Stoics receive special consideration by Favre, who finds in their pedagogical ideal an initiation to moral autonomy.[13] She protests that the Bible can lose none of its authority by the parallels she has drawn between Stoic and Christian moral teachings. In *La Morale des Stoïciens* she asks, "Because these faithful servants of God are in neither the Ancient or the New Testament, must one doubt that they have spoken and acted by divine inspiration? Was not the law of God written on their conscience and in their hearts?"[14] The answer Favre gives to these questions is compelling:

We would prefer a hundred times over to be excluded from the community of the faithful, along with these Christians of the heart, than to be admitted there with the narrow-minded people that set them aside... If we had to choose between the confidence, be it exaggerated, in the will and the inertia of a timid soul that awaits an action of grace (even to have the strength to wish for that), we would not hesitate for an instant to place ourselves on the side of the Stoics.[15]

Favre bases her response upon her observation that the moral ideal of the Stoics does not differ perceptibly from that of the Christian: to free the soul from all desires of a lower nature and to transform the soul into the likeness of God. Although Favre writes that only the "true Christian is superior to the Stoic," she concludes by asserting, "May a spiritual, charitable religion and a liberal education respectful of human dignity increase the number of true Stoics and of true Christians."[16]

The wholeness of each philosopher's teachings, the degree to which they approximate the full unity of moral law, is the criterion for Favre's evaluation of each philosopher's work. Cicero, for instance, is thought by Favre to neglect the inner moral life, to give a view of what humanity should be in the public domain rather than "the complete idea of perfection in itself."[17] Aristotle, in contrast, is cited by Favre for "the universality of his soul, open to all things and to everyone,"[18] an accomplishment that she attributes to his ideal of moderation. Aristotle's discussion of ethical principles and his wisdom in applying them to particular cases of conduct, make him, Favre states, "one of the most prodigious and most complete of geniuses."[19]

2. Woman's Moral Vocation

Women's vocation, Favre maintains, is the inculcation of moral virtue by precept and by example. She writes in *La Morale de Socrate*, "Woman's great vocation is to inspire the love of the good."[20] Women's role as the teachers of morality is thought by Favre to enhance women's lives and the society in which they live: "More than ever, in our democratic society in which our customs give to woman so much influence, woman needs to find her restraint within herself, to submit herself voluntarily to duty, to become respectable by her own respect of herself, and to inspire the love of the good by her simple and amiable virtue."[21] Favre describes women, not as the source of moral wisdom, but as the prompters who can encourage the soul in its quest to place itself in direct communication with "the great geniuses who are the glory of humanity."[22] By showing the side of moral philosophy that is accessible to everyone, by detaching what seems most fitting, women can instruct and raise in virtue even the youngest and most simple souls.

Woman is a topic of extensive study in each of Julie Velten Favre's books. Favre upholds the universality of virtue and the moral life. She affirms the capacity of women to attain the good, especially when aided by education. Favre also maintains, perhaps somewhat inconsistently, that woman is the complement of man, occupying a separate moral sphere and exercising different innate capacities.[23]

Socrates, in Favre's interpretation, viewed women as the equals of men in the home and in the state. Favre admits that Socrates often refers to women as inferior to men and that he attributes that inferiority to women's physical nature and intelligence. Yet, she explains, Socrates believed that women's weakness reflected the intentions of a divinity that had destined women, above all, to an inner life.[24] Women's "timidity," thus, was to make them better fulfill the function of guardian of the home and the family. Anxious and easily fearful, women could foresee danger, by dreaming of mishaps women could be watchful, economic and foreseeing, women could prepare for the future, vigilant and tender, women could keep evil at a distance. Favre asks, in *La Morale de Socrate*, "Who would dream of complaining of a weakness from which it is possible to draw so many advantages?"[25]

Socrates shows, moreover, that these weaknesses can be remedied so that women are not condemned irrevocably to moral inferiority.[26] Of particular interest to Favre is Socrates' remark that there are some women who are philosophers and courageous and others who are not.[27] Favre interprets this remark to demonstrate that Socrates recognized in women the courage that raises them above the weakness and timidity of their nature and up to the highest virtue: that of being so adequately the ruler of oneself that one is able to rule others as well.

A progressive outlook on women's education is attributed to Socrates. Favre writes that Socrates had resolved, in the broadest sense, the question of the education of women which, more than 2,000 years later, was still to give rise to so many hesitations and restrictions.[28] Socrates was convinced of the power of education to ennoble the soul. He also understood the powerful effect that women exercise indirectly over all that most concerns the human species. In the light of considerations such as these, he wanted, through education, to make women worthy of their great vocation.

Aristotle, Favre notes, claimed that women were inferior to men, seemingly deducing women's nature from women's social functions. Favre finds Aristotle's view to be far from the "lofty and more profoundly true doctrine of the master [Plato] who... renders such a noble testimony to the moral equality of the two sexes."[29]

Favre observes with a certain triumph that, despite the inferior condition in which civil law and the decline in morals had placed women, the Stoics still did not exclude women from freedom and moral virtue. The moral philosophy of Seneca, Epictetus, and Marcus Aurelius is universal in its claims and is addressed to the soul "independently of all distinctions of rank, of condition, and even of sex."[30] In *La Morale des Stoïciens*, Favre writes that Epictetus deplored the frivolous education of women and the degradation that was the consequence of such education. He had the sentiment of what women "ought to be," that is, of "the mission of woman and the moral height to which she can attain."[31] Seneca is noted for his comments on how Roman decadence had made women inferior, and for his admiration of the few women who had escaped women's general lot.[32] The Stoics, according to Favre, avenged women of their inferiority by inspiring in women the feeling of their dignity and calling upon women to exercise "the empire of virtue" over men and women. She pays special tribute to the women who responded to the Stoics' appeal: Arria, identified as the wife of Paetus, Arria the second, the wife of Thraséas, and Fannia, their daughter.

3. *The Great Human Family*

Consonant with Favre's conception of the unity of moral law is her claim that all humans are first citizens of the world and then members of their immediate family and state. "Man belongs neither to himself, nor to his family, nor to his friends: God made for him a more extended society to which each of its members owes his heart, his well-being, and his life,"[33] Favre writes in *La Morale de Socrate*. Socrates is distinguished from Plato and other moral philosophers precisely because he recognized himself as a citizen of the world. He saw, above the state, "the great human family of which the city is but a restricted image."[34] And although Socrates did not neglect civic virtue, Socrates held human virtue, including justice and kindness, to be the highest form of virtue. Favre comments with favor on Socrates' exhortation to extend hospitality and charity to the stranger, even if the stranger is one's enemy.[35]

Love and friendship are given considerable attention in Favre's moral writings, for they are understood as basic to the formation of the family, the state, and the "great human family of the world." Familial affection is presented as the most tender initiation to love of the non-self, because in it instinctual and rational love are combined. Man's love for woman is thought to ennoble woman so that she can be man's equal, and to complete man's being.[36] Favre objects to Aristotle's insistence on the superiority of maternal love and offers, instead, the idea that fathers who might replace mothers in the care of children would be no less tender.[37] In *La Morale d'Aristotle*, Favre critically assesses the "excessive" love that is shown by some mothers for their children and argues that such feeling is not always "directed and contained by reason."[38]

Positive justice, Favre claims in *La Morale des Stoïciens*, is justice that is inseparable from love.[39] She also links justice with love in *La Morale de Socrate:* "Justice is perfect only if it is united with the good, which is nothing other than love in action."[40] Although Favre finds that Socratic and Stoic concepts of justice coincide with her views, she offers serious criticism of Aristotle's distributive justice and compensatory justice.[41] Distributive justice, she writes, renders to each what is due in proportion to that person's rank and social standing.[42] Yet humans cannot judge the absolute value of any person. True justice can be exercised, therefore, only by indulgence and support for all, by honoring the human dignity in those who appear most worthy of being despised, and by refusing no one the benefits of charity. Compensatory justice differs from distributive justice because it considers all humans to be equal, but it, too, fails to reach true justice, for it is founded on the principle of proportion, which claims that the degree of punishment should be proportionate to the degree of wrong-doing. "In the name of the generosity which is but the true justice," Favre writes in *La Morale d'Aristotle*, "one should always suppose that he who does evil is blinded by ignorance or by passion."[43]

4. An "Ethics of Abundance"

Julie Velten Favre's moral philosophy might well be termed an "ethics of abundance." She argues strongly against those moral teachings which emphasize "negative virtue" by admonishing against moral failure. By repeating to children that humans are weak and incapable of doing good, Favre claims, one risks habituating children to less than is possible and to extinguishing in children the desire to make use of their strength.[44] What one must fear in education is not confidence in the strength of the will, but the inertia of a weak or self-satisfied will. Excess of the will is moderated by experience. A "paralyzed will," however, is difficult to remedy, for it is habituated to lament its condition and to hope for a miracle that will set it free.

Favre rejects, as well, the approach to moral philosophy that concentrates on balancing rights and wrongs.[45] This approach to conduct, Favre proposes, is satisfied with too little and neglects all that the moral life can accomplish. Negative virtue that limits itself to respect for the rights of persons and property, and to refraining from wrongdoing, is but a part of justice, which itself demands that we do all for our fellow men that is their due.

IV. CONCLUSIONS

Julie Velten Favre's own view of morality unites high ideals and the generosity of human spirit by placing foremost the inner duty to make choices that can lead to a virtuous life. "All the power and dignity of man are in his free will," she writes in *La Morale des Stoïciens*, "... it is necessary to persuade him that to will is to be able."[46]

NOTES

1. Belugou, L., "Une notice sur Mme. Jules Favre," in Favre, J., *La Morale de Plutarque (Préceptes et exemples)* (Paris: Paulin et Cie, 1909), p. xviii.
2. *Ibid.*, p. xxiv.
3. *Ibid.*, p. xxxvi.
4. *Ibid.*, pp. xliii, xlv.
5. *Ibid.*, p. xlv.
6. *Ibid.*, p. lxxxvii.
7. Favre, J., *La Morale d'Aristotle* (Paris: Alcan, 1889), p. 8.
8. Favre, J., *La Morale des Stoïciens* (Paris: Alcan, 1888), p. iv.
9. *Ibid.*, pp. iii, iv.
10. Favre, J., *La Morale de Socrate* (Paris: Alcan, 1888), p. iii.
11. Favre, J., *La Morale d'Aristotle*, p. 6.
12. *Ibid.*, p. 7.
13. Favre, J., *La Morale des Stoïciens*, p. 378.

14. *Ibid.*, p. iv.
15. *Ibid.*
16. *Ibid.*, p. ix.
17. Favre, J., *La Morale de Ciceron* (Paris: Fischbacher, 1891), p. 4.
18. Favre, J., *La Morale d'Aristotle*, p. 3.
19. *Ibid.*, pp. 8, 9.
20. Favre, J., *La Morale de Socrate*, pp. 229, 230.
21. Favre, J., *La Morale des Stoïciens*, p. 363.
22. Favre, J., *La Morale d'Aristotle*, p. 2.
23. Favre, J., *La Morale de Socrate*, p. 223.
24. *Ibid.*
25. *Ibid.*
26. *Ibid.*, p. 224.
27. *Ibid.*
28. *Ibid.*, p. 229.
29. Favre, J., *La Morale d'Aristotle*, p. 292.
30. Favre, J., *La Morale des Stoïciens*, p. 359.
31. *Ibid.*, pp. 359, 360.
32. *Ibid.*, p. 360.
33. Favre, J., *La Morale de Socrate*, p. 246.
34. *Ibid.*, pp. 246, 247.
35. *Ibid.*, pp. 247, 248.
36. Favre, J., *La Morale d'Aristotle*, p. 292.
37. *Ibid.*, p. 299.
38. *Ibid.*
39. Favre, J., *La Morale des Stoïciens*, p. 299.
40. Favre, J., *La Morale de Socrate*, p. 267.
41. Favre, J., *La Morale d'Aristotle, pp. 236–238.*
42. *Ibid.*, p. 237
43. *Ibid.*, p. 246.
44. Favre, J., *La Morale des Stoïciens*, pp. vii, viii.
45. Favre, J., *La Morale de Socrate*, pp. 250, 251; *La Morale d'Aristotle*, pp. 237, 244, 246.
46. Favre, J., *La Morale des Stoïciens*, p. vii.

13. Women Philosophers of the Seventeenth, Eighteenth and Nineteenth Centuries

MARY ELLEN WAITHE

The preceding chapters explore in some detail modern philosphy's indebtedness to women. It is appropriate to close this volume with brief descriptions of other women of the seventeenth, eighteenth, and nineteenth centuries who were also accomplished philosophers. These are women who were actively engaged in philosophical discourse and/or publishing. Like other philosophers of the period, those mentioned in this chapter were often also scientists, political theorists, social activists, educators, theologians, or professional writers. It was in multi-disciplinary domains that Laura Bassi and Mary Somerville explored the connections between the sciences; that Harriet Martineau and Clemence Royer advocated, respectively, mechanism and substantialism; that Harriet Taylor Mill advocated feminism and libertarianism; that Hortense Allart de Meritens claimed a common foundation for religion and science; and, that Christine Ladd-Franklin suggested improvements to Boolean algebra and began her analysis of color and visual perception. The contributions of these and other women philosophers of the period can be given only the briefest description here. All merit greater attention than can be given in this volume and all are worthy subjects of further research. Such a research agenda might include not only those who are discussed below, but also Marie Huber (1695–1753), Marie Agnesi (1718–1799), Sophie Germain (1776–1831), Marianna Bacinetti-Florenzi Waddington (1802–1870), Anna Tumarkin (fl 1875), Sophie Bryant (fl. 1888), and Hedwig Bender (fl. 1891), as well as the women who are named in the introduction to this volume.

Mary Ellen Waithe (ed.), A History of Women Philosophers/ Volume 3, 209–272.
© 1991 *Kluwer Academic Publishers. Printed in the Netherlands.*

I. THE SEVENTEENTH CENTURY

1. *Anna Maria van Schurman 1607–1678*

Born in Cologne, Germany, of Dutch parents, Anna Maria van Schurman received her early childhood education at home. The autobiographical *Eukleria; seu Melioris partis electio*[1] reports that she began studying Seneca's philosophy at age eleven and was taught by her father. Her early studies included the works of Plutarch, Pliny, Terrence, Xenophon, and other classical writers, as well as Augustine and other church fathers. As an adult, she numbered among her friends and colleagues Elisabeth, Princess Palatine of Bohemia, René Descartes, Marie le Jars de Gournay,[2] and Bathsua Makin. She was a prolific writer on diverse subjects, including philosophy and religion. According to Robertson, her works include *De Vitae Humanae Termino* (1639), *De ingenii muliebris ad doctrinam et meliores litteras aptitudine* (1641), later published in English as *The Learned maid, or Whether a maid may be a scholar?*[3] *Opuscula hebraeca, greca, latina, gallica, prosaica, et metrica*[4] which includes letters to Gassendi, Huygens, Makin, Voet, and others. According to her biographer, Una Birch (known as Pope-Hennessy), van Schurman is the author of *An Ethiopian Grammar.*[5] As noted by Anne F. Robertson,[6] Pope-Hennessy gives an incomplete source for this work, remarking only that it passed into the library of a Dr. Mayer. According to Robertson, this work may never have been published, rather, if it existed at all, may have been privately circulated.

Of philosophic interest is van Schurman's *The Learned maid, or, Whether a maid may be a scholar?* This pamphlet presents in classical rhetorical style an argument supporting the scholarly education of single women. The text appears in modern English translation in Angeline Goreau's *The Whole Duty of a Woman: Female Writers in Seventeenth Century England.* Goreau notes that van Schurman uses arguments which are

...often derived from some of the most traditionally restrictive attitudes or negative "received opinions" about women's nature. She argues, for example, that because of their "imbecility and inconstancy of disposition or temper," women are more in need of the "solid and continual employment" that learning can supply.

Furthermore, she does not question the assumption that women's "proper sphere" is in the home ... but uses it as an argument to demonstrate that "the study of letters is more convenient for them [women]."[7]

And while Goreau appears to take seriously van Schurman's comments about the natural intellectual inferiority of women, it is equally possible to see this as yet another version of the standard humility formula through which men's own assumptions about the natural inequality of women are used ironically in formal philosophical arguments by women to defeat those same unwarranted assumptions.

Van Schurman's *Whether a maid may be a scholar?* was widely circulated in Europe. Her influence may be seen in the writings of later women from Bathsua Makin and "Sophia" to Juliette Lambert Adam and Mary Wollstonecraft. Her work has seen many editions and translations and is widely available today.

2. *Bathsua Pell Makin: 1612–   ?*

Bathsua Pell was born in Sussex, England, of a family with strong ties to the aristocracy and to the academy. Although John Pell, her father, was a rector, she and two other children of Pell and Mary Holland achieved note: an older brother, Thomas, was attached to the Court of Charles I. A younger brother, John, allegedly the creator of the division sign, held chairs in mathematics in Amsterdam and Breda. In 1641, Makin joined the court of Charles I as tutor to Princess Elizabeth, who died nine years later at age fifteen. Makin is known to have taught Greek, Latin, Hebrew, French, and Italian to Elizabeth. In 1646, while she was at court, Makin wrote to Parliament, arguing that it ought to abolish debtors' prisons. *The Malady and Remedy of Vexations and Unjust Arrests and Actions*[8] argued on libertarian grounds that imprisonment for involuntary indebtedness, where there was no intent to defraud, was morally unjustified. She urged Parliament to strike down laws which permitted creditors and estateholders to have debtors and tenants imprisoned.

Makin was correspondent (in Greek) with Anna Maria van Schurman.[9] Makin's *An Essay To Revive the Antient Education of Gentlewomen*[10] appeared in 1673 and owes much to van Schurman's *The Learned Maid.*[11] And although it is clear that Makin much admires van Schurman, she goes beyond van Schurman in arguing for the education of women in law, business, and military strategy as well. She argues that advanced education in the liberal arts and sciences will not only advantage women and their families, but that it will have a trickle-down effect for the entire English nation as well. For, she says, a generation of intelligent, well-educated women will advance the general level of education of their children, who will in turn foster a higher degree of learning in subsequent generations. And although Makin argues that women ought not be educated merely in needle-work and painting, but in logic, mathematics, philosophy, and science as well, she is careful to claim that such education is justified primarily because it will enable women to be better helpmates to their husbands, better mothers and teachers of their children, and more consistent exemplars of piety and devotion. She is not advocating non-traditional careers for women. Rather, she sees advanced education of unmarried women as safeguarding against poverty and dependence upon the largesse of their male relatives. She sees education of married women as instrumental towards women becoming more useful wives and mothers. Education can provide insurance against impoverished old age for unmarried as well as married women. An educated wife, she says, ought to be able to successfully manage a husband's business during his illness or absence, as well as after his death.

Makin's *Essay* follows a form similar to van Schurman's *The Learned Maid* in that it considers objections to the claims it makes. It is not clear, however, where Makin acquired her knowledge of learned women from antiquity and the middle ages. The examples of learned women in various disciplines which she cites is reminiscent of Christine Pisan's *Cité des Dames*, and it is not at all unlikely that Makin would have been familiar with that work, as well as with other histories of philosophy which included references to women philosophers. After citing examples of educated women in a variety of disciplines, and after entertaining objections to the education of women, Makin briefly explores contemporary educational theory. She rejects the traditional Lilly's grammar in favor of that more recently developed by Comenius, in which Latin roots, accompanied by pictorial representation, are taught in sentential context. Referring to the education of "young gentlewomen of eight or nine," Makin proposes that this basic teaching of Latin be accompanied by basic

English grammar, so that the child's knowledge of her native tongue can be used in the acquisition of a general knowledge of grammar and rhetoric, to be followed by learning French and other Latin-based languages, Greek, and Hebrew. She advocates teaching natural sciences (botany and geology) and their applications in medicine, food preservation, and cooking, and teaching astronomy and geography, arithmetic, history, and philosophy.

3. *Elisabeth of Bohemia, Princess Palatine: 1618–1680*

Daughter of Frederick the Elector Palatine, who was briefly King of Bohemia, and Elizabeth Stuart, daughter of James I, Elisabeth fled with her family following the death of her father and the loss of the throne to exile at the Hague. At age twenty she refused accession to the throne, remaining instead at court in the Hague. Foucher de Cariel[12] represents Elisabeth as a young woman who sacrificed the throne as a result of her religious conversion to Catholicism, and who decided to forgo marriage in the pursuit of philosophy. According to Foucher de Cariel, this attachment to philosophy, and to Cartesian meditation, resulted in Elisabeth's retirement to the convent of Herford in Westphalia following Descartes' death. She lived the rest of her life there, first as coadjutrix, and later as abbess. A succinct biography and analysis of Elisabeth's philosophy is to be found in Beatrice Zedler's "The Three Princesses."[13]

Foucher de Cariel[14] groups the correspondence regarding Elisabeth, Descartes, and Kristina of Sweden, first reproducing the letters from Elisabeth to Descartes and interspersing them with summaries of Descartes' responses to the Princess. This group was written between May 6, 1643, and April 25, 1646. Next, Foucher de Cariel presents those letters amongst Descartes, Elisabeth, and Kristina during the period from July 10, 1646, through February 27, 1654. Letters between Elisabeth and her brother, one letter by Elisabeth to William Penn, and two to her sister are also included. This last grouping of correspondence dates from 1652 to 1680 and is the subject of some analysis by Dugas.[15] Although some of the correspondence is purely personal, describing, among other things, the Princess' recurring psychological depressions (Descartes once sent her Seneca's *On Happiness*, presumably for therapeutic reasons), there is a great deal of philosophical interest. Elisabeth challenges Descartes' account of the connection between soul as thinking substance, i.e., as mind, and the body. The ability of an immaterial substance to generate motion in a physical substance, is, according to her letter of May 6, 1643, not accounted for in sufficient detail by the metaphysics outlined in Descartes' *Principles of Philosophy*. Indeed, although most of the correspondence between Elisabeth and Descartes includes pleasantries and personal concerns regarding her court, her health, and their mutual acquaintances, moral philosophy, physics, aesthetics, philosophy of religion, and metaphysics are discussed in great detail. Her letters to Descartes take on the characteristics of questions and objections of the sort expected from an independent referee of a philosophy book. They are polite inquiries as to meaning, explanations of the ways in which some of Descartes' positions are confusing, contradictory, or simply inadequate, and explorations of the consequences of maintaining particular aspects of his doctrines. Princess Elisabeth offers comments and critical analysis of several of Descartes' works, including *Principles of Philosophy, Traité des Passions de l'âme*, and *Méditations Métaphysiques*. And although her inquiries and comments are knowledgeable and relevant, she makes no major contribution to Descartes' writings. Rather, as Zedler's summary of the interchange between Elizabeth and Descartes makes clear, Elisabeth functions as a knowledgeable, competent critic.[16] Of interest, as Zedler notes, is that Descartes frequently offers an inadequate response to her queries.

From the correspondence with Descartes we get a fair idea of Elisabeth's background in philosophy, for her letters refer to Aristotle, Socrates, Seneca's *On Happiness*, Epicurus, Gassendi, Machiavelli's *The Prince*, Bacon, and her friends and colleagues, Anna Maria van Schurman, Kristina of Sweden, and William Penn (whose moral, social, and political ideologies were reflected in the founding of Pennsylvania, and in the outlawing of slavery there). Indeed, she appears to have formed part of a group of women who studied philosophy.[17]

4. *Helena Lucretia Cornaro Piscopia: 1646–1684*

Helena Lucretia Cornelia was the daughter of John Baptist Cornaro Piscopia, Procurator of St. Mark's. She was viewed as a child prodigy and apparently owed most of her education to the efforts of her father. When she was quite young she became an oblate in the order of St.

Benedict. There are several sources available for study of Piscopia, including a publication by Nicola Fusco published by the United States Committee for Elena Lucrezia Cornaro Piscopia terentary.[18] According to her Benedictine biography,[19] she was fluent in Italian, Spanish, Latin, and Greek. When she was twenty-three years old she translated a devotional text of Lanspergius from Spanish into Italian. The first professor of philosophy at the University of Padua, Carlo Rinalin, was her private tutor in philosophy, and the locally eminent Fr. Hippolytus Marchetti was her tutor in theology. Unlike Laura Bassi, who decades later would defend her dissertation at Bologna, Helena Lucretia Cornaro Piscopia was examined for the Doctorate at Padua. The examination was held on June 25, 1678. She was thirty-two years old. For the examination Helena had to select the name of a classical philosopher. She chose Aristotle. The examiners then randomly selected passages from Aristotle's works. Piscopia was required to explain the passage, and identify and resolve the philosophic difficulties raised by it. The examination was conducted in public, in classical Latin, and apparently lasted an hour.

Helena Cornaro Piscopia is reputed to have found the many subsequent elections to honorary positions at educational institutions and academic societies inconsistent with her religious vows of humility. Her adult life both before and after the election to the doctorate was spent as a member of a religious order. Records of invitations to public disputations, proceedings in Italian and French religious academic circles about whether she could also be awarded a Doctorate in Theology, an engraving of her in the Museo Civico in Padua and a statue of her at the University of Padua indicate that her achievements as a philosopher and theologian were widely appreciated during her lifetime.

II. THE EIGHTEENTH CENTURY

1. *Laura Bassi Verati: 1711–1778*

Laura M. Caterina Bassi was born in the parish of S. Lorenzo di porta Stiera, Bologna, on October 29, 1711.[20] Our information about Bassi comes from an article by G.B. Comelli in the offical history of the University of Bologna.[21] Comelli reports that Laura learned Latin when she was very young and was viewed as a child prodigy.[22] The ecclesiastical authorities of Bologna persuaded her parents to educate their daughter. Cardinals who were on the faculty of the *Accademia Istituti Scientiarum Socia* of Bologna became her tutors. Laura later began studies at the Istituti and followed a typical curriculum which included speculative philosophy, logic, metaphysics, physics, astronomy, mathematics, medicine, surgery, law (probably canon law), and theology.[23] By age nineteen she had been studying at the Istituti only a short time but was reputed to have a mastery of philosophy equivalent to that of one who had been studying a decade. She applied for formal admission to doctoral candidacy, preparing a French and Latin version of her thesis proposal, and was immediately admitted to candidacy at the *Academia dei filosofi* of the Istituti.[24]

It was apparently around this time that Bassi considered marriage, for her biographer suggests that there was a dispute about the possibility of permitting a married woman to attend the university and to publicly defend a thesis. Whatever her plans may have been, she delayed marriage until after her defense in 1732. Her husband, Giuseppi Verati, was a physician and faculty member at the Istituto. The couple had five children. Their only daughter, Caterina (b. 1750), died at age seventeen. The oldest of their four surviving children, Giovanni (1738–1800), became a professor of theology and sacred scripture; the occupation of the second son, Ciro (1744), is not recorded; Giacomo (1743–1818) had a religious vocation, and the youngest child, Paolo (1753–1831) became a physics professor.[25]

While still in school and living with her parents, Laura conducted scientific experiments in the Bassi home for which the academic scientists of the Istituti awarded her a public acclamation on March 20, 1732.[26] On April 17, 1732, six months prior to her twenty-first birthday, she publicly defended a thesis of forty-nine hypotheses based on Aristotelian and Christian philosophy. They included six hypotheses of Logic, sixteen hypotheses of Metaphysics (including six on Being, four on Causation, three on God, and three on Angels), eighteen hypotheses of Physics (including six on Matter, five on Motion, and seven on Meteors), and nine hypotheses on Aristotle's *De Anima*.[27] The defense took place in the great hall of Bologna's City Hall, before the entire faculty of the Istituti, public officials, nobility, and the general public. In an elaborate processional, Bassi was escorted to her defense by a countess and a marquessa past a ceremonial honor guard.[28] For two and a half hours, Bassi defended her thesis by responding in Latin to questions and objections raised against it.

Comelli does not mention whether Bassi left any written works of philosophy. However, Alic notes that she published "many papers on Cartesian and Newtonian physics."[29] Alic, however, cites none of these publications. Scheibinger[30] names three papers on compression of air, and on bubbles. However, Bassi did teach natural philosophy (physics) at the Istituto.[31] It is likely that her teaching career, which began in 1732, would have ended or been suspended by 1738 with the birth of her first child. However, she may have continued teaching past the 1744 birth of her second child because her reputation as a scholar was widespread during her lifetime. Many medals, statues, and portraits of her are displayed in public places. There are also letters to Bassi from Voltaire in 1744 and 1745. In those letters Voltaire laments his inability to meet Bassi in Bologna and mentions Bassi and Émilie du Châtelet as "tabernacles" of philosophy.[32] Whether Laura Bassi Verati's fame was merely the product of her having been a woman in a male academic environment, and therefore having been viewed as a prodigy, or whether it was a result of her academic accomplishments and contributions to philosophy can perhaps best be determined through a more detailed study of her correspondence and other records in the archives of the University of Bologna. But whatever the source of her fame, Laura Bassi Verati clearly deserves mention as one of the eighteenth century's women philosophers.

2. *Catharine Sawbridge Macaulay-Graham: 1731–1791*

Catharine Macaulay, as she usually is referred to, was born in 1731 near Canterbury, England, to John Sawbridge and Elizabeth Wanley Sawbridge. Her mother died when Catharine was still an infant, and little is known about her early life. Hay, who is not the most reliable biographer, reports that Catharine's father seldom saw her, and refused to educate his daughters.[33] Whether and how Catharine Macaulay received a formal education is not known. However, her writings clearly evidence expertise in Latin and in history and a thorough knowledge of English literature and philosophy. She was nearly thirty before she married the physician George Macaulay. The couple had one child, a daughter. Dr. Macaulay died in 1766. Twelve years later, Catharine married the twenty-one-year-old surgeon's mate, William Graham.

Catharine was a prolific writer whose primary subject was political history. Her 3,500-page, eight-volume work *The History of England, from the Accession of James I to that of the Brunswick Line* was published over a twenty-year period. During that time, she also wrote three pamphlets: *Loose Remarks on Certain Positions to be found in Mr. Hobbes's Philosophical Rudiments of Government and Society*[34] (the English edition of *De Cive*),[35] *A Short Sketch of a Democratical Form of Government in a Letter to Signior Paoli* (published with *Loose Remarks*), and *Observations on a Pamphlet Entitled "Thoughts on the Cause of the Present Discontents"* (1770), a criticism of a pamphlet by Edmund Burke. Macaulay's 400-page *Letters on Education* was originally published in 1787,[36] reprinted in 1790,[37] and more recently in 1974.[38] I rely on the 1790 edition of *Letters*. I have not been able to obtain the *History*. Of those works which I have been able to obtain, only the criticism of Hobbes and the *Letters on Education* are clearly philosophical works. I therefore rely on the survey article by Boos and Boos for an assessment of the *History*.

According to Boos and Boos[39] Macaulay's *History of England* analyzes the politics of the Stuart succession and the dissolution of the French government. Her views are highly critical of the political philosophies of Hume, Burke, Hobbes, and others. She drew criticism from Samuel Johnson and from the philosopher and historian David Hume, who had published his own *History of Great Britain*.[40] Her commitment to the ideas of self-determination and human freedom led her to travel to France (1775) and to the United States (1785) to meet eminent revolutionaries including Benjamin Franklin, Mercy Otis Warren, James Otis Warren, John Adams, Abigail Adams, George Washington, and Martha Washington. Philosophical arguments apparently surface throughout her eight-volume *History*, and research to extract them from the *History* and to compare them to those appearing in her more explicitly philosophical writings would no doubt prove fruitful. Boos and Boos note:

> ...Macaulay's *History* was the first comprehensive anti-royalist history of its time, and by far the most detailed vindication of English opposition and dissent... Her revisionist *History* provided an alternative both to the narrowly sectarian religious accounts of

the previous century and to more accepted royalist histories, and was an important achievement in eighteenth century historiography and political thought.[41]

In her philosophical writings, Macaulay addresses many topics: she outlines a theory of women's equality, a theory of education, a theory of parentalism, and a contractarian theory of government. She considers slavery to be immoral, and she argues for determinism and against the idea of free will, as well as for a concept of a deity who works in mysterious ways.

The prevailing doctrine of sex-complementarity held that men and women were biological opposites whose fundamental differences complemented and completed each other's nature. Together, male and female formed a whole. The halves of this whole were physical, intellectual, and moral opposites: men were superior, women inferior to them. This natural inferiority provided the moral justification for the subjection of women by men. Macaulay disputed the logic of Rousseau's complementarian argument, claiming that

He sets out with a supposition, that Nature intended the subjection of the one sex to the other; that consequently there must be an inferiority of intellect in the subjected party; but as man is a very imperfect being, and apt to play the capricious tyrant, Nature, to bring things nearer to an equality, bestowed on the woman such attractive graces, and such an insinuating address, as to turn the balance on the other scale. Thus Nature, in a giddy mood, recedes from her purposes, and subjects prerogative to an influence which must produce confusion and disorder in the system of human affairs. Rousseau saw this objection; and in order to obviate it, he has made up a moral person of the union of the two sexes, which, for contradiction and absurdity, outdoes every metaphysical riddle that was ever formed in the schools. In short, it is not reason, it is not wit; it is pride and sensuality that speak in Rousseau... .[42]

Throughout Part I of *Letters* Macaulay criticizes the theory of sex complementarity. In her view the theory has immoral consequences even if one does not consider the unequal treatment of women to be immoral. By training females from birth that the admiration of men is the entire measure of women's self-worth, the theory of sexual complementarity, and Rousseau's application of it, induce vices of vanity and envy in women. The theory of sex-complementarity is inconsistent in this regard. On the one hand it specifies the virtues of women in a particular way; however, women who pursue that which is considered virtuous for women, can do so only by engaging in behavior which everyone recognizes to be vice. Macaulay precedes Concordet in her emphasis on the need for male education to include the same kind of training in virtue that women received. Macaulay believed that boys and girls should receive an identical education in a sex-integrated setting, rather than separate but equal education as Bathsua Pell Makin had proposed. In the first part of *Letters* Macaulay advocated a liberal upbringing for children with ample play time, opportunities for physical activity (to build strength and confidence), and responsibility for care of pets (to develop kindness for dependent creatures).

Macaulay also challenged contemporary accounts of parental rights and filial duty. In her *Loose Remarks on ... Hobbes* she argued against Hobbes' support of parental rights to commit infanticide by exposure, a practice which was not illegal in many countries:

> We know that the right of parents to expose their children has been the civil law of many countries; but that they have a natural right so to do is a bold assertion of Mr. Hobbes's, which nature and reason contradict.[43]

In her view, parental rights derive from a natural sentiment of care. Parental care in infancy creates in parents additional duties toward their children and reciprocal duties of children towards their parents to obey lawful, rational directives. Parents who neglect or abuse their children forfeit parental rights.[44]

Part II of the *Letters* reveals a curious admixture of elitist assumptions and egalitarianism. However, Macaulay's elitist assumptions appear to be grounded in an acceptance of contemporary scientific complementarian views about human anatomy and biology. Until recently, scientists and philosophers, as well as ordinary people, assumed that modern science was based on disinterested, objective observation and that its conclusions were therefore neither racist nor sexist. As Schiebinger has so adequately demonstrated, science, particularly anatomical studies and medical biology, have been grounded on sex complementarianist assumptions which in turn have led to sexist and racist interpretations of empirical data.[45] Macaulay, like her contemporaries, accepted as truths claims about anatomical and biological features of peasants and non-whites. She accepted as true scientific "evidence" of non-whites' greater tolerance for pain and lower intelligence when compared to whites. Nevertheless, despite these views, in Part II of *Letters* she considers slavery to be immoral. The third part of *Letters* presents Macaulay's views on immortality, determinism, the necessity of divine goodness, and the inability of humans to fully understand God's nature. She takes refuge in the concept of divine mystery rather than explain (as was then popular among philosopher-theologians) how a deity who was perfect and good can cause evil.

Macaulay's *Loose Remarks on Certain Positions to be found in Mr. Hobbes's Philosophical Rudiments of Government and Society...* counters Hobbes' monarchical theory of government with a more contractarian view. Macaulay takes issue with Hobbes' argument that individuals, once having transferred power to a monarch to become a "crude multitude", they have irrevocably contracted to delegate absolute authority to the monarch. (Macaulay, citing "Dominion" Ch. vii, art ii, p. 118 sq.) This quasi-empirical quasi-conceptual assertion by Hobbes was essential to his argument that absolute monarchy was morally justified and that the people had no moral authority to limit the power of the monarch. To Hobbes' assertion Macaulay responds:

> A Contract made by two contracting parties must be equally binding: therefore Mr. Hobbes's figure of the dissolution of the person does not serve his argument a whit; for if the person, viz. the people, dissolves, the obligation, if void of one side is so of the other.[46]

Macaulay argues that if one party fails to perform the duties stipulated in the contract, as a consequence of non-performance the party forfeits rights under the contract. The contract is dissolved and the parties can make another. Further, she denies Hobbes' assumption that the performance of the monarch under the contract can be vague and unspecified while performance of the people must be specific. The performance clause cannot be subject only to the interpretation of the contracting would-be monarchs and not to the interpretation of the contracting would-be subjects. The reason for this, Macaulay says, is that:

> ...the will of the contractor is necessary to the making of a lawful contract, and no rational person can give up his natural right to another, without proposing to himself more advantages than he could otherwise have enjoyed, had he not divested himself of that right.[47]

Catharine Sawbridge Macaulay-Graham was an unconventional eighteenth-century intellectual. Her primary interest was in history. However, she was familiar with and competently criticized the anti-libertarian, pro-monarchical philosophies of Hume, Hobbes, and Rousseau. Her *History of England* detailed the abuses and failures of the English monarchy at a time of its political decline. So great was the sting of her documented accusations that she drew fire from leading royalist apologists including Johnson and Hume. She was a firm believer in individual rights and in the equality of women. Her opposition to royalist and other structures of dominance led her to travel to the United States to meet its anti-monarchical revolutionaries, Benjamin Franklin, John Adams, George Washington, Martha Washington, James Otis Warren, and Mercy Otis Warren. It also led her to criticize the British slave trade in the West Indies and to demand equal educational and social rights for women.

3. *Sophia, a Person of Quality [pseud.]*: floruit *1739*

In 1739 the tract *Woman Not Inferior to Man or, A Short and Modest Vindication of the Natural Right of the Fair Sex to a Perfect Equality of Power, Dignity, and Esteem, with the Men* appeared, criticizing male Enlightenment philosophers who had argued that women were inferior to men. The influence of François Poullain de la Barre's *De l'égalité des deux sexes: Discours physique et morale* (1673) is noted by Bell and Offen, who also reproduce excerpts of Sophia's text.[48] Sophia argues against two related arguments for male supremacy. The first argument is that men are of superior reason, the second, that women are more driven by the passions than are men. Not only are men not of superior reason, she claims, but the arguments which they adduce to prove their superiority are not arguments at all, but the consequence of their own "passion, prejudice, and groundless custom." Men's claims to superior rationality fly in the face of empirical evidence of their lack of control over their sexual appetites:

> We know we have reason, and are sensible that it is the only prerogative nature has besow'd upon us, to lift us above the sphere of sensitive animals: And the same reason, which points us out our superiority over them, would light us to discern the superiority of *Men* over us, if we could discover in them the least degree of sense above what we ourselves possess. But it will be impossible for us, without forfeiting that reason, ever to acknowledge ourselves inferior to creatures, who make no other use of the sense they boast of, than basely to subject it to the passions they have in common with Brutes. Were we to see the *Men* every where, and at all times, masters of themselves, and their animal appetites in a perfect subordination to their rational faculties; we should have some colour to think that nature designed them for masters to us, who cannot perhaps always boast of so compleat a command over ourselves. But how is it possible for us to give into such a notion, while we see those very men, whose ambition of ascendency over us, nothing less than absolute dominion can satiate, court the most abject slavery, by prostituting reason to their groveling passions, suffering sense to be led away captive by prejudice, and sacrificing justice, truth, and honour, to inconsiderate custom?...[49]

Sophia notes that the arguments which men have offered, even if sound, are unjustly used against women because the premises are merely allegations made by other men, in favor of men, and therefore are biased and may be motivated by self-interest. Men's arguments have been arguments from other male authorities. Theirs are not even arguments grounded in clear and convincing empirical evidence (which Sophia discredits anyway, citing the effects of millennia of oppression and inadequate education of women). Nor are their arguments grounded in reason itself.

> Hitherto the *difference* between the *sexes* has been but very slightly touched upon. Nevertheless, the *Men*, biass'd by custom, prejudice, and interest, have presumed boldly to pronounce sentence in their own favour, because possession empower'd them to make violence

take place of justice. And the *Men* of our times, without trial or examination, have taken the same liberty from the report of other *Men*. Whereas to judge soundly, whether their sex has received from nature any real supereminence beyond ours; they should entirely divest themselves of all *interest* and *partiality*, and suffer no bare reports to fill the place of argument, especially if the Reporter be a *party* immediately concern'd.[50]

What is worse, she claims, is that the faulty logic and the introduction of bias demonstrate that those who make such arguments are themselves poor philosophers.

If a *Man* could thus divest the partiality attach'd to this self, and put on for a minute a state of neutrality, he would be able to see, and forced to acknowledge, that *prejudice* and *precipitance* are the chief causes of setting less value upon *Women* than *Men*, and giving so much greater excellence and nobility to the latter than to the former. In a word, were the *Men Philosophers* in the strict sense of the term, they would be able to see that nature invincibly proves a perfect *equality* in our sex with their own.[51]

Nor does Sophia claim expertise herself. Her argument in support of women's equality is not stronger or weaker because she is female: it stands or falls on its own merits, on the probative force of "rectified reason."

But as there are extremely *few* among them capable of such an abstracted way of thinking, they have no more right to act the judges in this matter than ourselves; and therefore, we must be obliged to appeal to a more *impartial judge*, one incapable of siding with any party, and consequently unsuspected on both sides. *This* I apprehend to be *rectified reason*, as it is a pure intellectual faculty elevated above the consideration of any sex, and equally concern'd in the welfare of the whole rational species in general, and in particular. *To this Judge* we leave our cause, by the decision of this we are prepar'd to stand or fall; and if, upon the evidence of *truth, reason* should declare us inferior to *Men*, we will chearfully acquiesce to the sentence. But what if we obtain a decree in our favour, upon impartial examination? Why then all the authority, which the *Men* have exerted over us hitherto, will appear an unjust usurpation on their side; for which nothing can make tolerable atonement, but their restoring to us the state of equality *nature* first placed us in...[52]

Sophia preceded Rousseau, and it is conjectural whether he was familiar with *Woman Not Inferior to Man*, or whether it prompted him to develop the character "Sophie" in marked contrast to his "Emile." According to Bell and Offen, Sophia drew an almost immediate response from "A Gentleman" in a pamphlet *Man Superior to Woman, or, A Vindication of Man's Natural Right of Sovereign Authority over the Woman*. They report:

> In 1740 Sophia replied with an even longer treatise, in which she demolished these arguments and stated her own. Her treatises were reprinted and adapted under similar titles in England throughout the next forty years.[53]

In addition, Bell and Offen mention several French translations. One of those translations, published in 1751, may have been by Madeline de Puisieux, who was closely connected to Denis Diderot, compiler of the *Encyclopédie*. If Mme de Puisieux was responsible for this translation, then Sophia may have been known to the young Rousseau, the creator of "Sophie," who was at about that time writing articles on music for Diderot's *Encyclopédie*, and who would soon begin his literary career.

4. (Marie) Olympe de Gouges (Marie de Gouzes): 1748–1793

Olympe de Gouges was born the daughter of a butcher in Montauban, France. She married a man named Aubry and had at least one son. De Gouges moved to Paris following an early widowhood. Her handwriting was illegible, and her spelling was phonetic, but soon she became a moderately successful playwright. During the period 1788–1791 she published a series of pamphlets and treatises arguing for political and legal equality for women, and for tax reform which would result in a redistribution of the national wealth and repayment of the national debt. Women continued to be excluded from participation in most of the popular societies as well as the universities. De Gouges repeatedly attempted to organize women's societies which were a combination of the intellectual *salons* and political activist groups.[54] Unlike other revolutionaries who argued for social and economic equality, she believed that a royal head of state could serve as a figurehead monarch in a popular democracy. In July 1793 she was arrested for attempting to circulate *Les Trois Urnes ou le Salut de la patrie* in which she suggested that a popular referendum decide the form of government for France. (The title itself is a pun: "urnes" means "cremation urns" as well as "ballot boxes." The title would translate loosely as 'The three urns or salute to the country.') Her trial took place in November of that year. Several days earlier, the National Convention outlawed clubs and societies for women. A partial trial transcript[55] indicates that it was her *Declaration of the Rights of Woman and Citizen*, as well as her plays and other works critical of the methods of the Revolution and the Terror, that led to her arrest. She was found guilty of being a reactionary royalist and was guillotined the day after the trial.

Olympe de Gouge's writings usually begin and end with an appeal to action. The central passages alternate a natural law theory with utilitarian constraints, peppering the argument with examples of contemporary abuses, pointing out the illogic of counterarguments offered by philosophers and other contemporary spokesmen for the *status quo*.

In 1788 Olympe de Gouges wrote three radical treatises. In *Lettre au peuple ou projet d'une caisse patriotique par une citoyenne* (Letter to the people, or project for a patriotic coffer by a [female] citizen)[56] she urged women of modest means to demonstrate their patriotism by voluntary contributions to the coffers of the state. De Gouges argued that such an action would facilitate an egalitarian redistribution of wealth as well as repayment of the national debt. In return, she urged the États Genéraux to recognize women's patriotism and legislate female equality. *Remarques Patriotiques par la citoyenne, auteur de la lettre au peuple* (Patriotic remarks by the [female] citizen, author of the letter to the people)[57] suggests other forms of voluntary taxation through which egalitarian redistribution of wealth might occur. Among other things, de Gouges urged luxury taxes on ownership of excessive jewels, horses, carriages, and fines on masters who injure their servants. Her tradition-shattering treatise *Réflexion sur les Hommes Nègres* (Reflection on black men)[58] claimed that there were no innate natural differences between blacks and whites. De Gouges argued that in the absence of such differences the underlying moral justification for socially differential treatment, particularly slavery, was lacking.

A non-philosophical 1789 pamphlet, *Projet d'un second théâtre et d'une maternité* (Project for a second theater and for a maternity hospital),[59] called for a competitor to the Comédie Française (to be called Le Théâtre Nationale) where non-mainstream feminist theatre could be produced. This treatise also argued that there was a need for a women's hospital in which "sanitary medicine" would provide an alternative to the deplorable conditions for women in public hospitals. That same year de Gouges wrote *Le Cri du Sage par une Femme* (The Call of the Wise by a Woman)[60] in which she urged the representatives of the clergy, nobility, and estate-holders convened by Louis XVI not to assume the truth of the doctrine of "couverture" (that the interests of women were included in that of men). A quarter-century later, the appearance of James Mill's "Article on Government," in which he argued that the interests of women were indeed "covered" by the interests of their male relatives, would stand in marked contrast.[61]

De Gouges' most famous and most philosophical work was her 1791 treatise *Les Droits de la Femme* (The rights of woman).[62] Dedicated to Marie Antoinette and modelled after the 1791 Constitution's preamble, *Declaration of the Rights of Man and Citizen*, it outlined constitutional principles of the rights of women. Women's rights were grounded, de Gouges claimed, on the natural law and the laws of logic. She called for full equal rights for women with social distinctions based only on requirements of general utility. In addition to full political equality, it called for equal rights and punishments under civil and criminal law. De Gouges demanded equal opportunity for employment, education, and holding public office. This remarkable document also called for women to have equal access to public programs, and for the right to outright ownership and control of property while married. A separate part of this treatise includes a draft of a model social contract between men and women which de Gouges offered as a replacement for conventional marriage vows which then provided the legal foundation of the family. It was the first legal treatise to argue in favor of a mechanism for proving legal paternity of illegitimate children. The language of the *Declaration* is markedly utilitarian, based in certain natural law assumptions. De Gouges urges women to oppose the

> *non sequiturs* [which male democratists] offer in contradiction to their principles, [to] courageously oppose the force of reason to the empty pretentions of superiority; unite yourselves beneath the standards of philosophy... .[63]

During the period that Olympe de Gouges was writing these brief works of legal and political philosophy, she continued to publish short plays, most of which were highly critical of revolutionary methods. Her final work was *Les Trois Urnes ou le Salut de la patrie*, in which she suggested that popular revolution risked reinstituting old privileges unless a referendum of all citizens decided the form of government for France. In *Les Trois Urnes...* de Gouges combined natural law views and utilitarian theory in support of a general societal reform. She reiterated her demands for women's political, social, and legal rights, beginning and ending the document with appeals to those who could effect such reforms. Acting on a tip from the printer, *Les Trois Urnes...* was confiscated by the agents of the Terror and Marie de Gouzes (as the court recorded her name) was placed under arrest on charges of being a royalist. Although the work was never published, there are revealing references to its contents in the transcript of her trial. The day after the trial, Olympe de Gouges was executed by guillotine.

5. *Mary Fairfax Somerville: 1780–1872*

Mary Fairfax was born in the last half of the eighteenth century of Scots parentage. Her first marriage, to the captain Samuel Greig, ended with his death. Several years later, she married her cousin, the physician William Somerville. The most authoritative sources, Martha Somerville[64] and Elizabeth Chambers Patterson[65] of Somerville College, Oxford University (a college named for Mary Somerville), report that Somerville was largely self-taught. A natural philosopher and experimental scientist living in an era when little distinction was made between the two by academicians, she taught herself Euclid's *Elements*, Bonnycastle's *Algebra*, Newton's *Principia*, and other mainstays of philosophy, mathematics, and science. She learned botany, astronomy, and geology and conducted experiments in solar refraction and geology. Margaret Alic reports that Pierre Laplace, unaware that until her remarriage Somerville had been known as "Mrs. Greig," complained to Somerville that:

> I write books that no one can read. Only two women have ever read the *Mécanique Céleste*; both are Scotch women: Mrs Greig and yourself.[66]

Ten years after Laplace made that comment to Somerville, The Society for Diffusing Useful Knowledge requested that Somerville prepare an English translation of Laplace's Newtonian-based theory that the solar system was a self-regulating, stable mechanism. In 1831 Somerville delivered much more than a translation. She prefaced Laplace's work with a lengthy historical and mathematical analysis of *Traité de Mécanique Céleste*, and contributed diagrams, sketches, derivations, and proofs of certain aspects of Laplace's theory.

Three years later, her *On the Connexion of the Physical Sciences*[67] was to result in the substitution of the term "scientist" for "natural philosopher" in intellectual circles. In it, Somerville offered a description of the physical sciences in a way which elucidated the common philosophical foundations for the sciences and contributed to the adoption of a common definition of the term "physical science." It was strongest in the subject of physical astronomy, but contained substantial analyses of mechanics, magnetism, electricity, heat, sound, light meteorology, climatology, geology, and elasticity in plate techtonics. The book saw five editions in only six years, and an additional five editions and translations into French, Italian, and German during the period from 1840 until Somerville's death in 1872. Remarkably, each edition was a revision which eliminated outdated material and included analyses of new discoveries, particularly in theories of magnetism and electricity.

Somerville's third, and most popular, work, *Physical Geography*,[68] was published in 1848. In it she described land, sea, and air masses, the animal and plant kingdoms, and social organization of the animal kingdom, including human social structure. She used this last description as an opportunity to criticize slavery and other forms of social and class difference and conflict. But the book affirmed that the earth was geologically older than religious authorities would have it. That view caused her to be denounced in the House of Commons. When she was ninety years old, she authorized the Darwinian evolutionary theorist Bates to revise *Physical Geography*, but required him to omit discussion of Darwin's theory from it. Alic[69] suggests that Somerville may have done this either because she believed Darwin to be mistaken or because she feared further censure. Although Mary Somerville was an authority on scientific developments, her final book, *On Molecular and Microscopic Science*,[70] written at age eighty-nine, was a pedantic and outdated account of atomic theory, plant physiology, and microscopic animal organisms.

Her early exclusion from academic societies changed following the publications of her works. The Royal Society, which excluded her from its sessions, erected a bust of her during her lifetime, and permitted her husband (who was a member) to read her papers there. The French *Académie des Sciences* published one of her early papers. The American Philosophical Society elected her a member in 1869. She received honors from the Royal Astronomical Society, The Royal Academy of Dublin, the Société de Physique et d'Histoire Naturelle de Genève, the Italian Geographical Society (Florence) (which awarded her its first Gold Medal), the Italian Academy of Science, the American Geographical and Statistical Society, the Royal Geographical Society (which awarded her the Victoria Gold Medal), and other academic and professional associations.

Mary Fairfax Somerville overcame the barriers of education, early widowhood, and exclusion from scientific societies before her early publications appeared. Alic reports that she was the first signatory to Mill's petition for women's suffrage.[71] Her professional life was as that of one of the last of the natural philosophers who lived during the period when philosophers of mathematics, metaphysics, cosmology, and science sought a unifying philosophical orientation and conducted scientific experimentation to "test" philosophical theories.

6. Anna Doyle Wheeler: 1785–1848

According to Bell and Offen,[72] Anna Doyle Wheeler was an Irish woman born to an "enlightened" family. At age fifteen she married the abusive Frances Massey Wheeler. Margaret McFadden, who has extensively documented Wheeler's biography,[73] notes that twelve years and six children later, Wheeler fled to the Isle of Guernsey and the protection of its governor, her uncle. Wheeler spent the next twenty years travelling around Europe. By this time, she had read many of the works of revolutionary utopian philosophers, and also the works of Mary Wollstonecraft.[74] An early Saint-Simonian group in Caen, France, counted her amongst its members. McFadden notes[75] that through Jeremy Bentham, Wheeler became acquainted with William Thompson and other utilitarians. Wheeler became closely associated with the utopian philosophers Robert Owen and Charles Fourier, and arranged exchanges of views among Fourierists, Owenites, and Saint-Simonians.

Thompson and Wheeler claimed that Charles Fourier's social philosophy shared the same basic assumptions as the utopian theories of Robert Owen and Saint-Simon. Wheeler's public life was spent developing a synthesis of these three social-political philosophies. From Wheeler's writings, we see that she considered herself to be not only a utopian, but a utilitarian. In her view, the philosophies of Saint-Simon, Owen, and Fourier provided the details of a political infrastructure for a Benthamite utilitarian society. In such a society "the greatest happiness of the greatest number" did not exclude the happiness of women, nor did it subsume women's happiness under that of males, or under that of the family unit. Wheeler published her own views in an 1830 article, "Rights of Women."[76] Bell and Offen cite[77] her "frequent contributions" to the Owenite Journal *The Crisis* in the form of translated articles by French socialists. A revision of her translation of "Call to Women" by the pseudonymous "Jeanne-Victoire" is reproduced by Bell and Offen.[78] Anna Doyle Wheeler worked hard towards having her philosophical views become a political reality. Towards this end, she gave a number of public addresses on the subject of utopian socialism, utilitarianism, equality, and women's rights. In public lectures she explained her position that the concept of "couverture" had consequences which were not utilitous: the consequences were that both men and women were degraded, kept in ignorance, and victimized by prejudice which pervasively characterized social institutions.

In 1814 Jeremy Bentham's student James Mill published an article on government in the *Supplement for the Encyclopedia Britannica*.[79] The article was reprinted in 1825 and privately circulated, but not republished. In it, Mill dismissed outright the question of women's rights, stretching the doctrine of "couverture" in marriage to assert paternalistically that women's interests were adequately represented through those of their husbands or fathers. In response to Mill's article, Wheeler and Thompson jointly wrote *The Appeal of One Half of the Human Race, Women, Against the Pretensions of the Other Half, Men, to Restrain Them in Political and Thence in Civil and Domestic, Slavery* (1825). Although only Thompson's name appears as author, the introduction clearly establishes that the work represents the joint efforts of Wheeler as well as Thompson, and she is considered by Pankhurst, Bell and Offen, and McFadden to be its joint author. The work is widely available in both a 1970 reprint edition[80] and in a 1983 edition with an introduction by Richard Pankhurst.[81] It is the 1970 reprint to which I refer whenever page numbers of the *Appeal* are cited. Competent biographical accounts appear in McFadden,[82] Pankhurst,[83] and Galgano.[84]

Thompson and Wheeler argue convincingly for a utilitarianism which is closer to Bentham's original (and in their perception, non-misogynist) utilitarianism. The first part of the *Appeal* examines James Mill's argument that women's political interests are represented through those of their male relatives and argues that a social system is not utilitous if it considers only the happiness of one half of the population, rather than that of the greatest number. The details and argument of this twenty-page part are nicely summarized by McFadden.[85]

Part II constitutes the central focus of their argument, and extends from page twenty-one to page 213. Here, Thompson and Wheeler entertain the hypothesis that their conclusion of the argument in Part I is not satisfactorily demonstrated. They begin with an examination of the "three great classes, or divisions, of women, whose interests or happiness are considered."[86] They consider all women without husbands or fathers, then, adult daughters living with their fathers, and third, wives. The extent to which the "interests" and therefore "happiness" of women lacking both husbands and fathers can be considered to be wholly involved in the interests of their non-existing relatives is nil, they claim. Mill's claim of "couverture" therefore cannot conceivably extend to these women, yet, the authors criticize, Mill excludes all women from political rights, even though it is clear that the interests of this group of women could not be "covered" by those of their fathers or husbands. To the contrary, the authors note, due to natural and social inequalities this class of women is in greater need of political equality than is any class of men. In their view, natural inequalities, such as physical limitations resulting from pregnancy and childbirth, are probably no greater than those suffered by men due to illness, accident, and disease. Nevertheless, they give the opposing prevailing view the benefit of the doubt here. Physical "inconvenience" and "indisposition" (as they referred to it) should be compensated for by social and political accommodations regardless of the sex of the person who suffers the "indisposition."[87] We may be able to distinguish Wheeler's views from Thompson's on the question of innate physical inferiority or limitations of women. In his "Introductory Letter to Mrs. Wheeler" at the beginning of the *Appeal* Thompson had suggested that women are physically weaker than men, particularly during "gestation" but denied that this is a basis for giving women unequal rights.[88] However, this distinction between the views of the two authors is far from certain, as there is no reason to assume that Wheeler did not approve the full manuscript including the prefatory letter.

Thompson and Wheeler next turn their analysis of Mill's argument to the case of adult daughters living within their fathers' households. If any group within a household has interests which are closely identical to that of the father it is adult sons.[89] Why are they not excluded from political rights under the doctrine of "couverture"? In fact, the interests of adult women are so completely unidentified with those of their fathers that they leave home as soon as possible. Even the law recognizes that parents have no direct control over the actions of children who have reached the age of majority.[90] The only sense in which the interests of families coincide with the interests of individual constituent members is the sense that families share prosperity. But this shared prosperity extends to the servants and also to family animals, the authors note.[91] Wheeler and Thompson insist that the interests of families are in all other respects to be distinguished from the individual interests of adult family members.[92]

Next Thompson and Wheeler examine the situation of married women, beginning with an examination of notorious marriage contracts, which, the authors claim, have no greater moral legitimacy than do slavery contracts.[93] To support their claim, they define a slave as

...a person whose actions and earnings, instead of being, under his own control, liable only to equal laws, to public opinion, and to his own calculations, under these, of his own interest are under the arbitrary control of any other human being, by whatever name called. This is the essence of slavery and what distinguishes it from freedom. A domestic, a civil, a political slave, in the plain unsophisticated sense of the word – in no metaphorical sense – is every married woman.[94]

For most women, the social dependence of women upon male privilege makes marrying the act which determines whether a woman starves or survives. Submission to "domestic despotism" is a choice made not in freedom, but of necessity.[95] It corrupts men while demeaning women, placing men in positions of power and authority, granting them privileges of extra-marital liaison never afforded to women, but for which men are never punished. Even if slavery of women promoted the happiness of men, it cannot be justified, as the enjoyment of pleasures by women are circumscribed by male fiat at home and by educational deficiencies even in the face of spousal acquiescence to women's intellectual and social pursuits.[96] No matter how many privileges husbands grant to wives, the lack of personal autonomy and the need to obtain male permission for every exercise of personal autonomy indicates that their interests are conflicting.[97] The authors ask: even if we assume that there is an identity of interests between husbands and wives, is there sufficient cause to limit the political or civil rights of one party and vest those rights exclusively in another party? Assuming the truth of the consequent, and asserting that women possess greater moral sensitivity to others than do men, Thompson and Wheeler recommend vesting those rights in women rather than in men![98] But this is a "straw man" argument, and the authors conclude that if that which is conducive to human improvement is utilitous, there is insufficient cause for excluding either men or women as rights-holders. They conclude that equal civil, criminal, and political laws are most conducive to promoting equal enjoyment, or happiness, among all adult members of the society.[99] The volume continues with calls for consciousness-raising among women as to their differential treatment, and recommends the establishment of an Owenite socialist state (rather than a Fourierist community) where rights and opportunities as well as goods are equally distributed.[100]

The Appeal received widespread distribution and parts of it were translated into French within a few years, according to Bell and Offen.

In this century, it has been discussed by Richard Pankhurst[101] and Margaret McFadden.[102] Thompson and Wheeler argued convincingly for a utilitarianism which was closer to Bentham's original utilitarianism. Unlike James Mill, they saw utilitarianism as consistent with female social and political equality. Their views were similar to those which would soon be published by other utilitarians, including John Stuart Mill and Harriet Taylor Mill. However, Thompson and Wheeler's agenda extended beyond providing a philosophical foundation for a social structure. They were impressed by the political philosophies of Fourier,[103] Saint-Simon, and Owen. These political theorists had large followings, and their views had given rise to a significant body of literature in which the details of an egalitarian social infrastructure were fleshed out with great specificity. Through her work to bring representatives of these social and political theories together, Wheeler paved the way for a synthesis of utopian and utilitarian philosophies. Through her political activism, Wheeler challenged women to demand their rights and to break down barriers to the realization of a utilitarian utopia in which women played a full and equal part.

III. THE NINETEENTH CENTURY

1. *Catharine Ward Beecher: 1800–1878*

Catharine Ward Beecher was an older sister of the novelist Harriet Beecher Stowe and was the daughter of the Calvinist theologian and evangelist Lyman Beecher and his first wife, Roxana. Her mother died of tuberculosis when Catharine was fifteen years old. One year later, Lyman married Harriet Porter. Catharine's education was a thorough one for the daughter of a New England Puritan. It emphasized religious studies, the great Roman and English poets, American literature, basic mathematics, and science, as well as the "female arts" associated with housework, child care, and becoming an intelligent helpmeet and companion to a future husband. Catharine attended a girls' middle school. Her parents, her aunt Mary, and, later, her stepmother reinforced school work with long hours of reading, writing, and discussion. A biography and a bibliography of her writings, including some jointly written works on home economics coauthored with her younger sister Harriet Beecher Stowe, can be found in Kathryn Sklar's *Catharine Beecher: A Study in American Domesticity.*[104]

Catharine Beecher became a prolific writer on diverse philosophical and practical subjects. Through eight of her writings she develops a comprehensive moral, religious, social and political philosophy. Beecher's philosophical writings merge religious and secular theories of ethics. She adapts the Scottish Common Sense Philosophy to Puritan virtues of self-denial and self-sacrifice. From this synthesis, she derives a duty of benevolent utility consistent with principles of justice. Catharine Beecher's sex-complementarian views of women's nature, reinforced by a Calvinist upbringing, led her to conclude that it is women's moral duty to work for the abolition of slavery. Nevertheless she was highly critical of the political methods of prominent female abolitionists including Angelina Grimké.

Letters on the Difficulties of Religion,[105] *An Address to the Protestant Clergy of the United States,*[106] and "An Essay on Cause and Effect in Connection with the Difference of Fatalism and Free Will"[107] are three of Beecher's writings on philosophy of religion. They evidence Beecher's dissatisfaction with the evangelical Calvinism of Lyman Beecher, her father. Her dissatisfaction with Calvinism was caused largely by the spiritual and social limitations which New England Puritanism placed on women.

Puritan theology, and in particular, Puritan epistemology, identifies "the common sense" as a faculty of the "sensitive soul."[108] The attribute which characterizes this faculty is its ability to distinguish truth from fantasy. Those who have confidence in the ability of the common sense know that they can correctly distinguish the true from the imaginary. Thus, Puritans escape the psychological impact of skepticism: uncertainty. According to Puritan epistemology, uncertainty about the truth of our perceptions does not prevent a person from relying on reasoned analyses of sensory data. Although it was Catharine's knowledge of Puritan theology which psychologically so distressed her as a woman, it was what led Catharine Beecher to become perhaps the earliest American proponent of Common Sense philosophy.

Berkeley is often credited with being the first European advocate of Common Sense philosophy because he denied the usefulness of a skepticism which forced us to deny the truth of sensory perception.

The Scottish philosophers Hume[109] and later Reid had argued that truths which all ordinary people know to be true (the incorporeality of mind, that humans have free will) cannot be undermined by Cartesian skepticism. These truths are first truths and, as such, are not susceptible to proof. They can be defended, however, by demonstrating the absurdity of their contrary. Common Sense philosophy was a rigorous form of realism, and as Flower and Murphey note, "It was a bridge between the Enlightenment and the pragmatists...".[110] Although the origins of its development may have been in Berkeley's epistemology, in nineteenth-century New England Common Sense became also a powerful social theory. This social theory included a philosophy of religion, a moral theory, a social and political philosophy, a philosophy of education, and an economic theory. Independent conscience played a central role in each. According to Reid,[111] conscience was the "moral faculty" through which each individual, endowed with free will, made moral judgments to act according to virtue. Common Sense philosophy asserted the connection between internal conscience and virtue and external, social morality. Conscience, not God, was the source of judgment on the morality of individual actions.

Beecher's Common Sense moral philosophy is decidedly grounded in a revision of Puritan ethics, as well as in the Common Sense moral psychology of Reid. Submission, self-denial, and self-sacrifice had long been considered characteristic virtues of women. They were also central virtues for Calvinist Puritanism. In *The Elements of Mental and Moral Philosophy, Founded upon Experience, Reason, and the Bible*[112] Catharine insisted that it was essential that these be moral virtues for everyone, particularly for social leaders. In this work Beecher adopts the rationalist view that the mind is the source of its own laws of reason and morality. In *Elements* Beecher supplements Common Sense rationalism with communitarian and utilitarian perspectives: minds exist in a social system in which each mind is dependent on other minds as sources of happiness. By promoting social virtue in others, one contributed to the development of the "greatest social happiness."

Cotton Mather and others had insisted that we be in the world but not be worldly. Beecher severely criticized Calvinist constraints on an individual's moral freedom through its inculcation of guilt and fear. In a fourth philosophical work, *Common Sense Applied to Religion, or the Bible and the People*, she claimed that concepts of original sin and religious conversion were Augustinian perversions.[113] In contrast, Beecher held that the real moral challenge is to live in the world and to be of it. The challenge is to overcome temptations through suffering, self-sacrifice, and self-denial and to lead others through education and example to a life of social and spiritual virtue.[114] In *An Appeal to the People on Behalf of their Rights...* Beecher claims that the choice of what is right and good is itself not a morally praiseworthy action. Only when the choice of what is right and good requires struggle, denial, and self-sacrifice is the act "a meritorious and praiseworthy act."[115]

An Appeal to the People on Behalf of their Rights as Authorized Interpreters of the Bible synthesizes much of Catharine Beecher's social and political philosophy with her moral and religious philosophy. In this work Beecher supports the Calvinist view that base desires must be controlled and denied. However, in her view, self-control and self-denial were to be supplemented by a principle of benevolent utility: the duty of the individual to sacrifice personal good to the greater good of the many. Beecher's duty of benevolent utility is a positive duty of individuals and not merely a duty of societies or of governments. The duty is to act utilitiously: to do that which is for the greatest good for the many. On Beecher's account, Calvinist religion and utilitarian philosophy should not be the greatest moral influences directing human action. Principles of religious benevolence and utility were subject to a principle she called "rectitude." Rectitude meant that personal sacrifice and self-denial for the good of others must be motivated by a desire to right social wrongs and by a commitment to principles of social justice. Referring to slavery, she wrote,

> One must not only choose to promote the greatest possible happiness, but must choose the right way of doing it.[116]

There is a positive duty to effect change that will lead to "the greatest happiness." However, the morality of the action cannot be judged on utilitarian grounds alone. Utility was constrained by the demands of justice and right. Utilitarian social practices must accord with principles of justice.

Through the development of her principle of rectitude, Beecher also enlarges her concept of a morally praiseworthy act. The action must not only have good (just and utilitous) consequences and be self-sacrificial, it must also be motivated by intentions and desires to achieve justice. Additional central elements of Beecher's concept of a morally praiseworthy act can be found in *An Essay on Slavery and Abolitionism with Reference to the Duty of American Females*.[117] Here Beecher develops two elements of her views on moral praiseworthiness. The first element is that an action which is morally praiseworthy must be one that evidences moral leadership which promotes moral development (increased virtue) in others. The second element is that an action which is morally praiseworthy must be one that treats wrongdoers with care and concern and with appreciation for those virtues which the wrongdoer does exemplify. In addition to developing these elements of morally praiseworthy actions, Beecher's *Essay...* also develops the idea of side constraints on utility.

Methods of securing justice, vehicles for disseminating truth, as well as policies for righting wrongs are themselves subject to moral side constraints. The *Essay...* is an open letter to Angelina Grimké in which Beecher criticizes the work of Grimké and others to popularize the actions of abolitionist societies. Beecher argues that social change must be effected through persuasion. However, persuasion must evidence kindness and respect for those whose views are attempted to be influenced. Using the abolitionist's efforts as an example, Beecher notes that the nature of prejudice is far more subtle than some reformers, including Grimké, acknowledged it to be. Beecher sets out the moral constraints on persuasion: attempts to change prejudice require treatment of the prejudiced person with concern and respect, and with a full acknowledgement of those virtues which the prejudiced person exemplifies.[118] The *Essay...* acknowledges that freedom for all is utilitous and will create the greatest happiness for all. Therefore not only is abolition utilitous but virtuous. She reminds abolitionists that morally virtuous ends do not justify means which themselves create moral evils.

Beecher gives two examples of what she considers to be evils created through the pursuit of the good. First, she addresses the establishment of a college for middle-class black men in a poor white town. Such actions do nothing to diminish prejudices, she says. Rather, they exacerbate another moral evil: class difference. By highlighting painful class differences not only is there a risk of backlash by the white community against the middle-class black male students and against the abolitionist movement, but there is also a risk that the moral arguments of the abolitionists will be perceived to be pretext for imposing northern cultural values on the South.

Beecher illustrates her point that morally virtuous ends do not justify means which themselves create moral evils with a second example: the appeal made by abolitionists that slaveholders living in states where emancipation is illegal nevertheless emancipate their slaves. Such an action, Beecher claims, places freedmen in jeopardy of "worse bondage." The "worse bondage" is not specified, but she presumably refers to the well-known risk that upon discovery, former slaves would be lynched as runaways, or would be reenslaved. Rather, she urges abolitionists to advise emancipatory-minded slaveowners to treat slaves as well as they do their family members, while working within the system; to change states' laws.

Calvinism held that the purpose of ethics is not merely to inculcate virtuous behavior in individuals, but to effect a basis for social cohesion and stability. Consistent with her Calvinist beliefs, Beecher insists that abolitionists respect Southern values, habits, and culture. She claims that respecting Southern culture while criticizing slavery and working to make emancipation socially and economically feasible for the South is morally virtuous.[119] Imposing Northern culture, norms, and mores is not. Such imposition is not only arrogant, but it has morally wrong consequences. It is divisive and generates regional hatreds and mistrust. Some slaveholders may be virtuous people who are blinded by custom and cultural norms. Yet they may act kindly towards their own slaves. These same slaveholders may fail to grasp the force of the moral argument against slavery. An abolitionist attack on the personal integrity and virtue of such a slaveholder is unlikely to change the slaveholder's convictions. Such criticism is likely to be perceived by Southerners as an evil onslaught upon the slaveowner's character.

The popular movement towards abolition, like the movement towards temperance, consisted largely of women. Towards the end of the *Essay...* Beecher challenges women to set the moral example for the men and for the nation by tolerating different opinions, by rejecting violent demonstrations as an instrument of change, and by working to defuse the anger surrounding abolitionism. She sets the challenge in the context of morality and cites the dissolution of the union as a risk should women fail to meet the challenge.

Catharine Beecher's moral, social, and political philosophy centers on her views of women's nature. In addition to the *Essay...* two other philosophical works regarding women capture her views: *The Duty of American Women to their Country*[120] and *The Evils Suffered by American Women and American Children: The Causes and the Remedy.*[121] In these two writings, Beecher sets out arguments supporting women's special duty to educate and to provide moral example through acts of benevolent utility involving personal sacrifice and self-denial. According to Beecher, women's nature is expressed through leadership in child rearing, in education, and in social reform. The home is an environment created by the woman. The family is a microcosm of the state. This much of her views on women's nature is clearly derived from her Calvinist beliefs. But Catharine Beecher also believed that women's moral duties did not end with their role as wives and mothers. Those duties extended beyond the home to the social state of which women were preparing their children to become virtuous, responsible members. The logical conclusion, drawn from Common Sense as much as from Calvinism, is that women must make the world a virtuous place by populating it with virtuous children and also by instilling virtue in others through teaching, persuasion, and example. To assist women in meeting their responsibilities, Catharine wrote many practical pamphlets and books directed at women of different classes from philanthropists[122] to educators[123] and servants.[124] Through these pamphlets we see that her position was that women, who are naturally more virtuous than men, must achieve hegemony outside the domestic sphere through activism to transform the social practices which men had instituted and which were inconsistent with virtue and morality. Although Catharine Beecher was a feminist and a believer in women's moral leadership and moral superiority to men, she adamantly opposed women's suffrage.[125] It was the duty of men to run the state; however, morally weak men must be led by women to understand and to fulfill their duty. In this regard, she frequently complained that the churches were not doing their part to provide the appropriate moral leadership.

Catharine Ward Beecher contributed to the development of an American moral, social, and political philosophy which originated in a revised and secularized Calvinism. In her later thought, Calvinism, with its emphasis on self-denial and self-sacrifice, became not merely or even primarily a theology, but the foundation for social ethics.

Beecher used the epistemology and methodology of Common Sense philosophy and incorporated its emphasis on the conscience as a moral faculty into her moral theory. In her view, utility was a philosophically sound measure of the morality of individual action, but utility was to be constrained by considerations of justice and right. Moreover, actions which were utilitous, just, and right were not morally praiseworthy in themselves. Actions became morally praiseworthy if they were motivated by the right intention (an unselfish desire to do good) and were performed in a manner which demonstrated care, concern, and appreciation for those who were affected by the act. Catharine Ward Beecher incorporated the prevailing complementarian views on women's nature into her moral, social, and political philosophy to derive a duty of women to bring about social justice through philosophical argumentation, moral example, selfless activism, and leadership.

Despite the comprehensiveness of her philosophical views, Catharine Ward Beecher is not remembered as a philosopher, nor as a theologian, nor as a social reformer. Rather, she is best known as the founder of a field of study which grew from her views of the central social importance of women as homemakers and educators: the discipline of home economics. Just as Common Sense philosophy was a bridge between enlightenment philosophy and pragmatism, so Catharine Beecher's work on the subject of home economics must be understood as an essential, pragmatic consequence of her philosophical views. With her sister Harriet Beecher Stowe, the author of *Uncle Tom's Cabin*, Catharine Beecher wrote the classic *Principles of Domestic Science*.[126] This and similar works sketch a "system of domestic management" to enable women to create the type of home environment which Catharine believed was essential to the development of virtue. Although many of Beecher's writings, including those on home economics, are not philosophical, they are firmly grounded in her Common Sense and Calvinist Puritan religious, social, moral, political, and educational philosophy. Her eight philosophical writings merit consideration and analysis as examples of mid-nineteenth-century American rationalist philosophy.

2. Harriet Martineau: 1802–1876

Harriet Martineau was born in Norwich, England, the sixth child of merchant-class Huguenot parents. She apparently was moderately ill throughout her childhood, had no sense of taste or smell, and had become deaf by the time she was in her mid-teens. The family became Unitarians, as did the local schoolmaster. Unitarianism was strongly frowned upon in the ecclesiastical city of Norwich.[127] When the school her brothers attended lost many pupils due to the schoolmaster's conversion to Unitarianism, the schoolmaster agreed to accept girls. Harriet's mother immediately placed her and her sister Rachel in the school. There, Harriet learned Latin, French, and studied English composition through a method that closely resembled the classical logic of rhetoric.

Although she was seriously ill for extended periods of her adult life, Harriet Martineau was a prolific author. Joseph Rivlin's bibliography[128] lists over 600 editions of her more than forty books, including many French, Dutch, German, Swedish, and Spanish translations. Her early publications earned her little, but in 1830 she won first, second, and third prizes for three essays in a Unitarian Association triple contest. One contest required writing an essay making Unitarianism appealing to Roman Catholics; a second essay contest was to make a Unitarian appeal for Jewish converts; and the third contest was for an essay directed at converting Moslems.[129] Martineau's published works include philosophy, natural history travelogues, devotional literature, poetry, novels and treatises on education, economics, home economics, theology, and other subjects. In part this diversity reflects her philosophic interests: Martineau seems always to have been seeking a unified philosophic account of science and of human nature. This quest was initially reflected by her Unitarian religious views, then by her analysis of religious knowledge and its implications for principles of moral philosophy, then by her later embracing of the philosophy of Auguste Comte.[130]

Martineau first became known as a philosophic writer when her essays on philosophy of religion and historical interpretation of religious epistemology began to appear in 1821. These essays were originally published in the journal *Monthly Repository*, and later in Volume 1 of her *Miscellanies*.[131] In this collection, Martineau writes about the development of religious sentiments and knowledge during a person's lifetime. This series of essays describe the logical and epistemological maturation of a person in their religious experience. In her preface she describes the sequence of that maturation which is more fully developed in the essays.

From occasionally remembering God, the worshipper proceeds to search for him, particularly by self-inquisition. Now he takes upon him his burden of self-consciousness, and is carefully, and often painfully, employed in settling points of belief and of conduct, fixing methods of observance, watching for manifestations (that is, virtues and vices) in others, and treating these manifestations... as ultimate facts.

This state is far superior to the former; for, though the love of manifestations is far below that of principles, it is far above that of forms.[132]

Throughout the *Miscellanies*, Martineau relates the type and degree of religious knowledge achieved by a person to moral philosophy as a source of knowledge of ideal human behavior. In her view, improvements in moral sensitivity to the needs of others, in abilities to be conscious of self, to be reflective, and to reason analytically, accompany greater knowledge of one's relationship to God and greater understanding of moral philosophy.

The highest condition of the religious sentiment is when it has attained repose; when the worshipper...sees nothing which is not full of God. In the serenity of this assured faith it is that men endure, at the call of duty, as a matter of course, the most protracted and the fiercest woes of life and of death. In this consciousness, – no longer of self, – but of God, it is that philosophers and philanthropists go forth through Nature and Society, to sound the processes of the one, and test the institutions of the other.[133]

The idea that religious epistemology implies moral philosophy is applied in Martineau's analysis of religious intolerance, the rights of factory workers in labor disputes, the slave trade, and involuntary commitment of the mentally ill, among other issues. In essays on these subjects Martineau traces the implications of her views of how we can know what rights are God-given human rights for the great social and political questions of her day.

Martineau's approach to the idea of progress in human knowledge and development closely follows that of Auguste Comte. Like Comte, she viewed that progress of individual persons as well as civilizations proceeds in three irreversible steps. The search for knowledge begins with theology, becomes metaphysics, and finally, positivism. Within each stage there is also a progression from the diffuse to the concrete to the absolute. Following Comte (and to be followed afterwards by Hegel), Martineau held that the development of the intellects of persons as well as the genius of a civilization is mirrored in analogous development of reason and the capacity for moral action (in persons), and in the development of sciences and of just, compassionate, institutional structures (in civilizations). In the theological stage, science and religion are indistinct; in the metaphysical stage they are separate, and natural science in its search for absolute knowledge dominates the structure of civilization. In the final, positivist stage, which historically accompanies the industrial revolution, the search for absolute metaphysical truths is abandoned for the study of lawlike relationships among individuals, among the sciences, and among cultures. Thus is born the science of sociology, an international industrial political economy, and, in contemporary parlance, the religion of secular humanism. Martineau soon expanded her analysis of religious epistemology and moral philosophy to focus on social philosophy. Her *Illustrations of Political Economy* appeared in serial publication of twenty-five parts beginning in 1832.[134] The collected essays were published in nine volumes in 1834.[135] At this point in her life, Martineau was part of the circle of philosophers and other intellectuals which included Unitarians and Utilitarians. The group assembled by her publisher Fox included other writers, among them Harriet Taylor, John Carlyle, and John Stuart Mill.[136] According to Hayek, Martineau was one of many in the group who talked about the indiscreet romance between Mill and Taylor. Apparently it is Martineau's participation in that gossip that caused Mill to want nothing to do with her or with her work when he refused to review her edition of Comte.[137] Martineau's translation and condensation of Auguste Comte's *Course de Philosophie Positive* appeared in 1853. The original eight volumes of Comte's published lectures were condensed to two volumes and translated. Many of Martineau's contemporaries, including Comte himself, praised Martineau's ability to translate from French to English the complex and often redundant contents of Comte's lectures without sacrificing either the original style or philosophic substance. It is the retranslation into French of

Martineau's English condensation of Comte that has become the standard French edition. The publisher's announcement of the second edition of the English translation reads in part:

> It is not for us to speak of the execution of this work: but we may fitly mention, that it was highly approved by the author himself, that, in his annual issue of his catalogue of works sanctioned by him, he substituted Miss Martineau's version for the original. In consequence of this her version has been, since his death, retranslated into French for the sake of its diffusion among the author's own countrymen.[138]

3. *Harriet Hardy Taylor Mill: 1807–1858*

Harriet Hardy was born in London, in 1807, a middle child among seven children of Harriet Hurst and Thomas Hardy. Little is known of her parents, other than that her father was a successful surgeon and male midwife of the lower aristocracy who provided good educations for all of his children. According to Frederick Hayek, the eighteen-year-old Harriet Hardy married a twenty-nine-year-old wholesale druggist, John Taylor, and had two children by him prior to meeting John Stuart Mill in 1830.[139] Her first philosophical writings can be dated to this year. According to Hayek,

> ...the variety of drafts and scraps on the position of women, on education and various social usages and conventions, which date from about the same period, [1830–1833] suggest that these problems must have been occupying her for some time. The most interesting of these essays which in parts curiously anticipates some of the arguments of *On Liberty*, is reprinted as Appendix II to the present volume.[140]

Harriet Taylor was part of a circle of Unitarian radicals and Benthamite philosophers, social theorists, and literary writers, which included Jane and Thomas Carlyle, William Johnson Fox, Harriet Martineau,[141] Eliza Flower, Sarah Flower, Southwood Smith, John Bowring, John Roebuck, John Stuart Mill, and others. The social and political views of various members of this group, including those of Harriet Taylor, were published in the Unitarian journal, the *Monthly*

Repository, and in the Utilitarian journal, *The Westminster Review*. According to Hayek, Taylor's contributions to the former journal began at about the time she met Mill (through Fox) in 1830.

Hayek notes[142] that an early draft of an untitled essay (paired with one by Mill: they had promised to write essays for each other) on the subject of marriage and divorce was on paper watermarked 1831. A later version was on paper watermarked 1832. The original was therefore probably written during the watermark year, or the following year at the latest. The essay on marriage and divorce is reproduced in Alice Rossi's edited work *Essays on Sex Equality: John Stuart Mill and Harriet Taylor Mill*. In her essay on marriage and divorce Taylor notes that women are educated only in order to "gain their living by marrying." According to Rossi,[143] Taylor's view was that once women had equal rights and access to education and employment, and enjoyed the same civil and political rights as did men, a woman's decision to have children would imply a right and responsibility to provide for them.

Women would have no more reason to barter person for bread, or for anything else, than have men. Public offices being open to them alike, all occupations would be divided between the sexes in their natural arrangements. Fathers would provide for their daughters in the same manner as for their sons.

All the difficulties about divorce seem to be in the consideration for the children – but on this plan it would be the women's *interest* not to have children – now it is thought to be the women's interest to have children as so many ties to the man who feeds her.[144]

The wisest and perhaps the quickest means to do away with its [marriage's] evils is to be found in promoting education – as it is the means of all good – but meanwhile it is hard that those who suffer most from its evils and who are always the best people, should be left without remedy. Would not the best plan be divorce which could be attained by any *without any reason assigned*, and at small expence, but which could only be finally pronounced after a long period? not *less* time than two years should elapse between suing for divorce and permission to contract again – but what the decision will be must be certain at the moment of asking for it – unless during that time the suit should be withdrawn.[145]

Those who are amused by evidence that Harriet Taylor Mill coauthored philosophical texts with Mill, should note that she is no mere student of his. An important difference is that Harriet Taylor's views on women's rights to employment were strongly opposed to those maintained by Mill. This is alarming in a married couple, and neither appears to have been able to convince the other respecting this subject. In his companion essay to Taylor's on marriage and divorce, and nearly four decades later, in his *Subjection of Women*[146] Mill maintained that by marrying a woman gave up all right to independent employment. In Mill's view, once a woman married, her career consisted exclusively of that of wife, mother, and counterpart to her husband. This issue appears to have been one which the couple could not adequately resolve for themselves. They did have nearly identical interests in writing philosophy and immensely enjoyed doing so together. On the one hand, consistent with his view that a wife was the husband's "intelligent" helpmeet, Mill acknowledged Taylor's joint authorship everywhere except on the title pages. This was in deference to the written request of John Taylor, Harriet's husband, who was at that time dying of cancer. Given John Taylor's request, his poor health, and the disapproving gossip, naming Harriet Taylor as coauthor would have appeared cruel and insensitive, and would undoubtedly have affected sales.[147]

According to Hayeck[148] the manuscripts of Taylor's essay on toleration of nonconformity appears on paper bearing an 1832 watermark. Following the system by which Hayek has dated other manuscripts in the Mill-Taylor collection, the essay was written in 1832, or 1833 at the latest. That dates the essay on toleration to within a year of the essay on marriage. If Taylor's 1832/3 essay anticipates *On Liberty* (which Mill specifically notes her to be coauthor and reviser of), it is in its focus on the social and political pressures against dissenting opinions.[149] For example, she says:

What is called the opinion of Society is a phantom power, yet as is often the case with phantoms, of more force over the minds of the unthinking than all the flesh and blood arguments which can be brought to bear against it. It is a combination of the many weak, against the few strong; an association of the mentally listless to punish any manifestation of mental independance. The remedy is, to make all strong enough to stand alone; and whoever has once known the pleasure of self-dependance, will be in no danger of relapsing into subserviency.[150]

On Taylor's account, the effect of suppression of dissent is that an inversion of values occurs: the virtuous tolerance of dissent is called vice, and vicious intolerance is called virtue. The result is a muddled uniformity of opinion and values codified as complex rules of decorum covering every aspect of human social interaction. In such a society, etiquette masquerades as ethics:

> Who are the people who talk most about doing their duty? always those who for their life could give no intelligible theory of duty? What are called people of principle, are often the most unprincipled people, if by principle is intended...accordance of the individual's conduct with the individual's self-formed opinion. Grant this to be the definition of principle, then eccentricity should be prima facie evidence for the existence of principle. So far from this being the case, 'it is odd' therefore it is wrong is the feeling of society... .

She continues in sarcastic reference to those who view themselves to be 'principled':

> They have been taught to think...so and so [is] right – others think so and so right – therefore it must be right. This is the logic of the world's good sort of people; and if, as is often the case their right should prove indisputably wrong, they can but plead those good intentions which make a most slippery and uneven pavement.
>
> To all such we would say, think for yourself, and act for yourself, but whether you have strength to do either the one or the other, attempt not to impede, much less to resent the genuine expression of the others.[151]

In addition to the untitled essays on marriage and divorce and on toleration of nonconformity, Taylor wrote at least six poems.[152] She substantially revised the first draft of Mill's *Principles of Political Economy*. The *Principles* were published under Mill's name alone, but Harriet had created many of the illustrative cases and an additional chapter on the future of the working class. During the winter of 1850–1851 Taylor wrote the essay *Enfranchisement of Women*. This work was apparently edited by Mill.[153] In addition, it is likely that she coauthored *On Liberty*, which was also published under Mill's name alone. The full extent of Taylor's contributions to *On Liberty* is unclear, although Michael Packe[154] holds the view that it was an elaboration on Taylor's views initially expressed in her essays on marriage and divorce and on toleration of nonconformity. According to Mill,

> ...there was not a sentence of [*On Liberty*] that was not several times gone through by us together, turned over in many ways, and carefully weeded of any faults, either in thought or expression, that we detected in it.[155]

Discussions of Harriet Taylor Mill's importance as a philosopher have focussed on the extent to which John Stuart Mill accurately represents her contributions to works which were published under his name alone. There are those who claim that Mill is an unreliable witness regarding Taylor, and those who find Mill a reliable, if somewhat smitten authority on her. In the former camp are those who portray Mill as an emotionally deprived child, raised to be a prodigious exemplar of Jeremy Bentham's and James Mill's educational philosophy.[156] They depict Mill as an adult who serially idolized his father, then Taylor.[157] These scholars sometimes describe Taylor as a shrill, domineering,[158] disloyal wife, who was callously insensitive to the effects on her long-suffering first husband of her public relationship with Mill.[159] On this account, Taylor was at most Mill's muse and copy-editor, someone whose intellect is rightfully compared to his and found lacking.[160] These unkind psychological portraits make good press. They depict Mill as a great thinker who single-handedly developed an important argument for personal and political autonomy, while remaining totally unautonomous as a spouse. In support of this portrait is cited a winter of depression which Mill suffered from in 1826, a quarter-century prior to his collaboration with Taylor!

In the latter camp are those who acknowledge that Taylor and Mill were mutual admirers whose intellectual compatibility quickly produced a strong emotional interdependence.[161] These scholars portray Taylor as a decent woman who was unfairly constrained in a loveless marriage to an equally decent man.[162] On this view, we ought to accept as truthful Mill's repeated claims of Taylor's philosophic as well as editorial contributions to works publicly attributed to him.[163] These claims appear not only in Mill's correspondence, and in his dedications to *Principles of Political Economy* and *On Liberty*, but in his manuscript list indicating "joint productions" of his publications.[164] Taylor's essays on marriage, toleration, and emancipation clearly demonstrate that she was a competent author of philosophy. Mill's testimony is knowledgeable, consistent, and reliable. I am not prepared to ignore it, particularly in light of the evidence of Taylor's own essays.

In my view, the position represented by the second camp has greater weight, in part because it is simpler and does not require us to concoct unkind psychological theories about both Mill and Taylor. The conclusion which I am drawn to is that Harriet Taylor was a competent libertarian feminist philosopher. Taylor appears to be a writer who publicly held feminist views on divorce and marriage which were more libertarian than those of Mill. In my view, Taylor was much more than Mill's muse and copy-editor. They were spouses and coauthors who held irreconcilable views on married women's rights to employment. In this and other respects, Taylor independently represented an important aspect of libertarian and feminist philosophy.

4. Jenny Poinsard d'Héricourt: 1809–1875

Little is known about the life of Jenny d'Héricourt.[165] According to Jeanne Deroin[166] Poinsard was d'Héricourt's family name. Offen reports that Poinsard was born in Besançon on September 10, 1809. Her clockmaker father was a Lutheran from nearby Héricourt. Her mother, Marguerite-Baptiste-Alexandrine Brenet, was a Calvinist of Swiss descent. She received an early education, apparently at home, but following the death of her father, she, her mother, and her sister moved to Paris, where at age eighteen she received her diploma of "Instructrice."[167] In her early twenties, Poinsard (who preferred to be known as "Jenny d'Héricourt"), married Michel-Gabriel-Joseph Marie. According to d'Héricourt's autobiography[168] he attempted to murder her early in their marriage so as to be free to marry another. This experience no doubt influenced d'Héricourt's view that divorce should be legalized in France. Following her separation, she published (under the pseudonym Felix Lamb) a novel against capital punishment. Her autobiography also alludes to another novel against adultery. She studied physiology and homeopathic medicine privately with the visiting president of the Medical Homeopathic Institute of Buenos Aires and received a diploma as a physician. In 1857, the *Revue philosophique et réligieuse* published her criticism of some of the philosophical and scientific foundations of homeopathic obstetrics.[169] Specifically, she objected to a then-popular system for immunizing newborns using injections of blood drawn from infected persons. In her view, many more infant deaths were caused by this method of immunization than would have occurred in its absence. She preferred inoculating mothers post-partum and then inoculating the child with the mother's blood several months later. Her autobiographical article claims that she received a diploma "maitresse sage femme." However, Offen[170] reports no success in confirming d'Héricourt's award of a diploma by La Maternité, nor by l'École des Sages-femmes (Port Royal Hospital), nor by the Paris Faculty of Medicine. And although the evidence documenting d'Héricourt's qualifications as a trained obstetrical nurse is lacking, her technical knowledge of obstetrics, pediatrics, and immunology is clear from her review of Croserio's text.

Offen reports that from 1855 d'Héricourt began publishing a series of feminist articles in the liberal Italian philosophy journal *La Ragione*, published in Turin. *La Ragione* was, Offen reports, edited by the rationalist philosopher Cristoforo Bonavino under the pseudonym 'Ausonio Franchi'. D'Héricourt's articles in *La Ragione* began in October 1855 and continued into 1857, according to Offen, and were discussed in the feminist revue *La Donna* (Genoa, 1855–56.) I have been unable to obtain copies of these articles. Both Offen[171] and Moses[172] indicate that d'Héricourt also published a series of articles against Proudhon in the *Revue philosophique et réligieuse* during the period December 1856 through February 1857. I have not been able to obtain that correspondence. According to Moses[173] d'Héricourt rejected outright the "exceptional woman" explanation resorted to by Proudhon and others to account for women who obviously did not fit misogynist conceptions of woman. In addition, d'Héricourt denied that feminists wanted special legislation to protect women from men. Rather, she asserted, feminists want all legislation to be common to both sexes.

In 1860, at age fifty, d'Héricourt published *La femme affranchie: résponse à MM. Michelet, Proudhon, E. de Giradin, A. Comte et aux autres novateurs modernes.*[174] An 1864 abridged English translation (by an unnamed translator) appeared as *A Woman's Philosophy of Woman.*[175] The work can properly be considered both philosophy of medicine, moral epistemology, and social/political philosophy. For example, in criticizing Michelet's argument that menstruation is proof that women are weak, diseased organisms, d'Héricourt (perhaps drawing on her obstetrical training?) counters:

> It is a principle in biology that *no physiological condition is a morbid condition*; consequently the monthly crisis peculiar to woman is not a disease, but a normal phenomenon.... It would be absurd to call a man perpetually wounded who should take a fancy to scratch the end of his finger every month.[176]

It is not only Michelet's philosophy of medicine which is erroneous, d'Héricourt claims, but also his methodology and philosophy of science:

> Michelet, therefore, has not only erred in erecting a physiological law into a morbid condition, but he has also sinned against rational method by making general rules of a few exceptions, and by proceeding from this generalization, contradicted by the great majority of facts, to construct a system of [social] subjection.[177]

The sources of moral knowledge, of knowledge of the nature of right and justice are not the masculist interpretations of the Book of Genesis. In interpreting Genesis, d'Héricourt says, Michelet and others like him wrongfully reason from the story of Eve's creation out of Adam's rib to the conclusion that God created woman inferior to man and intended woman to be subordinate to man. According to d'Héricourt, Michelet's arguments that women are physically, morally, and intellectually inferior to men are mistaken on several grounds. From the premise that male characteristics are the only characteristics relevant to assigning human rights, Michelet and others conclude that only males have human rights. Even if this argument were true, d'Héricourt contends, in order to restrict human rights to males it would have to be the case that men and only men had masculine characteristics. D'Héricourt asserts that women exemplify such characteristics as much as do males. According to d'Héricourt, what is most disturbing about misogynist arguments is not that they assume the truth of empirically false statements, nor that they misrepresent revealed truths, but that misogynist moral philosophy is grounded on epistemological, rather than logical, criteria. What Genesis teaches us, according to d'Héricourt, is that both man and woman are equally created creatures of God. It reveals to us the logical criteria for moral status: membership in the class of human beings. But Michelet and other misogynists read Genesis without realizing that woman is not created in man's image and likeness, but God's. Men and women are equally God's human creations, and it is this logical criterion, human nature, rather than purely empirical criteria like degrees of virility and amounts of physical strength, that is the proper criterion of moral status.[178] D'Héricourt concludes:

> Though that were true which I deny; that woman is inferior to you; though that were true which *facts* prove false; that she can perform none of the functions which you perform, that she is fit only for maternity and the household, she would be none the less your equal in right, because right is based neither on superiority of faculties nor on that of the functions which proceed from them, but on identity of species.[179]

> A human being, like you, [of] intellect, will, free will and various aptitudes, woman has the right, like you, to be free and autonomous, to develop her faculties freely, to exercise her activity freely; to mark out her path, to reduce her to subjection, as you do, is therefore a violation of Human Right in the person of woman – an odious abuse of force.[180]

According to Offen[181] Jenny d'Héricourt moved to Chicago shortly after the publication of *La Femme Affranchie*. There she worked with the leaders of the women's rights movement, including Kate Newell Doggett, Mary Livermore, Elizabeth Cady Stanton, and Susan B. Anthony. Her influence extended beyond America and France to Russia, Italy, and elsewhere.[182] During the decade which d'Héricourt spent in Chicago, she was a contributor to *The Agitator*. The great Chicago fire of October 1871 destroyed much archival evidence of the details of her years there. Her death in January 1875 is recorded in the *acte de décès*, January 12, 1875, in the Archives de la Seine, and her obituary was published in *L'avenir des femmes* (The Future of Women) on February 7, 1875.

5. *George Eliot (Marian Evans): 1819–1880*

An English woman who had little formal education, Eliot translated Feuerbach's *Das Wesen des Christentums* (The Essence of Christianity) in 1854.[183] Although her background in philosophy was scant, she was closely affillitated with the philosophers Herbert Spencer and George Henry Lewes. Eliot is known for her literary writings, for which there exists a large and accessible secondary literature. She is sometimes considered to be a philosopher whose *genre* was fiction. Her views on moral, religious, and metaphysical problems emerge through her literary works. Those views are summarized in one of the rare *Encyclopedia of Philosophy* articles about women philosophers (s.v. Eliot, George) as well as in *George Eliot: Romantic Humanist*.[184] Her philosophical orientation is variously identified with Feuerbach, Spinoza, Comte, and J.S. Mill. She held views on moral responsibility, free will, determinism, religious knowledge and faith, the nature of duty, the structure of society, and other philosophical issues. A thorough philosophical analysis of her *corpus* and of her method of developing her views in a literary form would be most welcome.

6. *Clemence Royer: 1830–1902*

Born in Nantes, Clemence Royer was known throughout the continent for her translation of Darwin's *Origin of the Species Through Natural Selection*.[185] To call her work a translation, however, obscures the fact that she heavily annotated and made extensive philosophic comment on the theory of natural selection and its implications for moral theory. In 1881 her major philosophic work, *The Good and the Moral Law; Ethics and Teleology*,[186] appeared. In this work, Royer develops both an atomistic metaphysics and a utopian, utilitarian ethics. According to the 1882 review of her *Le Bien et la Loi Morale; Éthique et Téléologie*, Royer's work surpasses Herbert Spencer's *The Data of Ethics* precisely because Royer presents a full-blown metaphysical theory which serves as the foundation for what can best be described as moral anthropology.[187]

According to Royer, just as the human species strives for survival and develops strength through the development of the intellect, so humans, viewed as moral agents, seek happiness, not only for themselves as individuals but for the larger social groupings of which they are a part. Basing her account of the development of morality on the ontological doctrine she calls substantialism, Royer claims that spirit and matter are both derived from the same noumenal "stuff" which is the foundational substance of the universe. Royer develops her account of substantialism in great detail. According to Royer this entity is conscious of itself and develops a vague idea of that space which it does not occupy. The first conditions of self-knowledge, that is, *a priori* knowledge, are part of the self-consciousness of the entity's own existence known through its sensation of physical contact with other entities as they limit the space of its existence. Those sensations of contact with other entities are perceived to be either enjoyable or painful. Royer represents algebraically the good and bad for an indefinite number of representative individuals and groups over time, in an infinite universe. She arrives at an algebraic representation of the absolute good for an infinite succession over time of an indefinite number of individuals, each of whom lives for a finite period in contact with a finite number of others. She asks how can we actually increase the amount of happiness in the universe?

To answer this question, Royer begins with a standard utilitarian account of the good. The good for each entity is represented as the sum of its enjoyable experiences multiplied by the intensity of each experience. The bad for each entity is represented as the sum of its painful experiences multiplied by the intensity of each experience. The moral good for each being consists in acting instinctively, which for humans means acting rationally in accordance with the law of human nature. That law is to seek the greatest happiness, which is the best interests of the greatest number of persons. The moral law, she argues, imposes an obligation on rational beings to increase human happiness by protecting and regulating the development of happiness-producing characteristics of the human organism. For each person, the moral law requires recognizing that the greatest happiness comes from sacrificing egoistic pleasures and the immediate well-being of one's person, family, and social group in order to promote the common human good. That means acting on sentiments of sympathy and universal fraternity. Seeking the good of all, rather than one's own good and the good of one's family or social group, will secure for the moral agent a totality of pleasure equal to or greater than those joys found in personal well-being or in that of one's family. In order to support individuals in their abandonment of moral egoism in favor of the common good, societies must support social institutions which teach and foster the development of humanistic sentiment. Eventually, Royer says, the humanistic instincts will become as integral a part of the organic makeup of future human beings as the egoistic instinct is of nineteenth-century human nature. In effect, she claims, instincts of universal beneficience can gradually become part of the heredity of the human race.

Clemence Royer's metaphysics and ethics merit study in their own right. But they also merit study in light of her contemporaries Hegel, Schopenhauer, Nietzsche, and Freud, as well as in light of those by whom she was undoubtedly influenced: Bentham, Mill, Spencer, Darwin, and Reid. She is an interesting barometer of late nineteenth-century moral philosophy as it was shaped by anthropology, physics, psychology, and politics.

7. *Juliette Lambert La Messine Adam: 1836–1936*

Born in Verberie,[188] Picardy, Juliette Lambert was educated by her father, who was a physician and a feminist, and by her maternal grandmother. She began her public career in 1856 with the pseudonymous publication (under the name "Juliette") of a letter to the editor of *Le Siècle*. At eighteen Lambert married Alexis La Messine, a government official. Two years later they reportedly had a child.[189] Lambert moved to Paris and was associated with a group of Saint-Simonians including Charles Fauverty and Charles Renouvier. Fauverty was the founder and editor of *La Revue Philosophique*.

Pierre-Joseph Proudhon's *De La Justice Dans la Révolution et dans l'Église* appeared in the spring of 1858.[190] The main thrust of Proudhon's book was against the church. However, two chapters were devoted to discussions of love and marriage. In them he argues that women were by nature physically, intellectually, and morally inferior to men. Proudhon claims that his proof of women's inferiority is mathematical: assigning weights to women's physical strength (weighted at 2 to a man's 3), he assigns the same social value to women: 2/3 of a man's value. But this value is overrated, he claims, and does not take into account twelve years of lost production by women due to menstruation, pregnancy, recovery, nursing, and child-rearing. After defining intellect in masculine terms ("virility") Proudhon assigns to women an intellectual weight of 2 to men's 3. On Proudhon's moral scale, women fare no better, lacking virtues of wisdom and courage, and lacking the intellect to have a conscience. Not surprisingly, women's comparative moral value is 2 to a man's 3. Multiplication of physical × intellectual × moral value of each sex mathematically proves that women's social value is 8 to a man's 27. Having thus demonstrated women's natural inferiority to men, Proudhon concludes that social, civil, and political equality was dangerous and a threat to French society. Women's unequal treatment was just, and the name of the institution which justly treated women unequally is marriage. Moses[191] reports that Juliette Lambert tried to convince the better-known Jenny d'Héricourt to respond to Proudhon. D'Héricourt eventually responded, despite an initial refusal. Four months after the appearance of Proudhon's *De la Justice...* Juliette Lambert published her own response, *Idées anti-proudhoniennes sur l'amour, la femme et le mariage.*[192]

Lambert dismisses Proudhon's arguments as *non sequiturs* (*coq-à-l'âne*), saying that his views on physical strength employ a "technology that borders on the obscene."[193] She states that freedom and equality based on equivalence rather than identity are necessary preconditions for the establishment of relationships which can be characterized as just.[194]

> It must be fully understood that, as society organizes itself, it creates parts corresponding to the degree of its own social development which must be increasingly perfect; these parts are "institutions." Primitive institutions were created for the purposes of strength, contemporary institutions arise instead for humanitarian reasons. The purposes of contemporary and future institutions are mutual aid, entitlements, and charity. Their goal is to spread knowledge, improve welfare, guarantee individual survival through community aid, care for the debilitated, the disabled and the ill.[195]

Lambert clearly accepts the theory of sex complementarity and corresponding functional equality. She says that the job of "brood hen" is a noble one, but it is not right for every woman. Nor does motherhood preclude outside employment. Her argument is multi-pronged. First, she argues that only productive employment emancipates adults. Vocational education for women can emancipate women by enabling them to identify themselves in terms of their productivity, instead of "posing as dolls before men," seriously playing the "stupid role" they have been socialized to play since childhood. Second, she argues that denying employment opportunities to women entices women to earn their incomes through prostitution. Legalizing broader avenues of employment for women without their husband's consent will not only help ambitious women resist the financial temptation of prostitution, but also resist the vices which idleness brings. Lambert lists a number of careers which are suitable for a woman.[196]

According to Moses, Lambert represents part of the move within social and political philosophy away from the utopian ideas of the Saint-Simonians and other sex-complementarians.[197] The Saint-Simonianism of Prosper Enfantin was an advance over earlier forms of sex complementarianism in that it justified full female participation in public life despite alleged innate moral differences between the sexes. Like the Saint-Simonians, Lambert acknowledged sexual differences and accepted the idea that women's virtues complement men's. Unlike the Saint Simonians, she did not call for the establishment of a utopian society in which women, as exemplars of "feminine virtue," would be valued equally with male exemplars of "masculine virtue." Lambert claims that so-called "masculine" and "feminine" virtues are found not only in members of each sex but within many individuals, and that the distinctions are not morally significant.

The third part of Lambert's argument for women's economic equality is an argument for moral autonomy. If the distinctions between the sexes are morally insignificant, there is no moral justification for society to allocate rights and opportunities based on sex. If moral autonomy is a charcteristic of men and if its exercise is a moral right of men, then it is also a characteristic and right of women. The exercise of individual autonomy is impossible in the absence of social and political equality and in the absence of equality of economic opportunity. Enforcement of alleged moral distinctions between the sexes through the imposition of constraints on women's employment is a threat to moral autonomy and therefore is a threat to freedom:

> Even if it were useful, concerning the organization of society, to be aware of those occupations that are more "feminine" and those which are more "masculine," it would however greatly endanger freedom to attempt to fix in advance the respective roles of men and woman and to imprison either in occupations according to their respective sex.[198]

Lambert develops an argument for women's autonomy:

> In a society created by men for their own benefit, woman was valued only as wife and mother; but if woman is a free individual, intellectually and morally vital, she has her own value and will make her own law. She will no more obtain her conscience and personal dignity from man than he obtains his own dignity and conscience from that which is external to him. Clearly, this is the doctrine of *immanence* (as Proudhon calls it) with respect to woman.[199]

Much later, she poses the rhetorical question "is woman an autonomous person?" The response is unequivocal:

> Woman, considered as woman, is an entity in herself: she is self-legislating within the context of natural law; in a word, she is a being. She comes to know the general laws to which she is subject and apprehends them by virtue of her understanding; she is therefore a knowing subject. Finally, she has free will and is the author of her own moral law; she is therefore autonomous.[200]

Lambert suggested that society acknowledge women's autonomy by replacing traditional marriage agreements (usually arranged by the families) with contracts between free and equal individuals in which each would be free to dispose only of his or her own property. The parties would determine the conditions of their association; divorce must be legal as a means of avoiding marital slavery. Her views on female autonomy lead her to renew her demands for social equality, particularly within the institution Proudhon had identified as an institution of just inequality: marriage.

8. *Christine Ladd-Franklin: 1847–1930*

Christine Ladd was born in Windsor, Connecticut, in the middle of the nineteenth century and gained eminence in philosophy of psychology and logic.[201] Her mother died when she was a teenager, and she was raised by relatives.[202] She studied Greek and mathematics at Wesleyan Academy in preparation for entering college. She spent two years at Vassar and graduated in 1869.[203] She taught secondary school for several years prior to seeking admission to the Johns Hopkins University graduate school in 1878. Some of her early published papers on mathematics had been noticed by the English mathematician Sylvester, who reportedly persuaded the graduate school to admit her on a special status. Although she entered Johns Hopkins in 1878, received a three-year fellowship (1879–1881), and completed all the requirements for the Ph.D. by 1882, the degree was not granted to her until 44 years later.[204]

According to Schneewind,[205] Ladd-Franklin taught logic at Johns Hopkins. She later taught logic and psychology for twenty years at Columbia University. Her writings evidence expertise in the logics of Boole, Jevons, McColl, Pierce, Ellis, Schroder, Delboef, Frege, Venn, and Wundt, the philosophy of psychology of Helmholtz, and the color and vision theories of Muller and Hering. Her interests in mathematical logic, and algebra and geometry in general, are represented by her "On the Algebra of Logic," published by the philosopher Charles S. Pierce, whose student she was.[206] This fifty-four-page article includes discussions of identical propositions in logic, on universalizability and its algebra (including expressions for conjoining and disjoining propositions and terms, on elimination of premises or parts thereof, on inferences from universals to particulars), on expressing the resolution of problems, and on constituting the universe of discourse. Throughout the paper, she draws on examples developed originally by Venn, Wundt, and others.

Ladd-Franklin is also known for her contributions to logic notation. In "The Reduction to Absurdity of the Ordinary Treatment of the Syllogism" she reduces the syllogism to a single formula in which its three statements form an "antilogism."[207] In addition, she developed a principle for recognizing valid forms of syllogism. She is the author of more than 100 articles on logic and color vision. A nearly complete bibliography is in Grinstein and Campbell's *Women of Mathematics*.[208]

Ladd-Franklin's interests in psychology, particularly the psychology of visual perception, are represented by her *Colour and Colour Theories*.[209] Improving on the theories of Muller (who repeated his lectures for her because Gottingen excluded women),[210] Hering, and Helmholtz, Ladd-Franklin formulated her own theory of color vision. It avoided Helmholtz's embarrassing need to consider yellow to be a combination of red and green, and Hering's need to consider red and green as complementary primary colors. Moreover, it was compatible with recent evolutionary theories in that it accounted for the evolution of the rudimentary brightness sense of some lower animals into a complete perception of the spectrum in humans. It also offered an explanation of certain forms of color-blindness in terms of incomplete development. It accommodated recent findings of light-sensitive iodopsin (in retinal cones), a modified form of the rhodopsin found in retinal rods. The geometric properties of the binocular fusion into a single retinal image appears to have initiated Ladd-Franklin's synthesis of mathematical logic, geometry, perception, and spectrography into theories of color perception. Her works on vision appeared in journals spanning a thirty-four-year period (1892–1926). They were collected in *Colour and Colour Theories*, which appeared in 1929.

9. *Hortense Allart de Meritens:* floruit *1850*

Hortense Allart de Meritens' *Novum Organum, ou Sainteté Philosophique* was published in Paris in 1857. A work of nearly 300 pages, it is part apology for the failures of previous philosophies to adequately demonstrate the existence of God and the moral imperative to be pious, while at the same time accounting for scientific advances which purport to supplant God with "Mother Nature." In her work, Allart de Meritens shows a thorough knowledge of the Pythagoreans, Plato, Aristotle, Plotinus, Confucianism, and Buddhism; Clement of Alexandria, Augustine, Descartes, Bacon, Leibniz, Constant, Locke, Spinoza, Machiavelli, Kant, Voltaire, Pascal, and Germaine de Staehl. Allart de Meritens describes her work as

> an attempt to understand natural religion as an object of science. The understanding of God and holiness, knowing God as we know life, and being pious as inevitably as we are mortal.[211]

Using a combination of "inspiration and observation" Allart de Meritens draws on philosophy of religion and moral philosophy and seeks inspiration through knowledge and understanding of these. She claims not to be dogmatic concerning God. She calls on her readers to acknowledge that there is an almost universal belief in a higher being. She urges us not to fear sensory illusion as Bacon does[212] because we have no need to rely on the senses for the kind of inquiry she is making. She urges us rather to follow Democritus and seek the source of laws of human action.

The first ten pages of Allart de Meritens' work are part exposition, but they are primarily a criticism of Bacon. In discussing Bacon's objections to philosophy she notes that in one respect she and Bacon agree: that philosophic inquiry has too often tied human experience to matter, rather than to spirit, and that an inquiry into human spiritual experience is also a proper subject for philosophic inquiry. Philosophers have always conceived of an infinite difference between the "phantoms" of the human understanding and divine understanding. The former, she says, are purely arbitrary abstractions, while the latter are true characteristics of the creator in all things such as he has determined. Here, Allart de Meritens suggests that there are written records (biblical?) of God's mental characteristics. Regarding God's attributes, she says, truth and utility are the same. Quoting Laplace's and Humbolt's comments on Herschel's astronomical findings, Allart de Meritens notes that even the astronomers agree that the likelihood of astronomical phenomena being organized as it is by chance is 1:200,000,000,000.

> Faced with the infinite unfolding before our eyes, who doesn't get the profound impression that God reveals himself there?...How these creations surpass our imaginations. The concept of God becomes greater with each of our [scientific] discoveries.[213]

Hortense Allart de Meritens was one of many women of the nineteenth century who were discussants of philosophy. Like her predecessors Cavendish and du Châtelet, and like her contemporaries d'Héricourt, Somerville, Royer, and Ladd-Franklin, Hortense Allart de Meritens was interested in the philosophical implications of recent scientific discoveries. Like her counterparts Masham, Astell, and Blackwell she believed that religious knowledge played a central role in resolving epistemological and metaphysical questions.

IV. CONCLUSIONS

The preceding chapters in this volume describe aspects of the works of some women philosophers of the seventeenth, eighteenth, and nineteenth centuries. Those descriptions are neither definitive nor complete. I have focussed on women who actually left important philosophical writings, and on women who through correspondence, commentary, or discourse partook of and contributed to the discipline. Sources which will facilitate further research about women's contributions to modern philosophy appear in the Bibliography.

The women who are discussed in this volume made contributions of varying importance to the discipline of philosophy. Most have made significant contributions to its literature. Some have professional and even academic affiliations with other disciplines. Their works often reflect the fact that philosophy itself has historically transcended disciplines. Their identification with other disciplines may have led earlier historians of philosophy to conclude that these women neither studied philosophy nor contributed to the ongoing philosophic dialogues of their day. However, their status as philosophers, whatever else their achievements may have been, ought not be overlooked by those who seek to understand the history of philosophy.

NOTES

1. Anna Maria van Schurman, *Eukleria: seu, Melioris partis electio. Tractatus brevem vitae ejus delineationem exhibens...* Altonae: C. van der Meulen (1673).
2. See Beatrice Zedler, "Marie le Jars de Gournay," *A History of Women Philosophers, Volume 2. Medieval, Renaissance and Enlightenment Women Philosophers: 500–1600*, Mary Ellen Waithe, ed. Dordrecht, Boston, London: Kluwer Academic Publishers (1989).
3. Anna Maria van Schurman, *The Learned maid, or Whether a maid may be a scholar?* London: John Redmayne (1659).
4. Anna Maria van Schurman, *Opuscula hebraeca, greca, latina, gallica, prosaica, et metrica.* Leyden: Elsevir (1642) and other editions.
5. Una Birch Pope-Hennessy, *Anna Van Schurman: Artist, Scholar, Saint.* London: Longmans, Green and Co. (1909), p. 195.
6. Anne F. Robertson, unpublished bibliography for Anna Maria van Schurman, personal communication.
7. Angeline Goreau, *The Whole Duty of a Woman: Female Writers in Seventeenth Century England.* Garden City, NY: Dial Press (1985), pp. 164–170.

8. Bathsua Makin, *The Malady and Remedy of Vexations and Unjust Arrests and Actions*, reprinted in Mary R. Mahl and Helene Koon, eds., *The Female Spectator*. Old Westbury, NY: The Feminist Press and Bloomington, IN: Indiana University Press (1977).

9. Makin-van Schurman correspondence published in van Schurman, *Opuscula hebraeca, latina, graeca, gallica, prosaica et metrica...* Lipsiae: M.C.F. Mullieri (1749), pp. 126–127.

10. Bathsua Makin, *An Essay to Revive the Antient Education of Gentlewomen*, facsimile reprint by The Augustan Reprint Society, Publication Number 202, Los Angeles: University of California Williams Andrew Clark Library (1980).

11. Anna Maria van Schurman, *The Learned maid; or Whether a maid may be a scholar?*

12. Louis Foucher de Cariel, *Descartes, La Princesse Elisabeth et la Reine Christine d'après des lettres inédites*. Paris: Felix Alcan (1909).

13. Beatrice Zedler, "The Three Princesses," *Hypatia* 4:1 (Spring 1989), pp. 28–63.

14. Foucher de Cariel, *op. cit.*

15. L. Dugas, *Une Amitié intellectuelle: Descartes et la Princesse Elisabeth*. Rennes: 1891.

16. Zedler, *op. cit.*, pp. 33–43.

17. Foucher de Cariel, *Descartes et la princesse Palatine, ou de l'influence du cartésianisme sur les femmes au XVIIe siècle*. Paris: Auguste Durand (1862).

18. Nicola Fusco, *Elena Lucrezia Cornaro Piscopia 1646–1684*. Pittsburgh: United States Committee for Elena Lucrezia Cornaro Piscopia terentary (1975).

19. *The Life of Helen Lucretia Cornaro Piscopia Oblate of the Order of St. Benedict and Doctor in the University of Padua*. Rome: St. Benedict's (1896), p. 63.

20. Plutarcho Marsa Vancells, *La Mujer en la Filosofía*. Madrid: Fragua (1976), p. 146.

21. G.B. Comelli, "Laura Bassi e il Suo Primo Trionfo," *Bologna, Istituto per la Storia dell' Universita di Bologna. Studi e memorie per la Storia dell' Universita di Bologna* (1912), pp. 197–256.

22. Comelli, *op. cit.*, p. 203.

23. Comelli, *op. cit.*, p. 201.

24. Comelli, *op. cit.*, p. 204.

25. Comelli, *op. cit.*, p. 199.

26. Comelli, *op. cit.*, p. 206.

27. Comelli, *op. cit.*, p. 210.

28. Comelli, *op. cit.*, p. 207.

29. Margaret Alic, *Hypatia's Heritage*. Boston: Beacon Press (1986), p. 136.

30. Londa Schiebinger, *The Mind has no Sex?* Boston: Harvard University Press (1989), p. 16.

31. Marsa Vancells, *loc. cit.*

32. Comelli, *op. cit.*, pp. 242–243.

33. Mary Hay, *Female Biography: or, Memoirs of Illustrious and Celebrated Women of all Ages and Countries*. Philadelphia: Byrd & Small (1807).

34. Catharine Macaulay, *Loose Remarks on Certain Positions to be found in Mr.*

Hobbes's Philosophical Rudiments of Government and Society. London: T. Davies (1767).

35. Thomas Hobbes, *Philosophical Rudiments concerning Government and Society.* London: J.G. for R. Royston (1651).
36. Catharine Macaulay-Graham, *Letters on Education.* London: 1787.
37. Catharine Macaulay-Graham, *Letters on Education.* London: Dilly (1790).
38. Catharine Macaulay-Graham, *Letters on Education.* London and New York: Garland Press (1974).
39. Florence Boos and William Boos, "Catharine Macaulay: Historian and Political Reformer," *International Journal of Women's Studies* 3:1 (Jan.-Feb. 1980) pp. 52–55. Hereafter as Boos and Boos.
40. David Hume, *History of Great Britain from the Invasion of Julius Caesar to the Revolution of 1688.* 6 vols. London: 1754–1762.
41. Boos and Boos, p. 55.
42. Catharine Macaulay-Graham, *Letters on Education.* London: Dilly (1790), Letter XXII.
43. Catharine Macaulay, *Loose Remarks*, p. 9.
44. *Op. cit.*, pp. 10–11.
45. Londa Schiebinger, *The Mind has no Sex? Women in the Origins of Modern Science.* Cambridge and London: Harvard University Press (1989).
46. Macaulay, *Loose Remarks*, pp. 7–8.
47. Macaulay, *op. cit.*, p. 8.
48. Susan Groag Bell and Karen M. Offen, eds., *Women, the Family, and Freedom: The Debate in Documents V. 1, 1750–1880.* Stanford: Stanford University Press (1983), pp. 26–27.
49. Sophia, a Person of Quality [pseud.], *Woman Not Inferior to Man or, A Short and Modest Vindication of the Natural Right of the Fair Sex to a Perfect Equality of Power, Dignity, and Esteem, with the Men.* London: 1739, p. 3.
50. Sophia, *op. cit.*, p. 7.
51. Sophia, *op. cit.*, p. 8.
52. Sophia, *op. cit.*, p. 9.
53. Bell and Offen, Vol. 1, p. 25.
54. Claire Goldberg Moses, *French Feminism in the 19th Century.* Albany: State University of New York Press (1984), p. 158.
55. D.G. Levy, H.B. Applewhite and M.D. Johnson, eds., *Women in Revolutionary Paris 1789–1795.* Urbana, IL: University of Illinois Press (1979).
56. Olympe de Gouges, *Lettre au peuple ou projet d'une caisse patriotique par une citoyenne*, in *Oeuvres* présentées par Benoite Groult. Paris: Mercure de France (1986).
57. Olympe de Gouges, *Remarques Patriotiques par la citoyenne, auteur de la lettre au peuple*, in *Oeuvres* présentées par Benoite Groult. Paris: Mercure de France (1986).
58. Olympe de Gouges, *Réflexion sur les Hommes Nègres*, in *Oeuvres* présentées par Benoite Groult. Paris: Mercure de France (1986).
59. Olympe de Gouges, *Projet d'un second théâtre et d'une maternité*, in *Oeuvres* présentées par Benoite Groult. Paris: Mercure de France (1986).

60. Olympe de Gouges, *Le Cri du Sage par une Femme*, in *Oeuvres* présentées par Benoite Groult. Paris: Mercure de France (1986).

61. James Mill, in *Encyclopedia Britannica*, suppl. 5th ed. (London: 1814), s.v. "Government." Reprinted as "The Article on Government," 1825.

62. Olympe de Gouges, *Les Droits de la Femme* Paris, n.d. [1791] Bibliothèque Nationale, E 5588, in *Women in Revolutionary Paris 1789–1795*, D.G. Levy, H.B. Applewhite and M.D. Johnson, eds. Urbana, IL: University of Illinois Press (1979).

63. *Ibid.*

64. Martha Somerville, ed., *Mary Somerville, Personal Recollections, From Early Life to Old Age: With Selections from her Correspondence.* London: John Murray (1873).

65. Elizabeth Chambers Patterson, *Mary Somerville and the Cultivation of Science, 1815–1840.* International Archives of the History of Ideas 102. Dordrecht: Martinus Nijhoff (1983).

66. Margaret Alic, *Hypatia's Heritage: A History of Women in Science from Antiquity through the Nineteenth Century.* Boston: Beacon Press (1986), p. 184, quoting Maria Mitchell, "Maria [sic] Somerville," *Atlantic Monthly* 5 (1860), p. 570.

67. Mary Somerville, *On the Connexion of the Physical Sciences.* 7th London edition. New York: Harper & Brothers (1846).

68. Mary Somerville, *Physical Geography.* 2 vols. London: 1848.

69. Margaret Alic, *op. cit.*, p. 189.

70. Mary Somerville, *On Molecular and Microscopic Science.* London: 1869.

71. Margaret Alic, *op. cit.*, p. 182.

72. Bell and Offen, *op. cit.*, p. 120.

73. Margaret McFadden, "Anna Doyle Wheeler (1785–1848): Philosopher, Socialist, Feminist," *Hypatia* 4: 1 (Spring 1989), pp. 91–101.

74. Bell and Offen, *op. cit.*, p. 120.

75. McFadden, *op cit.*, p. 93.

76. Anna Doyle Wheeler, "Rights of Women," *The British Co-operator* 1 (1830), pp. 1, 2, 12–15, 33–36.

77. Bell and Offen, *op. cit.*, p. 120.

78. Bell and Offen, *op. cit.*, pp. 146–147.

79. James Mill, in *Encyclopedia Britannica*, suppl. 5th ed. (London: 1814), s.v. "Government." Reprinted as "The Article on Government," 1825.

80. W. Thompson [and Wheeler], *The Appeal of One Half of the Human Race, Women, Against the Pretensions of the Other Half, Men, to Restrain Them in Political and Thence in Civil and Domestic, Slavery* (1825). New York: Lenox Hill (Burt Franklin) (1970).

81. W. Thompson [and Wheeler], *The Appeal of One Half of the Human Race, Women, Against the Pretensions of the Other Half, Men, to Restrain Them in Political and Thence in Civil and Domestic, Slavery* (1825). Introduction by Richard Pankhurst. London: Virago (1983).

82. Margaret McFadden, "Anna Doyle Wheeler (1785–1848): Philosopher, Socialist, Feminist," *Hypatia* 4: 1 (Spring 1989), pp. 91–101.

83. R. Pankhurst, *op. cit.*

84. M. Galgano, "Anna Doyle Wheeler," in Baylen and Gossman, eds., *Biographical Dictionary of Modern British Radicals* Vol. 1. Brighton (Gr. Br.) and Highland Hills (NJ): Harvester Press (1979), pp. 519–524.

85. Margaret McFadden, *op. cit.*

86. Thompson [and Wheeler], *op. cit.*, p. 27.

87. Thompson [and Wheeler], *op. cit.*, pp. 136–142.

88. W. Thompson, "Introductory Letter to Mrs. Wheeler," in Thompson [and Wheeler], *op. cit.*, p. x.

89. Thompson [and Wheeler], *op. cit.*, p. 38.

90. Thompson [and Wheeler], *op. cit.*, p. 45.

91. Thompson [and Wheeler], *op. cit.*, p. 48.

92. Thompson [and Wheeler], *op. cit.*, p. 48.

93. Thompson [and Wheeler], *op. cit.*, pp. 54–60.

94. Thompson [and Wheeler], *op. cit.*, pp. 65–67.

95. Thompson [and Wheeler], *op. cit.*, pp. 68–73.

96. Thompson [and Wheeler], *op. cit.*, pp. 73–82.

97. Thompson [and Wheeler], *op. cit.*, p. 95.

98. Thompson [and Wheeler], *op. cit.*, p. 129.

99. Thompson [and Wheeler], *op. cit.*, pp. 155–187.

100. Thompson [and Wheeler], *op. cit.*, pp. 189–200.

101. Richard K.P. Pankhurst, *op. cit.*

102. Margaret McFadden, *op. cit.*, pp. 91–101.

103. Anna Doyle Wheeler, Letter to Charles Fourier, 27 May 1833. Paris: Archives sociétaires (in the Archives Nationales): 10 AS 25, dossier 3.

104. Kathryn Kish Sklar, *Catharine Beecher: A Study in American Domesticity*. New Haven and London: Yale University Press (1973), pp. 331–34..

105. Catharine Beecher, *Letters on the Difficulties of Religion*. Hartford: Belknap & Hammersley (1836).

106. Catharine Beecher, *An Address to the Protestant Clergy of the United States*. New York: Harper & Bros. (1846).

107. Catharine Beecher, "An Essay on Cause and Effect in Connection with the Difference of Fatalism and Free Will," *American Biblical Repository* 2, no. 4 (October 1839).

108. Elizabeth Flower and Murray G. Murphey, *A History of Philosophy in America*. Vol. I. New York: Putnam's (1977), pp. 41–45.

109. David Hume, *A Treatise of Human Nature* London: 1739, 1740.

110. Flower and Murphey, *op. cit.*, p. 204.

111. Thomas Reid, *Essays on the Intellectual and Active Powers of Man*. Philadelphia: 1792.

112. Catharine Beecher, *The Elements of Mental and Moral Philosophy, Founded upon Experience, Reason, and the Bible*. Hartford: 1831.

113. Catharine Beecher, *Common Sense Applied to Religion, or the Bible and the People*. New York: Harper & Bros. (1846), p. 281, p. 337.

114. Catharine Beecher, *op. cit.*, pp. 30–37.

115. Catharine Beecher, *An Appeal to the People on Behalf of their Rights as*

Authorized Interpreters of the Bible. New York: Harper & Bros. (1860), p. 134.

116. Catharine Beecher, *op. cit.*, p. 203.

117. Catharine Beecher, *An Essay on Slavery and Abolitionism with Reference to the Duty of American Females.* Philadelphia: Henry Perkins (1837).

118. Catharine Beecher, *op. cit.*, pp. 4–6.

119. Catharine Beecher, *op. cit.*, pp. 40–42.

120. Catharine Beecher, *The Duty of American Women to their Country.* New York: Harper & Bros. (1845).

121. Catharine Beecher, *The Evils Suffered by American Women and American Children: The Causes and the Remedy.* New York: Harper & Bros. (1846).

122. Catharine Beecher, *Letter to Benevolent Ladies in the United States.* New York: 1849.

123. Catharine Beecher, *An Essay on the Education of Female Teachers.* New York: Van Nostrand and Dwight (1835).

124. Catharine Beecher, *Letter to Persons Who Are Engaged in Domestic Service.* New York: Leavitt & Trow (1842).

125. Catharine Beecher, *Woman's Profession as Mother and Educator with Views in Opposition to Woman Suffrage.* Philadelphia: Maclean (1872).

126. Catharine Beecher and Harriet B. Stowe, *Principles of Domestic Science: As Applied to the Duties and Pleasures of the Home. A Text Book for the Use of Young Ladies in Schools, Seminaries, and Colleges.* New York: J.B. Ford & Co. (1870).

127. For a description of the ecclesiastical and educational heritage of Norwich see Elizabeth Evasdaughter, "Julian of Norwich," in Mary Ellen Waithe, ed., *A History of Women Philosophers* Volume 2. Dordrecht, Boston and London: Kluwer Academic Publishers (1989), p. 191ff.

128. Joseph Rivlin, *Harriet Martineau: A Bibliography of her Separately Printed Books.* New York: The New York Public Library (1947).

129. Theodora Bosanquet, *Harriet Martineau: An Essay in Comprehension.* London: Frederick Etchells & Hugh Macdonald (1927), pp. 37–38.

130. Auguste Comte, *Cours de Philosophie Positive.* 6 vols. Paris: Bachelier (1830–1842), Bruxelles: Culture et civilization (1969).

131. Harriet Martineau, *Miscellanies* in 2 vols. Boston: Hilliard, Gray and Company (1836).

132. *Miscellanies, op. cit.*, p. v.

133. *Op. cit.*, p. vii.

134. Harriet Martineau, "Illustrations of Political Economy," 25 parts. London: C. Fox (1832–1834).

135. Harriet Martineau, *Illustrations of Political Economy.* 9 vols. London: C. Fox (1834).

136. F.A. Hayek, *John Stuart Mill and Harriet Taylor: Their Friendship and Subsequent Marriage.* London: Routledge & Kegan Paul, Ltd. (1951), p. 28.

137. *Op. cit.*, p. 89, p. 188.

138. Rivlin, *op. cit.*, p. 124.

139. F.A. Hayek, *John Stuart Mill and Harriet Taylor: Their Friendship and Subsequent Marriage.* London: Routledge & Kegan Paul, Ltd. (1951), pp.

22–23, 280–282.

140. Hayek, *op. cit.*, p. 26, material in square brackets supplied.
141. See discussion of Martineau, above.
142. Hayek, *op. cit.*, p. 57.
143. Taylor, in Alice Rossi, ed., *Essays on Sex Equality: John Stuart Mill and Harriet Taylor Mill*. Chicago and London: The University of Chicago Press (1970), pp. 85–86.
144. *Op. cit.*, p. 86.
145. *Op. cit.*, p. 85.
146. J.S. Mill, *Subjection of Women*. London: 1869.
147. Harriet Taylor Mill died before *On Liberty* appeared.
148. Hayek, *op. cit.*, p. 275, n. 4.
149. See Maurice Cranston, "Mr. and Mrs. Mill on Liberty," *The Listener* 9/10/59; pp. 385–386.
150. Harriet Taylor, quoted in Hayek, *op. cit.*, p. 275.
151. Taylor in Hayek, *op. cit.*, p. 276.
152. Three of Taylor's six surviving poems were published in the *Monthly Repository*: two published poems and one unpublished poem are contained in the Hayek volume.
153. Hayek, *op. cit.*, pp. 165–167.
154. Michael St. John Packe, *The Life of John Stuart Mill*. New York: Macmillan (1954).
155. Rossi, *op. cit.*, p. 40. quoting Coss. *Autobiography of John Stuart Mill*, p. 176, material in square brackets supplied by me.
156. Diana Trilling, "Mill's Intellectual Beacon," *Partisan Review* 19 (1952), pp. 116–120.
157. Ruth Borchard, *John Stuart Mill, The Man*. London: Watts (1957).
158. Knut Hagberg, "John Stuart Mill," *Personalities and Powers*. Sprigge and Napier, transl. London: John Lane The Bodley Head Ltd. (1930).
159. Jack Stillinger, ed., *The Early Draft of John Stuart Mill's Autobiography*. Urbana: University of Illinois Press (1961).
160. Gertrude Himmelfarb, *On Liberty and Liberalism: The Case of John Stuart Mill*. New York: Knopf (1974). Also: H.O. Pappe, *John Stuart Mill and the Harriet Taylor Myth*. Australian National University Social Science Monograph, 19. Melbourne: Melbourne University Press (1960).
161. R. Anschutz, "J.S. Mill, Carlyle and Mrs. Taylor," *Political Science* 7 (1955), pp. 65–67. See also Hayek, *op. cit.*, and Rossi, *op. cit.*
162. This appears to be the view of both Hayek and Rossi.
163. Virginia Held, "Justice and Harriet Taylor," *Nation* 213 (10/25/71), pp. 405–406. (Review of Rossi, *op. cit.*)
164. MacMinn, Hainds & McCrimmon, eds., *Bibliography of the Published Writings of John Stuart Mill*. New York: AMS Press (1970).
165. K. Offen, "A Nineteenth-Century French Feminist Rediscovered: Jenny P. D'Héricourt, 1809–1875," *Signs: Journal of Women in Culture and Society* 13: 1 (1987), pp. 144–158.
166. Jeanne Deroin, "Mme J. Poinsard d'Héricourt, maîtresse sage-femme de la

faculté de Paris," in *Almanach des femmes pour 1854*. London: J. Watson (1854).

167. K. Offen, "A Nineteenth-Century French Feminist Rediscovered: Jenny P. D'Héricourt, 1809–1875," *Signs: Journal of Women in Culture and Society* 13: 1 (1987), p. 146.

168. La Femme [pseud. Poinsard d'Héricourt] "Madame Jenny P. D'Héricourt," *Agitator*, May 1, 1869, p. 6ff.

169. Jenny d'Héricourt, "Critique de *Manuel homoeopathique d'obstétrique* par M. Croserio," *Revue philosophique et religieuse* 8: 29 (August 1, 1857), pp. 158–160.

170. Offen, *op. cit.*, p. 157, n. 28.

171. Offen, *op. cit.*, pp. 144–158.

172. Claire Goldberg Moses, *op. cit.*, p. 162.

173. Claire Goldberg Moses, *op. cit.*, p. 168.

174. Jenny d'Héricourt, *La femme affranchie: résponse à MM. Michelet, Proudhon, E. de Giradin, A. Comte et aux autres novateurs modernes*. Brussels: A. Lacroix, Van Meenen et Cie (1860).

175. Jenny d'Héricourt, *A Woman's Philosophy of Woman*. New York: Carleton (1864), fascimile reprint (Westport, CT: Hyperion Press) 1981.

176. d'Héricourt, quoted in Bell and Offen, *op. cit.*, p. 344.

177. d'Héricourt, quoted in Bell and Offen, *op. cit.*, p. 344, bracketed material supplied.

178. d'Héricourt in Bell and Offen, *op. cit.*, p. 343.

179. d'Héricourt in Bell and Offen, *op. cit.*, p. 346.

180. d'Héricourt in Bell and Offen, *op. cit.*, p. 347.

181. Offen, *op. cit.*, p. 147ff.

182. Offen, *op. cit.*, p. 149.

183. Ludwig Feuerbach, *The Essence of Christianity*. Marian Evans [George Eliot], tr. New York: 1957.

184. K.M. Newton, *George Eliot, Romantic Humanist: A Study of the Philosophical Structure of her Novels*. Totowa, NJ: Barnes & Noble Books (1981).

185. Marsa-Vacells, *op. cit.*, p. 143.

186. Clemence Royer, *Le Bien et la Loi Morale: Éthique et Téléologie*. Paris: Guillaumin et Cie. (1881).

187. "Y," Mme Clemence Royer, *Le Bien et la Loi Morale: Éthique et Téléologie*" *Revue Philosophique* 13 (1882), pp. 426–432.

188. Claire Goldberg Moses, *op. cit.*, p. 162.

189. Bell and Offen, *op. cit.*, p. 325.

190. P.-J. Proudhon, *De la Justice dans la Révolution et dans l'Église* (1858), in *Oeuvres complètes de P.-J. Proudhon*, ed. Bougle and Moysset, Vol. XII. Paris: 1935.

191. Claire Goldberg Moses, *op. cit.*, p. 163.

192. To prevent her estranged husband from confiscating her royalties (as permitted by law) the first edition was published under the name "Lamber." Her husband obtained her royalties, and the second edition was published under the name "Lambert."

193. Juliette Lambert [Adam], *Idées anti-proudhoniennes sur l'amour, la femme et le mariage.* 2nd ed. Paris: Dentu (1861) p. 44.

194. Juliette Lambert [Adam], *op. cit.*, p. 54.

195. Juliette Lambert [Adam], *op. cit.*, p. 75. Translation mine.

196. Juliette Lambert [Adam], *ibid.*

197. Claire Goldberg Moses, *op. cit.*, p. 167.

198. Juliette Lambert [Adam], *op. cit.*, p. 132. Translation mine.

199. Juliette Lambert [Adam], *op. cit.*, pp. 79–80. Translation mine.

200. Juliette Lambert [Adam], *op. cit.*, p. 128. Translation mine.

201. *International Encyclopedia of Psychiatry, Psychology, Psychoanalysis and Neurology.* New York: Aesculapius Publishers (1977), Vol. 6, p. 321.

202. *Notable American Women: A Biographical Dictionary.* Cambridge, MA: Belknap Press of Harvard University Press (1971), Vol. II, pp. 354–356.

203. *Dictionary of American Biography.* New York: American Council of Learned Societies (1961), Vol. 5, Part 1, p. 529.

204. *Notable American Women, op. cit.*, p. 354.

205. J.B. Schneewind, personal communication, 1989.

206. Christine Ladd, "On the Algebra of Logic," in *Studies in Logic by Members of the Johns Hopkins University (1883).* Edited by Charles S. Pierce. Reprinted in *Foundations of Semiotics.* Amsterdam and Philadelphia: John Benjamin Publishing Company (1983).

207. Christine Ladd-Franklin, "The reduction to Absurdity of the Ordinary Treatment of the Syllogism," *Science* 13: 328, pp. 574–576.

208. Louise Grinstein and Paul Campbell, *Women of Mathematics.* Westport, CT: Greenwood Press (1987).

209. Christine Ladd-Franklin, *Colour and Colour Theories.* 1929.

210. *International Encyclopedia of Psychiatry, Psychology, Psychoanalysis and Neurology. Loc. cit.*

211. Hortense Allart de Meritens, *Novum Organum, ou Sainteté Philosophique.* Paris: Garnier Freres (1857), p. 2. Translation mine.

212. Allart de Meritens, *op. cit.*, p. 6.

213. Allart de Meritens, *op. cit.*, pp. 18–19.

Bibliography

In addition to works cited in this volume, this bibliography contains references to works that will be of interest to readers. Where the works of male philosophers are widely available in modern editions, I have listed the probable editions used or cited by women philosophers who are the subjects of this volume.

Aaron, R.I. and Gibb, Jocelyn, eds. *An Early Draft of Locke's Essay, Together with Excerpts from his Journals.* Oxford: Clarendon Press, 1936.

Abreu Gomez, Emilio. *Sor Juana Inés de la Cruz.* Mexico City: Imprenta de la Secretaria de Relaciones Exteriores, 1934.

Abside 15:4 (1951). *Sor Juana Inés de la Cruz.* (Issue dedicated to Sor Juana Inés de la Cruz).

Agnesi, Maria Gaetana. *Propositiones philosophicae.* Milan, 1738.

—— *Analytical Institutions.* J. Colson, trans. London: Taylor & Wilkes, 1801.

Alic, Margaret. *Hypatia's Heritage: A History of Women in Science from Antiquity through the Nineteenth Century.* Boston: Beacon Press, 1986.

Allart de Meritens, Hortense. *Novum Organum, ou Sainteté Philosophique.* Paris: Garnier Freres, 1857.

—— *Lettres Inédites à Sainte-Beuve, 1841–1848.* Paris: Mercure de France, 1908.

André, Louis. "La Candidature de Christine de Suède au Trone de Pologne (1688)," in *Revue Historique* (1908) Vol. 2, pp. 209–243.

Anschutz, R.P. "J.S. Mill, Carlyle and Mrs. Taylor," *Political Science* 7 (1955).

Arckenholtz, J. *Mémoires concernant Christine, règne de Suède, pour servir d'éclaircissement à l'histoire de sa reigne et principalement de sa vie privée.* t. 1–4. Amsterdam & Leipzig, 1751–1760.

Arroyo, Anita. *Razón y pasión de Sor Juana.* 2nd ed. Mexico City: Porrua, 1971.

Astell, Mary. *A Serious Proposal To the Ladies for the Advancement of their true and greatest Interest.* By a Lover of her Sex. London: Printed for R. Wilkins at the King's Head in St. Paul's Church Yard, 1694.

—— *Letters concerning the Love of God Between the Author of the Proposal to the Ladies and Mr. John Norris, wherein his Discourse shewing That it ought to be entire and exclusive of all other Loves, is further cleared and justified.* London:

Published by J. Norris, 1695.

—— *Some Reflections upon Marriage Occasion'd by the Duke and Dutchess of Mazarine's Case*. London, 1700.

—— *Moderation truly Stated: or a Review of a Late Pamphlet entitl'd Moderation a Vertue with a Prefatory Discourse to Dr. D'Aveanant concerning His late Essays on Peace and War*. London, 1704.

—— *A Fair Way with the Dissenters and their Patrons*. London, 1704.

—— *An Impartial Enquiry into the Causes of Rebellion and Civil War in this Kingdom. In an examination of Dr. Kennett's Sermon Jan. 31, 1703–4 and vindication of the Royal Martyr*. London, 1704.

—— *The Christian Religion as Profess'd by a Daughter of the Church of England*. London, 1705.

—— *Pamphlet Attributed to Mary Astell: An Essay in Defence of the Femal Sex*. London, 1696.

Bacinetti-Florenzi Waddington, Marianna. *Taluui Pensieri*. Parigi, 1843.

—— *La Facolta di Sentire*. Montepulciano, 1868.

—— *Lettere Filosofiche*. Parigi, 1848.

—— *Filosofemeni di Cosmologia e di Antologia*. Perugia, 1863.

—— *Alcune Riflessioni sopra il Socialismo e il Comunismo*. Florence, 1860.

—— *Saggi di Psicologia e di Logica*. Florence, 1864.

—— *Della Immortalita dell'Anima Umana*. Florence, 1868.

—— *Saggio sulla filosofia dello spirito*. Florence, successori Le Monnieri, 1867.

Baillet, Adrien. *La Vie de M. Des-Cartes*. 2 vols. 1691.

Ballard, George. *Memoirs of Several Ladies of Great Britain*. London, 1752.

Barber, William H. "Mme du Châtelet and Leibnizianism: the genesis of the 'Institutions de Physique,'" in W.H. Barber, J.H. Brumfitt, H.A. Leigh, R. Shackleton and S.S.B. Taylor, *The Age of the Enlightenment*. Edinburgh and London: Oliver and Boyd, 1967.

Bartlett, Elizabeth. "The First Woman Poet in the New World," *New Orleans Review* 8 (1961), pp. 95–97.

Baylen and Gossman (eds.). *Biographical Dictionary of Modern British Radicals*. Brighton (Gt. Br.) and Highland Hills (NJ): Harvester Press, 1979.

Beecher, Catharine. *Letters on the Difficulties of Religion*. Hartford: Belknap & Hammersley, 1836.

—— *An Address to the Protestant Clergy of the United States*. New York: Harper & Bros., 1846.

—— "An Essay on Cause and Effect in Connection with the Difference of Fatalism and Free Will," *American Biblical Repository* 2: 4 (October 1839).

—— *The Elements of Mental and Moral Philosophy, Founded upon Experience, Reason, and the Bible*. Hartford, 1831.

—— *Common Sense Applied to Religion, or the Bible and the People*. New York: Harper & Bros., 1846.

—— *An Appeal to the People on Behalf of their Rights as Authorized Interpreters of the Bible*. New York: Harper & Bros., 1860.

—— *An Essay on Slavery and Abolitionism with Reference to the Duty of American Females*. Philadelphia: Henry Perkins, 1837.

—— *The Duty of American Women to their Country*. New York: Harper & Bros., 1845.

—— *The Evils Suffered by American Women and American Children: The Causes and the Remedy*. New York: Harper & Bros., 1846.

—— *Woman's Profession as Mother and Educator with Views in Opposition to Woman Suffrage*. Philadelphia: Maclean, 1872.

—— *Letter to Persons Who Are Engaged in Domestic Service*. New York: Leavitt & Trow, 1842.

—— *An Essay on the Education of Female Teachers*. New York: Van Nostrand and Dwight, 1835.

Beecher, Catharine, and Stowe, Harriet B. *Principles of Domestic Science; As Applied to the Duties and Pleasures of the Home. A Text Book for the Use of Young Ladies in Schools, Seminaries, and Colleges*. New York: J.B. Ford & Co., 1870.

Behn, Irene. *Der Philosoph und die Konigin – Renatus Descartes und Christina Wasa, Briefwechsel und Begegnung*. Freiburg/Munchen: Alber, 1957.

Beling de Benassy, Marie-Cecile. "A manera de apendice: Sor Juana y el problema del derecho de las mujeres a la ensenanza," in *La mujer en el teatro y la novela del siglo XVII. Actas de IIo Coloquio del Grupo de Estudios sobre Teatro Español*. Toulouse-Le Mirail: University of Toulouse-LeMirail, 1979.

Bell, Susan Groag, and Offen, Karen M. (eds.). *Women, the Family, and Freedom: The Debate in Documents*. 2 vols. Stanford: Stanford University Press, 1983.

Bentham, Jeremy. *An Introduction to the Principles of Morals and Legislation*. Printed in the year 1780 and now first published. London: T. Payne & Son, 1789.

Berkeley, George. *A Treatise Concerning the Principles of Human Knowledge*. Dublin: Printed by Aaron Rhames for Jeremy Pepyati, 1710.

Bernoulli, Johann. *Discours sur les lois de la communication du mouvement*. Paris, 1727.

Besterman, Theodore (ed.). *Les lettres de la Marquise du Châtelet*. 2 vols. Genève: Institut et musée Voltaire, Les Délices, Genève, 1958.

Bildt, Carl. *Christine de Suède et Cardinal Azzolino, Lettres inédites*. Paris, 1879.

Birch, Thomas, ed. *The Works of Mrs. Catharine Cockburn, Theological, Moral, Dramatic, and Poetical*. 2 Vols., with an account of the author's life. London, 1751.

Birch, Una Pope-Hennesy. *Anna Van Schurmann: Artist, Scholar, Saint*. London: Longmans, Green and Co., 1909.

Bjurstrom, Per. *Feast and Theatre in Queen Christina's Rome*. Stockholm, 1966.

Blackwell, Antoinette Brown. *Shadows of our Social System*. 1855.

—— *The Sexes Throughout Nature*. New York: G.P. Putnam, 1985, reprinted by Hyperion Press, 1976.

—— *Studies In General Science*. New York: G.P. Putnam, 1869.

—— *The Philosophy of Individuality, or The One and the Many*. New York: G.P. Putnam, 1893.

—— *The Social Side of Mind and Action*. The Neale Publishing Co., 1915.

—— *The Making of the Universe*. New York: The Gorham Press, 1914.

—— *The Physical Basis of Immortality*. New York: G.P. Putnam, 1876.

—— *The Island Neighbors, A Novel of American Life*. Harper and Brothers, 1970 (microfilm).

—— *Sea Drift; or, Tribute to the Ocean.* J.T. White and Co., 1902.

—— "Consciousness and Its Helpers," *Medico-Legal Journal of Michigan*, No. 1898.

—— "Exegesis of I Corinthians, XIV, 34, 35; and II Timothy, 11, 12," *Oberlin Quarterly Review*, July 1849.

—— "Relation of Woman's Work in the Household to the Work Outside," *Papers and Letters Presented at the First Woman's Congress of the Association for the Advancement of Women, New York, October, 1873.* New York, 1874, pp. 178–184. Reprinted in *Up from the Pedestal*, Aileen S. Kraditor, ed. New York: Quadrangle Press, 1968, pp. 150–159.

—— "How to Combine Intellectual Culture with Household Management and Family Duty," *Papers presented at the Second Congress of the Association for the Advancement of Women, Chicago, October 15–18, 1874.* Chicago: Fergus Printing, 1875. Reprinted in *Woman's Journal* November 7, 1874.

—— "Sex and Work," *Woman's Journal*, March 14, 1874.

—— "The Wisest Way," *Woman's Journal*, August 19, 1876.

—— "Marriage and Work," *Papers read at the Third Annual Congress of the Association for the Advancement of Women, Syracuse, October 13–15, 1875.* Chicago: Fergus Printing, 1876, pp. 27–35.

—— "Comparative Mental Power of the Sexes Physiologically Considered," *Papers read before the Fourth Annual Congress of the Association for the Advancement of Women, Philadelphia, October 4–6, 1876.*

—— "History and Results of the Past Congresses," *Papers Read before the Association for the Advancement of Women at its Tenth Annual Congress, held at Portland, Maine, October, 1882*, p. 39.

—— "Heredity," *Papers Read before the Association for the Advancement of Women at its Eleventh Annual Congress, held at Chicago, Illinois, October, 1883.* Buffalo: Press of Peter Paul and Bro., 1884, p. 14.

—— "The Comparative Longevity of the Sexes," *Proceedings of the American Association for the Advancement of Science*, Philadelphia, 1884, p. 515, and *Papers read before the Association for the Advancement of Women, Twelfth Annual Congress, held at Baltimore, Md., October, 1884.* Buffalo: Peter, Paul and Bro., 1885, pp. 41–55.

—— "Where is the work of women equal, where superior, where inferior to that of men?" *Papers read before the Association for the Advancement of Women, 16th Congress, Detroit, Michigan, Nov., 1888.* Fall River, MA: J.H. Franklin, 1889.

Blom, John J. *Descartes – his Moral Philosophy and Psychology.* New York: New York University Press, 1978.

Bold, Samuel. *A Discourse Concerning the Resurrection of the Same Body: With Two Letters Concerning the Necessary Immateriality of Created Thinking Substance.* London: S. Holt for A. & J. Churchill, 1705.

—— *Some Considerations On the Principal Objections and Arguments Which have been Published against Mr. Lock's Essay of Humane Understanding.* London: A. & J. Churchill, 1706.

Boos, Florence, and Boos, William. "Catharine Macaulay: Historian and Political Reformer," *International Journal of Women's Studies* 3: 1 (Jan.–Feb. 1980), pp. 52–55.

Borchard, Ruth. *John Stuart Mill, The Man.* London: Watts, 1957.

Bosanquet, Theodora. *Harriet Martineau: An Essay in Comprehension.* London: Frederick Etchells & Hugh Macdonald, 1927.

Boyle, Robert. *The Christian Virtuoso: Shewing, That by being addicted to Experimental Philosophy, a Man is rather Assisted, than Indisposed, to be a Good Christian. The First Part.* By T.H.R.B. Fellow of the Royal Society. London: In the Savoy, Edw. Jones, 1690.

Bryant, Sophie. "On the Nature and Functions of a Complete Symbolic Language," *Mind* XXIII (1888), pp. 188–207.

Burke, Edmond. *A Philosophical Enquiry into the Origin of our Ideas of the Sublime and Beautiful.* London, 1787.

Burnet, Gilbert, Bishop of Salisbury. *An Exposition of the Thirty-nine Articles of the Church of England. Written by Gilbert, Bishop of Sarum.* London: R. Roberts for R. Chiswell, 1699.

[Burnet, Thomas] Master of the Charterhouse. *Remarks upon an Essay concerning Humane Understanding: In a Letter Addressed to the Author.* London: M. Wootton, 1697.

—— *Second Remarks upon an Essay Concerning Humane Understanding. In a Letter address'd to the Author. Being a Vindication of the First Remarks, against the Answer of Mr. Locke. At the End of His Reply to the Lord Bishop of Worcester.* London: M. Wootton, 1697.

—— *Third Remarks upon an Essay concerning Humane Understanding: In a Letter Address'd to the Author.* London: M. Wootton, 1697.

Calhoun, G.D. "Un triangulo mitológico idolatro y cristiano en *El Divino Narciso* de Sor Juana," *Abside* 34 (1970), pp. 373–401.

Callmer, Christian. *Konigin Christina, Ihre Bibliotekarie und ihre Handschriften.* Stockholm: Acta Bibliothecae Regiae, 1977.

Campagnac, E.T., ed. *The Cambridge Platonists: Selections from Whichcote, Smith and Culverwel.* London, 1901.

Cassirer, Ernst. *Descartes-Lehre-Personlichkeit-Wirkung.* Stockholm: Behrmann Fischer Verlag, 1939.

Caudet, Francisco. "Sor Juana Inés de la Cruz: la crisis de 1690," *Cuadernos Americanos* (Mexico) 222 (1970), pp. 135–140.

Cavendish, Margaret, Dutchess of Newcastle. *Philosophical Fancies.* London, 1653.

—— *Philosophical and Physical Opinions.* London, 1655 and 1663.

—— *Natures Pictures drawn by Fancies Pencil to The Life.* London, 1656 and 1671.

—— "Femal Orations," *Orations of Diverse Sorts.* London, 1662.

—— *Philosophical Letters: or, Modest Reflections upon some Opinions in Natural Philosophy, maintained by several famous and learned Authors of this Age.* London, 1664.

—— *The Life of the thrice Noble, High and Puissant Prince William Cavendishe, Duke, Marquess, and Earl of Newcastle.* London, 1667.

—— *Grounds of Natural Philosophy.* London, 1668.

—— *The Description of a New World, called The Blazing World.* London, 1666.

—— *Poems and Fancies.* 2nd ed. London, 1656.

—— *Worlds Olio.* London, 1655.

—— *Observations on Experimental Philosophy.* London, 1666 and 1668.

Cazden, Elizabeth. *Antoinette Brown Blackwell, A Biography.* Old Westbury, NY: The Feminist Press, 1983.

[du Châtelet, Émilie]. "Lettre sur les Éléments de la Philosophie de Newton," *Journal des Sçavans*, September 1738, pp. 534–541.

—— *Response de Madame *** à la lettre que M. de Mairan, Secrétaire perpétuel de l'Académie Royale des Sciences, lui a écrite le 18 février sur la question des forces vives.* Brussels, 1741.

du Châtelet, Émilie. *L'Essay sur l'optique* in Ira Wade, *Studies on Voltaire*. Princeton, 1947, pp. 188–208.

—— *Dissertation sur la Nature et la Propagation du Feu.* Paris: Prault, fils, 1744.

—— *Institutions de Physique.* Paris: Prault, fils, 1740.

—— *Principes Mathématiques de la Philosophie Naturelle.* Paris, Desaint & Saillant, 1759.

—— *La Fable des abeilles*, in Ira Wade, *Studies on Voltaire*. Princeton, 1947, pp. 131–187.

—— *Réflexions sur le Bonheur* in *Opuscules philosophiques et littéraires, la plupart posthumes ou inédits*. Paris: Suard et Bourlet de Vauxcelles, 1796.

—— *La Grammaire Raisonnée*, in Ira O. Wade, *Studies on Voltaire With Some Unpublished Papers of Mme du Châtelet.* New York: Russell & Russell, 1947.

—— *Lettres Inédites De Madame La Marquise Du Châtelet à M. Le Comte D'Argental.* Paris, 1806.

Chavez, Ezequiel Adeodato. *Sor Juana Inés de la Cruz.* 2nd ed. Mex. City: Porrua, 1970.

Chodorow, Nancy. *The Reproduction of Mothering.* Berkeley: University of California Press, 1978.

Christophersen, H.O. *A Bibliographical Introduction to the Study of John Locke.* New York: Burt Franklin, 1968 reprint of 1930 edition.

Clark, M.L. "The making of a Queen: The education of Christina of Sweden," *History Today* 28 (178), pp. 228–235.

Cockburn, Catharine Trotter. *The Works of Mrs. Catharine Trotter Cockburn, Theological, Moral, Dramatic, and Poetical.* Thomas Birch, ed. 2 vols. With an account of the author's life. London, 1751.

Coignet, Clarisse. *Biographie de Mme Lemonnier, fondatrice de la Société pour l'enseignement professionnel des femmes.* Paris, 1866.

—— *Catherine de Médicis et François de Guise.* Paris: Fischbacher, 1895.

—— *Cours de morale à l'usage des écoles laïques.* Paris: Le Chevalier, 1874.

—— "Le Droit dans l'antiquité," *Revue Politique et Littéraire* 15 (1875), pp. 1107–1112.

—— "Le Droit romain dans les temps modernes" *Revue Politique et Littéraire* 15 (1875), pp. 1136–1140.

—— *L'Evolution du protestantisme français au XIXe siècle.* Paris: Alcan, 1908.

—— *François Ier, portraits et récits du seizième siècle.* Paris: Plon, 1885.

—— *Un Gentilhomme des temps passés, François de Scepeaux, sire de Vieilleville, 1509–1571: Portraits et récits du seizième siècle, reigne de Henri II.* Paris: Plon, 1886.

—— *De Kant à Bergson: réconciliation de la religion et de la science dans un spiritualisme nouveau.* Paris: Alcan, 1911.

—— *De l'affranchissement des femmes en Angleterre.* Paris, 1874. Excerpted from *Revue politique et littéraire* 13 (1874), pp. 1066–1073, 1043–1049.

—— *De L'éducation dans la démocratie.* Paris: Delagrave, 1881.

—— "De l'enseignement de la morale dans les écoles laïques," *Revue politique et littéraire* 13 (1874), pp. 854–855.

—— *De l'enseignement public au point de vue de l'Université, de la commune et de l'État.* Paris: Meyrueis, 1886.

—— *La Morale dans l'éducation.* Paris: Delagrave, 1883.

—— *La Morale indépendante dans son principe et dans son objet.* Paris: Bailliere, 1869.

—— "Le Mouvement des femmes en Angleterre: le suffrage politique," *Revue politique et littéraire* 13 (1874), pp. 251–255, 274–280.

—— *Ou allons-nous?* Paris: Paulin et Cie, 1903.

—— "Le Père Hyacinthe et la morale indépendante," *Revue politique et littéraire* 19 (1877), pp. 1092–1095.

—— *Principe et dernières consequences de la réforme Sabatier.* Paris: Dole, Girandi et Audebert, 1905.

—— *Rapport présenté à la Commission de l'enseignement communal...sur la première declaration, "l'enseignement est libre," applicable à l'organisation de l'enseignement primaire.* Paris: Dupont, 1870.

—— *Rapport présenté au nom de la Commission des dames chargés d'examiner les questions relatives à la réforme de l'instruction primaire...suivi d'un appendice par Mme. Fanny Ch. Delon.* Paris: Dupont, 1871.

—— *La Réforme française avant les guerres civiles, 1512–1559.* Paris: Fischbacher, 1890.

—— "Le Suffrage politique pour les femmes en Angleterre," *Revue politique et littéraire* 16 (1875), pp. 251–258, 274–280.

—— *Victor Considérant, sa vie, son oeuvre.* Paris: Alcan, 1895.

—— *Francis the first and his times.* Translated by Fanny Twemlow. London: R. Bentley, 1888, and New York: Scribner and Welford, 1889.

—— *A gentleman of the olden time, François de Scepeaux, sire de Vieilleville, 1509–1571; portraits and stories of the sixteenth century during the reign of Henri II.* London: R. Bentley, 1887.

Comelli, G.B. "Laura Bassi e il Suo Primo Trionfo," Bologna: Istituto per la Storia dell' Universita di Bologna. *Studi e memorie per la Storia dell' Universita di Bologna* 3 (1912): pp. 197–256.

Comte, Auguste. *Cours de Philosophie Positive.* 6 vols. Paris: Bachelier, 1830–1842.

Conway, Anne. *The Principles of the Most Ancient and Modern Philosophy.* Glen Rock, NJ: Gerritsen Women's History Microfilm Collection.

—— *The Principles of the Most Ancient and Modern Philosophy,* Peter Lopston, ed. The Hague: Martinus Nijhoff, 1982.

Cooke, George W. *George Eliot: A Critical Study of Her Life, Writings and Philosophy.* London 1883.

Coudert, Allison. "A Cambridge Platonist's Kabbalist Nightmare," *Journal of the History of Ideas* XXXVI: 4 (Oct.–Dec. 1975), pp. 633–652.

Cranston, Maurice. *John Locke: A Biography*. New York: MacMillan, 1957.

—— "Mr. and Mrs. Mill on Liberty," *The Listener* 9/10/59, pp. 385–386.

de la Cruz, Sor Juana Inés. *Obras Completas*. Mexico City: Porrua, 1975.

—— *A Sor Juana Anthology*, A.S. Trueblood, trans. Cambr.: Harv. Univ. Pr., 1988.

—— "La respuesta a Sor Filotéa de la Cruz," in Margaret Sayers Peden, trans., *A Woman of Genius, an Intellectual Autobiography*. Salisbury, CT: Lime Rock Press, 1982.

Cudworth, Ralph, Master of Christ's College, Cambridge. *A Treatise concerning Eternal and Immutable Morality*. London: J. & J. Knapton, 1731.

—— *The True Intellectual System of the Universe: The First Part: Wherin, All the Reason and Philosophy of Atheism is Confuted: and Its Impossibility Demonstrated*. London: R. Royston, 1678.

Culverwel, Nathanael. *On the Light of Nature*. Edinburgh 1857.

—— *An Elegant and Learned Discourse of the Light of nature, With severall other Treatises*. London: T.R. and E.M., 1654. London: by Tho. Roycroft for Mary Rothwell, 1661.

Cunningham, Gilbert F. "Sor Juana's 'Sueño,' " *Modern Language Notes* 83 (1968), pp. 253–261.

De Beer, E.S. *The Correspondence of John Locke*. Oxford University Press edition in 8 vols. Oxford: The Clarendon Press, 1976–1985.

Deroin, Jeanne. "Mme J. Poinsard d'Héricourt, maîtresse sage-femme de la faculté de Paris," *Almanach des femmes pour 1854*. London: J. Watson, 1854.

Descartes, René. *Passiones Animae per Renatum Descartes*. Amstelodami: Apud Ludovicum Elzevirium, 1650.

—— *Principia Philosophiae*. Amstelodami: Apud L. Elzevirium, 1644.

—— *Meditations de Prima Philosophia*. 2nd. ed. Amstelodami: Apud Ludovidum Elzevirium, 1642.

Desmaizeaux, Pierre. *Recueil de diverses pièces sur la philosophie*. 2 vols. Amsterdam, 1720.

Dictionary of American Biography. New York: American Council of Learned Societies, 1961.

Dugas, L. *Une Amitié Intellectuelle: Descartes et la Princesse Elisabeth*. Rennes, 1891.

Duran, Manuel. "El drama intelectual de Sor Juana y el anti-intelectualismo hispánico," *Cuadernos Americanos* (Mexico) 129 (1963), pp. 238–253.

Edwards, Samuel. *The Divine Mistress*. New York: David McKay Company, 1970.

Egan, Maureen. "Evolutionary Theory in the Social Philosophy of Charlotte Perkins Gilman," *Hypatia* Special Issue on the History of Women in Philosophy 4: 1 (Spring 1989), pp. 102–119.

Ehrman, Esther. *Mme du Châtelet*. Leamington Spa, UK, Dover, NH: Berg, 1986.

Eliot, George. *The Works of George Eliot*. 20 vols. Cabinet edition. Edinburgh and London, 1878–1880.

—— *The George Eliot Letters*. 7 vols. G.S. Haight, ed., New Haven, CT and London, 1954–1955.

Essen-Möller, E. "La Reine Christine. Étude Médicale et Biologique," *Hippocrate*, 1937.

Favre, Julie Velten. *Montaigne, moraliste et pédagogue*. Paris: Fischbacher, 1887.

—— *La Morale d'Aristotle*. Paris: Alcan, 1889.

—— *La Morale de Ciceron*. Paris: Fischbacher, 1891.

—— *La Morale de Plutarque (Préceptes et exemples) avec les discours de MM. Chantavoine, Lemonnier et Joseph Fabre prononces aux obsèques de Mme. Jules Favre et Une notice sur Mme. Jules Favre par Mademoiselle L. Belugou, Directrice de l'École Normale Supérieure de Sèvres*. Paris: Paulin et Cie., 1909.

—— *La Morale de Socrate*. Paris: Alcan, 1888.

—— *La Morale des Stoïciens*. Paris: Alcan, 1888.

Flexner, Eleanor. *Mary Wollstonecraft. A Biography*. New York: Coward, McCann and Geoghegan, Inc., 1972.

Flower, Elizabeth, and Murphey, Murray G. *A History of Philosophy in America*. 2 vols. New York: Putnam's, 1977.

Flynn, Gerard Cox. "The alleged mysticism of Sor Juana Inés de la Cruz," *Hispanic Review* 28 (1960), pp. 233–244.

—— "A revision of the philosophy of Sor Juana Inés de la Cruz," *Hispania* 43 (1960), pp. 515–520.

—— "Sor Juana Inés de la Cruz: Mexico's Tenth Muse," in J.R. Brink, ed., *Female Scholars: A Tradition of Learned Women Before 1800*. Montreal: Eden Press Women's Publications, 1980, pp. 119–136.

Foucher de Cariel. *Descartes, La Princesse Elisabeth et la Reine Christine d'après des lettres inédites*. Paris: Felix Alcan, 1909.

—— *Descartes et la princesse Palatine, ou de l'influence du cartésianisme sur les femmes au XVIIe siècle*. Paris: August Durand, 1862.

Fox, Margaret Fell. *Woman's Speaking Justified*. 1677.

Fox Bourne, Henry Richard. *The Life of John Locke*, 2 vols. Scientia Verlag Aalen, 1969, reprint of the edition London, 1876.

Frankel, Lois. "Damaris Cudworth Masham: A Seventeenth Century Feminist Philosopher," *Hypatia* Special Issue on The History of Women in Philosophy 4: 1 (Spring 1989), pp. 80–90.

Franklin, Christine Ladd. "On Some Characteristics of Symbolic Logic," *American Journal of Psychology* 2 (1889), pp. 543–567.

—— "The Reduction to Absurdity of the Ordinary Treatment of the Syllogism," *Science* 13 (1898), pp. 574–576.

—— "Minor Logic," *Journal of Philosophy, Psychology and Scientific Methods* 9 (1912), pp. 580–585.

—— "Bertrand Russell and Symbolic Logic," *Bulletin of the American Mathematical Society* 25 (Nov. 1918), pp. 59–60.

—— "The Antilogism," *Psyche* (1927), pp. 100–103.

—— *Colour and Colour Theories*. London: K. Paul, Trench, Trubner & Co. Ltd., 1929.

—— *Colour and Colour Theories*. NY: Arno Press, 1973.

Fusco, Nicola. *Elena Lucrezia Cornaro Piscopia 1646–1684*. Pittsburgh: United States Committee for Elena Lucrezia Cornaro Piscopia Terentary, 1975.

Gabbey, Alan. "Anne Conway et Henry More: Lettres sur Descartes (1650–1651)," *Archives de Philosophie* 40 (1977), pp. 379–404.

Galeazzo, Gualdo Priorato. *Historia della Sacra Maesta di Christina di Svetia.* Roma, 1656.

Galgano, M. "Anna Doyle Wheeler," in Baylen and Gossman, eds., *Biographical Dictionary of Modern British Radicals.* Vol. 1. Brighton, UK, and Highland Hills, NJ: Harvester Press, 1979, pp. 519–524.

Gallagher, Catherine. "Embracing the Absolute: The Politics of the Female Subject in Seventeenth Century England," *Genders* I (1988), pp. 24–39.

Gerhardt, C.I. *Die philosophischen Schriften von Leibniz.* 7 vols. Berlin, 1875–90.

Germain, S. *Oeuvres philosophiques de Sophie Germain.* H. Stupuy, ed. Paris, 1896.

Gilligan, Carol. *In a Different Voice.* Cambridge: Harvard University Press, 1982.

Gimbernat de Gonzalez, Ester. "Los romances filosóficos de Sor Juana Inés de la Cruz," Sacramento, CA: *California State University Department of Spanish and Portugese* 9 (1980/81), pp. 47–53.

Godoy, Emma. "Juana Cosmica," *Abside* 37 (1973), pp. 225–228.

Goreau, Angeline. *The Whole Duty of a Woman: Female Writers in Seventeenth Century England.* Garden City, New York: Dial Press, 1985.

Gosse, Edmund. "Catharine Trotter, the Precursor of the Bluestockings," *Transactions of the Royal Society of Literature of the U.K.* XXXIV (1960), p. 90.

Gouges, (Marie) Olympe de. *Les Droits de la Femme.* Paris, no date [1791]. Bibliothèque Nationale, E 5588.

—— *Declaration of the Rights of Woman and Citizen* reprinted in D.G. Levy, H.B. Applewhite & M.D. Johnson, eds., *Women in Revolutionary Paris 1789–1795.* Urbana, IL: University of Illinois Press, 1979.

—— *Lettre au peuple ou projet d'une caisse patriotique par une citoyenne*, in *Oeuvres* présentées par Benoite Groult. Paris: Mercure de France, 1986.

Goulding, R.W. *Margaret (Lucas) Duchess of Newcastle.* London 1925.

Grant, Douglas. *Margaret the First. A Biography of Margaret Cavendish, Duchess of Newcastle, 1623–1673.* London 1957.

Groult, Benoite. *Olympe de Gouges, Oeuvres.* Paris, Mercure de France, 1986.

Guralnicjk, Elissa. "Radical Politics in Mary Wollstonecraft's *A Vindication of the Rights of Woman*," in Carol H. Poston, ed., *A Vindication of the Rights of Woman: An Authoritative Text, Background, The Wollstonecraft Debate, Criticism.* 2nd ed. New York: W.W. Norton Co., 1988, pp. 308–317.

Hagberg, Knut. "John Stuart Mill,"*Personalities and Powers.* Sprigge and Napier, transl. London: John Lane The Bodley Head Ltd., 1930.

Hay, Mary. *Female Biography: or, Memoirs of Illustrious and Celebrated Women of all Ages and Countries.* Philadelphia: Byrd & Small, 1807.

Hayek, F.A. *John Stuart Mill and Harriet Taylor: Their Friendship [Correspondence] and Subsequent Marriage.* London: Routledge & Kegan Paul Ltd., 1951.

Held, Virginia. "Justice and Harriet Taylor," *Nation* 213 (10/25/71), pp. 405–406.

van Helmont, Francis Mercury. *Seder Olam.* London, 1684.

d'Héricourt, Jenny. "La Bible et la Question des Femmes," *Revue philosophique et religieuse* 8 (1857), pp. 16–38.

—— "Critique de *Manuel homoeopathique d'obstétrique* par M. Croserio," *Revue philosophique et religieuse* 8 (1857), pp. 158–160.

—— "Le Christianisme et la Question des Femmes," *Revue philosophique et religieuse* 9 (1857), pp. 27–45.

—— *La femme affranchie: résponse à MM. Michelet, Proudhon, E. de Giradin, A. Comte et aux autres novateurs modernes.* Brussels: A. Lacroix, Van Meenen et Cie., 1860, microfiche reprint in Gerritsen Collection of Women's History, Glen Rock, NJ: Microfilming Corporation of America.

—— *A Woman's Philosophy of Woman.* New York: Carleton, 1864; facsimile reprint, Westport, CT: Hyperion Press 1981; microfilm reprint in History of Women microfilm collection, Woodbridge, CT.

—— ["la Femme" pseud. Jenny d'Héricourt]. "Madame Jenny P. D'Héricourt," *Agitator*, May 1, 1869, p. 6.

Himmelfarb, Gertrude. *On Liberty and Liberalism: The Case of John Stuart Mill.* New York: Knopf, 1974.

Hiriart, Rosario. "America's First Feminist," *Americas* 25 (May, 1973), pp. 2–7.

Hobbes, Thomas. *De Cive: The English version entitled in the first edition. Philosophical Rudiments concerning government and society.* H. Warrender, ed. Oxford: Clarendon Press, 1983.

Holland, Nancy. "Gender and the Generic in Locke," presented at the Pacific Division meeting of the American Philosophical Association, March 1986.

Huet, Pierre-Daniel. *Commentarius.* Amsterdam, 1718.

Hume, David. *A Treatise of Human Nature.* London, 1739, 1740.

—— *History of Great Britain from the Invasion of Julius Caesar to the Revolution of 1688.* 6 vols. London, 1754–1762.

Iltis [Merchant], Carolyn. "Madame du Châtelet's Metaphysics and Mechanics," *Studies in History and Philosophy of Science* 8 (1977), p. 30.

International Encyclopedia of Psychiatry, Psychology, Psychoanalysis and Neurology. New York: Aesculapius Publishers, 1977.

Janik, Linda Gardiner. "Searching for the metaphysics of science: the structure and composition of madame Du Châtelet's *Institutions de Physique*, 1737–1740," *Studies on Voltaire and the Eighteenth Century* 201 (1982), pp. 85–113.

Johnson, Dale A. *Women in English Religion 1700–1925.* New York and Toronto: Edwin Mellen Press, Vol. 10, 1983.

Jolley, Nicholas. *Leibniz and Locke: A Study of the New Essays on Human Understanding.* Oxford: Clarendon Press, 1984.

Junco, Alfonso. "La carta atenagórica de Sor Juana," *Abside* 37 (1973), pp. 286–307.

Kant, Immanuel. *Gedanken von der wahren Schatzung der lebendigen Krafte,* in *Immanuel Kants Werke.* Vol. 1. Ernst Cassirer, ed. Berlin, 1922, pp. 1–187.

Kargon, Robert. *Atomism in England from Hariot to Newton.* Oxford, 1966.

Kendall, Kathryn McQueen. "Friends or Rivals? Two Versions of the Same Tale," unpublished 1984 draft of doctoral dissertation, "Theatre, Society and Women Playwrights in London from 1695 through the Queen Anne Era," University of Texas at Austin, 1986.

Kenworthy, Patricia. "The Spanish Priest and the Mexican Nun: Two Views of Love and Honor," Wendell M. Aycock and Sydney P. Cravens eds., *Calderon de la Barca at the Tercentenary: Comparative Views.* Lubbock, TX: Texas Tech Press,

1982, pp. 103–117.

Kersey, Ethel M. *Women Philosophers: A Biocritical Source.* New York, Westport CT, and London: Greenwood Press, 1989.

Kimball, Gayle. *The Religious Ideas of Harriet Beecher Stowe: Her Gospel and Womanhood.* New York and Toronto: Edwin Mellen Press, Vol. 8, 1982.

King, Peter. *The Life of John Locke, with extracts from his Correspondence, Journals and Commonplace Books.* London: H. Colburn, 1829.

—— *The Life of John Locke, with Extracts from his Correspondence, Journals and Commonplace Books. A new edition with considerable additions.* London: Henry Colburn and Richard Bentley, 1830.

Kinnaird, Joan K. "Mary Astell: Inspired by Ideas," in D. Spender, ed., *Feminist Theorists.* London: Women's Press, 1983, pp. 28–39.

Kristina, Queen of Sweden. A Personality of European Civilisation. Stockholm: National museum exhibition catalogue 305, 1966.

[Kristina] *Drottning Kristinas Självbiografi.* Stockholm, 1967.

—— *Maxim l'Ouvrage de Loisir.* Stockholm: Kungliga Biblioteket, D.682.

Ladd, Christine. "On the Algebra of Logic," in *Studies in Logic by Members of the Johns Hopkins University 1883.* Edited by Charles S. Pierce. Reprinted in *Foundations of Semiotics.* Amsterdam and Philadelphia: John Benjamin Publishing Company, 1983. For additional works see "Franklin."

Lambert [Adam], Juliette. *Idées anti-proudhoniennes sur l'amour, la femme et le mariage.* 2nd ed. Paris: Dentu, 1861.

Lamprecht, Sterling Power. *The Role of Descartes in Seventeenth Century England,* in *Studies in the History of Ideas,* edited by the Department of Philosophy of Columbia University. New York: Columbia University Press, 1935.

Laplace, Pierre Simon. *Traité de Mécanique Céleste.* Paris: Chez J.B.M. Duprat, 1798, 1852.

Le Doeuff, Michele. "Women and Philosophy" in Toril Moi, ed., *French Feminist Thought.* London: Basil Blackwell, 1987, pp. 181–209.

von Leibniz, Gottfried Wilhelm. *Die philosophischen Schriften von Gottfried Wilhelm Leibniz.* 7 vols. Hrsg. von C.J. Gerhardt. Berlin: Weidmann, 1875–90.

—— "Mr. Leibniz's Second Paper Being an Answer to Dr. Clarke's First Reply," in S. Clarke, *The Leibniz-Clarke Correspondence.* H.G. Alexander, ed. Manchester: Manchester University Press, 1956.

Leiva, Raul. *Introducción a Sor Juana: sueño y realidad.* Mexico City: Universidad Nacional Autonoma, 1975.

Leonard, Irving A. "The *Encontradas correspondencias* of Sor Juana Inés," *Hispanic Review* 23 (1955), pp. 33–47.

Letters and Poems in Honour of the Incomparable princess, Margaret, Dutchess of Newcastle. London, 1676.

Levine, George. "Determinism and Responsibility in the Works of George Eliot," *PMLA* 77 (1962), pp. 268–279.

Levy, D.G., Applewhite, H.B., and Johnson, M.D. eds., *Women in Revolutionary Paris 1789–1795.* Urbana IL: University of Illinois Press, 1979.

Lindroth, Sten. *Svensk Lardomshistoria. Stormaktstiden.* Stockholm, 1975.

Locke, John. *An Essay Concerning Human Understanding.* Alexander Campbell

Fraser, ed. 2 vols. New York: Dover, 1959.

—— *Mr. Locke's Reply to the Right Reverend the Lord Bishop of Worcester's Answer to his Letter, concerning some Passages Relating to Mr. Locke's Essay of Humane Understanding: in a Late Discourse of his Lordships, in Vindication of the Trinity.* 1697.

—— *The Works of John Locke.* A new edition, corrected. 10 vols. London: T. Tegg, 1823.

—— *An Essay Concerning Humane Understanding.* In Four Books. London: Printed for Thomas Basset, and sold by Edw. Mory, 1690.

—— *The Reasonableness of Christianity, As delivered in the Scriptures.* London: for Awnsham and John Churchill, 1695.

Lopez Camara, Francisco. "El cartesianismo en Sor Juana y Siguenza y Gongora," *Filosofia y Letras* (Mexico) 20 (1950), pp. 107–132.

Lowrey, Charles E. *The Philosophy of Ralph Cudworth: A Study of the True Intellectual System of the Universe.* New York: Phillips and Hunt and Cincinnati: Cranston and Stowe, 1894.

Lund, Christopher C. "Os sonetos filosóficosmorais de Gregorio de Matos e Sor Juana Inés de la Cruz." *Barroco* 4 (1972), pp. 77–89.

Macaulay, Catharine. *Loose Remarks on Certain Positions to be found in Mr. Hobbes's Philosophical Rudiments of Government and Society, with a Short Sketch of a Democratical form of Government in a Letter to Signior Paoli.* London: Printed for T. Davies, 1767.

Macaulay-Graham, Catharine. *History of England.* 8 vols. London: J. Nourse, 1763–1783.

—— *Letters on Education.* London: Dilly, 1787.

—— *Letters on Education.* London: Dilly, 1790.

—— *Letters on Education.* London and New York: Garland Press, 1974.

—— "From Letters on Education," in *A Vindication of the Rights of Woman: An Authoritative Text, Background, The Wollstonecraft Debate, Criticism.* 2nd ed. Carol H. Poston, ed., New York: W.W. Norton Co., 1988, pp. 205–212.

MacMinn, Hainds, and McCrimmon. *Bibliography of the Published Writings of John Stuart Mill.* New York: AMS Press, 1970.

McFadden, Margaret. "Anna Doyle Wheeler (1785–1848): Philosopher, Socialist, Feminist," *Hypatia* 4: 1 (Spring 1989), pp. 91–101.

de Mairan, M.D. *Dissertation sur l'estimation et la mesure des forces motrices du corps. Mémoires de l'Académie des Sciences (1728).* 1730.

—— *Lettre à Madame *** sur la question des forces vives, ou Résponse aux objections...dans ses Institutions de physique.* Paris 1741.

Makin, Bathsua. *The Malady and Remedy of Vexations and Unjust Arrests and Actions,* reprinted in Mary R. Mahl and Helene Koon, eds., *The Female Spectator.* Old Westbury, NY: The Feminist Press and Bloomington, IN: Indiana University Press, 1977.

—— *An Essay to Revive the Antient Education of Gentlewomen.* Facsimile reprint by The Augustan Reprint Society, Publication Number 202. Los Angeles: University of California Williams Andrew Clark Library, 1980.

Mandeville, Bernard. *The Fable of the Bees: Or Private Vices, Public Benefits.* Sixth edition. London, 1729.

Mansfield, Sue. *John Stuart Mill: The Subjection of Women*. Illinois: AHM Publishing Corporation, 1980.

Marsa-Vancells, Plutarco. *La Mujer En La Filosofía*. Madrid: Fragua, 1976.

Martineau, Harriet. *Miscellanies*. In two volumes. Boston: Hilliard, Gray and Company, 1836.

—— "Illustrations of Political Economy," 25 parts. London: C. Fox, 1832–1834.

—— *Illustrations of Political Economy*. 9 vols. London: C. Fox, 1834.

—— *Positive Philosophy of Auguste Comte*. New York, London, 1858.

Masham, Damaris. *A Discourse Concerning the Love of God*. London: For A. and J. Churchill at the Black-Swan in Paternoster-Row, 1696.

—— *Occasional Thoughts in reference to a Virtuous or Christian Life*. London: for A. and J. Churchill at the Black-Swan in Paternoster-Row, 1705.

Mathers, S.L. Macgregor. *The Kabbalah Unveiled*. London: Routledge & Kegan Paul, 1888.

de la Maza, Francisco. *Sor Juana Inés de la Cruz ante la historia*. Revised by Elias Trabulse. Mexico: Universidad Nacional Autonoma, 1980.

Mendez Plancarte, Alfonso. *Sor Juana Inés de la Cruz: El sueño*. Mexico City: Imprenta Universitaria, 1951.

Merchant, Carolyn. *The Death of Nature: Women, Ecology and the Scientific Revolution*. San Francisco: Harper & Row, 1980.

—— "The Vitalism of Anne Conway: Its Impact of Leibniz's Concept of the Monad," *Journal of the History of Philosophy* XVII: 3 (July 1979), pp. 255–269.

—— "The Vitalism of Francis Mercury Van Helmont: Its Influence on Leibniz," *Ambix* 26: 3 (November 1979), pp. 170–183.

Meyer, Gerald. *The Scientific Lady in England*. Berkeley 1955.

Mill, James. s.v. "Government," in *Encyclopedia Britannica*, suppl. 5th ed. London, 1814. Reprinted as "The Article on Government," 1825.

Mill, J.S. *Principles of Political Economy*. 2 vols. 1848.

—— (Untitled essay on marriage) in A. Rossi, *Essays on Sex Equality: John Stuart Mill and Harriet Taylor Mill*. Chicago and London: University of Chicago Press 1970.

—— *On Liberty*. London 1859.

—— *Utilitarianism*. London 1863.

—— *The Subjection of Women*. London 1869.

Mintz, Samuel. "The Dutchess of Newcastle's Visit to the Royal Society," *Journal of English and Germanic Philology* 51: 2 (1952), pp. 168–176.

Monk, Samuel H. *The Sublime: A Study of Critical Theory in Eighteenth-Century England*. Ann Arbor: The University of Michigan Press, 1960.

Montross, Constance M. "Virtue or Vice, the *Respuesta a Sor Filotea* and Thomistic Thought," *Latin American Literary Review* 9 (1980), pp. 17–27.

Moses, Claire Goldberg. *French Feminism in the 19th Century*. Albany: State University of New York Press, 1984.

Nervo, Amado. *Juana de Asbaje*. Madrid: Biblioteca Nueva, 1910.

Newton, Isaac. *Principles of Mathematical Philosophy*. 2nd ed. London, 1713.

—— *Principles of Mathematical Philosophy*. 3rd ed. London, 1726.

Newton, K.M. *George Eliot, Romantic Humanist: A Study of the Philosophical Structure of Her Novels.* Totowa, NJ: Barnes & Noble Books, 1981. The Macmillan Press Ltd., 1981.

Nicholson, Marjorie H. *Conway Letters.* New Haven: Yale, 1930.

Noble, Dorothy. "La influencia ternaria en algunas obras de Sor Juana," *Abside* 39 (1975), pp. 145–164.

Nordstom, Johan. "Cartesius och Drottning Kristinas omvandelse," *Lychnos*, 1940.

Norris, John, Rector of Bemerton, near Sarum. *Cursory Reflections upon a Book call'd, An Essay concerning Human Understanding.* In *Christian Blessedness.* London: S. Manship, 1690.

—— *An Essay Towards the Theory of the Ideal or Intelligible World. Designed for Two Parts. The First considering it Absolutely in itself, and the Second in Relation to Human Understanding.* London, 1701.

Notable American Women: A Bibliographical Dictionary. Cambridge, MA: Belknap Press of Harvard University Press, 1971.

Oestreich, Gerhard. *Neostoicism and the Early Modern State.* Cambridge and New York: Cambridge University Press, 1982.

Owen, Gilbert Ray. "The Famous Case of Lady Anne Conway," *Annals of Medical History* 9 (1937).

Packe, Michael St. John. *The Life of John Stuart Mill.* New York: Macmillan, 1954.

Paloma, Dolores. "Margaret Cavendish: Defining the Female Self," *Women's Studies* 7 (1980), pp. 55–66.

Pankhurst, Richard K.P. "Anna Wheeler: A pioneer socialist and feminist." *The Political Quarterly* 25: 132–143.

Pappe, H.O. *John Stuart Mill and the Harriet Taylor Myth. Australian National University Social Science Monograph 19.* Melbourne: Melbourne University Press, 1960.

Passmore, John A. *Ralph Cudworth: An Interpretation.* Cambridge: Cambridge University Press, 1951.

Patterson, Elizabeth Chambers. *Mary Somerville and the Cultivation of Science, 1815–1840. International Archives of the History of Ideas 102.* Dordrecht: Martinus Nijhoff, 1983.

Paz, Octavio. *Las peras del olmo.* 3rd ed. Barcelona: Seix y Barral, 1974.

Perez, Maria Esther. *Lo americano en el teatro de Sor Juana Inés de la Cruz.* Eastchester, NY: Eliseo Torres, 1975.

Perry, Henry Ten Eyck. *The First Duchess of Newcastle and her Husband as Figures in Literary History.* Boston, 1918.

Pfandl, Ludwig. *Sor Juana Inés de la Cruz, la Decima Musa de México. Su vida. Su poesía. Su psique.* Francisco de la Maza, ed. Tr. Juan Antonio Ortega y Medina. Mexico City: Universidad Nacional Autonoma, 1967.

Pierce, Charles S. *Studies in Logic.* Members of the Johns Hopkins University (1883). Amsterdam and Philadelphia: John Benjamins Publishing Company.

Pintard, René. *Le Libertinage érudit dans la première moitié du XVIIe siècle.* t. 1–2. Paris: Boivin, 1943.

Pleten, Magnus von, ed. *Queen Christina of Sweden. Documents and Studies.* Stockholm: Analecta Reginensa 1, 1966.

Popkin, Richard H. "Menasseh ben Israel and Isaac La Peyrere, II" *Studia Rosenthaliana* XVIII: 1 (January 1984), pp. 12–20.

Poullain de La Barre, François. *De l'égalité des deux sexes: Discours physique et moral.* Paris, 1673.

—— *De l'éducation des dames pour la conduite de l'esprit dans les sciences et dans les moeurs.* Paris, 1674.

Proudhon, P.-J. *De la Justice dans la Révolution et dans l'Église (1858),* in Bougle and Moysset ed., *Oeuvres complètes de P.-J. Proudhon,* Vol. XII. Paris, 1935.

Puccini, Dario. *Sor Juana Inés de la Cruz. Studio d'una personalita del Barocco messicano.* Rome: Ateneo, 1967.

Pufendorf, Samuel. *On the Law of Nature and Nations.* Oxford, 1703.

Rabil, Albert. *Laura Cereta: Quattrocento Humanist.* Binghamton, NY: Medieval & Renaissance Texts and Studies, 1981.

Radcliffe, Mary Anne. *The Female Advocate.* Hildesheim and New York: Georg Olms Verlag, 1980 facsimile of 1799 edition.

Ranke, Leopold von. *The History of the Popes – their Church and State and especially of their conflicts with Protestantism in the sixteenth and seventeenth centuries.* 3 vols. London: George Bell & Sons, 1906.

Reid, Thomas. *Essays on the Intellectual and Active Powers of Man.* Philadelphia, 1792.

Reyes, Alfonso. *Las letras de la Nueva España.* Mexico City: Fondo de Cultura Economica, 1948.

Ribot, Th. Review of Coignet, Clarisse, "Cours de morale a l'usage dans écoles laïques," *Revue politique et littéraire* 15 (1875), pp. 759–760.

Rich, Adrienne. "Compulsory Heterosexuality and Lesbian Existence," *Signs, Journal of Women in Culture and Society* 5: 41 (1980), pp. 631–666.

Rivers, Elias L. "El ambiguo *Sueño* de Sor Juana," *Cuadernos Hispanoamericanos* 63 (1965), pp. 271–282.

Rivlin, Joseph. *Harriet Martineau: A Bibliography of her Separately Printed Books.* New York: The New York Public Library, 1947.

Robin, Richard S. *Annotated Catalogue of the Papers of Charles S. Pierce.* Cambridge, MA: University of Massachusetts Press, 1967.

Rosenroth, Knorr von. *Kabbalah Denudata.* 1677.

Rossi, Alice S., ed. *The Feminist Papers: from Adams to de Beauvoir.* New York: Columbia University Press, 1973.

—— *Essays on Sex Equality: John Stuart Mill and Harriet Taylor Mill.* Chicago and London: The University of Chicago Press, 1970.

Rousseau, J.-J. *Julie, ou la Nouvelle Héloise.* Paris, 1761.

—— *Émile.* Paris, 1762.

Royer, Clemence. *Le Bien et la Loi Morale: Éthique et Téléologie.* Paris: Guillaumin et Cie., 1881.

Sabat de Rivers, Georgina. *El Sueño de Sor Juana Inés de la Cruz: tradiçiones literarias y originalidad.* London: Tamesis, 1976.

—— "Sor Juana y su Sueño: antecedentes científicos en la poesia española del siglo deoro," *Cuadernos Hispanoamericanos* 310 (1976), pp. 186–204.

Sarasohn, Lisa. "A Science Turned Upside Down: Feminism and the Natural

Philosophy of Margaret Cavendish," *The Hunting Library Quarterly* 47: 4 (1984), pp. 289–307.

Schiebinger, Londa. *The Mind has no Sex? Women in the Origins of Modern Science.* Cambridge and London: Harvard University Press, 1989.

Schons, Dorothy. *Bibliografía de Sor Juana Inés de la Cruz. Bibliográficas Méxicanas, Monograph 7.* Mexico City: Seria de Relaçiones Exteriores, 1927.

Schurman, Anna Maria van. *De Vitae Humanae Termino.* 1639.

—— *De ingenii muliebris ad doctrinam et meliores litteras aptitudine.* 1641.

—— *Opuscula hebraeca, greca, latina, gallica, prosaica, et metrica.* Leyden: Elsevir, 1642.

—— *Eukleria; seu, Melioris partis electio. Tractatus brevem vitae ejus delineationem exhibens.* Altonae: C. van der Meulen, 1673.

—— *The Learned maid, or Whether a maid may be a scholar?* London: John Redmayne, 1659.

—— *Opuscula hebraeca, greca, latina, gallica, prosaica, et metrica,* Leyden: Elsevir 1642, and other editions.

Scott, N.M. "Tenth Muse," *Americas* 30 (Feb. 1978), pp. 13–20.

Scudéry, Madeleine de. *Discours pour et contre l'amitié tendre.* 1653.

Serafin, Silvana. "La Respuesta sor juanina: Ippotesi interprative," *Rassegna Iberística* 13 (1982), pp. 3–15.

Shen, Eugene. "The Ladd-Franklin Formula in Logic: The Antilogism," *Mind* 36 (1927), pp. 54–60.

Sklar, Kathryn Kish. *Catharine Beecher: A Study in American Domesticity.* New Haven and London: Yale University Press, 1973.

Smith, Hilda. *Reason's Disciples.* Urbana-Champaign, 1982.

Somerville, Martha. *Mary Somerville, Personal Recollections. From Early Life to Old Age: With Selections from her Correspondence.* London: John Murray, 1873.

Somerville, Mary. "On the magnetizing power of the more refrangible solar rays." Communicated by W. Somerville, M.D., F.R.S., Feb. 2, 1826, *Philosophical Transactions of the Royal Society of London* CXVI (1826), p. 132.

—— *The Mechanism of the Heavens.* London, 1831.

—— *Preliminary Dissertation to the "Mechanism of the Heavens" by Mrs. Somerville.* London, 1831.

—— *A Preliminary Dissertation on the Mechanism of the Heavens.* Philadelphia, 1832.

—— *On the Connection of the Physical Sciences.* London, 1834, 1835, 1836, 1837, 1840, 1843, 7th London ed. New York: Harper & Bros., 1846.

—— "art. VII. – 1. Ueber den Halleyschen Cometen. Von Littrow. Wein, 1835. 2. Ueber den Halleyschen Cometen. Von Professor von Encke. Berliner Jahrbuch 1835 & c. & c. & c." *Quarterly Review* LV (December 1835), pp. 195–223.

—— "Experiments on transmission of the chemical rays of the solar spectrum across different areas. Excerpts from a letter of Mrs. Somerville's [sic] to Mr. Arago," *Comptes rendus* III (1836), pp. 473–476.

—— *De la connexion des sciences physiques où expose et rapide de tous les principaux phenomènes astronomiques, physiques, chimiques, géologiques, et météorologiques, accompagné des découvertes modernes, tant français qu'étrangers. Traduit de l'Anglais, sous l'auspices de M. Arago, par Mme T. Meulien.* Paris, 1839.

—— *Physical Geography.* 2 vols. London, 1848.

Sophia, a person of Quality [pseud.]. *Woman Not Inferior to Man or, A Short and Modest Vindication of the Natural Right of the Fair Sex to a Perfect Equality of Power, Dignity, and Esteem, with the Men.* London, 1739.

Soul Mates: The Oberlin Correspondence of Lucy Stone and Antoinette Brown, 1846–1850. Oberlin College Press, 1983.

Spinoza, Benedict (Baruch). *Tractatus Theologico-Politicus.* Amsterdam, 1670.

Squadrito, Kathleen M. "Mary Astell's Critique of Locke's View of Thinking Matter," *Journal of the History of Philosophy* 25: 3 (July 1987), pp. 434–439.

Stephan, Ruth. "A Note on Christina and her Academies," *Queen Christina of Sweden – Documents and Studies.* Magnus von Pleten ed., Stockholm, 1966, pp. 365–371.

Stillinger, Jack. *The Early Draft of John Stuart Mill's Autobiography.* Urbana: University of Illinois Press, 1961.

Stillingfleet, Edward. *The Works of That Most Eminent and Learned Prelate, Dr. Edw. Stillingfleet, Late Lord Bishop of Worcester. Together with His Life and Character.* 6 vols. London: J. Heptinstall for H. & G. Mortlock, 1710–13.

—— *A Discourse in Vindication of the Doctrine of the Trinity: With An Answer to the Late Socinian Objections Against it from Scripture, Antiquity and Reason. And A Preface concerning the different Explications of the Trinity, and the Tendency of the present Socinian Controversie.* 2nd ed. London: J.H. for Henry Mortlock, 1697.

—— *The Bishop of Worcester's Answer to Mr. Locke's Letter concerning Some Passages Relating to his Essay of Humane Understanding, Mentioned in the Late Discourse in Vindication of the Trinity. With a Postscript in answer to some Reflections made upon that Treatise in a late Socinian Pamphlet.* London: J.H. for Henry Mortlock, 1697.

—— *The Bishop of Worcester's Answer to Mr. Locke's Second Letter; Wherein his Notion of Ideas Is proved to be Inconsistent with it self, and with the Articles of the Christian Faith.* London: J.H. for Henry Mortlock, 1698.

Stolpe, Sven. *Fran Stoicism till Mystik. Studier i Drottning Kristinas maximer.* Stockholm, 1959.

—— *Drottning Kristina.* Stockholm: Askild & Karnekull, 1982 (1960–61).

—— *Drottning Kristina Maximer Les Sentiments Héroïques. Acta Academicae Catholiquae Suecianae* 1. Stockholm: Bonniers, 1959.

—— "Kristina-studier," *Credo, Katolsk tidskrift* 40: 4 (1959), pp. 203–315.

Sunstein, Emily W. *A Different Face, The Life of Mary Wollstonecraft.* New York: Harper and Row, 1975.

Taylor Mill, Harriet. "Enfranchisement of Women," in A. Rossi ed., *Essays on Sex Equality.* Chicago: University of Chicago Press, 1970.

—— Untitled Essay on Marriage. In A. Rossi, ed. *Essays on Sex Equality.* Chicago: University of Chicago Press, 1970.

—— Untitled Essay on Tolerance. In F.A. Hayek, *John Stuart Mill and Harriet Taylor: Their Friendship [Correspondence] and Subsequent Marriage.* London:

Routledge & Kegan Paul Ltd., 1951.

Thompson, William [and Anna Doyle Wheeler]. *The Appeal of One Half of the Human Race, Women, Against the Pretensions of the Other Half, Men, to Restrain Them in Political and Thence in Civil and Domestic Slavery.* New York: Lenox Hill, 1970 reprint of 1825 edition.

—— *The Appeal of One Half of the Human Race, Women, Against the Pretensions of the Other Half, Men, to Restrain Them in Political and Thence in Civil and Domestic Slavery.* London: Virago, 1983.

Thurloe, John. *Thurloe State Papers.* 6 vols. London, 1648–1667.

Thurman, Judith. "Sister Juana: the price of genius," *Ms.*, April 1973, pp. 14–21.

Todd, Janet. *A Dictionary of British and American Women Writers 1660–1800.* London, 1984.

Tomalin, Claire. *The Life and Death of Mary Wollstonecraft.* New York: Harcourt Brace Jovanovich, 1974.

Trilling, Diana. "Mill's Intellectual Beacon," *Partisan Review* 19 (1952), pp. 116–120.

Truchet, J., ed. *La Rochefoucauld Maximes.* Paris: Editions Garniers, 1967.

Valentin, Hugo. "Drottning Kristina av Sveriges Judiska forbindelser," in J. Fischer et al., eds., *Festskrift...David Simonsens.* København, 1923, pp. 213–237.

Vermeylen, Alphonse. "El tema de la mayor fineza del amor divino en la obra de Sor Juana Inés de la Cruz," *III Congreso Internacional de Hispanistas*, México City 1968, pp. 901–908.

Voltaire. *Éléments de la philosophie de Neuton.* Paris, 1738.

—— *Correspondence and related documents.* Th. Besterman, ed., Genève, Banbury and Oxford, 1968–1977.

Wade, Ira. *Voltaire and Madame du Châtelet.* Princeton: Princeton University Press, 1941.

—— *Studies on Voltaire With some Unpublished Papers of Mme du Châtelet.* New York: Russell & Russell, 1947.

Waithe, M.E., ed. *A History of Women Philosophers, Vol. 1. Ancient Women Philosophers: 600 B.C.–500 A.D.* Dordrecht and Boston: Martinus Nijhoff, 1987.

—— *A History of Women Philosophers, Vol. 2. Medieval, Renaissance and Enlightenment Women Philosophers: 500–1600.* Dordrecht, Boston and London: Kluwer Academic Publishers, 1989.

—— "On Not Teaching the History of Philosophy," *Hypatia* Special Issue on the History of Women in Philosophy 4: 1 (Spring 1989), pp. 132–138.

Wardle, Ralph M., ed. *Collected Letters of Mary Wollstonecraft.* Ithaca: Cornell University Press, 1979.

Ware, Malcolm. *Sublimity in the Novels of Ann Radcliffe: A Study of the Influence upon her Craft of Edmund Burke's Enquiry into the Origin of our Ideas of the Sublime and Beautiful.*

Weibull, Curt. *Drottning Christina. Studier och Forskningar.* Stockholm: Natur och Kultur, 1931.

Wheeler, Anna Doyle. "Rights of Women," *The British Co-operator* 1 (1830), pp. 1, 2, 12–15, 33–36.

—— Letter to Charles Fourier, 27 May 1833. Paris: Archives sociétaires (in the

Archives Nationales): 10 AS 25, dossier 3.

Whitelock, Bulstrode. *A Journal of the Swedish Embassy in the Years 1653–1654*. 2 vols. Reeve, ed. London, 1855.

Wieselgren, H. *Drottning Kristinas bibliotek och bibliotekarier före hennes bosättning i Rom. Vitterhetsakademiens Handlingar* (Stockholm: Norstedt) 33: 2 (1901).

von Wolff, C.F. *Vernunsstige Gedancken von Gott, der Weld und der Seele des Menschen, aus allen Dingen uberhaupt* (1720). Ulrich von Suhm, translator, 1736.

Wollstonecraft, Mary. *A Vindication of the Rights of Men*, with an Introduction by Eleanor Louise Nicholes. Gainesville: Scholars' Facsimilies and Reprints, 1960.

—— *A Vindication of the Rights of Woman: An Authoritative Text, Background, the Wollstonecraft Debate, Criticism*. 2nd ed. Carol H. Poston, ed. New York: W.W. Norton Co., 1988.

Woolf, Virginia. "The Dutchess of Newcastle," in *The Common Reader*. London, 1929, pp. 98–109.

Xirau, Ramon. *Genio y figura de sor Juana Inés de la Cruz*. Buenos Aires: Editorial Universitaria de Buenos Aires, 1970.

"Y". "Mme Clemence Royer, *Le Bien et la Loi Morale: Éthique et Téléologie*." *Revue Philosophique* 13 (1882), pp. 426–432.

Yolton, John W. "Locke's Unpublished Marginal Replies to John Sergeant," *Journal of the History of Ideas* 7 (Oct. 1951).

—— "Locke and the Seventeenth-Century Logic of Ideas," *Journal of the History of Ideas* 16 (Oct. 1955).

Zamora Pallares, Dionisia. *Sor Juana Inéz de la Cruz y la educacion de la mujer*. Mexico City: Seminario de Cultura Mexicana, 1963.

Zedler, Beatrice. "Marie le Jars de Gournay," *A History of Women Philosophers, Volume 2. Medieval, Renaissance and Enlightenment Women Philosophers: 500–1600*. Mary Ellen Waithe, ed. Boston, London and Dordrecht: Kluwer Academic Publishers, 1989.

—— "Three Princesses," *Hypatia* Special Issue on the History of Women in Philosophy 4:1 (Spring 1989), pp. 28–63.

Zetterwall, Monica. "Role playing in maxim form – a comment on Queen Christina's maxims," *Scandinavian Studies* 2 (1985).

Index